Riding
Storm Out

A Season of St. Louis Inner City High School Football

By David Almany

Copyright © 2010 By David Almany
All Rights Reserved
Heart of the Ozarks Athletics, LLC

To order additional copies of this work, contact
Heart of the Ozarks Publishing, P.O. 20501, St. Louis, MO 63139

ISBN: 978-1-4507-0252-2

ACKNOWLEDGMENTS

You should always thank your *family* first, eliminating any potential fatal oversights. So be it done. Your support is recognized and appreciated. Others who were of help in what often seemed a lonely and endless endeavor: The family of Roosevelt High School who gave me open access to anyplace I wanted to stick my nose; Principal *Terry Houston*: a man of boundless energy; head football coach *DeAndre Campbell*: his passion for his job allows him to embrace his life's calling with an unbridled vigor; as fine a group of assistant football coaches as you will find on any high school staff; *Darren West*: whom I could always count on for a quick and well placed witted quote; *Darren Wade*: the hard working assistant who never sought the spot light, even if it had a way of finding him; *George Simmons*: a wise and venerable teacher of life, and a wonderful companion around dinner time; the members of the *2008 varsity football team*: as the years pass, may you look back fondly on a special year. *Kevin Kraus*: for his ability to uncover my numerous misuses of the English language, eliminating the many times my prose went amiss, askew and astray. I hope you found them all. To *my runners*: when the firing starts, some guys cut and run, while others stand and fight. You stood tall. I will never forget your show of courage. And finally, a special thanks to *the good ole boys* who five short years ago gave to me the nudge I needed to remove myself from the "rut" my life had become. See you at the Rodeo.

CHAPTER 1
PROLOGUE

People.
People important to you, people unimportant to you, cross your life,
Touch it with love and carelessness and move on.
There are people who leave you and you breathe a sigh of relief and
Wonder why you ever came into contact with them.

There are people who leave you and you breathe a sigh of remorse and
wonder why they had to go
And leave such a gaping hole.

Children leave parents; friends leave friends.
Acquaintances move on.
People change homes. People grow apart.
Enemies hate and move on. Friends love and move on.
Think on the many who have moved into your hazy memory...

I believe in God's master plan in our lives. He moves people in and out of each other's lives and each leaves a mark on the other.
You find you are made up of bits and pieces of all who have touched your life, and you are more because of it...you would be less if they had not.

—Lois A. Cheney

By the spring of 2008, all components for the "Perfect Storm" educational style were in precise alignment: abysmal student performance and test scores, a shrinking student enrollment, labor and management strife, a financial short fall of mind boggling proportions, a splintered and divided city government who had turned the city public schools into a political football - resulting in staff and student morale that was at an all time low - coupled with a citizenry that had lost it's concern for public education. All factors combined, it made for the absolute worst of times for the St. Louis, MO Public School System (SLPS). Support for public education in the "Best Baseball City in America," was about as popular as a warm $9 bottle of Budweiser beer on a humid summer night at Busch Stadium. As the St. Louis Cardinals and Major League Baseball launched into the season's opening day ceremonies in April of 2008, a ritual of tradition and adoration that in St. Louis ranks second only to the celebration of Christmas, the future and very survival of public education in the city of St. Louis was teetering on a slippery slope of public apathy. Parents and students with the financial resources to abandon this sinking vessel, had by the spring of 2008, made their way to the lifeboats.

However, surprising to me, and shocking to my preconceived notions of reality, I found within the decay of a once proud school system, a group who had no intention of bailing out on their neighborhood high school. I found a group of Roosevelt High School Roughriders who, figuratively speaking, were *"Riding The Storm Out."*

Perception is reality. Or is it?

I spent 12 months following the 2008 St. Louis, Missouri Roosevelt High School Roughriders football team. I witnessed the highs and lows, the joys and sorrows, the trials and tribulations of 40 young men, five coaches, and a principal. This group earned my respect as they endured through daily challenges that would immediately derail most of us before we finished our first morning cup of coffee. This group which I grew to admire had the capacity to shrug their collective shoulders and soldier on, no matter the obstacles - stoically accepting the hand dealt them as one of the necessary daily chores required for survival in a disengaging inner city environment.

At its peak, the St. Louis Public School's facilitated four public high schools to serve students on the south side of the city. For years, through an intricate system of red lining real estate procedures and de facto segregation housing patterns, Roosevelt was mostly devoid of African American students. By 2008, that had all changed. Today, Roosevelt High School – the only public high school left on the south side - is 80% black. The majority of the rest of the school's 20% enrollment is made up of first generation immigrants of Oriental, African or Eastern European descent – "right off the boat" was the common terminology of south side neighborhood old timers - most having left dangerous and chaotic environments in their native lands to settle in one of South St. Louis' rapidly developing immigrant neighborhoods. In 2008, virtually no white children of American birth attended RHS. Multi generational white families of South St. Louis simply refused to send their children to the St. Louis Public Schools. It is a decades old problem, deeply and bitterly rooted in the forced busing of the early 1980's.

I grew up in the St. Louis area, moved away for 30 years, spent a career as a public school educator, and returned in the summer of my 48th year. The neighborhood changes were startling. Three decades had completely reshaped the South St. Louis area I had once known. The starkest image, the one that hit me immediately, was not the complete racial change in demographics that the area had undergone, but the abandonment of the large and elaborate brick structures that at one time were the lifeline and the anchors of the south side communities: the neighborhood public schools. Neighborhood after neighborhood that I cruised through on a warm August 2006 afternoon, contained boarded up school buildings. As these structures had fallen into states of disarray and disrepair, it appeared that the community's very foundation had crumbled along with the buildings. It was obvious to my eyes that the breakdown of the social institutions that held the area together, providing fiber and stability; the family, the school and the church, were now gone, draining the very life from the South St. Louis neighborhoods.

As I drove along the dying streets on that day in 2006, I felt a sense of nostalgic sadness, a sense of the passing of a great time - a grandeur that would never come again. Where once stood stoic but solid neighborhood elementary, junior high and high schools, now could only be found graffiti covered abandoned brick shells. The gutters drooped, the paint peeled; the windows were long ago broken out, and the playgrounds as empty as the dreams of the citizens of European ancestry- German, Irish, Italian, Czech and Pole- who had abandoned these once thriving and teeming ethnical neighborhoods. The life of the buildings, along with the valuable copper pipe, had been ripped out by forces and agents of change who did not understand what these neighborhood schools had once bound together: the sense of community that had fostered a special and safe place to raise a family, grow old and die. It was very depressing. I felt as outdated as the buildings; my memories as dead as the August lawns along the empty streets, now overrun by the summer weeds of neglect.

Once, not long ago, in my mind's eye at least, these same streets had teemed with the vibrant sounds of summer night life in ethnic St. Louis neighborhoods: transistor radios blaring the sounds of Cardinal baseball games into the sticky stillness of humid summer nights, broadcast over the 50,000 watt wavelengths of KMOX Radio – the voice of Cardinal Nation – propelling the game to far reaching outposts throughout the South and Midwest. Hall of Fame broadcasters Harry Caray and Jack Buck were at the microphones, calling the play by play descriptions of the heroes of our youth - Musial, Brock and Gibson - while neighbors, family and friends sitting on row house stoops listened intently; all the while discussing the latest developments in that night's game, "Can you believe we needed a pinch hitter and he left McCarver, his best lefty, on the bench? McCarver owns Drysdale. What was he thinking? We will never win the pennant with Keene as manager."

By the time of my 2006 nostalgic drive, both Harry Caray and Jack Buck were dead; Bob Gibson and Lou Brock were advancing into the late throes of middle age; Stan "The Man" Musial had just celebrated his 84th birthday and KMOX Radio no longer broadcast Cardinal games. Busch Stadium had even been torn down and a new and supposedly improved "Green Cathedral," albeit of the same name, was erected just to the south of the old ball yard's hallowed ground, in what had once been a parking lot. At least the owners, in a small concession and tribute to tradition, did move Musial's statue, the oft used site of rendezvous - "you get the tickets and I will meet you at Musial's Statue at 7:00" - to a place of prominence outside of the new structure.

The neighborhoods I had once known were now almost gone, devoid of any human spirit or community engagement. The pulse was faint, the area dying.

But as 2006 progressed into 2007, and then 2008, I would learn that I was wrong, and in this case, blatantly wrong; an error based on my failure to look beyond the obvious. I learned the validity of the cliché "the more things change, the more they stay the same." Example: Once Stan "The Man" Musial held the collective adulation of the great city. In his place now was Albert "El Hombre" Pujols, a circle unbroken. In time, I began to understand that my initial perception of the death of public education on the South Side was indeed, not reality.

Fast forward to 2008 and enter the Roosevelt High School Roughriders football team as they charge smack into my middle aged, judgmental and preconceived world. Once RHS became a part of my daily life and as time allowed for introspection and a clearer and less judgmental view of the Roosevelt community, my perception swung 180 degrees. What I found, once I peeled back the layers of neglect, became a personal inspiration in the resilience of a community of people who would not quit. I saw pride and determination - in some cases against all odds - to overcome a harsh and dangerous environment. I learned that the word "overcome" was the operational term for the successes I found at Roosevelt High School. Abandoning their neighborhood was not a viable option for this group. Setting up roots and fighting for a better life was. The school and the community: teachers, students, coaches, administration and parents, did not yearn for their children, as so many St. Louis inner city parents before had, the supposed greener educational pastures that boarding the desegregation bus daily and following the migration to the more affluent suburban schools offered. Instead, the leaders of Roosevelt High School chose to dig in their collective heels and create their own legacy, in their own neighborhood.

Where many outsiders saw only urban decay, the family of Roosevelt High School saw opportunity and potential. In time, with experience reshaping and sharpening my vision to 20/20, I began to see the same. For me, the opportunity to spend time observing the dynamics of this cast of modern day visionaries was a perception changing experience. I grew to admire them as individuals, pull for their collective successes; and in the end, as the football season drew to a close and as the senior class began its journey into the adult world, watch as time closed an important chapter in each and every one of our lives.

But back to the summer of 2006, when I first formulated in my mind the idea of an expose on the St. Louis Public Schools (SLPS), a much maligned organization. I would learn in due time that the SLPS is criticized for many valid reasons. The Missouri State Department of Education in 2007 - the year before my 12 months with the Roughriders- had taken the unusual step of pulling the district's accreditation. This extreme action was based upon years of pathetically abysmal standardized test scores, along with financial mismanagement on almost every level of the system. In accordance with this state legislative approved action, the city's elected Board of Education was removed and the district was placed under the direction of a Special Appointed Board of Education (SAB) whose members were appointed by three different governmental bodies: the Governor, the Mayor and the City Alderman. The outcry from the parents of city students, to this action, was loud and long. The disenfranchisement of the voters by the removal of the elected Board set off a firestorm in the city that was flamed with angry cries by African American constituents of racism. But the leaders at the State Department of Education insisted in a non-compromising voice, that it was time for action. No longer did something need to be done about the condition and performance of the SLPS, but now, *had to be done*. Most in power concurred with this damning assessment. Years of infighting had left the school system a public embarrassment and a yoke around the neck of the downtown movers and shakers who preached that urban renewal would never become reality in the city of St. Louis until the problems with the SLPS were addressed and rectified. Six Superintendents in five years, wasted funds and resources, a militant teachers union that was not in the mood to accept school closings or cuts in pay and benefits that district administrators claimed was the only feasible hope of staving off bankruptcy (a balanced budget was nothing more than a pipe dream and not even discussed by district bean counters) had led to the very real possibility of total financial collapse, leading to the complete and immediate shut down of the city's public schools.

Into this "Perfect Storm"- and into my life - rode the Roosevelt Roughriders football team. For anyone with a soft spot for the underdog, they were a story waiting to be told.

Chapter 1: Prologue

My initial vision of what I wanted to chronicle was a story to be based on high school athletics in the St. Louis Public High League (PHL), a circuit that contained all eleven (by 2008, the number had grown to 13) of the city's public high schools. My background, I felt, gave me the insight to be a successful recorder and storyteller of such a tale. I was a long time high school boy's basketball coach of, I humbly insert, some success and renown, a track coach, a building principal for 15 years, a classroom teacher for the 15 years prior, an athletic director, and currently, after my retirement from the State Public School System, a college track and cross country coach at a St. Louis area Catholic University.

But first, I had to find a story. I spent two years looking. I read the area high school sports blogs religiously, daily poured over the high school sports section of the St. Louis Post Dispatch and attended as many PHL high school sporting events in person as possible. At many a game, I was - with a sometimes exceptionally lonely referee, teacher or administrator- the only white person in the crowd.

I looked at the soccer team at Soldan International Studies High School, the baseball team at a high school I will not identify by name; and the girl's basketball team at Metro High School, along with the football team at Roosevelt. The soccer team at Soldan would have been an interesting study because of the squad makeup; almost all team members were first generation immigrants and English as Second Language (ESL) students. I backed away for two reasons; Soldan was a "magnet" school, drawing students from throughout the city – I wanted to do an analysis of a neighborhood school – and two, I don't like soccer. The baseball team I followed briefly was just bad. I have no other way to sugar coat an assessment of their ability and skill level. The abandonment and decline of baseball in the inner city has been well documented. If you don't believe this to be true, I suggest you sometime take in a PHL baseball game. Metro's girl's basketball team looked initially promising. The Metro team was in the middle of what would be a run of consecutive state championships and the coach was a personal friend. Metro's student body demographics eventually steered me away. Metro is far and away the most academically decorated school in the St. Louis system; the favorite Son in a field full of red headed orphans. Metro is also a magnet school where admission is based upon a merit test, tempered somewhat by racial make up. Such a student body does not represent a true inner city school population. I felt it important to avoid this type of manipulated student achievement if I was to get a true snapshot of what an inner city high school student faces in a day to day battle for an education, always in reach of the forces of the temptations found in the streets of the big city. I wanted to dissect the lives of students who attended traditional neighborhood schools. I wanted to see both the good and the bad of such a populist arrangement.

That left Roosevelt and its football team. I liked several aspects about the Roughriders: it was a neighborhood school and had a team that had suffered through a few 0-10 seasons over the past decade, but in recent years had seen a re-emergence of success and an upward turn of fortunes under the guidance of a young and upcoming coach. I was told by one PHL observer "they are tough little rascals." I had attended several Roosevelt football games in the 2006 and 2007 seasons, and confirmed in person what I had been told: the Roughriders were a fun team to watch. Led by their interactive and enthusiastic coaches, the squad displayed spirited play and enjoyed at least some shred of community support; a factor sorrowfully absent from the other PHL contests in the many and various sports I had attended. I also felt comfortable as an observer and recorder of a football team based on my personal background. I had played college football, felt I possessed an understanding of the game at a level at least above that of the average fan and I still immensely enjoyed attending and watching games. In the end, my choice was crystal clear; it would be Roosevelt High's football team.

Contacting the proper officials and following the appropriate chain of command to gain access and approval of my project, along with trying to convey my vision of what this endeavor would produce, I feared would be difficult. In addition, I would need to convince total strangers that this out of the blue request from a middle aged white guy for an all out access pass to their football team was a good idea. Again, I was dead wrong. It turned out to be one of the easiest chores I encountered in the whole production of this project.

In March of 2008, I sent an e-mail outlining what I was proposing. I used the Roosevelt High School web site to get the e-mail addresses for the Principal, the Athletic Director and the Head Football Coach. I then sent an electronic message to all three. Part of my communication read as follows:

Chapter 1: Prologue

"For the last several years I have watched as a spectator the performance of the Roosevelt Roughriders Varsity Football team. I have been impressed with the tenacity displayed by your players and your coaches.

I want to present to you a project I have been formulating over the past few months. I would like to follow your team, beginning this upcoming summer, through the completion of your 2008 season. I would like to focus on the young men and players on your squad and gain an insight into their daily lives as they pursue their academic and athletic goals. My long range plan is that the Roosevelt Roughriders would make a very compelling story that I would want to turn into a book. Obviously; your coaches, teachers and school administrators would be an integral part of this project. It matters not to me if your team goes 10-0 or 0-10. The pursuits and challenges facing your players, coaches and staff is what interests me.

The assimilation of where I want to go with this idea is right now only in the "drawing stages." The directions my inquiry could take at this point in time are numerous. I am intrigued by the fact that you are a neighborhood school and that the demographics of the student clientele you serve is so evolving. I am sure this phenomenon presents many challenges to both you and your staff. I would not want to lose sight of your student athletes, and they would remain the focus of my writing."

Several days later, I received a response back via e-mail from DeAndre Campbell, Head Football Coach at Roosevelt High School. "I like your idea. When can we meet," was the direct response, the very one I had hoped to receive.

On Friday morning, April 11, 2008 I walked into Roosevelt High School at 8:50 am for a 9:00 am meeting with Mr. Terry Houston, the principal of RHS. Thirty years experience in public education told me immediately that something was wrong. My antenna was raised. As I walked through the metal detectors, voiding my pockets of any contraband that would raise the ire of these now mandatory school contraptions, I heard the ominous sound of the school tardy bell. After so many years in school buildings, I have developed a Pavlovian response to the "sound of the bell;" I immediately turn and place my back to the nearest corridor wall and begin a 180 degree vision span of my environment. Sounds wacky, but it is time proven for survival in a hallway about to be overrun with teenagers.

Instantly, doors of classrooms flew open, Security Guards lined up at the entrance to the school auditorium- which was directly across the hall way from where I stood sentry- and the students began to quickly file into the Auditorium. It was very apparent that a school-wide assembly was going to take place. This gave me the opportunity to view the student body as they paraded by my duty post, which I found interesting as I watched the dress, the body language and the outward behavior of approximately 1200 teenage students; but also perplexing, as in five minutes I was supposed to meet with the building principal. My initial thought was that there had been a crossing of the proverbial wires between my having made the appointment through a secretary the previous week; or Mr. Houston had simply forgotten about our conference.

I walked to the school's administration office, just up the hallway from my post, proceeding with no due haste, all the while careful not to turn my back to the student body. I was directed to a seat in the outer office by the receptionist. Precisely as the clock struck 9 am, a door with the label of "Principal" on it opened and, from an inner office, emerged a man, who through his demeanor was obviously the occupant of the Principal's Office. Approaching to shake my hand was Mr. Terry Houston, Principal of Roosevelt High School.

I had been previously informed that I would like Mr. Houston. "Mr. Houston gets things done," I was told on more than one occasion. A stocky and well built man of around my age, Mr. Houston introduced himself, shook my hand and motioned that we could meet in an adjoining conference room.

I decided to give Houston an "out." "Look," I began, "I know how busy you are and it looks like you are getting ready for an assembly, perhaps it would be better if we rescheduled," I offered.

"No, no, no," was Houston's rapid fire deep voice response. "You made time to come see us; we will make time to see you." Thus began my association with Mr. Houston, a man who I would be told many times over the next 12 months by students, teachers, parents and community members- was "a man of vision."

In thirty years of my tenure in public education, the most frustrating change I have seen in the day-to-day operation of a public school is the totally asinine restraints that legality and fear of liability through litigation has placed upon public education. We, as educators in the 21st Century, have become shackled with the restraints cultivated by the often unfounded fear of litigation. Nothing gets done anymore - unless the school lawyer gives the ok. I worked for a Superintendent in a small Missouri district who could not scratch his butt without first calling the school lawyer. It was maddening, it was frustrating and it led me to find - at his request, I might add - another job. (My Superintendent's attorney, to show how good she was at fee driven advice, also represented the Wentzville, MO School District. She billed that small district over $200,000 for her work in representing the district in a 2004 case involving two cheerleaders who had been suspended from school for 10 days for allegedly consuming alcohol before a football game. $200,000! Over a suspension! In perhaps one of the greatest understatements in history, a school insurance representative was quoted as saying that these types of situations could be better handled in house and not by lawyers in court). With that type of legal boogey man hanging over any innovative or new idea in education, it is easy to see why the very bureaucratic red tape that hamstrings any educator who wants to think outside the box; has driven many of our brightest, creative and best young teachers, right out the school house doors and into less maddening - and better paying - professions.

Against this backdrop, I approached Mr. Houston with an introduction of my project at Roosevelt, with caution. I attempted to create empathy - we are all in this together, a "one front line fighter" to another type of camaraderie. I went into a spiel about how I understood FERPA laws and the need to protect student privacy and how I was asking, as a total stranger, to be allowed inside the very closed areas of student and coach interactions that might create privacy concerns, but was an absolute necessity for me to have any hope of producing the story I sought. I sensed Mr. Houston was not interested - nor had the time to listen - to me babble on and on about my vast knowledge of school privacy laws.

"What is it you need," he injected.

"Total access to your school," was my answer.

"You've got it," was his immediate response.

I was stunned. That is it? I don't have to have parental permissions slips signed and filed in triplicate in the offices of all the appropriate Assistant Superintendents? I don't have to offer my first born as collateral to some high dollar Law Firm? I don't have to sign 25 pages of documents that no one ever reads, killed an acre of trees to produce, and will help some poor lawyer afford a bigger house at the Lake? "That is it," I said out loud, in a flabbergasted reaction bordering on shock.

Mr. Houston leaned across the desk and said in his best Virginia bred, son of a Baptist Preacher Man drawl; "We have nothing to hide at Roosevelt High School. We are what you see. Good and the bad, take a look for yourself. The door here is always open. Now, I hate to rush, but I have an awards ceremony to attend. Feel free to stay or walk around anywhere you want to go. And," added in a voice he threw over his left shoulder as he walked out the office door, "Good look with your project." And gone he was to the Senior Awards Program. Yes, I thought, I do believe Mr. Houston gets things done around here.

During my initial meeting with Roosevelt Head Football Coach DeAndre Campbell, I made sure that he understood I was making no promises about producing a book on the season. I confided in him the obvious; I am no John Feinstein and I was not even sure if I could secure a publisher. We'd probably never get rich off of any book royalties, nor could I guarantee that Denzel Washington would portray Coach Campbell in the forthcoming movie version of my bestselling book. What I could state confidently was that I had done my homework and felt there was a story here that needed to be told, that his work with the Roosevelt Roughriders was a tale that the citizens of the community needed to hear. I also assured Coach Campbell that I would never hang him - or anyone at Roosevelt - out to dry, and that in due time he and his players would grow to trust me and the comfort level that would develop between us would allow me to become invisible as the season wore on. I would not, I assured Coach Campbell, become a distraction.

I repeatedly over the next 12 months reassured everyone at Roosevelt that I was not looking to write a negative expose on the evils and overemphasis on high school athletics; that instead my initial view was that the Roughriders were a source of pride and had created a positive impact upon the school and community. I was not out to write another _Friday Night Lights_. The popularity of the movie by the same name was immense, but most do not realize that the movie was released more than 15 years after H. G. Bissinger's writings hit the bookstore shelves. Bissinger followed the 1988 Odessa, TX Permian High School Football team from summer camp to the completion of their season. He had moved his family from the East Coast to West Texas, enrolled his children in the local public schools and had become a member of the Odessa community. His book - the movie projected a much kinder bent on the town and the team – was often critical of a school that held as its highest priority the success of its football team.

In football crazed Texas, overemphasis on athletics - in particular high school football - was an often heard complaint by educators. Bissinger chronicled the actions of coaches that seemed out of sync with mainstream educational standards: playing student athletes when they were hurt, insensitive to the pressure that high stakes football had placed on the shoulders of mere teenager boys, casting aside injured players like last week's trash; and a troubling theme throughout Friday Night Lights – the book version at least - the blatant racism aimed by some of the team's white coaches at the black athletes of Permian. When the book was published the following fall, the Odessa community was outraged at what many saw as a betrayal by Bissinger of the community's trust. The author canceled a return trip to Odessa to hype the publication, because several book stores reported that they had received death threats against Bissinger if he returned to Odessa.

When I first met with Coach Campbell, I assured him that Roosevelt High School was far removed from the fanatic atmosphere of an Odessa Permian level program, and that if anything the opposite was true; most PHL football programs were dying a slow death from apathy. I also pointed out that there would be no public interest in another negative story about the St. Louis Public Schools. There are more than a sufficient number of such stories already out there. For my efforts at Roosevelt to blossom into a story that people would want to read, I needed to spin a positive tale with a Don Quixote slant; accompanied by a heavy emphasis on the accomplishments of a group not afraid to tilt at the numerous bureaucratic windmills that had hamstrung the SLPS for years. A good shot in the arm of "emphasis," I pointed out to Campbell, would be therapeutic for his program and it was my hope that my writing could bring positive attention to his student athletes and the work done by he and his coaching staff.

One last important component that factored into my selection of the Roughriders as the subject of my work was my view of the special status football-led by a strong leader in the position of head coach - can achieve within the social hierarchy of a school and a community. For me, as an old basketball coach, the previous statement is hard to swallow, let alone verbalize. However, over the years, I have seen the occupants of the office of head football coach, often more than any other school position, have the stage needed to forge their will upon a program, a school, and a community. Their labors, evaluated through their team's on field successes and failures, toiling under the relentless glare of the community spotlight, often make the man holding this position the most accountable public figure in the community.

As a high school principal, I always said that nothing fostered a smooth and positive start to a school year more than a successful football team. I will not try and rationalize or justify such a statement. As a professional educator, in theoretical analysis, I can not. But from a pragmatic view, backed by 30 years of experience, I can testify that such a statement rings with a resounding truth. In many small communities, the collective psyche and self esteem of not only the school, but the entire community, rises and falls with the Friday night successes of the town's high school football gladiators. These youth, the best that the community has to offer, are often led by an outsider, the head coach - a mercenary selling his skills to the highest bidder with the promise of gridiron glory. Right or wrong, this phenomenon is part of our culture, pure Americana.

I spent a year after retiring from the Missouri Public School system as a High School Principal in Pocahontas, AR; a community of 6,000 tucked away in the Ozark foothills of the Northeast section of the state. The positive effect on the community and the loads of community support for education, derived directly due to the long standing successes of the PHS Redskins football team, was to say the least, amazing. Every Friday evening, from early September until Thanksgiving, 84 sophomore, junior and senior boys dressed in their beloved and revered red uniforms of PHS, set to do battle, home and away, before 5,000 adoring fans. Serving in auxiliary functions, but in the eyes of their parents and families no less important roles, were the cheerleaders and the band. Both groups were award winners and worked long hours to contribute to the pageantry and festive environment that was Friday Night High School Football in Pocahontas, AR.

Chapter 1: Prologue

I had several long discussions with very talented teachers on my staff that didn't understand the necessity for such worship at the figurative alter of Coach Williams and his boys; for merely playing a kid's game on Friday night. What they so logically would point out to me was the obvious: what a young man learned in Chemistry class that morning would be the vehicle he would ride to life's future successes or failures, and in the long run, it really didn't matter who won Friday night's football game. A goal line stand in the last two minutes of a close football game will not pay the rent 20 years down the road. I agree. But a chemistry lecture will never draw 5,000 community fanatics. That is just the way it is.

The key to the positive role that football played in this particular school was simply the man in charge. Coach Dave Williams had built a program for nearly 30 years that was anchored on unbending discipline. He was a winner, but he was not about winning. He was about doing things the right way, and the community respected him for it. On Coach William's team, you behaved or you didn't play. As I pointed out to my many talented teachers, "when you have a problem in class- be it academic or behavior based -with a football player, you don't bring the issue to me for solution, you take it to Coach Williams; and the nonsense stops- immediately." This, in my opinion, is the key to the educational defense of high profile athletics in our school systems. If the right person occupies the role of leader, an educator committed to impacting young lives through the athletic lessons of teamwork, discipline, and diligence, then athletics will be the positive high profile activity that so many in the public judge a local school by. That is the reality of the educational world we live in.

After meeting Coach Campbell in the Spring of 2008 and discussing with community people their impression of how his work and success with the athletes on his team had effected and impacted community perception of Roosevelt High School, I knew I had found my story. His role as an inner city coach was a mixed lot when compared to his contemporaries in smaller towns and affluent suburban communities. Campbell was not under the constant community pressure to produce consistent winners. He also did not receive the benefits and support from an adoring public when the fruits of his labors ripened into gridiron triumphs, allowing for the chest swelling civic pride that accompanies successful high school football programs in smaller communities. Despite performing on a different stage, in his own way, it was obvious to me that DeAndre Campbell was having a positive effect upon his young players lives that easily transgressed the wins and losses of a brief three month fall football season.

My research and involvement on a daily basis with Roosevelt High School has forced me to re-examine my own view of race and the dynamics it has played in the downfall of the St. Louis Public School system, and more importantly - and painful through personal introspection - in the relationships I have in my own daily personal and professional life. To deny the importance of the racial implications that thread throughout this story of Roosevelt High School would be very blind on my part. In many ways, race is by far the most important sociological phenomena to dissect when attempting to paint a portrait of the Roosevelt High School Roughriders. Race became a constant dynamic in the relationships I developed, and assumptions I drew, as I came to know the primarily African American family of Roosevelt. To not re-examine my own particular views and conditioned responses to racial issues in America in 2008 would have been very shallow on my part, and would have done a great disservice to what the people at Roosevelt are accomplishing with the direct rebirth of a school and the indirect rebirth of a neighborhood. But deep personal delving into racial relations and beliefs amongst those of us who feel an educated aloofness to the uninformed bigot can open a door to a dark and brooding room found inside of us all – a very uncomfortable state of consciousness - resulting in a desire to return to our disconnected but superior frame of mind as quickly as possible.

We, as a society, have come a long way from the volatile years of my youth, the 1960's. We are without a doubt more racially sensitive as a society on the surface today than we have ever been. Comments and subjective racial stereotyping opinions given freely and accepted by the mainstream public 30 years ago would bring instant censure to those that spoke them today. Still, we are a nation and a people who are searching for answers to the role race plays in 21st Century America. Or is it beyond even that? Should the issue of race in America be taken even a step further? Should we as a society realize that we can not answer the questions of racism in our lives until we know the right questions to ask? My experience at Roosevelt has led me to conclude that as a society, we are still searching for the right questions to ponder in our search for racial enlightenment, the answers to which are still light years removed form our collective social grasp.

As I write these thoughts in the year 2009, our nation has for the first time in history elected a candidate of African American family lineage to the Presidency of the United States of America. Yet we are still a people not comfortable with the dynamics of race and the role it plays in our everyday life, including how it affects the education we provide to our young.

One question continued to reappear in my mind with haunting regularity as I worked on this project: was desegregation of the SLPS a good move? If viewed as a single issue focused on the segregated pre-1980 system within the context of a racist motivated conspiracy to keep neighborhoods segregated by making an end run on the landmark Supreme Court's 1954 Brown v Board of Education decision which outlawed the premise of separate but equal schools; then yes, desegregation of the public schools, has been good for the city of St. Louis. But, if viewed through a pragmatic lens, we must conclude that the current system that serves the children of the city of St. Louis is a complete failure in its attempts to provide students anything close to a quality "free and appropriate" education. Furthermore, the schools of the city of St. Louis are more segregated now than at any time since 1954's Brown v Board decision.

As I have studied the desegregation process in urban school districts since Brown v Board, the end result has been absolute and identical in every urban school district in America. When busing for desegregation purposes is enacted as law, a system has developed in each and every case that has produced a more segregated school system than when court mandates were put into place to try and rectify racial imbalances in public education. The bottom line, and I found it held true in every major city I researched in the year 2008, white parents will not send their children to a public school where their child is not a member of a clear racial majority.

In many cases, especially amongst white educators, we are very quick to pat ourselves on the back for breaking away from the moral burden of past racism that so defined the legacy of the previous generations of educational leaders. In 2008, we know the politically correct phrases to use and we are quick to rise up in self righteous indignation to any inference made that would suggest racism based insensitivity was behind any action we took in regard to the executing of our duties as professional educators.

In 2007, I recruited two African American track athletes to the St. Louis Catholic University I coach for. Both young men were very talented, but came from vastly different cultural backgrounds than the large majority of our students. The University where I work is very diverse and prides itself as such. However, many of our black students are products of middle class families – proof of the positive effects of 1970's affirmative action programs, many of us liberals like to point out - and attended one of the numerous private high schools in the St. Louis area. In contrast, my two recruits were from southern states and black public school backgrounds. As I told a Vice President of the University, "my kids are city black kids, not suburban black, like the majority of our black students. They come from a completely different background and culture than what you are used to seeing on this campus."

Two weeks after the Fall 2007 arrival on campus of these two young men, they came to me upset and ready to quit school and go home. They complained to me that they were being singled out and treated differently than other students and thus felt uncomfortable when on campus. Neither lived in the dorms, but when they would visit friends who did, the Resident Assistants would tell them to leave or call security to have them removed, under threat of arrest. The two athletes claimed that their behavior was appropriate, but had been told that dorm residents, especially female residents, were "uncomfortable" with their presence. My two runners said that white visitors were never asked to leave, disregarding and despite the constant overt (drunken) actions of many of these white non-residents, behaviors in obvious violation of dorm rules.

After I confirmed with other students – both white and black - who lived in the dorm in question that this type of unfair treatment of these two young men was indeed occurring, I requested a meeting with the Dean of Students and the Dorm Supervisor.

At the beginning of the meeting, it was made very clear to me, and angrily so, that no one on the dorm staff was a racist and no student would ever be treated in a negative way based on their race or appearance. This was before the particulars of concerns of these two young men had even been addressed or discussed.

When I asked what the two had done to receive such a harsh welcome, I was told "they make some of the girls uncomfortable."

I asked how, and I was told one of the girls heard a rumor that one of these two athletes had stolen an IPod at an off campus party. I was shocked. That was it? That was the justification for being ordered to leave university property or face arrest? I then had several phrases stated to me that my athletes had earlier complained about, but I found hard to believe that any educational leader in the 21st century would be dumb enough to state – even if they believed them: "they don't fit in here," and "they don't belong here."

It only got worse. I was told by a mid-20ish Assistant Dorm Director that he had turned me in to the University's Athletic Director for an NCAA rules violation for paying for the lunch of one of these young men. I denied paying for any athlete's lunch and asked where he got this information. He proceeded to tell me that he watched this particular young man everyday when he went through the cafeteria line, and twice he had seen him not pay for his meal and later he had seen me go through the line and assumed I had paid for both mine and the athlete's lunch bill. He turned this "information" over to the Athletic Director to "protect this institution." (This explained an earlier meeting I had endured with an angry Athletic Director who told me it was "all over campus that you have broken NCAA rules" in order to recruit athletes of this caliber. He didn't say "black" athletes, but we both knew whom he was referring to). The Assistant Dorm Director also confirmed that he watched me every time I ate lunch, when these black athletes I coached were present, to see if and how much I was paying when I handed over money to the cashier. I was now angry. He also told me that I needed to understand how to "handle these types." I informed this $50,000 a year private school educated theater major that I was running a school full of students who would have cut my throat in a New York minute when his mommy was still wiping his butt.

"You watch every student and coach who goes through the line, or just the black kids and the coaches who have black kids on their teams," I asked? The answer to my rhetorical question, although unanswered, was obvious. His assumption was also crystal clear: black city kids couldn't possibly afford to pay for their own lunch, especially if they also happen to be good athletes.

For me, I now had a first hand understanding of the hostility these two young men felt when on the University's campus. I seldom - if it could be at all avoided - ever ate in that cafeteria again. I felt very uncomfortable knowing that an Assistant Dorm Director, who now held the self appointed position as head of the University's NCAA compliance efforts and was running his own sting operation in order to assure proper maintenance of NCAA codes, was staring suspiciously at me as I ate my lunch. I now had first hand experience as to the meaning of the legal term "hostile environment."

After the revelation of this cafeteria "sting operation," I informed the Dean of Students that I now felt that these two young men were being subjected to a hostile environment based upon their skin color, and that if they were two of my white cross country runners from the suburbs, instead of two kids with dreadlocks from the inner city, that we would not be having this discussion about their presence making white girls uncomfortable, nor would they be "eyeballed" in the cafeteria to ensure NCAA compliance.

Unleashed was a fury I had not anticipated. I was immediately told that my comments were "personally insulting" to **her** (the Dean). She made not one inquiry of the Dorm Supervisor as to why these young men were being subjected to this type of scrutiny and treatment, nor what could be done to make them feel less harassed and more at ease on campus; only that **she** was insulted.

At the time of our meeting, the Jena Six situation in Louisiana, where six young African American males had been charged with assaulting a white student and were given what many felt were disproportionate punishments based on their race, was a hot issue on college campuses across the nation. Student organization on our campus had taken up the call for support and "Free the Jena Six" posters and t-shirts were all the rage in the dorms and on campus building bulletin boards. A poster even hung on the wall in the Dean's Office where we met on that September afternoon. Never one smart enough to know when to quit, I fired one final parting shot across the bow, "maybe instead of worrying about the Jena Six, we ought to take a look at what is happening right here on our own campus," I opinioned. Needless to say, that comment did not endear me any to this now riled up Dean. Hence forth, I felt as welcome in her office as an intoxicated Cubs fan in the left field bleachers at Busch Stadium.

I learned a valuable lesson from this experience: we do not risk exposing ourselves to the painful self introspection that would result from true soul searching of our own personal behavior in regard to racial stereotypes if we focus all of our energies – fueled by a righteous indignation and moral outrage - but intellectually centered upon less personal issues, such as racial injustice found in the far off state of Louisiana.

I will include myself in the above realization. As white educators, working in the public eye, where the dynamics of race will always be factored in by those judging our actions (or inactions), we are quick to deny that any decision made by us is ever racially motivated or compromised. This knee jerk reaction to show the superior quality of color blindness that we possess, is often done before we even inquire as to the feelings and thoughts from the individual(s) who feels slighted. Racism is taken off of the table of debate before it can even be considered when often the perception of its existence is viewed by at least one party as the primary reason for the conflict in question. For the progressive and white liberal leaders of our 21st century educational systems, racial bias resulting in unfair and unequal treatment based on simple skin color, would never happen in our enlightened world and on our morally sound watch. Such despicable actions are reserved only for the ignorant and the racists; for the rednecks and uneducated hood wearing bigots safely located in distant lands like Louisiana.

Both of the above mentioned young men returned to their homes in the South at the Christmas break. Neither ever came onto our campus again. I cannot say I blame them.

In 1993, I was the building principal of a small school where a young male student had recently been diagnosed as HIV positive. His mother had dealt with her personal and family grief by immersing herself in the AIDS education movement. In 1993, there still was a sense of hysteria that led many to believe through fear and ignorance that those infected with the virus needed to be quarantined to stop the spread of the deadly disease through causal everyday contact.

The mother of this boy had developed a national reputation in her crusade to educate the public on her son's illness. She had, to say the least, impressive media contacts. One day in 1993, I received a note to call ESPN in Bristol, CT. At first, I suspected a set up by colleagues and friends, but I dialed the number anyway. The message was legit. The ESPN show *Outside The Lines* was producing an episode on AIDS and its impact on sports. This was only several years after Magic Johnson's shocking announcement to the world that he was infected with the AIDS virus. AIDS and its effect upon athletics was still a hot and emotional public issue, and a growing concern in the world of sports. Many Americans, polls showed at the time, still held irrational fears of HIV infection through common daily contact with carriers.

The previous basketball season, several neighboring schools had refused to play our school, if the infected young man was allowed to participate in contests played by our 7th grade boy's team. Being a small town where any controversy can erupt into a full blown crisis, the fall out - fueled by this boy's mother and her media friends - had been overwhelming. The incident received regional wide media coverage. ESPN, with a well placed tip from the boy's mother, was now sending a crew to record how our school had stood behind this young man, informing the balking neighboring schools that we would forfeit before we would remove him from our roster. Eventually, we went on and played the contests after the infected young man voluntarily - rather nobly I thought - removed himself from the team. We found out later that the resistance to his participation was not coming from the players of opposing schools, but from the school's adults: most notably, parents and School Board members.

When I met in my office with a producer from ESPN, he gave to me some remarkable insight into how the media manipulates a story to fit its preconceived notions. "You know we already have this story written," he told me before his crew had even interviewed one of our students. "It is about the ignorance found in small towns and how the good work of one lady helped your small town overcome this ignorance." He candidly told me that he and his crew had spent the previous day on school grounds of one of the neighboring schools who had refused to play us and our infected student the previous year. "Our storyline is to show this school (our rival) in as negative and biased a light as possible. Yesterday, we interviewed at least 10 of their players and only one told us he was afraid of catching AIDS through contact on the basketball court with your boy. We are only using one interview in the show and guess which one it will be?"

Chapter 1: Prologue

I have tried throughout this project to retain a stance of neutrality and objectivity as I recorded my year with the Roughriders. It was hard; and I will not claim a 100% success rate. None the less, I have made a substantial effort to let this story tell itself. I have tried to let the facts lead where they may. Sometimes this made me uncomfortable. None the less, I have made a conscious effort to not bend reality to fit some preconceived story line I had concocted in my own mind. I have taken no liberties with the facts in order to mold this saga into a more interesting, heartwarming or dramatic tale. The story of the 2008 Roosevelt High School Roughriders football team, as Coach Darren West loved to tell his chargers, "it is what it is, dude." But I will admit, in time I grew fond of the individuals whose lives make up this story.

By the Spring of 2008, the St. Louis Public Schools found itself floundering at an all time low water mark. The very survival of the district was suspect, many predicting within years, if not months, an impending doom and total systemic collapse. Into this educational abyss I walked - and found the exact opposite of what I had assumed. The reality I found was a dedication to the education and future of young people - on a front line, grass roots level - that should be awe inspiring to anyone who still believes in the populist dreams that are built upon the foundation of a free and public education.

Our public schools today are not burdened by a lack of modern day educational heroes; just a lack of knowing where to find them. They are out there. Within the St. Louis Public School System - an organization infested with political agendas that find little time or resources for the education of students - I found heroes. I found at Roosevelt High School teachers, coaches and administrators whose one simple daily goal was to make a positive impact on the lives of their students; one child at a time. <u>Riding the Storm Out: A Year of Inner City High School Football</u> is their story.

David Almany
December, 2008

CHAPTER 2
THE 2007 SEASON

It is better to look ahead and prepare than to look back and regret.
— Jackie Joyner-Kersee

Poor people have poor ways.
— Anonymous

Here's to the crazy ones, the misfits, the rebels, the troublemakers, the round pegs in the square holes... the ones who see things differently — they're not fond of rules... You can quote them, disagree with them, glorify or vilify them, but the only thing you can't do is ignore them because they change things... they push the human race forward, and while some may see them as the crazy ones, we see genius, because the ones who are crazy enough to think that they can change the world, are the ones who do.
— Steve Jobs

Strength, quickness and agility training in the new millennium have revolutionized high school sports, especially football. In the dark ages of the pre 1970's, football was viewed as a game of survival. Conditioning and mental toughness were the hallmarks of champions. Size was secondary. Iconic Coach Paul "Bear" Bryant won an NCAA National Championship at the University of Alabama in 1965 with an offensive line whose average weight was 190 pounds. Weight training in 1965 was considered taboo, as the prevailing belief during this time was that lifting weights made an athlete too "muscle bound," limiting quickness and agility, thus rendering the athlete's strength useless against a smaller and quicker opponent. To produce championship caliber play with such small stature players, the sport required an inhumane conditioning system that if used today would lead to charges of abuse and child endangerment. To develop toughness, water breaks during three hour summer practices, held under a boiling sun, were not allowed. Practice sessions were long on torturous drills and short on common sense. Hydration was not considered important enough to offset the weakened competitive spirit that a drink in practice would produce. It was common policy for coaches to give their players, in the middle of 100 degree two a day summer camp practices, salt pills to replace the potassium an athlete lost in sweat. Lawyers today would salivate at such an idiotic, dangerous, and libelous practice.

Today, all has changed. The advantage that leverage through body size brings to both offensive and defensive line play is paramount to any successful football team, at any level. In 1975, not one player in the National Football League had a listed weight of over 300 pounds. By 1990 there were 39. By 2002 the number had exploded to 327. Why? Cynics could point to illegal drugs such as steroids, but a more pragmatic answer would lie with the rule changes that have taken place at both the professional and amateur levels. In the late 1970's, the fundamental rules of blocking were changed. Before, blockers were not allowed to extend their arms and lock their elbows. Such rules put the emphasis for lineman on quickness and agility. With the rule changes allowing the arms of the blocker to extend and "lock up" a defender, body mass and brute strength now trumped quickness.

In 2008, even at the small college level, lineman under 300 pounds are a rare find. Roosevelt's projected starting offensive line for 2008 will average over 250 pounds, yet in many games, the Riders will be outsized along the line of scrimmage. And it is not just size alone. Improvements in the science of developing not only bigger, but also quicker and more agile athletes, today dominate the game of football. Personal trainers and nutritionists, even on the high school level, are now common place. Through intricate drills - with sometimes complex, sometimes simple equipment - the science of athletic training has produced athletes whose physical prowess today dwarfs that of previous generations.

"Bigger, Faster, Stronger" has become more than just a motto, it is a way of life for any modern high school football program that aspires to compete on the highest level. Twenty years ago, a well structured year round strength and conditioning program was the staple of only the elite high school football programs. Today, to have such a regimen in place is a commitment that no longer separates the winners from the losers, but will now only allow a program to avoid doormat status as a homecoming scheduling favorite. No longer is a strength and conditioning program at the high school football level a guarantee for success, but for many, it is only a stop gap measure to starve off ineptness. In simple terms, if you don't lift, you don't win.

High schools, with access to the needed funds, have made financial commitments to their athletic programs that have fueled the construction of special training facilities. A carpeted weight room with wall to wall mirrors and the latest in strength training equipment- accented by row after row of dumbbells, benches and free weights - staffed by coaches well breasted in the latest scientific training methods is now considered a basic requirement for membership in the upper echelon of high school football programs. Many high octane high school football teams even have at their disposal indoor training and practice facilities that assure a good indoor workout or practice regardless of outside weather conditions.

In early May 2008, located in the basement of the school, approximately 30 Roosevelt Roughriders football team members voluntarily lift weights in a converted shower room within an old physical education changing room. To call the area a weight room would be a stretch in generosity. The lighting is poor, the walls and floors bare concrete. The room is abundant with the moisture and the accompanying moldy smell common to the subterranean areas of old buildings. The cramped quarters necessitate that the full body Olympic style lifts, so popular in today's world of strength training– dead lift, cleans and squats – be done in an adjacent hallway.

A quick visual survey of the after school session showed how serious the players are about strength training. Quarterback Arlando Bailey, his powerful body glistening with sweat, did incline dumb bell presses seated on a folding chair. Linebacker George Bell, rippling with muscles that go undetected when he is viewed walking down the hallway between classes in civilian attire, did repeat sets of bench presses; each set consisting of 10 reps. Running back Antonio Carter takes the old school approach, endlessly executing the perfect form pushup. Judging from the lean and muscular development of his upper body, this long time simple staple of physical training is still effective. Offensive center Tyler Clubb, under the watchful eye of Coach Campbell and his hand held video recorder, executes dead lifts, hoisting a barbell holding 300 pounds of plate weights to waist level, dropping the bar and repeating the movement, conscious throughout to employ the proper lifting technique.

The atmosphere of the training session is punctuated and enhanced by teammate's cries of encouragement and the heavy erythematic base beat of rap music blaring from an unseen source, deep inside one of the many old and battered lockers that line a far wall.

Arlando Bailey will be the quarterback of the 2008 Roughriders. He is one of the team's most advanced football talents. "Has Division I potential written all over him," is Coach Campbell's spring 2008 evaluation of Bailey, paying him the ultimate tribute – he has the skills to be considered as a potential recruit at the highest level of college football. Bailey has taken a path less traveled to arrive as a Roosevelt team leader. He attended multiple public city elementary and middle schools as he and his mother moved on a regular basis, sometimes as much as three times in one school year. When Bailey was twelve years old, two monumental changes occurred in his life: he became a rarity amongst the Baptist dominated African American St. Louis church culture as he began to attend a Mennonite Church and he was "adopted" by a South St. Louis Caucasian couple, Ron and Cathy Hutcherson. Bailey calls the Hutchersons, "my God Parents." In reality, the Hutchersons have no legal claim on Bailey. He simply chooses to live with them, while his Mother retains legal custody of him.

Bailey is a well groomed and well spoken young man. His dress would please many a parent of today's teenagers. His conservative appearance is highlighted by a personal dress code favoring pants pulled up to the waist and a pullover polo shirt. At an age when peer pressure is so influential in an adolescent life, Bailey appears to be comfortable in his personal march to the beat of a different dress code drummer. His selected attire goes against the grain of the hip hop, thug look so preferred by many of his Roosevelt contemporaries.

Bailey sports fine, soft facial features, accentuated by a youthful appearance of several years younger than his current age of 17. No leader of a football team wants to be labeled "baby face," but the description is an apt one for Bailey. He does not, as he has been told many times, have the body of a quarterback. His stocky and powerful build is more within the mode of a hard hitting linebacker than a pin point throwing quarterback. Bailey appears to be "leg heavy," large thighs that are thickly muscled. He is the constant target of good natured ribbing from teammates who like to point out his "fat ass" gives him more of a lineman's body than that of a quarterback.

Once on the field, Bailey's unexpected ability to scramble from the passing pocket when his pass blocking breaks down becomes a strong attribute in his personal football arsenal. College coaches comment often that the QB has "good feet." Not the classic 6'3" drop back passer, Bailey becomes agitated when a visitor once again makes the pronouncement of his unlikely position based upon his physical appearance. His defiant intent is clear in his prognosis of his best suited position on the gridiron: "I am a quarterback. I did not want to play running back at CBC (his former school), I do not want to play running back here and I do not want to play running back in college. I am a quarterback," he states.

In a "man bites dog" unlikely sequence of events, Bailey chose of his own free will to leave a prominent private high school to transfer to Roosevelt. Bailey began his high school career by enrolling and attending his freshman and sophomore years at Christian Brothers College (CBC), an all-boy's Catholic high school that has for years produced a large number of St. Louis' civic leaders. The expensive education provided by CBC is grounded in the firm belief that those chosen by God to be blessed with special gifts of intellect have a moral and civic duty to use their blessings for the betterment of humanity.

Being African American made Bailey a minority on the large and well maintained campus, located on Highway 64 in the suburban St. Louis West County area. Conversely, living with a white couple also set him apart from the few black CBC students. But his coup de grace for establishing Bailey as unique amongst his highly motivated peers at CBC was religion. A black student with white adopted parents, while regularly attending Sunday services at a Mennonite Church, placed the stout muscular young man from the inner city in a category all to his own at the private school.

"We had required religion classes at CBC," Bailey recalls. "Everyone in class thought that if I lived with Mennonites then I didn't have electricity or ride in cars. They all thought I was Amish. I am not Mennonite, but I like to go to church with them every Sunday and I find several (church members) really cool."

The Hutchersons espouse a deep rooted faith grounded in solid religious beliefs. Several years ago, they made the hard decision to forsake their long time membership in the Baptist Church. The move was precipitated by the gnawing feeling that the Hutchersons personal pacifist beliefs were no longer in sync with the more mainline foreign policy beliefs expressed in their Baptist Church. "We made the change from the Baptist Church to the Mennonite faith because we were looking for a way to express our feelings against the War (on Terrorism). Baptists talk about peace, Mennonites live it. We try very hard to live in harmony. We do not believe in conflict and we do not believe in violence," explains Ron.

Cathy detailed Arlando's role in the family spiritual arrangement. "One of the few rules we have is that each Sunday morning we will go to church as a family. We don't force our beliefs upon Arlando, but we do want him to be exposed to the spiritual side of life."

When describing his junior year emergence into the vastly different world of Roosevelt, Bailey details an assimilation that required a contentment fostering self confidence, a process that in the early stages caused some anxiety. "When I came to Roosevelt, I didn't mind telling (people) what I thought. I love to argue, but I think I can do it in a way that is not demeaning or confrontational. I don't mind being different. It took some time after I got here (Roosevelt), but now students and my teammates accept me for who I am. I am viewed as a smart guy and good student, but I don't think the other students look down on me or hold that against me. My nickname around school is "CBC." But I don't think that is negative. I view it as a positive."

Bailey's relationship with Ron and Cathy has also evolved over time. "We met Arlando when he was in the 5th grade," says Ron, a slightly built and soft spoken man employed in the field of computers. "I taught a Sunday School class at the Third Baptist Church, located downtown at Grand and Washington. Arlando was one of my students. I felt a bond to him immediately. He was just so much more aware, on just a different level, than the other students his age. He just seemed to have remarkable potential."

Neither the Hutchisons nor Arlando can put an exact time on when he took up full time residence with the childless couple. "He first stayed with us over the Christmas break of his 5th grade year," says Cathy. "He knew that he was welcome any time and it just slowly progressed that he was with us more and more. We were very careful not to overstep our bounds and we have always respected the rights and the privileges of Arlando's mother, but he was just a kid we felt like we could have a (positive) impact on his life."

A defining moment in Bailey's deepening involvement in the lives of the Hutchersons came during the summer after his 6th grade year. "He was coming back from a camp for city kids held out in a rural area," remembers Cathy. "When the bus brought him back to the drop off point, he had no way home. He called and we went and picked him up at the bus station, and it was just like 'now you are with us.' We just kind of fell in love with each other."

By the time Bailey had entered middle school, the Hutchersons questioned the education the bright young man was getting at his public school, Fanning Middle School. "He was not challenged," says Ron, a contention that Arlando quickly seconds. "I was bored."

Despite repeated trips to Fanning to speak with administrators and counselors, Ron felt their concerns were not being heard. "For Arlando's sake, we decided to look elsewhere for his 7th grade year."

As so many St. Louis city parents have done over the last generation that "elsewhere" became the city's Catholic school system. Arlando was enrolled in the prestigious and often lauded Loyola Academy, a middle school of all African American male students, located in the inner city St. Louis area. The school, steeped in the many success stories of its graduates, is staffed and run by the Jesuit order of Catholic Priests. "They had a longer school day," says Arlando, "and we had to work in every class. The teachers were tough and it was hard, but I learned more there in two years than I ever thought possible."

Cathy reaffirms the positive assessment of Loyola. "He thrived on the challenge. Arlando really grew as a student in his two years at Loyola." Iron fisted academic discipline, instilled by the Jesuits seemed to fit well with the serious student Arlando found emerging within himself.

After several years of bouncing between the home of his mother on the North side and the home of the Hutchersons - located right across the street from Roosevelt High School - by the time Bailey was ready to start his freshman year of high school, it was pretty well assumed by all involved that his permanent residence was now with Ron and Cathy. "He can come and go as he pleases, and there are times that he has," said Ron.

Twice since the initial visit during his 5th grade Christmas vacation- when he first moved in with the Hutchersons- Bailey has returned to his mother's house for extended time periods. But Arlando was careful not to sever his lifeline to the white couple who had befriended him, as he continued to keep a room and some of his belongings at their home. Bailey maintains that he has always felt a strong tie to the middle class couple. "I moved back with my mom for most of my 6th grade year, but it just didn't seem to work. And I didn't want to go back to Fanning for 7th grade. Ron and Cathy helped get me into a much better school. I have always felt comfortable living with them."

Bailey was always athletic – an accomplished basketball player from the youth leagues all the way through middle school – both the Hutchersons and Bailey say that athletics played no role in his decision to attend the well known and long time athletic power, CBC. "Several of my friends from Loyola were going there and I felt it was a good fit for me." Upon arrival, Bailey did immerse himself into the Cadets' gridiron program. A recent move from the school's long time home campus in the city, to a multi million dollar new campus in the suburban West County area, had made CBC one of the fastest growing and exclusive high schools in the area. Always known for it's athletic programs –NBA star

Larry Hughes who was a late 90's CBC graduate, lead the Cadets (the school formally required military training and uniforms for all students, a policy long ago abandoned) to a state title his senior year. Hughes then had a one year stop over at St. Louis University before launching a long and lucrative NBA career.

To upgrade its football program, CBC in 2001 made the headline grabbing move of hiring legendary football coach Bob Shannon to lead the Cadets. Shannon, an African American, had built his reputation as a no-nonsense disciplinarian and father figure at East St. Louis High School in Illinois, a school which serves a community consistently at the top of any negative national crime report ranking. Shannon won numerous state titles with the Flyers and established for himself a national reputation as a visionary leader of black male youth. While in constant competition with the East Side street forces: drugs, gangs, pimps and any other low life dreg of society that can manage to leech to the under belly of the street culture, Shannon, through his powerful personality, taught his players to pull themselves out of the ghetto by their own jock straps. He demanded that they use football as a means to an end – a college scholarship and a ticket out of the East St. Louis Projects. Shannon was considered a national hero and was lauded by many, including the President of the United States, Bill Clinton, as such.

Unfortunately, Bailey and the legendary coach never meshed. "I wanted to play quarterback, he wanted me at running back. I didn't want to be a running back, I wanted to be a quarterback. But that is not why I left. I could have quit football and stayed at CBC, if football had been the only concern. I liked CBC, but the ride (to the county school) got old. I had to get up at 5 am each morning, " said Bailey.

The Hutchersons looked at several options as alternatives to returning to CBC for Arlando's junior year. "We were ready to pay the money to send him to a different Catholic high school in the city, but then Ron lost his job, and all of a sudden, paying the expensive tuition to a private school was no longer an option we could afford," says Cathy. Home schooling was even discussed, but abandoned because of Ron's insistence that Arlando would suffer socially with the isolation that the home school option would come burdened with. As the summer vacation of 2007 drew to a close, Roosevelt became a last and perhaps only educational option left for Arlando.

"It was tough at first," says Bailey of his initial days at Roosevelt "It was so much different than what I was used to. I was right back in with some of the neighborhood guys I had known in 6th grade at Fanning, and they were going nowhere."

The Hutchersons also had many anxiety laced concerns with moving Arlando back to the public schools. "We had such a bad experience with Fanning, and we had no reason to believe Roosevelt would be any different," says Ron. At first, it wasn't. "After the first couple of weeks of school," remembers Ron, "Arlando called us one day during school, and was very unhappy." His plea to his God Parents was direct and to the point, "get me out of here," was the message that came through loud and clear over the cell phone that September 2007 afternoon.

With no other viable educational options available until at least the end of the first semester, the trio had to buckle down and make the best of what had the makings of a bad educational situation. What was perceived by Ron and Cathy as a lack of concern for Arlando's class schedule by some at Roosevelt, resulted in dismay and frustration on the part of the Hutchersons. "He was not in the upper level classes where he should have been," says Ron.

Several trips to the Roosevelt High School counselor's office did not elicit the class changes that they had sought for Arlando. That, however, changed after a visit to the office of Principal Terry Houston. "I spoke with Mr. Houston and immediately Arlando was given classes we were all much happier with. Things were much better after that," said Cathy.

With academics and their importance duly noted, all sides agree, the dynamic that launched Arlando Bailey into the fast track of acceptance by his peers at Roosevelt High School, was football. Witness Bailey's interaction with his teammates for only a short duration, and an observer will know at once that the soft spoken young man with a linebacker's body has the difficult-to-demarcate quality common to all successful gridiron field generals: leadership.

Bailey was an unexpected gift that fell on Coach Campbell's doorstep on the eve of the start of summer camp in August of 2007. "When my mom (Cathy) came up and talked to Mr. Houston before I enrolled, she never even mentioned football to him, so nobody really knew who I was when I showed up for practice the first day of summer two a days last August (2007)."

After only a few practices with Bailey on the roster, the coaches knew they had a quarterback competition on their hands. The incumbent QB entering the 2007 season was popular senior Miguel Allen. Most college scouts considered Allen to be Roosevelt's best athlete and the 2007 team's top collegiate prospect.

"We always wanted to move Miguel out of the quarterback slot," said Coach Campbell, "because he was our best athlete. We wanted to be able to line him up all over the field, sometimes in the backfield, some times flanked out wide, (to) take advantage of his (multitude of) talents by getting him the ball in different spots on the field. We couldn't do that with him as a quarterback. But he was also our best quarterback (before Bailey arrived) and we needed to keep him there. When Arlando showed up, it opened up the position. But we had spent the whole offseason working with and developing our offense around Miguel at quarterback. Arlando needed time to learn the system. We had planned to continue to be primarily a team that ran the ball, but with Arlando, we saw he was a much better passing option than Miguel. Arlando's joining the team made us pause and say, 'hey, we've got something here.'"

From the NFL all the way down to the lowest peewee league, every football coach knows that nothing can tear a team apart at the seams and create locker room dissention quicker than a full blown quarterback controversy.

"We were very much aware that we needed to tread lightly with the situation," said Coach Campbell. "Miguel was a neighborhood guy. He was our leader. The others looked up to him." That made Bailey about as popular with Allen's senior classmates as a hard working meter maid. But, after an opening season disappointing and dispiriting 12-8 loss to conference foe Vashon, which saw an injury to Allen, the coaches were forced into a move necessitated by Allen's incapacity.

"It is a good thing Arlando is a quick learner," said Coach Campbell, "because by Week II, we had decided he was our man at quarterback. Miguel couldn't go and we had no other choice."

Allen's 5 for 12 passing performance in the opening loss were not considered dreadful by the coaching staff. However, all sides knew that not only would the team benefit, and Allen's collegiate stock would rise, if upon his return from the injured list he was moved to his more natural positions of running back and wide receiver.

The coaches set about the task of convincing not only Allen, but also his loyal teammates, that Allen's position move was a win-win situation for everyone. "I knew I was ready," said Bailey, who showed no hesitation in accepting the early season challenge as the Roughriders starting QB.

The strategy for Bailey's first start in Week II appears on the surface similar to that of the Super Bowl bound Chicago Bears of 2006. The Bears kept a tight leash on their beleaguered quarterback, Rex Grossman, employing a conservative run oriented offense in their march through the NFC. Grossman's explicit orders from the Bear's coaches in 2006 were simple; "just don't get us beat. Let the defense win the game." In his first start, Bailey threw only 3 passes, completing two, in a 12-6 win over Miller Career Academy.

Coach Campbell says that the comparison to the Grossman situation in Chicago and Bailey's with the Roughriders is not accurate; that a different set of circumstances limited Bailey's passing attempts in his debut as the starter. It was not a lack of confidence in Bailey, but the limited time he had to learn the offense- a lack of practice repetitions - that limited his passing attempts against Career Academy to only three.

By Week three, an unbridled and better acclimated Bailey was ready to burst onto the PHL gridiron scene. In a 29-6 win over Sumner- lead by former Roughrider Coach Sorrel Harvey - Bailey completed 9 of 11 passes for two touchdowns. By the following week, after a 59-0 pounding of Soldan - the team coached in 2006 by now RHS Principal Houston - everyone in the PHL was buzzing about Bailey's remarkable stats. Completing 18 of 22 passes against the Tigers of Soldan, the Roughriders emerging star was now the talk of the PHL football circles.

Terry Houston, Principal of Roosevelt High School, had the distinct experience in October 2006 of concurrently wearing two time demanding hats. After his appointment as Roosevelt's latest in a long line of Head Masters, Houston simultaneously finished out the 2006 season as head football coach of the PHL's Soldan Tigers, while tackling the monumental task of cleaning up Roosevelt High School.

Houston, 50 years of age, was born and raised in Virginia. As an undergrad at Virginia State University, Houston played varsity football. After graduation, he entered the ranks of public education, landing an assignment teaching and coaching in the Petersburg, VA Public School system.

Married in 1984, Houston's career has followed a nomadic course ever since. He explains the reason for the numerous moves: "My wife works for the federal government. She is the real breadwinner of the family. I just make chump change compared to her. When she receives a job promotion requiring a move, I just pack up and follow." His wife's developing career has led to more job transfers and teaching reassignments in more states than Houston can remember. "We were in Colorado Springs before my wife's transfer here (St. Louis) in 1997. I went to work for the SLPS in December of 1997." Stints as an assistant football coach at several PHL schools were endured until Houston settled into a home at the PHL's Soldan High School in the Fall of 2000.

After several seasons as an assistant coach, Houston became the head coach of the Tigers for the 2002 season. He also was working in the evenings and the summers in graduate school, attempting to earn his administration certification. Degree in hand in 2004, Houston vacated his health and PE teaching slots to become an Assistant Principal at Soldan High School. He continued in his role as head coach of the football Tigers. On October 6, 2006, Houston took on perhaps the most daunting challenge in a school system full of daunting challenges: the Principal at what many considered the worst high school in one of the worst school system in the country, St. Louis Roosevelt High School.

Speaking with the older students of Roosevelt, whose tenure as Roughriders spans to the pre Mr. Houston days, a stark picture quickly emerges of a school that was overrun by out of control students; dominated by multiple neighborhood gangs who had taken control of the school hallways. Senior football player Quadricous Sanford in 2006 transferred to Roosevelt from South Panola High School in Batesville, MS, several months before Houston's arrival. "Mississippi was bad," Sanford says in a thick southern drawl, "but this place (Roosevelt) was wild. I come here and dudes are spitting on the floor right in the hallways, tearing up things and just being crazy. I say 'why you do that, this is our school, why you tear it up.' Mr. Houston comes in and all that changed. Here now we got discipline, not only in football, but also in school. Mr. Houston come in and just start(ed) kicking the gang members out. He tells us all the time 'there is only one gang here now, the Roosevelt Gang, and everyone here is a member.'"

Houston states the condition he inherited in quantitative terms: "Our first point of emphasis when I came here was to hold people accountable for their behavior. We had 38 identifiable gangs at Roosevelt in 2006. Today (April, 2008) we can't identify one (active) known gang in our hallways. If some of our students are in gangs, they are keeping it quiet. They know if they throw signs or participate in any identifiable gang activity while in our building, they are gone. No second chances. No gray area. If you are in a gang, you will not go to school here, and if you in any way display your membership in our building, you are gone. The gang members, we had zero tolerance for them. That is non negotiable here at Roosevelt High School."

As Houston continues to describe the improvements in his school, his passion and pride for the transformation of Roosevelt is obvious by the rising emotion in his voice. "You want to fight, you will not go to school here. You commit a type one offense at Roosevelt High School, fighting or dealing with drugs on school grounds, you are gone. No second chances," he emphatically declares.

Houston's second chore, after securing safety in the hallways of RHS, was to get students to school on a regular basis, and then into class in a timely manner. "Attendance was at 60% when I came and it took kids 20 minutes to get to class and clear the hallways each hour," Houston remembers. "We started school at 7:20 am. An hour later there would still be 200 kids out in front of the building or hanging out in the hallways or auditorium. Nothing good or productive is going to come from that (scenario). We stopped that right away."

Addition by subtraction was Houston's next strategy in reshaping the attitude of the Roosevelt student body. "We identified the kids that had no reasonable chance to graduate, the ones that had only a few credits and were already 18 or even 19 years old. They were in educational limbo and they knew it. Nothing good was going to come from carrying them on our rolls and having them in our classrooms. We got them into programs that better fit their needs, helped them to get a GED or get into an alternative school setting."

According to Houston, the data supports the validity of his efforts. "This year (2008) we plan to graduate 225 students. Last year it was 140. I have had some people upset with me for the hard line we have taken on fighting, gangs and school safety, but that is the way it is going to be here at Roosevelt. You have to understand that we couldn't keep doing the same thing that was being done. We were failing our students, sacrificing their future. We had to change."

Houston feels that the changes he initiated in 2006 have not only made the school safe, but brought back to the South Side neighborhood a feeling of community pride for Roosevelt High School. "We are starting to show pride in our school and our kids are proud to go to school here," Houston said. "We want Roosevelt High School to be a place that every kid feels safe. To do that, you have to hold people -students, teachers, myself, and everyone in our building- accountable." Houston's emphasis on the word "accountable" sends a clear message of who is in charge at Roosevelt High School.

Houston targeted from the beginning of his tenure at Roosevelt the importance of rebuilding relationships with the area residents, returning Roosevelt to the critical role it once played in the stability of the area neighborhood. The blocks surrounding Roosevelt's campus retain a large section of white residents. Few, if any, of these long time south siders, send their children to Roosevelt. Those with high school age children enroll them in the private schools, not at Roosevelt. The majority of Roosevelt's African American students do not live in the immediate vicinity of the school, but to the east or to the north. For many years, the community perception and acceptance of the Roosevelt student body's daily track into their neighborhood was at best, leery. Houston says, "we want to once again be the anchor of the neighborhood, the social institution that gives the community an identity."

Houston admits that he has a long way to go to insert RHS back into its once prominent rank in the community, but the success of his efforts may well be the last chance for the survival of Roosevelt High School. "For us to survive, we have got to be a true neighborhood school, not just an educational warehouse for kids from another part of town. When I came here, the community viewed our students almost like an invading army that would march through each morning and retreat each evening. The area citizens were afraid of our kids. It was important that we showed the neighborhood that our kids were good kids and it was also (important) that we show our kids that being respectful, and (to) behave appropriately, would in the long run make Roosevelt a better school."

Robert Ashton, President of the Tower Grove Neighborhood Association, confirms the recent tenuous relationship between Roosevelt and the neighborhood. "Before Mr. Houston," Ashton stated at a community meeting in December, 2008, "it was a problem. We viewed the students here as a (detriment) to the area. We felt that their presence hurt business and that their behavior scared area residents. But over the last couple of years, Mr. Houston and the school have reached out and it has allowed us to build bridges and start dialogue with the schools."

Ashton can point to several areas of quantitative improvement. "The trash the students used to leave on the streets and in the yards as they would come and go each day was a problem that upset many of our residents. That has improved a great deal the last two years, and I give Mr. Houston credit for that. He has gotten us involved in the school and the school has gotten involved in the community. Mr. Houston meets with us once a month to get our input and to ask for our assistance. Nobody ever reached out like that to us before. The last two years the school has held a barbeque in May for the students and the area citizens, giving each group a chance to interact. Before Mr. Houston, letting all the kids out of school and into the neighborhood could have never happened without a whole lot of police to keep order. The Roosevelt kids were just too wild. The last two years, the behavior of the kids has been so good (at the barbeque) it really impresses our area (residents)," says Ashton.

Houston reaffirms that the improved relations between the community and the school did not just happen. "We are a neighborhood school," explains Houston. "We need the support of the community for our school to reach its potential. All of our people: students and staff have worked hard in this important area."

White parents not willing to send their children to the SLPS is an obvious problem for the district. Census data for the south side enrollment area that Roosevelt serves, depicts a population of over 65% percent white. Yet, few white students attend Roosevelt High School. Houston sees that as a challenge. "All we can do is try everyday the best we can to educate our students the best way we know how. We can do a better job of that with the support of the neighborhood. If because of that we begin to attract more students that are now in private schools, that is a plus. But we can not make parents send their child here. What we can do is show them that we are a good school with a hard working staff committed to helping every child succeed. If we can do that, and then continue to do that, parents will see that, and parents, who can now afford other educational options for their child, will start to trust us with their child's education. But we have to first earn that trust and that is what we try to do everyday, with every bit of our effort, down here at Roosevelt High School."

Area educators began to sit up and take notice of the transformation that was occurring at the south side school. In the spring of 2008, Houston was named Principal of the Year by the St. Louis Association of Secondary School Principals (SASSP). The selection area encompassed the entire St. Louis metropolitan area and approximately 100 high schools, a laudable start for a first time building principal.

Houston brims with energy and enthusiasm for his favorite topic, public education. Despite a youth spent growing up in an impoverished background, Houston's parents allowed no excuses for neglecting an education. His parents would not tolerate such nonsense. Raised by a father who himself had dropped out of grade school, Houston and his siblings had education and its social enabling power drilled into their belief system from an early age.

Houston's father, Thomas Houston, was raised in Alabama. The man without an education himself, never the less hammered home the importance of a college degree to all four of his children. Foregoing college was simply not an option for any of Thomas Houston's offspring. "I remember as a child, around the age of 6 or 7, my dad used to preach that you're going to college, you're going to college," Houston told the St. Louis American, a weekly black St. Louis Newspaper. "I used to tell people that I was going to college before I even knew what college was."

The Principal takes the same approach with the students of Roosevelt High School. "I tell them 'when you graduate, you need to be thinking about college, trade school or the military,'" Houston said. "Don't graduate and think that McDonald's will be a career for you, unless that is the best that you can do."

Houston's message is reaching its intended audience and resounding with the Roosevelt clientele. At an April, 2008 senior awards ceremony, a senior student stood to address her fellow classmates. Her statement to her peers was a riveting endorsement of what Houston had preached long and hard to the Class of 2008: "I'm always going to remember one thing Mr. Houston said, 'They can take your glasses, your shoes, your watch, and your earrings, but they can't take what you know.'"

Houston and his wife, Deborah, are the parents of three children: Tiffany, a freshman at Jackson State University; Terry Jr., a sophomore at Southeast Missouri State University; and Thomas, a junior at Lindenwood University. In addition to his Bachelor's Degree from Virginia State, Houston has earned a master's degree in education leadership from Saint Louis University. In the spring of 2008, he was finishing work for a doctorate degree in education from Lindenwood University in St. Charles, MO.

Possessing a strong spiritual side that he is not afraid to show and share, Houston gives passionate witness to his religious faith and how it guides him through the trials and tribulations found at his inner city school. Houston states: "Nothing, nothing can be done anywhere without faith. I really believe in Philippians 4:13, 'All things are possible through Christ Jesus who strengthens me,' which means that coming to a place like Roosevelt, when people said that I couldn't, I knew that I could. When people said that the kids couldn't, I knew that we could."

The Roosevelt Headmaster has obviously put on a few pounds since his days as a star running back in the late 1970's at Virginia State University, but the enthusiasm he shows for his job as head man at RHS deters any concern that his energy level is not up to the task of running a tough inner city school. A knock on his closed office door on a warm May 2008 day uncoils him from his desk chair quicker than an Albert Pujols line drive home run leaving Busch Stadium. As Houston throws open the door, a young lady appears. "Mr. Houston, Raymond is upset," she says. From behind his messenger, stands Raymond, a tall lean young man.

"Raymond," Houston blurts out, "speak up son, what you need." The young man stares at his feet and mumbles an inaudible request. "Speak up boy, how can I help you if I can't hear you," implores Houston.

"Mr. Houston, she going to flunk me in Science," the young man pleads in a now clear baritone voice, deceptive of his slight and youthful appearance. "I did the work, but she going to flunk me anyway, and I got to graduate" the boy relates in a voice now rising with emotion.

"No, no, no," Houston responds in rapid fire, "nothing going to keep you from walking across that stage in a few weeks, Raymond. You've come too far. You get here by 7 tomorrow morning and we will get this fixed. Don't stress out on me now Raymond, just be here at 7."

The young man and his female moral supporter depart Houston's Office with an obvious sense of relief. "Now where were we," says Houston, returning to an interrupted conversation with a visitor.

All in a days work for the head Roughrider. "Never want to forget," Houston says, "the students and their future are why we are here. Nothing is more important to me right now, than what is important to the child, right now."

Roosevelt Assistant Principal Joe Kenney brings a different perspective to the Administrative Staff at Roosevelt. He began his duties at RHS in the Fall of 2007. Kenney had previously run the Alternative School for a predominantly white suburban high school. Prior to that assignment, he had been a literature teacher. Keeney has no athletic participation or coaching experience on his resume'. He grew up in North St. Louis and graduated from the exclusive boy's private school - and Roosevelt district football foe - Chaminade. Kenney is also the only white administrator on the RHS staff.

"I view athletics as a means to keep kids in school. Without football, many of Coach Campbell's players would have dropped out," says Kenney. "Coach Campbell and his staff play an important role in their players' education. The discipline they show on the field (will) carry over to the classroom. The success they have on the field brings positive recognition to our school. That closeness that the coaches can develop on the field is at a different level than a classroom teacher can. Coach Campbell has moved on from coaching his players in just football, but is now coaching them in life. Mr. Houston gives that same commitment to our students and staff. He "coaches" us all with the same passion that Coach Campbell does with his players. It is about life and it is about preparing our kids to do well in life."

The 5th week of the 2007 season saw the return from injury of Allen, and the Roughriders unveiled a two quarterback rotation system. "There were times when we wanted Miguel in the game and there were times when we needed the talents of Arlando at quarterback. Each brought something special to the plate and we tried to maximize the talents of both," says Campbell of his midseason signal caller deployment.

The two headed quarterback model led the Riders to an easy 43-6 win over their one time south side neighborhood rival, Cleveland. The Dutchmen, no longer a south side neighborhood school; and not even the Dutchmen anymore, but were known now as the Admirals of the Cleveland Naval ROTC Academy, a magnet school that the year before had abandoned its' long time south side "castle," moving to the north side of the city. Cleveland Naval ROTC was struggling mightily to keep its doors open. By the end of the 2006-2007 school year, enrollment was at a free fall and class rosters listed less than 300 students. Cleveland was also the alma mater of Roosevelt Head Coach DeAndre Campbell.

Campbell is a young coach, but embraces much of the same gung ho enthusiasm and drive of his mentor, Principal Houston. Campbell possesses the vigor needed to tackle the herculean task of building and maintaining an inner city high school football program.

"I had a great experience as a student at Cleveland," said Coach Campbell, Class of 1994. "I was born on the north side and always attended city schools up there until I came south to Cleveland for my high school years." After graduation, Campbell landed a football scholarship at tiny Missouri Valley College in Marshall, MO. "I had very good coaches throughout high school and college, but I never really thought about coaching myself. Like a lot of guys, I thought I was headed to the NFL. My major at Missouri Valley was mass communications. I did a lot with production of video and producing for television. I had very good practical experience in my undergrad training, but when I moved back to St. Louis after graduation, the job market was pretty sparse. So I started to substitute teach for (the) SLPS."

Maybe it was fate, but as the new millennium dawned on the Gateway City, the anemic job market for mass media production specialists that forced Campbell to search for what ever means of employment subsistence he could find, led him straight into what he now considers his true calling, coaching football with inner city kids. "There is so much potential in these kids at Roosevelt. I could see it right away and knew that working with kids in this school system is where I needed to be."

Initially, Campbell bounced around to several schools and positions, as he gladly took whatever non-certified position was available in the SLPS. Without the proper teaching certification, his options were limited to lower level assistant teaching and assistant coaching slots. Aspiring for much higher levels in the SLPS, Campbell spent his nights, weekends and summers finishing up the college course work he needed to achieve the proper credentials to certify him for full time teaching and head football coaching positions. "In 1999, before I even had my certification, I taught math at an Alternative School," said Campbell, alluding to a special school for students who can not exhibit the proper behavior in a regular school setting. "That was an eye opener. You get to see the kids everyday whose behavior was denying them an education, so they came to us. We were the end of the line. If they didn't make it with us, they were not going to make it. A lot of them didn't make it, but a few did, and that was always a good feeling; knowing that you had given them a future, a chance."

With certification firmly and finally in hand, Campbell spent the 2002, 2003 and 2004 school years at Beaumont High School on the city's north side as a PE teacher and assistant football coach. As if right on cue, in 2004, the job he had always dreamed of, head football coach at his alma mater - Cleveland ROTC Naval Academy - became vacant. With a plan of bringing back the past gridiron glory to the south side school, Campbell made an all out blitz in his attempt to secure his first head coaching position. "I was ready," he says in 2008. "I had served my time as an assistant in the SLPS. I had studied hard. I had gone back to school and gotten my certification. I had prepared myself. I was very confident I could do the job. I didn't get it. I was surprised. I was hurt. I thought for sure I would be the head coach at Cleveland," Campbell states in a voice that four years later still cracks of bitterness.

"I don't know why they passed on me. They just said they wanted to go another direction. They hired a guy from the suburbs, from Clayton, who I understood had a few connections with some of the influential alumni of Cleveland. It just was not meant to be."

After the bitter disappointment at what he perceived as a personal rejection by a school he was proud to call his alma mater, Campbell took a year off from coaching in the PHL. "I needed some time, so I volunteered to help with the JFL, the little league football program. It was good for me. I needed to step back and get some perspective. In 2005, I was ready to jump back in and I took a job as an assistant coach with (PHL rival) Career Academy. Then Coach (Sorrel) Harvey decided to leave Roosevelt and go back to his alma mater, Sumner. That created an opening I jumped at and I was hired as the head coach here at Roosevelt for the 2006 season."

Although he does not say so, the implications from Campbell are clear: things worked out for the best. On September 28, 2007 the Roughriders of Coach Campbell pounded Cleveland, the school that had left him standing at the alter three years before, by the score of 43-6. It was the Roughriders fourth consecutive lopsided win over an overmatched PHL foe.

"Team First" and "Family" are two sound bites heard constantly around the Roosevelt football program. These two cornerstones are instilled daily by Coach Campbell into the heads of his young players. "We have a large number (18) of seniors for this year (2008)," Campbell stated. "These are my guys. This is my team. We function as a disciplined unit, both on and off the field. We will accept nothing less from any of our players or any of our coaches. We are accountable for the actions of this team. Coach Harvey's kids are now gone. My mark is on these guys."

"We will be disciplined" is an oft sounded mantra for any new football coach when taking over a downtrodden program. However, an inner city football program creates its' own special challenges to a coach trying to instill order into the unstructured lives of his teenage athletes.

"Before Coach Campbell, a lot of guys just would not show up for practice, or if they did show up it would be late," states senior running back Antonio Carter. "Now, guys don't practice, they don't play."

Attempts to increase participation levels while at the same time requiring escalating hours of commitment to a developing football program can be a catch 22 that has derailed many a new coach. Do you lower your standards to keep less committed athletes on the team? What if mass player mutiny results from the demands of a disciplined program and not enough bodies are left to fill 11 uniforms on game day? Such anxiety laced questions have been faced over the years by many a new head coach who suddenly realizes the reality and the accountability of being the "head man." But not the case, according to Campbell, of his early days as the head coach at Roosevelt. "From day one, we made it very clear what we wanted. The ground rules were in place and if you did not follow them, you were not going to play for Roosevelt. I never considered doing it any other way. It is the way I have been taught as a player and I will never coach any other way."

The senior class members of the 2008 Roughriders football team have seen the important role that discipline can play in a developing a winning attitude. "We lead by example," says senior center Tyler Clubb. "We count on each other. If you are not at weight lifting, then you are letting your teammates down. The younger players see what we are and how hard we work and they follow. Actually, I hate to say it, but so far this offseason the younger guys are outworking us seniors. They are really pushing us."

Clubb's testament on the revival of the Roughriders, built upon the rock solid foundation of old school discipline, is proof that Campbell's philosophy of hard work is taking root. According to Campbell, the vision he is instilling in his players is part of a program hell bent on taking no short cuts in developing a legacy that will long outlast the departure of any one particular senior class.

For a coach to demand a year round commitment to a football program in the inner city raises obstacles not found in the suburbs and private schools; namely transportation to and from workouts, and the need for continued after school employment for many players, even during the season. "Kids here don't have cars," says Campbell. "Many ride public transportation to and from school. Kids here also have to work, not just to have money to play around with, but many times to help put food on the table for their families. I can't be as demanding of them as coaches in other environments can. What we ask them to do is sacrifice. Make our team a family. If you are a family, you find ways to work things out. That is just how it is in the city. We all sacrifice. We all make do.

We all work together. If football is important enough to you, you can still take care of the (family) things, and still have time to be a part of our team. You just have to want it pretty bad. And most of our kids find a way."

So how did it work out, this hard nosed attempt by a first time head coach to instill discipline into a program that most at RHS in 2006 say was drastically needed? "We never lost one kid in that first year (2006) because he wouldn't live up to our behavior expectations," says Campbell. "They do what we ask and they expect nothing less from us than high expectations. The players bought in right from the start."

Campbell seeks role models that he can hold up as examples of the possibilities for an inner city athlete willing to strive for the best. "Right over there is Charles Ali," Campbell pointed out on a warm summer evening in 2008, during a break in a 7 on 7 scrimmage between Cleveland and Roosevelt. "He comes down here all the time when he is home and talks to our kids. He played for me when I was an assistant coach. Now he is in the NFL with the Cleveland Browns. He made it (to the NFL) the hard way. He was an undrafted free agent out of a low profile program (Arkansas-Pine Bluff). But now he is playing with the best in the world and making a great salary. And he started right here in the PHL, just like these kids out here tonight. To see someone who has made it in the league back here, well, that lets our kids dream. They see his success and they think, 'if he can make it, so can I.'"

The 2007 week 5 thrashing of Cleveland carried two significant statistics that forced now leery PHL opponents to sit up and take notice of: the debut of the two headed quarterback passing duo of Allen and Bailey, complimented by the punishing ground game led by junior running back Antonio Carter. The quarterbacks combined for 9-10 passing for 168 yards and three touchdowns and Carter rushed for 189 yards on only 12 carries.

In a weird statistical quirk, no Roughrider forward pass attempt during the game ever hit the ground. The lone non- completion was an interception thrown by Bailey. "Right off Xavier's (Walker) hands," Bailey bemoaned almost six months after the near perfect night of passing. "He should have had it," Bailey said with a shrug.

A hot discussion topic amongst PHL football enthusiasts in both 2007 and 2008 centered around the debate as to who was the best running back in the PHL, Gateway Tech's sophomore AJ Pearson or Roosevelt's senior Antonio Carter. A college coach succinctly summed up Pearson's style as such: "Watching him run is like watching clean water flow over rocks in a creek. His style is natural and effortless." The star sophomore was already being called one of the top Class of 2011 recruits in the nation. A limitless future was predicted for the 6'2" multi talented running back. Pearson's running style was effortless, at times appearing almost too easy. He was a top of the line Cadillac possessing a level of potential stardom most at Roosevelt could not relate to.

Carter, on the other hand, was a four wheel drive pickup; with a lot of mud under the chassis. Unlike Pearson, Carter was not a glider; he was a slasher. He didn't flow; he attacked. While Pearson appeared to have hitched a ride onto a first class charter jet on his way to stardom, Carter took the city bus to work each day, lunch pail in hand - the people's choice for best running back in the PHL. As Carter liked to point out about his more acclaimed rival, "the dude ain't ever beat me on the field."

Couple Carter's God-given athletic talent with his humility and a courage level described by another coach as "more guts than a fish market" and Carter would seem to have a perfect football pedigree and a future well beyond the confines of Roosevelt High School and the Public High League. Only one problem area can be found on Carter's football resume: he stands, with shoes on, only 5 feet 4 inches tall and weights a slight 140 lbs. Carter's RHS coaches emphasize his great team attitude. They tell college suitors that he would run through a brick wall if asked to. However, as college scouts are quick to point out, the hole in the brick wall the diminutive Carter would make, would be a small one.

Of all the athletes under Campbell's tutelage, Carter had proved to be the hardest for the coach to get to know. "Antonio is quiet kid. He let's his playing talk for him," said Campbell. "It is nice to see a kid like that. He got none of that chest pounding 'look at me' that so many players today have. They see it on Sports Center every night and think, 'I guess if you are a star, that's how you have to act.' But not Antonio."

Carter, always calm on the field and off, appears to a visitor to be in constant contemplation of his next move. He would politely answer questions asked by a visitor, but the answers were guarded. Most Roughriders knew little about the life of their star running back away from the gridiron. "I know he lives with his Mom right now somewhere off Grand," said Arlando Bailey. "I also heard his dad is moving back from the north side and that Antonio might be moving with him. He don't say much, and I don't know what he does away from school, but I know on the field the dude's got your back and I know he is one hell of a running back. That's good enough for me."

Against Cleveland High School in 2007, Carter rushed for an eye-popping average per carry of 15.8 yards. Balance and the spreading of the offensive wealth were fast becoming trademarks of Coach Campbell led teams. "Coach Campbell, he is all about the team, not the individual," said Carter. "It was much different when we were freshmen. Then it was like, we got our stars and everybody else just stay out of the way and don't mess things up for the stars. But Coach, he believes in the team. Everybody contributes, everybody gets their chance. Who knows how many yards I could have had against Cleveland last year if Coach had given me the ball 30 times. Maybe 300? Maybe 350? But I don't care about that, because with us, it is all about team. Discipline, that is what we needed and that is what Coach Campbell brings to us everyday," said Carter. "We go to class, we behave, or we don't play. I played a lot as a freshman with Coach Harvey and we won the conference. But it was not like it is now. Guys just did what they wanted. Gangs were a problem here, not only in the school but even on our team. Coach Campbell and Mr. Houston put a stop to that. Before, there was no pride in being a football player, like there is on our team now. Coach Campbell came in and he said, 'we are going to win with or without you. If you don't take care of grades, if you don't come to practice and work hard every day, then we will go on without you. We will play freshmen if we have to. But you will take care of business on a day to day basis or you will not be on this team.' That is the way it is with Coach Campbell."

After leading the Roughriders in rushing in 2007 with 947 yards on 99 carries, punctuated by 10 rushing touchdowns, Carter is readying himself for a breakout senior season. "Coach Campbell says I will go for two dimes (2000 yards) this year."

Such a productive year might put Carter on the radar screens of college recruiters, who had during his junior year been mostly lukewarm in their expressed interest in his post high school football skills. Grades will also be a problem for Carter, perhaps a bigger hindrance than his lack of height and bulk. Carter offers, without prompting, his dismal score of 14 on the ACT college admissions test. Coupled with a below average GPA of "somewhere around 2.0," the chances of Carter making it through the NCAA Academic Clearinghouse to qualify for a Division I or Division II football scholarship are almost nil.

Coach Campbell and Antonio both realize that Carter's college football career will most certainly require a two year stop at a Junior College, where the earning of a two year Associates Degree would qualify him to finish his career at a four year NCAA school with two years of football eligibility remaining. The JUCO route is a path that is not that uncommon for Roosevelt athletes. "We are sending three of this years' seniors (Class of 08) on to junior colleges. That is the only path they can choose due to their grades," says Campbell in May of 2008. "So many of our athletes get serious about school too late, we have got to start convincing our athletes that from the day they walk in as freshman they have to start right then working on the academic skills they will need if they are to play big time college football."

Carter is a perfect example of educational seriousness taking root too late. "Antonio right now is a very serious student, taking difficult classes," Campbell states of a junior class load that consists of Spanish, American History, Chemistry, Algebra II, and Literature. "But it is not going to happen for him right away. He will have to do what many great players had to, go the JUCO route. It is not easy, but it can be done, if the player wants it bad enough."

Before settling in at Roosevelt, Carter spent several years bouncing in and out of the City-County Desegregation program. He attended his 7th grade year in the suburban Parkway School District. "Was a fashion statement out there," says Carter. "It just was not for me. I just didn't feel like I belonged and the bus rides and all were just too much if you wanted to play sports."

The next year, he moved in with his father and completed junior high school in North St. Louis County, attending the almost all black Riverview Gardens schools, a district that had compiled almost as dismal a record as the SLPS, and who in 2008 was in danger of suffering a similar fate, a state takeover of the district. "Lots of fights," is the summation Carter gives of his year at Riverview Gardens. "For high school, I wanted to come back to the neighborhood. I wanted to go to Roosevelt."

Earning the respect of the one group any successful running back must court - his offensive line - is a task Carter can check off as completed. "Antonio never complains or blames us if we do not get our blocks," says senior center and offensive line captain Tyler Clubb. "I have seen him get absolutely blown up in the backfield because one of us missed our block and he never says a word. He just picks himself up and comes back to the huddle. That is why we work so hard for him, get him the blocking he needs to get 100 + yards a game. Antonio deserves it. He is a great teammate."

When watching Carter carry the football in either practice or game situations, his tenacity immediately jumps out at the viewer. His running style is fast and furious. Carter seeks out contact and has great balance after taking a hit from a defender; pin balling away from the contact and continuing in a north/south direction up the field. The Roosevelt coaches are also quick to point out to college scouts that Carter is a more than adequate pass receiver and a fearless blocker.

Carter steadfastly maintains that his demure size and academic challenges will not keep him from attaining his dream of a Division I Scholarship. "Missouri has talked to me," said Carter in June of the summer before his senior year. "They have talked to me about Junior College and getting my grades together and then transferring and playing for them. I have heard a lot from Ohio University. They have talked to me about some Junior Colleges in California where they could put me. I will make it. It might just take me a couple of extra years, but I will make it."

Beaumont was the next 2007 victim of the now raging Roosevelt stampede, falling by a score of 38-6. Now more than halfway through the 2007 schedule, the Riders stood with a record of 5-1. After the initial toe stubbing against Vashon to open the season, Roosevelt was now rolling full speed ahead. But ominous storm clouds were gathering on the horizon. The 2007 PHL season for Roosevelt was now almost complete. A date with Gateway Tech remained. But up next was the first district tilt, a battle with the private all boys school

Chaminade, followed by three more district matchups, with only the week 9 date with Gateway Tech involving a PHL member. Due to a quirk in the state playoff system, Roosevelt was in a five school district instead of four, one of only two out of the 60 statewide football districts that would require teams to play a fourth and extra district game.

District play would be as coaches liked to say, "for keeps." The final four games of the season would decide if Roosevelt would qualify for the 16 team single elimination tournament that would lead to the late November crowning of a state champion. Everything done in the first six weeks no longer mattered. Everyone had a clean slate, a fresh start. District play would be the beginning of the "second season."

The start of District play had been the downfall of many a Public High League football team over the previous 20 years. A powerhouse in the early season PHL games, the top dog of the PHL would emerge unscathed from league play, with bared teeth flashing in anticipation of the first district encounter and the chance to show that this is the year the PHL will put the bite back into city football. But seldom in the last generation had it materialized as such. After the first week of district play, and a solid ass whipping administered by a superior county and/or private school squad, the PHL top dog would lick its wounds, and with tail between its legs, crawl back to its demoralizing residence of inferiority within the world of area high school football. Many PHL coaches, when asked to predict the day that the PHL would regain football superiority, would shake their heads in an unknowing fashion that displayed worn out resignation.

For Roosevelt to achieve the dream of advancing beyond district play, they would have to improve to the level of the long time county powers assigned by the MSHSAA as district foes. The road to the Dome and a state championship would not go through the PHL patsies that Roosevelt spent the first half of the 2007 season pounding on. The road to the promise land always went through the county powerhouse district foes, back loaded at the end of Roosevelt's 2007 schedule: Chaminade, Kirkwood and McCluer North. It was a riddle that few PHL teams had solved over the prior twenty years.

The Missouri State High School Activities Association was one of the last states to institute a statewide football playoff system to determine a state champion, holding it's first such event in 1967. Originally, only four teams from each of three classes were invited to participate in the playoffs. In 1967, to determine the three champions, schools were divided into classes based on school enrollment. Because of the small number of districts in each class (4) and the accompanying large number of teams assigned to each district (as many as 35), no head to head competition to determine the qualifiers was held. Instead, a complex points system was introduced. Factors weighted in included strength of schedule, determined by the enrollment and win-loss records of opponents. With only 12 teams from over 300 football playing schools to be chosen, one loss, even in the first game of the season, pretty well doomed any chance of a school making the playoffs. It was also not uncommon for a school to go through the 9 or 10 game regular season schedule undefeated and not make the playoffs. Everyone was at the mercy of the number crunching computers.

As the years rolled by, the state association tweaked the system, often in a futile attempt to quiet the critics (think BCS). More teams were allowed to make the playoffs by adding more rounds to the tournament bracket and increasing the number of classifications based upon school enrollment. A major change occurred in 1987, when the point system was done away with and District round robin play was implemented. Each school was now placed in a four team district, based on geographic location, and would play the other three district opponents during the last three weeks of the regular season. The winner of this "second season" would advance on into state play. District championships were now decided on the field, which seemed to be a factor that most everyone favored. The new system did play havoc with traditional conference schedules, dependent upon how many conference opponents were now also district rivals. In some cases, it became mathematically impossible for each conference school to play each other in a round robin schedule to decide a true conference champion.

A major criticism of the district playoff system is that it assigned teams on a two year basis, strictly on geographic location; and did not take into consideration how many top teams were being placed in the same district. These overloaded districts created a competitive disadvantage, with many top schools ending the season short of the playoffs. It has not been unusual over the years to see some districts begin play the last three weeks of the season with all four members sporting unblemished 7-0 records. The reverse also happened on numerous occasions: a team would enter the district with an 0-7 record, and through a combination of playing well at the right time of the year and having been placed in a weak district, march undefeated through the last three weeks of the season and enter the state level playoffs sporting a ghoulish record of 3-7. Still, most agreed that the district round robin system of determining the winner on the field was superior to the old point system.

By 2007, the state had increased the number of classifications for football to six (seven if you count the 32 small enrollment rural high schools, mostly in the northwest corner of the state, which battle for the 8-man football title). The four smallest classes in the 11 man game were divided into 16 districts, each comprised of four schools. This setup required district survivors to play and win four games beyond district play to claim a state title. The two largest classes in the state, known by MSHSAA jargon as Class 5 and Class 6, were comprised of the schools with the largest enrollments. As in the four smaller classes, four teams were assigned to each of 8 districts in Classes 6, with the exception to this mathematically "tidy" arrangement being Class 5.

In 2007, to make up for the odd number of teams in the state, Class 5 would have two districts comprised of five teams and those 10 schools would start District play one week earlier than the other 78 Districts around the state. Assignments were for a two year cycle with each team playing each district opponent under a two year home and away arrangement. For the 2006 and 2007 seasons, based on an enrollment of just over 1200 students, the Roughriders were assigned to Class 5, District 3, and fell into one of the two above mentioned five team districts.

For Roosevelt, and the other Public High League teams, the start of District play signaled the time for the collective inferiority complexes of the city teams to kick in. Once Roosevelt and the other PHL teams stepped out of conference play, many considered the playing field to no longer be level. For over 20 years, PHL schools had seen their neighborhood talent raided by the county schools through a court ordered voluntary desegregation program. Most top city athletes were targeted while still in junior high, and to stay within the rules that prohibited recruiting by high school coaches, would through an intermediate have it made known to them and their parents that they would be wise to cast their football playing lot with a certain public school in the county.

Private schools also found the city a friendly and lucrative area to "find" students with uncommon athletic ability. Better facilities, better coaching, a better education – the abandonment of the PHL was an easy sell to the impressionable youthful athletes of the city. It soon became a given that most athletically talented city kids would somehow find a path to the county and private schools. The few talented athletes that did stay in the city were the late bloomers, those who somehow fell between the cracks of the intricate recruiting system.

City coaches cried long and hard that these raiding parties were engaging in illegal recruiting. The benefiting private and county schools would smugly claim that they were simply interested in diversifying their student bodies, and with a sly wink and nod, blow off any accusation of recruiting by the shady claim of a mere coincidence that a large majority of the city black students in their school just happened to be star athletes.

Because of the talent drain of the PHL schools by these forces, the city schools had known nothing but 20 years of lopsided beatings when competing against the private and county schools, ironically thrashings frequently administered by teams with rosters stocked with athletes who were St. Louis city residents.

"We have got to get our kids over the mental block of competing against the county schools," said Coach Campbell, in the summer of 2008. "We can play with these county schools. We have to, if we are ever going to get to the Dome and play for a state championship. Our kids know this. We are getting better. The play in the PHL is getting better every year. I think the coaching is better now than what it was when I came in seven, eight years ago. We have a group of good young head coaches in the league now. We are all tight. We talk all the time. The PHL is on the way back, man. Vashon proved last year that it can be done. They made it all the way (in 2007) to the semifinals of Class 4."

Much has been made by the St. Louis sports media of the talented backfields and ineffective line play found in PHL teams. Campbell sees change in this critical area of the game as the blue print for returning the PHL football programs to prominence. "Our line play this year, especially on offense, will carry us as far as we go," said Campbell in the spring of 2008. "We are getting better. If we don't, we will never beat the county schools."

Quarterback Arlando Bailey has the unique perspective of having transferred in from a county power, CBC. "The speed of the game in the PHL took me a while to get use to last year," said Bailey. "The athletes in the PHL are so much faster than what I saw at CBC." Then why can PHL schools not compete with county schools come district playoff time? "Their line play is so much better," said Bailey.

Assistant Head Coach Darren West, whose duties included overseeing the Roughriders Offensive Line, sees the discrepancy not in racial terms, but as mind set. "Why can't we have an outstanding offensive line," West asked his Roughrider linemen in the Summer of 2008? "Don't give me this stuff that black schools can't beat a white school at the line of scrimmage. Go watch East Side (East St. Louis, IL High School, the area's top ranked team). They are all brothers and watch them block. Same with Normandy. They pancake people and, once again, all brothers."

"But coach," injected one player, "We have a white guy (Tyler Clubb), maybe that's the problem?"

"Hadn't thought of that," said West with a mischievous grin.

Coach Campbell points hopefully to the results of three years of intense weight training by his incoming Senior class. "We were at a distinct and obvious disadvantage when we first got here, when playing against county schools, because we didn't have a structured weight program. The linemen at the county schools would just flat out whip our butts on the line because they were stronger than our kids. I don't care how fast your backs are, if you can't win the war on the line of scrimmage, your offense is going nowhere. We feel this season (2008) will be the first year that our kids are going to be as strong as the guy across the line of scrimmage, when we get to district."

Watching Roosevelt athletes compete in 2008 against PHL rivals Career Academy and Cleveland ROTC in 7 on 7 summer play, where the athletes were adorned in only shorts and tee shirts, the physiques of the Roosevelt players were strikingly more developed than their opponents. The effect of the emphasis placed upon strength training by Coach Campbell and his staff was obvious – the Roughriders looked like men competing against boys. "We think it will make a difference and so do our kids. We never miss a lifting session, even in the summer," said Coach Campbell, gesturing to several weight benches and a squat rack, that, due to the summer remodeling of the Roosevelt building, had found a new home outside of the football field concession stand. "We will be out here all summer," said Campbell. "We pull them (equipment) out of the concession stand to lift and then store them back in after we are done, and we pray it don't rain."

Any Coach who is to survive in the city system, learns quickly the importance of improvising when coaching in the St. Louis Public High League.

As Coach Campbell struggled with the monumental task of convincing his players that this was the year that they could compete with the suburban schools, those who had been around the PHL long enough to remember the pre-busing days, were quick to point out that there was a time when the shoe was on the other foot.

George Simmons serves as an assistant coach at RHS. He was the head coach at Cleveland High School 15 years prior when a young running back named DeAndre Campbell came under his wing. Simmons's association with the PHL goes all the way back to the 1964 and 1965 seasons, when he was a star lineman for the now defunct former PHL member, O'Fallon Technical High School. When asked about the county dominance of the city schools, Simmons shoots a visitor one of his famous impish grins, and points out with relish, "there was a time when those cats in the county were scared to death of us. Wouldn't set foot in the city."

Ask George Simmons for a lunch date and he quickly seizes control of the situation. "Hodaks. Best fried chicken on the South Side. Eat there once and you will know why. Between Jefferson and Interstate 55. What time?"

Simmons looks like a man who would know good fried chicken. He also looks like an offensive line coach. The veteran Assistant Coach of the Roughriders would be a favorite of broadcaster, and throw back proponent of old school football, John Madden. Close to 40 years of coaching in the PHL has left not only an indelible mark upon the man who fits perfectly the descriptor of "grizzled," but also upon the countless city youth who have learned the trade of a football lineman while studying the craft under Simmons's persistent and unyielding, nose to the grindstone style of teaching. For four decades, his deep voice has boomed across countless barren city football practice fields, while garnering the attention - and more importantly - the respect of several generations of PHL players.

Simmons informs a visitor, "I have seen it all. The good times, the bad times, and a lot of times in between. And you know what, the more things change the more they stay the same. Winning football games is still about blocking and tackling. You can have all the different looks and gadgets you want, all the fancy bells and whistles, don't matter. If you control the line of scrimmage, you control the game," theorizes Simmons, endorsing a philosophy that would make any old line coach proud.

If you were making a football movie and had placed a call to Central Casting for a line coach, George Simmons would be the guy they would send over. If you want to learn about football in the trenches, along with some enlightening social perspective, spend an afternoon with Simmons in a South Side chicken joint. Simmons over a free lunch will gladly discuss everything from pass blocking technique to the racial divide in the city of St. Louis - or even better - be on the football field and spend a pre-season practice watching him apply his teaching skills through a methodology heavily dependent upon the use of praise, criticism and humor.

All punctured for emphasis with an occasional profanity.

Despite the age difference, Simmons has a rapport with his players that is the timeless ingredient common to all successful teachers and coaches. In a head spinning rapid fire dialogue, Simmons can kid, scold, and praise in a way that attracts the attention of his players without diminishing the obvious respect they have for him as their coach. Simmons also has a unique relationship with his Roosevelt boss, Coach Campbell. "I was DeAndre's head high school football coach at Cleveland Naval ROTC," explains Simmons. "Was he one of my favorites? No. I treat 'em all the same, but I do owe DeAndre. He caught a pass off his shoe tops to win the district title for me in overtime back in '93. I told him after he came back and got in the (SLPS) system, 'you get a head coaching job and I will come work for you.' When he came to Roosevelt, I was helping out over at Vashon and those dudes at the "V" were not real crazy about me coming to the South Side to coach, but hey, a promise is a promise and like I said, he won me my first district title."

Campbell, as well as Simmons, both declare a comfort level with their reversal of roles. The student has become the teacher, the mentor the subservient. "We think a lot alike," says Campbell. "There is no better line coach out there than Coach Simmons."

Although Simmons' title is officially that of Head Junior Varsity Coach, it is obvious with a casual observation of a Roughrider practice that Simmons is a leader, not a follower. He and Varsity Assistant and Head Line Coach Darren West have a give and take relationship fostered by constant good natured practice field banter between the two.

"Give me a defensive end, I don't care who. Any defensive end I have coached can sack the quarterback," the younger West loudly boasted at a 2008 pre season practice. The two coaches were putting their small number of lineman through pass blocking and pass rushing drills.

"Give me an offensive tackle that can shut him up. I am tired of listening to it. Rene, get up there," barked Simmons in response to the gauntlet thrown down by the younger coach. Simmons' pupil, talented junior lineman Rene Faulk, easily manhandled the overmatched and undersized junior varsity defensive end chosen by West for the drill. After Faulk's decisive win, Simmons glared across the line of scrimmage at West. "That's all you got? That's it? You talk all this shit and that is all you can send?" Simmons then breaks into a deep and hearty laugh. "Man-Child," he says to Faulk, "get out of there. Give me another lineman. Coach West, you got any more, send them." The players feed off the energy of the two coaches separated by two generations and 35 years of age, but bound by a common passion each possess for their chosen avocation of coaching.

"Here he comes," counters Coach West. And so it continued, for the rest of the morning practice, as it did most days, the "smack talk" between the two coaches.

In July 2008, with the Roosevelt school building shut down for summer repairs, the coaching staff resorted to hauling water to the field for the players. Simmons secured a 25 gallon jug, filled to the brim with ice water, exclusively for use by his linemen. The tempting liquid treasure rested on the side of the practice field on the tailgate of Simmons' well worn Ford pick up truck. In the midst of a late summer practice, under the relentless and boiling afternoon sun, the veteran coach spots a running back trying to sneak an undetected quick drink from the linemen's stash. "You little piss ant, get out of my water," the ever vigilant Simmons barks from half a football field away. "Get your own damn water. That's for real men, for linemen. Take your pansy ass over and drink out of the hose. You don't deserve to drink with the linemen."

"It is a young man's game," Simmons will relate later when discussing his evolution as a coach. "It's changed some and I've changed with it. Dads are not around anymore. They used to be. So many of these kids have no direction, and no discipline. But we can still give (the athletes) discipline and direction on the football field, and that is why I am here. I just want to do a good job and want to help Campbell win, but I also want to have an impact on these boys. Get'em thinking. Get them planning for their futures. Too many of them have no plan."

Simmons has a plan, and it is short term. "I use to coach year to year. Now I say it's day to day," he chuckles. Simmons has been retired from the full time teaching ranks for three years. His role at Roosevelt is classified as part time. "I tried the retirement stuff for a while," Simmons says. "But I got in a slump. Lay on the couch all day, watch the same TV shows at the same time every day. I got stale with the retirement gig real quick."

Simmons suffers from several serious health concerns, most notably high blood pressure and diabetes. He explains to a waitress at Hodaks that he had been to see his doctor that morning and the doctor was not happy with his lack of discipline with the prescribed diet Simmons has reluctantly been placed on. By passing on dessert, he calculated, he would hold his sugar intake to a level that would allow for mashed potatoes with his fried chicken. "And don't even bring the broccoli out here," he tells the waitress. "Just the mashed potatoes and don't hold back on the gravy, either."

Simmons graduated from the now closed O'Fallon Technical High School in the spring of 1966. "I was supposed to go to Vashon out of junior high. But that year some kid got stabbed at Vashon and I said 'I ain't going to Vashon.' I took the test for O'Fallon Tech and scored, I guess, good enough to get in there." Simmons did not play football until his junior year of High School. "A coach found me in PE class my sophomore year. I was the class dodge ball champion. I was very quick on my feet, but I only weighed about 170 pounds back then," Simmons states. (A conservative estimate of his present weight would be double that of Simmons's dodge ball glory days.) "The coach in PE was also a football coach and he kept working on me and finally I decided to go out for the team. Football got me going. I also wrestled and I went to Northeast Missouri State (now Truman State) on a wrestling scholarship. I graduated with a degree in physical education and I came back to St. Louis to teach. That was in 1971, and I have been here ever since. This will be my 38th consecutive year of coaching in the PHL."

With an initial teaching job at Central High School, Simmons not only worked with the wrestlers, but also the school's football team. He later transferred to Northwest High School and eventually took over the school's long time state championship wrestling program. By the early 90's, he had landed the head football coaching position at Cleveland Naval ROTC Academy. One of the young charges now under Simmons' care was a quick and game savvy running back named DeAndre Campbell.

"The schools are really different now, so much more so than they were when I started out. I wouldn't say better or worse, just different," says Simmons. The veteran coach is asked about the problems besetting the district he has served for so many years. "Too many different directions. How many Superintendents have we had in the last four years, five, six? Now we are getting another new one. New ideas, new way to do things, so we start all over. Change is not bad, but we never get anything done because we are always starting over."

Simmons is asked to address the "white flight" phenomena that over his 35 plus year tenure, has plagued the SLPS and totally reshaped the demographics of the district. "The white kids are all gone, but it's not just them, it's a lot of good kids, white and black, who have either gone to the county schools through Deseg or have gone to the private schools. It will only turn around in the city when the test scores go up. People need to see the good. Look what is happening at Roosevelt now. A bunch of kids who are neighborhood kids, go right by Roosevelt everyday on their way to school at places like Kirkwood or Mehlville. Why? Because their parents think they can get a better education there than here, and I can't blame them for that. But things will turn around when those kids start driving by Roosevelt every morning and see the improved facilities. See a new 8 lane track. See new lights on the football field. Then they and their parents read about Roosevelt and how things are getting better here. We have the Principal of the Year for the whole St. Louis area leading our school. They read about how the test scores have gone up. How Roosevelt kids are graduating and going on to good colleges. How the gang bangers are no longer allowed at Roosevelt. How the community has rallied around the school and given us the support we used to never find."

"When all that happens, those city kids going to Kirkwood and Mehlville will start asking themselves, 'why am I riding this bus three hours a day. I could be at Roosevelt and its right down the street.' That is when the parents of the white kids will say, 'why am I paying $10,000 a year to send my kids to a private school when they can get just as good an education here on the south side and it costs me nothing?' People say white parents will not send their kids to the city public schools. That is not true, look at Metro, they have lots of white kids."

A magnet school, Metro, with numerous national awards and recognition bestowed upon its students, has been long recognized as the top academic public high school in the city. Competition for a seat in the freshman class is fierce. The merit test, used to determine admission, assures the school of a high quality clientele. It is also the only city school whose racial breakdown is similar to that of the city population as a whole, 50/50.

Simmons continues, "It is too simple to say white parents won't send their kids to predominately black schools. If the test scores improve, the good kids, white and black, will come back. If they (test scores) don't, then the system can not survive, and maybe it shouldn't."

Many PHL athletes, over several generations, have benefited immensely from the guidance and wisdom of George Simmons. If not for a PE Class Dodge Ball Championship won years ago, in a school that today no longer even exists, Simmons may have never found his true life calling, impacting the lives of young men through football. As Simmons says, "things just always seemed to work out for me."

Roosevelt's first district game in 2007 was against Chaminade, an exclusive all boys' prep school in St. Louis County. No matchup anywhere in the high school football universe could have produced more startling and contrasting lifestyles than those lived by the members of these two district opponents. In exchange for the $18,000 + a year tuition fee at Chaminade, parents were ensuring a world class college prep style education for their sons. For nearly 100 years, the school had produced many of St. Louis' future lawyers, doctors and business leaders. The school also offered a boarding option and attracted many foreign students. The tab per year for a student who boarded on the South Lindberg Blvd. campus totaled over $34,000 a year.

The Roughriders traveled to Chaminade with all the false bravado they could muster, but it was not enough to overcome the inferiority complex that so exasperated Campbell. "We entered the game 5-1, but our kids just do not think we can win when we step outside the PHL, and it cost us that game," lamented Coach Campbell the following spring. "We have got to change that. Our kids get overwhelmed by the facilities. We should have won that game. We get Chaminade, who knows, our confidence grows and maybe we run the table." Instead, Roosevelt fell behind early, tried to rally late, but allowed numerous mistakes to derail an offense that had been practically unstoppable for five weeks, losing the 2007 District opener by a score of 14-7.

Behind 14-0 late in the fourth quarter, the Roughriders used a touchdown pass from Bailey to Antonio Carter to climb within a possession of tying or winning the game. The Riders defense, however, could not make the crucial defensive stand needed to return the ball to the offense. Chaminade ran out the clock to win what many Roosevelt players and coaches viewed as the make or break game of the 2007 season. Carter, who rushed for 150 yards on 19 carries, 8 months later, still felt the sting of the defeat. "We moved the ball all night on the ground, we just couldn't put the ball in the end zone."

Arlando Bailey went the entire game as the signal caller for the Roughriders, but attempted only 7 passes, five for completions. The time tested statistic that so often determines the winner of a football game, the battle of the turnovers, doomed the Riders. Roosevelt lost four fumbles, compared to no turnovers for Chaminade. "I lost the game," Quarterback Bailey stated bluntly, in the spring of 2008. "I think about that game all the time. It motivates me. We should have won. Next year we will win games like that in District. We were better than them and it still hurts that we did not win," Bailey states about a Chaminade team that would finish the season 7-3, 3-1 in the district.

Although one loss does not eliminate a team from the district title hunt and the accompanying dreams of a state playoff berth, before 2008, it did take a team's destiny out of its own hands. Once a team lost in the district portion of the schedule, it now not only has to take care of business and win the rest of its games, but would also need help. Week II of 2007 district play for the Roughriders would get no easier, as they would return home to host the Stars of McCluer North High School.

McCluer North, much like Roosevelt, had seen a recent dramatic shift in the racial makeup of its student body. Over a period of 20 years the school, located in North St. Louis County, had seen many of its' white students abandon the public school system for private schools, or a move west to booming St. Charles County. It was, by 2008, a problem being addressed by all public school districts in North St. Louis County. Once predominantly, if not totally all white, the North County schools, in sports such as football and basketball, now sported rosters heavily laden with African American athletes. An abundance of talented and athletic players had made the North County schools a fertile and favorite recruiting ground of Division I football coaches. Because the North County schools already possessed a large home grown African American student population, they were not included in the voluntary busing of city black students. North County schools were not an attendance option for St. Louis City minority students.

Athletic talent, specifically the speed that black athletes provide, was the common denominator between the PHL teams and the powerhouse Suburban North Conference members. The differences, however, were distinct. Due to a much more stable tax base, facilities were of a higher quality in the North County schools, than what would be found in the Public High League. Many felt this factor tipped the athletic scales in the favor of the county schools. Others would say in a low whisper that the coaching in the Suburban North, with a large quantity of white coaches, was at a higher level than that found in the PHL. Another factor attributed to the coaching disparity of the two areas was the inability of the PHL to retain talented young black coaches who, after gaining experience in the PHL, would, upon the first opportunity, bolt to the County schools. "A young PHL coach comes in and does a good job, he won't be long in the City and will soon be (employed) at a Suburban North school," said one PHL insider. "The South and West County schools steal our players and the North County schools steal our coaches. But you can't blame the coaches. Better facilities, better pay, better stability. Who wouldn't go? But let me tell you something else, the North County Schools remind me a lot of the PHL a generation ago. All the white kids are leaving. With them go the community support and the tax base. Check back in a few years and see if McCluer North looks a whole lot different than Roosevelt does now."

One current Roughrider with a McCluer North connection was defensive linebacker and offensive guard George Bell. He had attended middle school in the McCluer district when he lived with his mother in North St. Louis County. Bell was slated to attend North High School, when the summer before his freshman year he made the decision to move to the South Side and live with his Dad- a former football player in the 1980's at the PHL's McKinley High School. It is a move Bell says he has never regretted. Soft spoken with fine features set off by a baby face, which gives both the illusion of a boy much younger than Bell's 17 years, and a personality much more timid than the ferocity Bell exhibits from his position on the gridiron. Bell, a starter at Roosevelt since his freshman year has, by the spring of his junior year, found his way onto the radar screen of Division I College Coaches. Bell is somewhat unique from his teammates who have received recruiting inquiries in that he is not sure that football will be a part of his college experience. "It will not be the deciding factor in where I go to school," said Bell.

Wanting to major in either Sports Medicine or Orthopedics, Bell knows that a heavy class load in college will be difficult to balance with a commitment to athletics that a college football scholarship would demand. With a deceptively lean body, the 5'10", 210 pound Bell, who runs the 40 yard dash in a very respectable 4.7, is not sure he can play at the Division I level. "I am interested in the University of Arkansas for their undergrad program," Bell comments on the Fayetteville school, a big time football program and a member of the Southeastern Conference. But Bell admits he has not received any encouragement in the way of recruitment by the Razorback football staff. "If it (playing college football) works out, fine, if not, I will just concentrate on academics."

Bell speaks in a soft, high pitched voice. On the football field, in the heat of battle and when Bell gets excited, his voice pitch will rise even several more octaves. Picking out George's distinctive voice in the midst of multiple players voicing their opinions is easy. Bell is not shy about stating his opinion to questioning opponents or teammates. He may be the best trash talker on the team. He is defiantly the most creative. At a summer workout he gladly, and without prompting, decided to ride fellow lineman and teammate Rene Faulk. Bell had overheard a visitor ask to interview Faulk. "Hey, Man-Child, what you going to tell them, 'you too dumb to remember the plays, you smell bad and we got no helmet big enough to fit your head?' That about it, right Man-Child," Bell chided the hulking junior lineman, much to the laughter and delight of his teammates. The frustrated Faulk just shook his head in resignation. No need to take on the king of trash talkers in front of a visitor.

A young man who impresses a stranger immediately with his logical introspective analysis, Bell is sold on Roosevelt, Coach Campbell and Principal Houston. "It has changed so much for the better here since my freshman year," observes Bell. "We have dedicated teachers here. Nobody talks about that. My teachers here are always pushing me, always telling me I can do better. When people talk about teachers at our school, they always think our teachers don't care; they are just here to get a pay check. But that is not true. I went to school in the County. I know. Teachers here do care and they do try and get the students to learn. And the school is so much better since Mr. Houston got here. Right away he threw the gang (members) out. We used to have fights every day. Nobody fights here now. If they do, they are gone."

Bell also throws praise in the direction of Campbell. "Coach Campbell has made us a family. When I was a freshman, it was all about the "stars". Now it is about the team. Coach Campbell says, 'we all win together and we all lose together.' When we suffer, we all suffer together. There is not another school I would leave Roosevelt to go to. No place could be better for me than right here. I am a Roughrider."

Bell aspirers to live a faith based life. "I am a Christian. I have been raised that way. I try to have my life reflect my beliefs." Bell is also a leader. Before each game, he lead his teammates through pre game stretching, his authoritative voice barking out the cadence for each exercise. Following the pregame preparation, Bell would gather his teammates - all but Muhammad Dukly, the place kicker from Guinea, who was a devout Muslim - into a tight huddle in the end zone and lead them in prayer.

"George Bell is the kind of young man we want the community to see," says RHS Principal Terry Houston. "He is what we want a Roosevelt graduate to be."

Bell's teachers and coaches predict a bright future for him beyond football. Fast forward twenty years and the sharp image of a successful George Bell is easy to bring into focus. Bell is provided a hypothetical scenario that in many ways succinctly sums up the educational decision faced by so many St. Louis City parents over the past generation: In 25 years, Bell is asked, you have the resources to send your 14 year old son to any high school in the St. Louis area, would you send him to Roosevelt? "If Mr. Houston and Coach Campbell were still here, yes I would," Bell answers with no hesitation.

McCluer North humbled the Roughriders in week 8 of the 2007 season by the score of 28-0. Any post season success for Roosevelt would again have to be put off for at least one more year. An offense that had been high octane for 5 consecutive weeks as it ran roughshod over the PHL opposition was held to only 117 yards rushing and 60 yards passing. Fifty yards of offense came on one play, the only completion of the night for Miguel Allen, now back to splitting the snaps with Bailey. The junior QB fared no better, completing only one pass. It would prove to be the low water mark for Bailey's junior season. "I got yanked," Bailey recalled the following April, the memory of being benched midgame in favor of Allen still frustrating Bailey. "It was homecoming and I was so mad, after the game I didn't even go to the dance. It was the low point of my season."

But Campbell and his players could take solace in the fact that Week 9 would see a return to PHL competition, with an away game at Gateway Tech.

In perhaps Roosevelt's best played game of the season, the Roughriders prevailed in a thriller over the Jaguars, winning in overtime by a score of 20-14. With the score tied at the end of regulation at 14-14 - Gateway having failed on a conversion kick with 5 minutes remaining in regulation - Roosevelt used a ten yard run by Antonio Carter to grab the overtime lead. The defense then stiffened to hold Gateway out of the end zone, insuring one bright moment for the Riders in what, to that point, had been a dismal district season.

Leading the defense against Gateway Tech, with 10 tackles, was the fiercely loyal and true Roughrider, George Bell.

Now mathematically eliminated from the district title race, the Roughriders would end their season attempting to play spoiler as they hosted the undefeated Kirkwood Pioneers. A Suburban West Conference member, Kirkwood has a long and storied history as a St. Louis high school football power. It had a less storied history of racial harmony.

The community of Kirkwood found itself pushed reluctantly into the national spotlight on three separate occasions within a four year period. The first riveting story to ensnare the nation's interest and place its collective focus on the St. Louis community was the unlikely and amazing story of Shawn Hornbeck. While riding his bike on a fall Sunday afternoon in 2002, 11 year old Shawn vanished without a trace from his rural home in Richwoods, MO; a poor enclave in the Ozark Foothills, approximately 70 miles southwest of St. Louis.

After an initial intensive and wide spread search turned up no leads and no suspect; the story, as so often happens, faded from public view. Local rumors around the rural community of Richwoods swirled with alleged information on the youth's disappearance. One theory had him run over by an automobile while riding his bike, and the body hidden to foil any investigation into the accident. Another favorite: Shawn had been murdered after accidently stumbling upon a meth lab hidden in the woods. While the stories made for good dialogue, in reality, not one credible piece of information came forward about Shawn's disappearance until an amazing and bizarre chain of events led to Hornbeck's discovery at an apartment in Kirkwood on the afternoon of January 12, 2007, four and one half year's after his initial disappearance.

The police had come to the low rent apartment complex in search of another pre-teen boy, 12 year old Ben Owenby, who had, days before, disappeared from the small St. Louis area town of Beauford. Amazingly, the police found not only Ben in the apartment, but also Shawn.

As both youths were reunited with overjoyed parents and an entire metropolitan area joined the families in giving thanks for the unexpected miracle ending to their personal nightmares, Kirkwood resident Michael Devlin was arrested and charged with kidnapping and the sexual assault of both boys. Devlin was immediately demonized in the eyes of an outraged community. The soft spoken and non-descript over weight middle aged pizza parlor manager had lived openly with Hornbeck for the past four years, passing him off as his son. He later pled guilty and was sentenced to multiple life prison terms, with no possible chance for parole.

Kirkwood's other two forays into the national news did not have the same happy and uplifting endings. Instead, two violently explosive and what seemed like senseless murders of police officers and community servants, committed by two African American Kirkwood citizens, brought to the forefront, exposing to public scrutiny, the upscale community's long and simmering racial divisions.

In the summer of 2005, the day after the fourth of July holiday, a young Kirkwood African American man, Kevin Johnson, in cold blood, gunned down Kirkwood police officer Sgt. William McEntee. Earlier in the day, Johnson's 12 year old brother had died from what was later determined to be a heart aliment. Kevin Johnson felt that the police, upon their arrival at the home of the stricken 12 year old, had not done enough to help save his brother's life. Johnson was enraged at the police who seemed more interested in finding and arresting him (Kevin) for an outstanding warrant, than giving aid to his dying brother.

Later that afternoon, Johnson spotted Officer McEntee - who had earlier been at the Johnson house when 12 year old Joseph (Bam Bam) had died - sitting in his patrol car talking to several neighborhood youth. Johnson walked up to the officer and without warning other than the comment "you killed my little brother," shot McEntee, execution style, in the back of the head.

Relationships between the city's black residents and police, already strained, now were on the brink of boiling over. After the shooting, black residents complained of a heightened police presence in their neighborhood. Many felt the aggressive police response bordered on harassment.

After one mistrial, Johnson was found guilty at a second trial of capital murder and sentenced to death. Many black citizens, while not justifying the actions of Johnson, felt that his mental state of mind, compromised by the death of his young brother only several hours before, should have been enough of a mitigating circumstance to avoid a death sentence. The jury disagreed. From comments posted in local papers and internet chat rooms, so did most white Kirkwood citizens.

Two and one half years later, in the early evening hours of February 7, 2008, 52 year old lifetime Kirkwood resident and businessman, Charles "Cookie" Thornton walked into a Kirkwood City Council meeting armed with two hand guns. Concealing the weapons was a sandwich type sign board which read "The unrest in Meacham Park (Kirkwood's black neighborhood) will continue until the racist plantation mentalities of the Kirkwood officials are addressed."

By the time of his entry into the council chambers, Thornton had minutes before already killed a Kirkwood policeman in the city building parking lot. A later released police video of the council meeting, documents Thornton's actions. "Everybody stop what you're doing! Hands in the air!, Hands in the air!" Thornton is heard to say. He then can be seen approaching another on duty officer, who was seated in the audience. Thornton killed him with one shot, continuing to shout "Hands in the air."

Thornton next shot and killed the city Project's Manager, before turning his guns on Mayor Mike Swoboda. Thornton shot the Mayor in the head twice from point blank range. (Miraculously, Swoboda survived the shooting and seemed to be making steady rehabilitative progress, only to die from complications of the shooting six months later.) Thornton then shot and killed two city council members. Next Thornton made eye contact with Councilman Timothy Griffin, who had sought cover, along with others, behind the council table.

Griffin later told police that he said, "Cookie, I've known you a long time." According to the St. Louis Post Dispatch, Thornton turned away and set his sights on City Attorney John Hessel, who pleaded repeatedly, 'Cookie, don't'". According to the Post, "Hessel threw chairs at Thornton, and kept him at bay for several seconds before running out of the chamber. At that point, there was a brief pause in the booming rounds from Thornton's guns."

Police officers responding to the ensuing distress call entered the council chambers. In the background could be heard another series of short bursts of gunfire. Thornton had been mortally wounded in the city council chambers by responding Kirkwood Police Officers. Within minutes, five people were shot dead by Thornton – three city officials and two police officers.

Thornton was a former star Kirkwood High School athlete. He was a distinguished high school basketball player for the Pioneers. In track and field, Thornton was a state champion his senior year in the triple jump. Thornton went on to a stellar career, and earned a degree at Northeast Missouri State University (now known as Truman State). He was so successful at the Kirksville, MO school that he was elected to the school's Athletic Hall of Fame. After college, he returned to his home neighborhood and started a construction company.

Thornton had, for years, railed against the majority white power structure in Kirkwood. He charged that racism was behind what he claimed was an overzealous harassment of his construction business by the city of Kirkwood. A total of over $20,000 in parking tickets and code citations had been issued to Thornton. He also leveled claims at city officials that he had been discriminated against when his company did not land lucrative city contracts.

Over the years, Thornton spent tens of thousands of dollars in legal fees in the filing of numerous federal law suits against the city – all of which were eventually dismissed before ever reaching trial. Financial records showed that Thornton was in serious financial debt, mortgaged to the hilt, in order to fund his legal challenges. According to the St. Louis Post Dispatch, "He (Thornton) had used his parents' two homes like a personal ATM, getting hundreds of thousands of dollars in loans, then squandering it all. The dump trucks he bought for his demolition and asphalt business had been repossessed. About a year before the killings, the IRS took out two liens against Thornton for more than $200,000."

The murders polarized not only Kirkwood, but the entire St. Louis area. Opinions were divided clearly upon racial lines. Kirkwood had, for years, been one of the St. Louis Metro's areas most affluent cites. Blacks who lived within the city limits were mostly confined to a small area known as Meacham Park. In the early years of the decade, the city of Kirkwood had used Imminent Domain condemnation procedures to tear down a large part of the once thriving black neighborhood. In its place was built a huge shopping center, anchored by such retail box store giants as Target, Home Depot and Wal-Mart. Many African American residents saw this lucrative real estate deal that had mostly denied them, the original land owners, a share of the economic largesse that the deal produced, as a composite of the long standing shoddy treatment of black Kirkwood residents by an uncaring white majority power structure.

In many ways, the two murderous rampages in Kirkwood came to symbolize the lack of consensus and communication in regard to the racial tensions that continued to plague the St. Louis Metropolitan area. Where whites saw needless murders of civil servants, horrific acts that had wrecked lives and left behind mourning widows and children, many area black leaders, while not justifying the murderous acts, asked for at least a realization from whites that these were reactions of desperate and frustrated men who felt no connection or confidence in the ability of the system to better their lives. "Let's look at the root of the problem," was the message that black area leaders repeatedly conveyed in the aftermath of both killing sprees.

Social scientists would editorialize, in the months that followed each of the murders, that in many ways St. Louis held the rank as the most racially divided city in America. Using the racial segregation of the city's public schools, along with its dismal record in regard to student achievement as a barometer to measure the level of racial strife in the city, experts once again pointed out that the city of St. Louis would not overcome it's racial disharmony until something was done to "fix" the SLPS.

The 2007 season ended for the Roughriders the same as it had started: disappointing bookend defeats that left coaches and players questioning what it would take to drive the team over the hump of mediocrity.

Kirkwood dominated a dispirited Roosevelt team, crushing the Roughriders in a season ending encounter by a score of 42-6. Adding to the humiliation was the location of the mismatch: Roosevelt's home turf. In retrospect, the contest was more one sided than the final score would indicate. Down 35-0 at half time, Roosevelt suffered the indignity of playing the fourth quarter under the "mercy rule," a high school standard that requires a running clock in the second half of a game when one team has taken a lead of 35 points or more. The rule is intended to speed the game and end the carnage for the overmatched foe as quickly as possible.

Roosevelt's only score in the game came on the last play of the 4th quarter, a meaningless 20 yard pass from senior Miguel Allen to senior Deven Palmer.

Statistically, the game was no contest. So bad and one sided that, for the only time in the 2007 season, the Roosevelt coaching staff neglected to submit their squad's final game statistics to the local media.

During the off season, the Roosevelt coaches would often use the overwhelming dominance that Kirkwood had showed in manhandling the Roughriders in an attempt to motivate the players, tugging at their collective pride. After watching the team's sluggish beginning to one 2008 practice, with a dispirited obligatory jog around the long ago abandoned cinder running track surrounding the football field, an assistant coach ripped into the team: "You out here cutting corners," he screamed. "You think Kirkwood is cutting corners? I don't think so. They beat you 42-6 on your own field. And why? Because they were more disciplined than you," was the summer mid morning practice commentary leveled at the unmotivated Roughriders. The Coach was only getting warmed up. "They destroyed you on your own field. The embarrassed you on your own field. And you are out here cutting corners? They whipped your sorry asses all over your own field. They came into your house and stole your manhood, made punks out of you. And you out here cutting corners? You couldn't score on them until the last play of the game and then it was against their "D" team. Not their "B" team. Not their "C" team; but their "D" team. And you are cutting corners? Seniors, where is your pride? We had better get some senior leadership out here or we are going to be running until we get to Chicago."

Mental or Physical? Why can the city schools not compete when they step outside of the PHL to play the top county and private schools? For Roosevelt and its fellow PHL brethren, it was a question that must be addressed if city schools are to once again climb to the top of the area high school football ladder. "The gap is closing," states Campbell.

In the Spring of 2008, as city wide elections approached, the political and economic leaders of each of the city's racial groups bunkered down - blacks in the north and whites in the south - with no dialogue of compromise in sight. As the growing abyss of lack of understanding and brotherhood between white and black citizens continued to widen unimpeded, the stalemate of the racial divide in the city of St. Louis had become so solid it seemed that the only agreement city white and black leaders could reach consensus upon was that neither side could find a common ground with the other. Dialogue, while oft started, never materialized into any tangible positive change.

Set against this backdrop of racial disharmony, the Roosevelt Roughriders football team, within the bowels of the old school and under the steady watch of the coaching staff, lifted weights.

Junior Tyler Clubb, the undersized center and linebacker, grunted and strained through his workout. A stereo, buried somewhere in a locker, blared its rhythmic base pounding and wall shaking vibrations. As Coach Campbell videotaped each lift, Clubb reached deep into his own physical and mental reserves to do one more set of dead lift reps. Coaches and teammates alike offered shouts of encouragements as Clubb grimaced and grunted to repeatedly lift the bar bell, holding several hundred pounds of weight plates, from an old and dirty gray mat that was placed in the stairwell outside the locker room - a sort of poor man's make shift lifting platform. After 50 continuous minutes of circuit weight training, and before reporting to an auxiliary gym with his fellow offensive linemen for another 30 minutes of pure torture - known to the linemen as quickness drills - Clubb was asked about his relationship with his fellow Roughrider football teammates. "These guys are my brothers," said Clubb. "There will be 18 of us seniors next year. We have been together since our freshman year. I'd take a bullet for anyone of them and I believe they would do the same for me."

Tyler Clubb is one of two white players on the Roosevelt Roughrider football roster.

Clubb has attended city schools all of his life. He and his family are long time South City residents. "My dad went to Roosevelt." Clubb said. Tyler's father, Jim, is of the last generation of white students to attend city schools before the forced busing of the early 80's sent white city students scampering en mass to the private city schools, or a move to the suburbs. Clubb's presence on the football roster at Roosevelt is unique in ways beyond the color of his skin. He does not attend Roosevelt during the school day. Tyler has been enrolled in the SLPS's magnet school program since entering Kindergarten. He currently attends Central Visual and Performing Arts Academy High School, his interest is music.

Magnet schools were set up as part of the 1980's voluntary busing program to attract and retain students, especially white students, in the city public schools.

Each magnet school would be built around a special theme. Enrollment, based in part on race, would be open through application to any city student, white or black; along with white county students. The theory was that the special and unique curriculum of the "magnets" would attract white students from the county to voluntarily enroll in the city schools, as well as keep many white students in the city schools and out of the private schools. It was a colossal failure. While many black students took advantage of the opportunity to be bused daily to more affluent county schools, few whites – either city or county residents- enrolled in the city public school magnets.

Central and Visual Performing Art Academy is housed in the old Southwest High School building, one mile west down Arsenal Street from Roosevelt. Clubb takes advantage of a unique PHL athletic policy, approved by the Missouri State High School Activities Association, for the benefit of the city's magnet school system. If a student attends a magnet school that does not offer a certain sport, then that student is eligible to participate in that activity at his neighborhood school. (As Roosevelt would painfully learn during the 2008 season, this arrangement did not include non-SLPS Charter Schools.) Clubb's family residence is in the Bevo neighborhood, just down Morganford Road, from Roosevelt High School. Because his magnet school, CVPA, does not have a football team, each day Clubb catches the activity bus outside of his school at Arsenal and Kingshighway and spends the late afternoon hours at Roosevelt with his football playing "brothers."

"I have never felt different or left out because I am white," said Clubb. "I really don't know most of the white kids in my neighborhood. I spend most of my out of school time either working (at an area bowling alley) or with these guys at Roosevelt. Coach Campbell has made us a family."

Clubb would like to dream of a college football career although his undersize body, despite hours of strength training, would limit his options to sub Division I level programs. With outstanding ACT test scores, Clubb does not have to do the tap dance around NCAA eligibility standards that now so preoccupy the worries of many of his senior Roosevelt teammates. "A lot of these guys just didn't take school serious until the last couple of years (of high school). Now they want to play ball in college, but grades are a problem for them. I hope the younger guys are watching and have learned their lessons. You have got to take care of grades from the start, if you want to play on the next level," says Clubb, sounding much like a junior Coach Campbell.

Sending their son to play football at an almost all black inner city school, should not give one the impression that Clubb's parents, Jim and Nita, are modern day liberals, the kind visible throughout the trendy areas of the city; driving hybrid cars adorned with anti war and diversity promoting bumper stickers while wearing an Obama tee shirt. Nor should one deduce that the Clubbs are intent upon using their son's education to make a social statement about the importance of school desegregation and racial diversity. In reality, almost the opposite is true.

"I will admit," says Jim, "Tyler is in the city schools because we cannot afford the private school option, nor are we in a position to move to the county. I was not in favor of Tyler doing this (playing football) at Roosevelt. He had never played football before. His first experience with football was when he went over to Roosevelt to start practice his freshman year. He didn't even know how to put his equipment on. I called the coach at the time and said 'look, this is a white kid. Is this going to be a problem?' I was very uneasy about him being the only white kid. I was afraid he was going to get hurt. I remember taking him to practice the first day of his freshman year and I drove him around to the back of the school to get to the locker room. There were all of these black kids milling around in the lot, being loud, pushing and shoving, and lots of roughhousing. It looked like an out of control mob to me and I let Tyler, my son, out to walk right through the middle of the whole bunch. There was not another white kid there. I admit, I was really uneasy about the whole setup."

Jim decided it would be prudent for him to stay and watch that first day's practice from the stands. "Two players get into a fight right in the middle of practice on the field. I mean a fist fight. They were really going at it and the coaches that were at Roosevelt at the time did nothing to break it up. It was almost like they wanted them to fight."

Tyler's mother Nita agrees that it was not an easy decision to let Tyler join the Roosevelt football squad that freshmen year. "It was his idea. We didn't encourage him at all. We are not big 'sports' people, so it was not like we were pushing him. But it was something he wanted to do, so we gave it our (reluctant) blessing."

Like many freshmen new to the sport, Clubb had to endure through an adjustment period. "He even quit football once," says his Mother. "He walked right off the field in the middle of practice. But the next day he went back and as the (freshman) year went on, it got to be easier and easier for him. Now, football is all he wants to talk about. Football has really come to define the person Tyler sees himself as."

The Clubbs are in a position to view and evaluate the city school system from a perspective most white city residents cannot, that of a parent. They are candid with their observations. "There have been many things over the last 13 years about the city schools we have not liked," says Jim. "Many times we have not felt like Tyler has been challenged in his school work. He has had some good teachers and he has had some bad ones. We have always voiced our opinion when were not pleased with things."

When asked if he would have sent Tyler to a neighborhood school such as Roosevelt, if the magnet school option had not been available, Jim answers with no hesitation, "No. I would not feel comfortable for his safety at Roosevelt. I would not feel safe with his being one of the few white kids in the school." But when the subject turns to football, the parental perception of Roosevelt takes a full,180 degree swing to the positive. Jim says, "Playing football at Roosevelt has been a great experience for Tyler. We are very proud of how hard he has worked and we are proud of his achievements. We do not miss a game."

Mrs. Clubb seconds the positive assessment of the Roughrider football program. "Tyler's self esteem is so tied to football. He is very proud of what he has achieved and how good the team has become. He has made very good friends with the boys on the team. They are at our house all the time. Sometimes after games, they will come over and stay until they go to school the next Monday morning. They are all such nice kids, just typical teenage boys. But oh my can they eat! I call them 'eating machines.'"

Clubb, which Tyler likes to point out is a great name for an offensive lineman, would like to major in computers in college. He would use either his music talents or his football playing skills beyond high school if either, or both, would help him secure a college scholarship. But what, he is asked, if he had to pick between music and football? What if he had to choose between Roosevelt and CPVA? What if the rules were changed and he could not play football for

Roosevelt unless he abandoned his music at CVPA and enrolled as a full time student at Roosevelt? Clubb, showing no hesitation, responds decisively to the hypothetical questions: "I couldn't get to Roosevelt fast enough. I wouldn't give up the experience I have had playing football at Roosevelt for anything. It has been very good for me to see that we, as whites and blacks, are not that different. I don't even think about there being only two white guys on the team. We all bleed Roosevelt Red. We seniors are a band of brothers."

So what lessons can be gleaned from the feel good story of Tyler Clubb, the white kid known affectionately by his black Roosevelt teammates as "White Chocolate?" To paraphrase his parents, it would be this: The beauty and educational value of athletics lies in the premise that everyone; regardless of racial, social, or economic differences; compete on an even playing field, void of social prejudice and discrimination. For Tyler, the football field at Roosevelt High School became his own personal proving ground, allowing him to earn not only the respect of his black teammates but, more importantly, his own self respect. The football driven self esteem he has nurtured - due to his participation at Roosevelt, Tyler will tell you, is priceless. In due time, Clubb morphed from a scared 14 year old freshman into a self confident 18 year old team leader. He earned the respect of his teammates - and later their friendship - not because he is white, but because he showed a grit and drive that allowed him to endure. Along the way, he also willed himself into a pretty good football player.

Once Tyler was accepted as a teammate, the racial divide between his culture and that of his black teammates melted away, in essence, bridged by a camaraderie forged through endless hours of shared toil on the football field. Athletics teach youth a valuable lesson: respect is earned and lasting friendships are built, not on skin color, but as the end result of equals working together, striving toward a common goal.

Watching Clubb joke and banter in good natured fun with his black friends at a 2008 football practice, is a stark image in contrast to a much different scenario his father witnessed that summer evening four years prior: a timid and unsure 14 year old white boy, on his way to his first football practice at Roosevelt High School, walking gingerly through what his father perceived as a "threatening mob" of young black men in the Roosevelt High School parking lot. Over the next four years many of those same young men who comprised the perceived "threatening mob" would become like brothers to Clubb, teammates he would now "take a bullet for."

By developing a strong rapport with his African American teammates, Clubb's experience as a Roughrider is perhaps a glimpse into the future, and the utopian hope, of a someday truly desegregated and color blind public school system.

But the most important lesson taught by the uplifting football experience of Tyler Clubb is the proof once more that any real change within the SLPS will be initiated from the grass roots level, not the downtown administrative offices. St. Louis educational leaders, constantly hindered by the racial strife that polarizes the city; could learn a few lessons in racial harmony and respect from Tyler Clubb and his Roosevelt Roughriders teammates.

One of the many forms of madness that had invaded the minds of urban city leaders across the United States by 2008 was the asinine and no holds barred civic recruitment of professional sports teams. Nation wide, Municipal leaders were climbing over each other to offer rich professional sports team owners hundreds and hundreds of millions of tax payer dollars to build state of the art stadiums for millionaire players to showcase their skills, while playing the games of children.

The nation witnessed city after city line up with ever increasing frenzy and ferocity to outbid each other with public funded handouts to entice professional sports teams to abandon one city for another. Amazingly, this gypsy like movement and mercenary attitude of professional teams did little to dilute the fanatical outpouring of support shown once the team's move was completed and a new home base established. Ridiculous prices for everything from tickets, to hot dogs, to parking were simply accepted as the price to be paid for the privilege of being a "big league city." Nothing could deter the loyalty of the smitten "fan" of the new home team. Unfortunately, this loyalty was not a two way street. St. Louis would discover such in the spring of 2008, due to its own case of flirtation and a souring love affair with its own lured team, the professional football Rams.

St. Louis had previously been through a nasty public "divorce" and abandonment by an NFL team. From 1960 to 1987, the Gateway to the West had been home to a National Football League entry, the St. Louis Football Cardinals. The Cardinals franchise was one of the original NFL founding clubs, established in 1919. For years the franchise was a distant second in popularity in the Windy City, playing second fiddle to the cross town rival Bears, owned and coached by the legendary George Halas. In 1960, the Bidwill family, owners of the Cardinals, fled Chicago, moving the team south to set up shop in St. Louis.

The team played first in the old Sportsman's Park on North Grand Avenue, until moving downtown in 1966 to the newly constructed and state of the art Busch Stadium. The love/hate relationship between the Bidwills and St. Louis sports fans lasted until 1987, when the city fathers declined the team's demand for a public funded football only stadium. Frustrated by second tier status to the beloved baseball team sporting the same nickname, and tempted by the promised financial windfall of a new suitor, the Bidwill family shifted the Cardinal franchise to Phoenix, AZ.

During their St. Louis tenure, the Big Red - a name contrived to help separate the baseball and football teams of St. Louis whom uniquely shared the same nickname - was well known throughout professional sports for their fumbling and bumbling ways. Playoff seasons were few and far between. In their 27 year history in St. Louis, the Cardinals never won, nor hosted, a post season playoff game. From ridiculous draft choices (in one of their last drafts as St. Louis residents, the team's player personnel officials used a first round draft choice to select an unknown quarterback from Colorado State named Kelly Stouffer, eliciting the classic disbelieving comment from one St. Louis reporter: "My God, they drafted a girl"), to questionable coaching hires; all cumulating in one losing season after another.

The Big Red became the modern day version of a previous St. Louis loveable losers, the St. Louis Browns baseball team. The former major league entry in the American League had made St. Louis, for a half a century, a two team major league baseball city. The Browns also played second fiddle to the big brother they shared a stadium with, the Cardinals.

As with the Browns - before their move to Baltimore in the mid-1950's, to be renamed the Orioles - the Big Red continuously complained about the lack of support from the St. Louis sports community. No matter the level of their success, the football team always perceived themselves to be in the shadow of the city's flagship professional sports franchise, the baseball Cardinals.

For the St. Louis sports fan, the football Cardinals were a diversion to be endured between the fall World Series and the start of spring training in February. Conversely, their baseball playing counterparts were given rank worthy of a god; a true city icon and civic treasure. In the early 1980's, Big Red All Pro quarterback Neil Lomax complained to the media that the baseball Cardinals mascot, Fredbird, was held in higher esteem and was more popular with the area fans than he, a high profile quarterback. By the late 1980's, the Big Red were off to the desert, and into the waiting arms of a group of Phoenix civic leaders, promising the moon - at tax payer expense, of course – in exchange for a coveted entry in the National Football League.

Many social scientists find it hard to ethically or economically justify the corporate handouts given to professional sports teams, while the public infrastructures: schools, roads, bridges, health care, are so woefully underfunded. Joseph L. Bast, president of The Heartland Institute, a nonprofit research and education organization based in Chicago, Illinois, was one of many who were questioning the sensibility of this full bore spending spree form of corporate welfare. "All available data suggest that continued public investment in sport stadiums is madness. Sports subsidies don't produce economic benefits sufficient to justify their public subsidies. At best, they are an inefficient and unfair way to attain such 'intangible' benefits as civic pride or urban identity. They unfairly burden those who don't follow professional sports or who can't afford to watch live games," wrote Best.

By the year 2000, athletic venues costing at least $200,000,000 each, had been built - or were being built - in Baltimore, Charlotte, Chicago, Cincinnati, Cleveland, Milwaukee, Nashville, San Francisco, St. Louis, Seattle, Tampa, and Washington, D.C. Stadiums were in the planning stages for Boston, Dallas, Minneapolis, New York, and Pittsburgh.

Renovations of existing stadiums were underway in Jacksonville and Oakland. Total estimated cost of these massive projects by the year 2006: $7 billion- most of the funding supported on the hardworking middle class backs of tax payers, many of whom ironically could not afford the ticket price to see a game in these new palaces.

Bast used data to back up his claims. "Less than a decade earlier, in a very controversial finding, this sizeable public investment is being made for an industry that is puny compared to almost any other sector of the U.S. economy. For example, annual sales reported by Sears Roebuck & Co. are approximately thirty times the entire revenues of Major League Baseball. Chicago, home of five professional sports franchises, derives less than a tenth of 1 percent of its personal income from professional sports. Indeed, there isn't a single county anywhere in the U.S. where professional sports accounts for more than one-half of 1 percent of that county's private-sector payroll."

In the mid 1990's, in a deal that many felt had been secretly brokered in back room smoke filled meetings resulting in commitments of large amounts of public tax waivers and abatements without approval of the voters; the Los Angeles Rams agreed to abandon their west coast tinsel town home of over 40 years and move their franchise to St. Louis. Fellow NFL member franchise, the Raiders, had recently also moved from Los Angeles to Oakland, leaving the Rams as the sole tenant of the Greater Los Angeles area. What could facilitate the abandonment of the nation's second largest market which the Rams now had all to themselves, enticing the move to the much smaller Midwest market of St. Louis? How about a blank check, which is just what many St. Louis area taxpayers felt the Rams had been given.

Critics felt that the Rams were presented by civic leaders, not only a key to the City, but also the combination to the City bank vault. There were voices of dissent, apart from the civic leaders who had become cheerleaders for the Rams and supporters of pacification of anything Ram management deemed as unacceptable to a move. They questioned the city throwing millions and millions of dollars – cash viewed by some as nothing short of bribe and extortion money - at wealthy owners of a football team, while the city's schools and other social institutions were so woefully under funded.

The new home of the Rams, the lynch pin in securing their move from the West Coast, the TWA Dome, was under construction before St. Louis had even secured an NFL team. In 1994, city leaders insisted that St. Louis would be one of two cities awarded NFL expansion franchises that year. With a stadium already half built, St. Louis was jolted by an announcement that the NFL's two newest members would call the cities of Jacksonville, FL and Charlotte, NC home. With a multi hundred million dollar stadium already in the oven, St. Louis politicians found themselves in quite a quandary.

St. Louis then turned its collective gaze west to Los Angeles, and one of the more storied franchises in the illustrious history of the NFL, the Rams. With a stadium half built and no team secured to play in it, St. Louis leaders were in a bad negotiating position, and both they and the Rams knew it. To entice the Rams move to St. Louis, both sides knew the city would have to pay dearly, and they did. Because of the weakness of their position, the city agreed to a potentially fatal escape clause that, in 20 years, would give the Rams a chance to break its lease with the city of St. Louis, once again entertaining offers from would be suitors wanting to move the team from St. Louis to their own city.

St. Louis Post Dispatch columnist and humorist Bill McClellan described the strange marriage between the Rams - "our second wife" - as the writer referred to the current home team. McClellan, tongue in cheek, differentiates the current St. Louis NFL entry from "our first wife," the Big Red: "We went to Los Angeles for our second wife. We built her the stadium we had refused to build Big Red. We threw money at her. That's the only reason she married us, and we knew it. She was a head-turner. A Super Bowl winner, the Greatest Show on Turf. We were out of our class. A paunchy, middle-aged guy with a comb-over out there on the dance floor with a supermodel. Now we can see the end. Right there in the marriage contract she made us sign; it says the stadium she plays in has to be in the top 25 percent of all NFL stadiums by 2015. There are 32 teams in the league. So our stadium has to be in the top eight. That seems almost impossible. According to a recent story in this newspaper, three stadiums are currently under construction, and that means that 20 of the 32 stadiums will be newer than ours in 2015 — and that's if no others are built between now and then."

In 1995, the first year the Rams called St. Louis home, the club played the first two months of home games at the old home of the Big Red, Busch Stadium, as they waited for the TWA Dome to be completed. In October, 1995, the Rams christened their new palace with their first home game in a structure built to the tune of $280 million.

Finances for the new stadium came from 100% public funding. The Rams did not put in one dime. The package to lure the Rams with the free stadium offer was a combined effort of several levels of government. 50% of the debt was backed by the state of Missouri through an annual general fund appropriation. The tax payers of St. Louis County accepted 25% of the cost, generated by proceeds from a 3.5% hotel/motel tax. The final 25% was raised by the city of St. Louis with funds generated by activities at the city owned downtown Convention Center, adjacent to the new dome.

And the largesse was not just limited to the owners. The explosion of televised sports through cable, and the activism of player labor unions in the 1980's and 90's, had led to the elimination of the hated reserve clause. A monopolistic practice that tied a player through a life time contract with any team who held his rights, to play for what ever amount of money the team offered, or not play at all - had created a free agent market that produced spiraling lucrative contracts for star players and journeyman alike. For a point of reference, think about this: retired Ram Running Back Marshall Faulk, in 2005, his last active year in the NFL, earned over six times the amount of money with one rushing attempt (which on the average would require some where in the range of five seconds of his effort) as the entire football coaching staff at Roosevelt High School combined would earn in extra duty stipends for 12 months of mentoring youngsters like Faulk's nephew, Roosevelt High School lineman, Rene Faulk.

Once an NFL team settled in its new home, the supply and demand nature of the product of the National Football League forced cities to continue unabashedly courting their new resident, or the fickle lover would cast a straying eye in the direction of another star struck city without a team. As mentioned by McCellen, the contract the Rams signed with the city of St. Louis - a document reputed to be so large it took three huge three ring binders to house it - required that their stadium (the Dome) be in the top 15% of NFL venues, or the team by the year 2015, could break it's lease and move to another city. This would leave St. Louis elected officials with ownership of a 66,000 seat domed stadium with no tenant, sans an occasional tractor pull; a terrifying thought for St. Louis civic leaders, to say the least.

Whatever it would take, and by 2008 it was estimated to be in the tens of millions of dollars, to improve the team's domed stadium to meet the upgrade demands of the lease, the city - or more accurately the tax payers - would have to pay, or the Rams would be gone.

By the spring of 2008, other ominous factors were pointing to a wavering Rams commitment to St. Louis. In late winter, long time team owner - and St. Louis native - Georgia Frontiere had died. The team was now owned by her son and daughter, Chip Rosenbloom and Lucia Rodriguez, both lifelong Los Angeles residents. Suppose the Southern California city made a pitch for the return of its wayward team? It was well accepted that it was just a matter of time - and lining up another civic supported stadium deal - before the NFL was back with a franchise in the city of Los Angeles, arguably next to New York - which had two franchises - the most important and lucrative TV market in the nation. For the National Football League to not have a team in Los Angeles followed no economic rhyme or reason. Were the Rams not the logical choice? Would St. Louis be spurned again by an NFL team?

Although the new brother and sister ownership team gave public statements of their support in keeping the Rams in St. Louis, by the Spring of 2008 it was obvious to even the most casual of observers that the Rams had the leverage needed to once again put the economic squeeze on the city. If St. Louis wanted to retain a team past the year 2015, they had better be prepared to pony up one heck of an expensive tax payer supported offering. More complicating was the assessment by the end of the 2008 season that the Rams were arguably the worst team in the NFL. Despite supporting a team that had over the two previous years won only five of 32 games, if St. Louis were to retain the Rams, they had better be ready to pay a steep price.

Once again a little perspective: By 2005, the Rams were complaining that the turf in their domed stadium - a tax payer supported building don't forget, that was for all practical purposes handed to the Rams on a silver platter upon their move to St. Louis in 1995, was old and worn. The Rams demanded that it be replaced at taxpayer expense.

Tom Anselm of Florissant, MO, saw the hypocrisy of the Rams as well as the good done (as will be discussed later in Chapter 4) by the philanthropist group *PHL, Inc.*, the volunteer group that had worked miracles in refurbishing the playing fields for St. Louis Public High League teams, all having been accomplished with volunteer labor and donated funds. PHL, Inc. had asked for no tax payer support. Anselm had evaluated the relative merits of each and wrote in a letter to the editor of the St. Louis Post Dispatch the following poignant comments: "The good news is that someone (PHL, Inc.) finally is doing something instead of complaining about how hard it is to do something. The bad news is that it took a group of private citizens to make it happen. The people at *PHL, Inc.* are to be congratulated and supported. Speaking of support, am I mistaken or do we not have a professional football team in St. Louis? Why haven't we heard that the Rams have pitched in with a generous grant of cash to aid the process of (high school) field renovations? It would be natural for the Rams to make a donation, especially since we (tax payers) are paying $168,000 for new artificial turf for the Rams."

In addition to the dome Stadium, the Rams, upon their arrival in St. Louis, were also built - once again on the public tax dime - a practice facility in the North St. Louis County burg of Earth City. No expense was spared in facilitating the Rams players with the most modern and comfortable state of the art athletic training venue to be found in the St. Louis area. The setup at Rams Park, as the facility was known when it was built - and later renamed Russell Training Center after a hefty monetary contribution to the Rams by the huge manufacturer of athletic equipment and apparel of the same name - contained team offices, training and injury rehabilitation facilities, meeting rooms, and several practice fields, of both the indoor and outdoor variety.

To be competitive in the modern new era of the NFL, players by 2008 were committed to year round training. Drinking beer and working odd jobs - which was the common off season routine for NFL players in the 1950's and 1960's - and then using training camp to play one's way into shape, was as out of vogue in the NFL of the 21st century as team and player loyalty to its home town fans. The money for all involved – players and owners - was too great, the investment too immense. To train otherwise would net the player a quick ticket out of the modern day NFL. To maintain peak performance and fitness - attained under the watchful eye of the Rams large professional training and conditioning staff - most Rams now made St. Louis their year round home.

In May of 2008, the high salaried stars of the Rams – some of the elite and best football players in the world - could be found daily at the Ram's Earth City facility, protecting their careers and their high dollar salaries by intently preparing for the upcoming season.

Meanwhile, that same May, another St. Louis football team, quietly and without fanfare, also prepared diligently for the 2008 season. Deep within a tired old brick school building, crumbling under the weight of years of neglect and indifference at 3230 Hartford Street – home since 1925 of Roosevelt High School, off the corner of Grand and Arsenal and just to the east of Tower Grove Park, the Roosevelt Roughriders trained in a facility that was as Spartan and sparse as the Rams was exquisite and excessive. In a converted shower room, a group of young men, self labeled as a band of brothers, lifted weights with a dogged determination, preparing and dreaming of a destined glory they believed to a man, come fall football season, would be theirs.

CHAPTER 3
A HISTORY

A generation which ignores history has no past and no future.
— Robert Heinlein

There is no accountability in the public school system - except for coaches. You know what happens to a losing coach. You fire him. A losing teacher can go on losing for 30 years and then go to glory.
— Ross Perot

In the first place, God made idiots. That was for practice. Then he made school boards.
— Mark Twain

In every child who is born under no matter what circumstances and of no matter what parents, the potentiality of the human race is born again, and in him, too, once more, and each of us, our terrific responsibility toward human life: toward the utmost idea of goodness, of the horror of terrorism, and of God.
— James Agee

In the glory years of long ago, they once stood throughout the south side of the great city. Architectural monuments to a school system that educated the masses; although in the strictest practice of the day's legal racial segregation. Anchors of the community, these modern day Bastilles stood a tall and constant vigil, a source of comfort for its neighbors and inhabitants and a lasting reminder of the accomplishments of its graduates. Through their arch doorways passed several generations of St. Louis citizens who would come of age in these buildings, developing the skills and knowledge which would produce many a local, regional and national leader.

In St. Louis, the neighborhoods had been for many years clearly marked, white in the south, black in the north. With the exception of periodic spirited athletic competition through the Public High League– post 1954 Brown v. Topeka Board of Education - little did the two sides mix, nor collaborate. An educational pattern was thus established that throughout the city of St. Louis still holds true today, two separate worlds, each to its own, with one major change. Today the separation between white and black students is not the locals of north and south, but separation between public schools and private schools. With very few exceptions, white parents within the city limits of St. Louis long ago abandoned the St. Louis Public School System.

From the dawn of the 20th century, until the early 1980's and the onslaught of forced busing in the white dominated south area of the city, the heartbeat of the community flowed through the corridors of the four neighborhood high schools. Local pride was rooted deep in the academic and athletic accomplishments of the Cleveland High Dutchmen, the Southwest Longhorns, the McKinley Goldbugs and of course, the Roosevelt Roughriders, the school off the corner of Arsenal and Grand.

Cleveland High School opened in 1915. With its Jacobethen style architecture, similar in style to castles built in England in the 17th century, the school building became the most famous landmark in the "Dutchtown" area of South St. Louis. The students of Cleveland came from a community predominated by decedents of German-American immigrants. (The area's residents never were Dutch. The misconception came from the use of the German term "Deutschland" or "Fatherland" to describe their neighborhood, a term many non-German St. Louis citizens mispronounced as "Dutch".) When forced busing became mandated in 1980, Cleveland was hit the hardest and the swiftest. From a 98% white enrollment, overnight the school saw its' African American population rise to 45%. Chaos was imminent and immediate. Reports of race wars, harassment, and accosting of white girls by black males and roving gangs of blacks taking control of the school hallways spread through the Dutchtown community like wildfire. Police were dispatched to the school on a daily basis to break up fights that occurred between whites and blacks. Permanent security within the building was given dramatic increase in numbers. White parents immediately began to pull their children from Cleveland and enroll them in one of the many parochial schools which were already in abundance on the south side, but who were now swelling to the brink with new students. Many white parents who could not get their children into an area private school simply pulled up roots, family tradition be damned, and moved to the county, the beginning of the "white flight" phenomena that would doom the future of the south side public schools.

Despite far reaching efforts to try and bridge the racial abyss and to build lines of co-existence – Cleveland High School went so far as in 1981 to name two homecoming queens; one white and one black, each escorted by a male of their own race, by 1984, Cleveland was closed as a neighborhood school, its' students shuttled off to the west and absorbed into the student body of Southwest High School.

When its doors opened in 1935, Southwest High School became the newest of the city's four Southside high schools. The home of the Longhorns, located at the corner of Arsenal St. and Kingshighway, was considered a modern marvel. The school served the city's world famous Italian neighborhood known as The Hill. Southwest also drew students from the upper class neighborhoods of St. Louis Hills, South City and Holly Hills. At the time, if the city had a high school that could be labeled as attended by affluent students, it would have been Southwest. White flight hit the school before even the court ordered busing programs of 1980. Southwest was, by this time already beginning to see the demographic makeup of its student body change, as more blacks moved within the fringes of its northern residency area. By 1992, Southwest would also see its doors shuttered and its students, by this time mostly black, sent to schools in the north.

McKinley High School opened in 1904. Located on Russell Blvd, it had always been the "blue collar" high school on the south side. The students of McKinley tended to be from poorer families than students enrolled in the south side's other three public high schools. McKinley was the most lacking of any city school in terms of athletic facilities, even less equipped than the black schools on the north side. The "we can overcome anything" attitude, adopted out of necessity by the school's athletic teams, became a rally point which is still to this day cherished by McKinley Alumni.

The Goldbugs had no home field, home court, running track or baseball diamond. In short, McKinley had no athletic facilities. They practiced and played wherever they could find an open field or an open court. The track team ran sprints in the school's third floor hallway. The football team practiced in a vacant lot, a scant 50 yard open space. This practice field, it was joked, was often harder than the school parking lot. In fact the Goldbugs, when heavy rains made their grassless practice area unusable, did at times have its football team practice on the campus's concrete parking lot.

Despite these many handicaps, the Goldbugs won more than their share of PHL football titles in the 50's, 60's and 70's. McKinley was also the Southside high school located the farthest north, and the first to encounter a shift in population that would by the early the 1970's see a growing black percentage in the make up of the Goldbug student body. McKinley closed its doors in 1988, its students transferred to Southwest.

Constructed in 1925, Roosevelt High School was named for the former American President, Theodore Roosevelt. Its nickname, the Roughriders, derived as a tribute to "Teddy's" legendary hard fighting unit that stormed San Juan Hill in the Spanish American War of 1898, with the future near sighted President leading the charge. The school's yearbook for years was known as the "Bwana" - Swahili for "Master" - a name given to Roosevelt by tribesman during his many big game safaris to Africa. In 1985, in a gesture to political correctness and simplicity, the Annual's name was changed to "The Roosevelt High School Yearbook." The newest yearbook to be found in the school library archives was produced in 2000. No one at the school can give an explanation about the demise of a publication that had, for 75 consecutive years, documented life at the school.

Roosevelt High School was built on 20 acres that had previously housed the Holy Ghost Cemetery, a burial ground founded in 1845 and said to hold the remains of many of the victims of a cholera epidemic that sweep the city in 1849. The cemetery was also at times known as Picket Cemetery. By the time construction of the Roosevelt building began in 1923, the cemetery had been long abandoned, some of the bodies exhumed and reinterred, while others were simply left unattained for years. Stories abound of residents of the area complaining during the construction of Roosevelt, that human bones were being drug home by dogs, or collected by children playing at the construction site. For years the students of Roosevelt have passed down, from one class to the next, the stories of the unused 4th floor of the building being haunted by the ghosts and spirits of Picket Cemetery.

The school building was designed by St. Louis Public School Architect RA Milligen. Its construction was described by the district leaders as "English Renaissance." Its trade mark bell towers, reminiscent of Czarist Russia and a dominant structure of the Tower Grove neighborhood, are considered a local landmark. The brick building itself has remarkably withstood the test of time. The four story structure remains basically unchanged, while witnessing the days of the Roaring 20's, the Great Depression, the Second World War, the Korean War and the upheaval Social Movements of the 1960's. While the building remains the same, the clientele that stroll its hallways has undergone a transformation of 180 degrees.

The other South Side high school buildings have not fared as well in withstanding the test of time. Today The Castle, as Cleveland High School was affectionately known, stands empty, a sullen reminder of all that has gone wrong with an urban school system that many experts call the worst in the nation. The Castle last housed city students during the school year of 2005-2006. Despite a grass roots effort, spearheaded by a group of Dutchman Alumni known as the *Alliance to Save Cleveland High School*, making a passionate pitch to save their treasured school from the wrecking ball, the prognosis for future survival of the south side landmark is grim. SLPS bean counters point to the rapid decline of the infrastructure of the building, combined with the almost non existence of south side students enrolled in the public schools; coupled with skyrocketing costs incurred in maintaining a building close to 90 years of age. Due to these prohibiting problems, SLPS leaders see little chance of the doomed building ever reopening as a public high school.

The buildings that once hosted McKinley High School and Southwest High School are still in use as public school buildings, but under new configurations and not as neighborhood high schools. McKinley has been converted to a Middle School magnet, McKinley Classical Middle School. Southwest, once the home of the PHL's most dominant football program, now houses a "magnet school" – Central and Visual Performing Arts Academy. Due to lack of student interest, CVPA does not even field a football team. Its game field is still maintained by the SLPS and is used for "home games" for various PHL football teams who do not have a football field on their own campuses.

Only Roosevelt High School, standing where it has since it opened in January, 1925, at the corner of Hartford and Gravois - on the southwest corner of Tower Grove Park – operates as a neighborhood high school. The Tower Grove Park neighborhood that houses Roosevelt has seen, in recent years, an urban renewal of its own. Many young Caucasian white collar types have been drawn to the area's cheap, but well maintained, housing. Most residences are of solid brick architecture. Despite many of the dwellings being over 100 years of age, they are solid in structure and make good investments for young and upward bound city dwellers.

Attendance zones for Roosevelt High School by 2008 encompassed the entire south St. Louis area. Where once four public neighborhood High Schools had served the needs of south side students, Roosevelt now stood alone, its enrollment numbers nowhere near the levels of the 1950's and 60's. The sheer size of the boundaries that Roosevelt currently serves, makes its designation as a neighborhood school misleading. Few of today's current Roughriders come from the neighborhoods surrounding Roosevelt. White families, who still maintain a racial majority of the population on the south side of the city, do not send their children to the public schools, especially Roosevelt High School. Most students enrolled at Roosevelt in 2008 are bused to the school from minority neighborhoods to the north and the east of the school.

The neighborhoods surrounding Roosevelt were originally settled by the French in the early 1700s. Grazing land for the self sufficient farms that developed in the surrounding areas was viewed by law as common communal land.

Farming land was divided into long narrow tracts. Around 1800, the practice of communal land for grazing was dissolved and private ownership of tracts were sold and recorded. By the 1850s, German immigrants had taken over a majority of the area. These German Catholics, many of who had fled Germany during the 1848 civil war, found the rich soil and rolling hillsides ideal for dairy farming. As the farmers prospered, they began to build huge and expensive homes. The area was soon divided into blocks and the agrarian economy was, by the late 1800's, gone, replaced by merchants and business men. A local historian from the Tower Grove East Neighborhood Betterment Association describes the homes that still dominate the neighborhood as structures that were "built on the four-square plan. The typical house is a pyramid, or hipped roof, on a two-story cube. Often a pressed brick or limestone course separates the stories. The original developers then varied the theme through detail choices. Attention was heavily focused on the entry, cornice and windows. Buyers would often choose the architectural elements from pattern books that illustrated multiple styles of windows, doors, stairways and fireplace mantels. Thus the interiors of the homes in Tower Grove East are full of surprises. The often austere exterior facades typically hide a wealth of richly designed entries with carved fretwork, built-in hall benches, mirrors and bookcases, wood paneling, stained-glass windows and elaborate staircases."

Sagging - the style of wearing oversized trousers well below the hip line - has, over the last 15 years, become a fashion trend favored by many inner city male teenagers. Sagging has become the cultural equivalent of the long hair statement made by rebellious youth of the 1960s and 70s. Students of today's hip hop generation continually push the limits of the outrageous, with how low and loose their pants hang, before the long arm of authority- often in the form of an assistant principal - reaches out to pull the wearer back into some range of the parameters of respectability and cultural acceptance. It has become a constant cat and mouse game between those who set and enforce polices, and the youth that resist the implementation of society's norms.

In 2008, a sign is attached to every classroom door at Roosevelt High School, asking students before they enter the classroom: "Are your pants pulled up?"

Someone walking out of a time warp from 20 years ago and seeing such a sign on a public school classroom door would do a double take of amusement, with a quizzical nod to question the sanity of those running the school. The hallways of Roosevelt High School have witnessed, since 1925, this ongoing struggle between the conformity to culturally accepted standards demanded by the established adults in command, and the non conformity born of the urge of a teenager's need for exuberance and rebellion.

The first generation of Roughriders came of age in the "Roaring" 1920's, amidst the rising hem lines that signaled to many adults of that era the end of acceptable society. It was also the time of the explosion of the availability of the automobile to the masses. The freedoms now afforded 1920's teens by this unprecedented mobility surely placed the fear of rampant youthful immorality into the minds of many a parent of these first Roosevelt Roughriders.

Students of the 1930's and 1940's, decades overpowered by two monumental generation defining events- the Great Depression and World War II – matured to the anti-social emergence of folk hero gangsters. Many teenagers found a romantic urge to emulate these outlaws with behavior considered outside accepted norms and laws. Further upheaval to society's basic unit, the family, occurred when so many fathers were marched off to war, and the nation was rocked with an explosion in juvenile delinquency. Yearbooks validate that the Roosevelt students of the 1950's were part of the popular "greaser" look. Rolled up sleeves of white t-shirts and leather jackets, worn in an attempt to look "cool", was the uniform of a generation of "rebels without a cause," coming of age in time of unprecedented national financial prosperity.

More documenting photos from Yearbooks and newspaper clippings show that the hippie movement and youthful revolution of the mid 60's also found its way to the home of the Roughriders. Stylish long hair for males, and the prevalence of short skirts for females, give visual proof that, by the end of the 60's, the non-conformity of the Age of Aquarius had indeed arrived in the Halls of RHS.

By 1970, a widening generation gap, between child and parent, student and school leader, had become a national reality. Festered by a lack of communication and understanding, as in no other time in our history, many a parent and child found themselves helplessly and hell bent on a collision course of values that would manifest itself in the societal divisiveness of the Vietnam War Protests, the Civil Rights Movement and the explosion of the main stream drug culture - a societal phenomena that still rivets through today's society.

Even the nation's 1980's return to conservative polices, embedded in American culture by the popularity of the Reagan years, failed to protect the nation's adults from the outlandish styles of the young generation. By the 1980's, with the second wave of the British invasion in full force, a cross Atlantic import that brought the "punk" look to the youth of America; adults had again a reason to shake their heads in astonishment at the younger generation. A glance through historical pictures archived of Roosevelt High School in the 1980's also shows the evolving face of diversity as the student body at the south side school became more and more minority dominated.

The popularity of rap music, as could be predicted, is very popular amongst RHS students of the New Millennium. An entire sub culture and lifestyle for inner city African American teens has been spawned through the dress and music of this fad. As historically documented over the years, styles born within the cultures of inner city youth will, in due time, invade the affluent suburban enclaves and catch favor with the white teenagers who live in these markedly non urban communities. Sagging, to the consternation of many suburban parents and school leaders, is now as deeply ingrained in the youth culture of the suburbs as it is in the city.

The more things change, the more they stay the same, and the hallways of Roosevelt High School have seen it all. Conformity to non-conformity, that rite of youthful passage to dress and behave in an outlandish manner has, without fail, raised the ire and righteous indignation of each succeeding generation of parents. The evidence of "this misguided youthful generation" is recorded and portrayed in yellowing photographs, hidden safely in cedar chests stowed away in attics of the homes of now middle aged pillars of the community; proof that Mom and Dad had their "outlandish" days as well. Grandparents of 2008 shake their collective heads in amazement when they hear their own children admonish the dress, behavior and music of their off-spring as gaudy, outrageous and disturbing. Memories and visions conjured up by grandmother and grandfather are of today's teachers, executives and city leaders in a another life - and another time - when the folly of their own youth was manifested and expressed by Afro hair styles, bell bottom jeans and outlandish flower child style clothing. The care free 1960 and 1970's, where the mantra was: if its fun do it, and if it is really fun do it twice; was a time that most who came of age during the Woodstock years managed to experience, survive and move on. Many of these legions of wayward youths of the "Hippie Age" have matured into the successful leaders of today's society. When it comes to the style and fashion of the young, the biblical reminder that "this too will pass," is sage advice that will bring relative acceptance - and perhaps maintain to some degree parental serenity - when dealing daily with the folly of the younger generation.

For the last 80 years, Roosevelt students have traveled through its stately corridors on a sometimes bewildering four year journey; a junket marked equally by the memorable and traumatic events of their high school years. The heartfelt prayer of each following generation of parents has remained constant: "God help me survive these four years with a trace of my sanity in tact." Most have had their prayers answered, affirmed by their offspring's climactic Graduation Day walk across the hallowed RHS auditorium stage. With the completion of this milestone, comes the emergence onto the other side, the real world of adult responsibility. In a poetically just circle unbroken, in a few short years, these young adults will themselves be immersed in parenthood, and their roles flipped to one of concerned and bewildered mothers and fathers.

When Terry Houston took over as Principal at Roosevelt, he put an immediate emphasis on appearance. "It is not an issue of trying to dress and look 'white,'" says Houston. "It is a matter of making it in this world. I want every one of our graduates to go to college, join the military or go to trade school. We have too many (of our students) ending up working dead end jobs; or worse, in jail or dead."

Houston's view on student dress code issues is grounded in a pragmatic view. "I want our kids to dress with pride and with an eye on success. How you look matters. Nobody is going to hire a gang banger if they have any other choice. No investment, no return. Our job is to prepare these kids for life. Prepare them to take care of their families. Live up to their responsibilities as a father or a mother, a husband or a wife, a son or a daughter. You are not going get the good jobs or get into the good colleges with your pants down (and) showing your rear end."

A strange scene involving the stylish "saggers," was played out at the beginning of most every Roughrider football practice. For the team's coaches, getting

Roosevelt football players to practice on time was a constant struggle; getting them fully adorned in the proper football practice gear, a near impossibility. Team members who forgot their football shorts or practice pants, would run the obligatory two pre practice laps dressed in the shorts they had worn to school that day. With the garment several sizes too big and of a length to almost reach the wearer's ankles, the shorts, while running, were next to impossible to keep from falling down around one's ankles. To keep the shorts on required committing one hand to a securing grip. Watching this battle was one of the many amusing sights for an outsider not in tune with the style of the inner city youth of 2008.

So what happened to the athletic powerhouses that had once adorned the Public High League teams with area wide admiration and respect? How had feared programs whose ferocity once put the shakes into the collective knees of the suburban schools, been turned into dispirited shells of their once lofty status, now pitied by the county rivals while ridiculed and all but abandoned by their once proud neighborhood boosters? What had happened to the swagger? The answer was simple: the 1981 court ordered "voluntary" city-county desegregation program. The process was intended to bring desegregation to the south side city schools. Instead, it doomed a whole generation of poor St. Louis City students, mostly black, to not only a sub par education, but to an embarrassment of an athletic program that cared little about them or their self esteem.

In 2003, the weekly alternative newspaper the St. Louis Riverfront Times (RFT), did an expose on the miserable conditions of Public High League teams and placed the blame squarely on the shoulders of the voluntary desegregation program. The report focused on the drain to the city schools of over 10,000 city students who now attended school in predominantly white St. Louis County districts. The sudden improvement in the success levels of the athletic programs of these county schools, especially in football, was undeniable. They had found a gold mine of athletic talent, and despite their often and loud public denials of recruiting for athletic gain, mined the seemingly inexhaustible vein for all it was worth.

The RFT reported on the PHL glory days as such: "From the 1960s through the '80s, the Public High League dominated St. Louis-area football. Lawrence Walls, who retired in 1998, presided over a dynasty at Sumner High School, beginning in 1971. Only Bob Shannon's East St. Louis Senior High program in Illinois rivaled Sumner during Walls' reign, as the Bulldogs won state titles in 1973, 1982, 1990 and 1991 and made it to the championship game five other times between '74 and '89. Beaumont consistently challenged Sumner for the city championship, while teams from McKinley, Soldan and Cleveland also won PHL titles. All those schools produced dozens of players who went on to successful college and pro careers — the list of stars is headed with names like Lorenzo Brinkley Sr., who starred at Beaumont in the '60s and then at Missouri, and Demetrious Johnson, who played at Soldan and Mizzou before going on to the NFL. On Friday nights, PHL games were raucous, celebratory events, with games held at either Soldan, Gateway or the old Southwest High — the only schools in the city with fields at the time. Hundreds of students, parents and alumni filled the stands, dressed in team colors. School bands provided vibrant halftime shows, and almost every PHL matchup was a cross-town rivalry."

Although RFT's facts were sometimes a little on the loose side – Friday Night games were seldom played in the PHL as only Gateway (formally O'Fallon Tech) had lights - the statistics were irrefutable. When the voluntary desegregation program began in force in 1982, over the next ten years, St. Louis County schools won seven state football championships and finished runner up another 13 times. Many of these juggernaut teams were powered by St. Louis city student/athletes who boarded a bus each morning for the long ride to the county schools.

Current Sumner High Coach, Sorrel Harvey, was coach in 2002 of the Roosevelt Roughriders and stated his views of the transfer program, "The Public High League was one of the strongest athletic conferences around Missouri. When desegregation happened, a number of good athletes, a number of good students, got involved. Not having the number of students, the competitiveness in the league went down." As a player in the 1970's, Harvey had been a member of some of the most dominant teams in the city's long and gloried gridiron history. In 1974, Harvey was a running back for a Sumner team who won the large school state championship with a 35-0 massacre of Columbia Hickman.

Such glory days are now just a distant memory for anyone associated with the PHL football programs.

The Riverfront Times reported the following statistics on the number of city players on county school rosters: "All those county teams have significant numbers of transfer students on their rosters: Mehlville has 36 transfer students in its 90-player program, or 40 percent; Parkway Central has 23 transfers on its varsity (nearly 50 percent). Seven of Pattonville's 35 junior and senior players – 20 percent – are transfers; the numbers are similar at Webster Groves, where 7 of the 34 juniors and seniors are transfers, including Darrell Jackson, the area's top player. One rival coach says the Mehlville football team could be called 'the St. Louis All-Stars.'"

The paper then turned it's focus to facilities. "The disparity in facilities offered by city and county schools remains, in 2008, stark. While city schools have always lagged behind their county rivals in terms of money and equipment, the gap has only widened since desegregation. The football stadium at Roosevelt High School was built to hold hundreds of fans who no longer show up for home games. The grass on the field is brown and worn, trampled down to patches of dirt between the hash marks. The grass stretches all the way up to the stands on the north side and to a ratty chain-link fence to the south; a circular path of trodden dirt approximates the expensive 400-meter tracks that surround typical county football fields. The field at Gateway Tech is equally threadbare, worn down by four-times-a-week practices, and games on Friday nights and Saturday afternoons."

Few experts, be it coaches, reporters, or building administrators would mention the word race; but the assumptions were clear: blacks bring the speed and athletic ability to the Suburban schools that their home grown all white student bodies cannot provide. Schools like Mehlville would start an entire line of big and strong local white athletes, and an entire backfield of black city transfer students. The combination was lethal. White county schools that fell just outside of the desegregation area, were stark reminders of the importance of speed in football. Fox High School, just outside the St. Louis County line and located in Jefferson County, therefore not eligible to receive black city students, but still forced into a conference and a district schedule that saw them yearly competing against county schools who did receive city student athletes, was a prime example of the effect that the desegregation program had on area high school football.

Fox High School would regularly churn out outstanding linemen, one particular example being Mike Wells, who went on to star at the University of Iowa and in the National Football League. But, due to lack of backfield speed, the Warriors suffered through many 0-10 winless seasons in the 80's and 90's.

As could be expected, charges of illegal recruitment were leveled loud and long by both PHL and out state rural coaches, whose teams had to compete in conference, district and state play against these recently retooled county suburban schools. According to the Missouri State High School Activates Association (MSHSAA), the rumors were next to impossible to prove. Others charged that the Association simply turned a blind eye to a problem they knew existed, but felt would be near impossible to police or enforce. MSHSAA Director Becky Oakes told the Riverfront Times in 2002, that "Trouble is, there's virtually no way to pinpoint the motivation behind a transfer. There are so many ways in which people can try to influence kids to change schools," Oakes said. Her point is well made. As long as a student was wise enough – perhaps after receiving lessons from county suitors - to the rules, gaining eligibility after a desegregation transfer was not that difficult of a task. If the student filled out the transfer form listing the necessitated move for academic reasons, along with a subsequent denial of any influence for athletic reasons, the student would almost always be found eligible for athletics at the county school he or she transferred to.

Another problem with stopping athletic recruitment through the voluntary desegregation program was the number of individuals who operated with no official concrete tie to a particular suburban school. These "street agents" would often develop relationships with one particular suburban school, and perhaps that school's coach, and would use their influence and connections to steer players to that program. With the rapid development of youth programs in the different city Recreation Programs, such as Boys and Girls Clubs, outstanding athletic talent could, and often was, labeled at an early age, sometimes before the athlete had even reached junior high. There was no question that high school coaches in the suburban schools knew where the talent could be found, and who could help them secure it.

Even if recruitment for athletic reasons was occurring, and most everyone thought it was, Oakes felt there was little her state organization could do to curtail it. "In some cases it may be intentional," says Oakes. "In a metropolitan area like St. Louis or Kansas City, it's easy to take place. There are so many schools, and you also have the voluntary transfer program and the whole "choice issue." That sets up a scenario where it's easier for kids to pick or have something suggested to them. We're not a policing-type organization," Oakes said. "We rely on the schools to monitor themselves, and they do a pretty good job." Many high school coaches around the state of Missouri would have begged to differ with Ms. Oakes' assessment of the honesty in the self monitoring of suburban programs. These schools were, year after year, growing stronger and more successful with the immense help of talented athletes who rested their heads each evening on pillows in domiciles located within the boundaries of the St. Louis Public Schools.

The Riverfront Times, in its 2003 expose, found that schools that did recruit had little to fear from the MSHSAA. "In the past five years, no team in the state has been sanctioned by MSHSAA for recruiting, and only three students have been declared ineligible for transferring for athletic reasons. None of those three students were involved in the local desegregation plan," the paper reported. "If coaches at the school a student is transferring to are found to have exerted undue influence, by promising a spot in the starting line-up or offering free shoes or equipment, the school faces sanctions, but ultimately the decision of whether to punish an offending coach lies with the individual school districts, not the MSHSAA. 'It goes back to local control,' says Rick Kindhart, an MSHSAA staff member 'We deal with the administration, the administration deals with the coach. That's who the coach works for. The coach is not a member [of the MSHSAA], the school is.'"

Not everyone involved in the administration of suburban programs took such a "hear no evil, see no evil approach." A Pattonville Administrator involved directly with his St. Louis County's school district's participation in the desegregation program, stated what many felt was the obvious. Brian Simmons said, "That doesn't mean it (recruiting) doesn't happen. Everybody's doing it," said the former football coach. Although he sympathized with the bitterness and resentment felt by many city coaches and officials, he saw benefits for students through better facilities, equipment and academics; in other words, a path to a brighter future. "Is it a bad thing? Yeah," says Simmons. "Is it a good thing? Yeah. It's not that county schools are taking students out of the city, It's voluntary. Parents decide that the county schools have much more to offer."

This "end justifies the means" argument was seen by many in the city system as a mere rationalization and a classic what comes first, the chicken or the egg analogy. "Our programs are down because you stole all of our talented kids, not because our programs went down and our talented kids then decided to leave," city league coaches would often wail to the deaf ears of both city and county school district leaders.

Terry Houston, Principal of Roosevelt High School, attended a Historical black College (HBC), Virginia State, graduating in 1982. Houston was on the tale end of the "glory days" of segregated higher education systems found in the southern states like Virginia. A system that was once the law of the land was, by the early 80's, slowly eroding away. Football teams sponsored by HBC were at one time almost the equivalent in talent, if not in state resources, of the powerhouse state Universities of the Southeastern Conference (SEC). Many years in the 1960's, considered the zenith of football prowess at HBCs, as many future NFL stars could be found on the roster of Alabama State as at the University of Alabama, at Grambling as at LSU. In spite of the landmark court ruling of Brown v. Board, which in 1954 overturned all Jim Crow segregation laws; the pace of desegregation of southern universities and its athletic programs, even into the mid 1970's, was slow and dominated by obvious quotas as to how many black athletes could be found on a roster, how many could start - and in some cases, quarterback in particular - what positions black athletes could play.

Many famous and infamous humorous anecdotes have come out of this era, as well as several landmark college contests that today are given much credit for the quickening pace of desegregation in American society. Noted funnyman and college basketball coach Abe Lemons was a maverick in the 1960's, at least a decade ahead of his time, as he played many African American basketball players at white southern universities, first at Oklahoma City, and later at Texas Pan American and the University of Texas. Lemons when asked if he were given a quota for the number of blacks he could have on the court at any one time, wisecracked: "Its one at home, two on the road and three when we are behind." Once, at the University of Texas, Lemons claimed he was told by an administrator that there were grumblings from powerful forces in the ranks of the alumni and the state legislature that he had too many blacks on his roster and that he need to recruit more "Whites." "So," said Lemons in retelling one of his favorite stories, "I spent the whole off season recruiting Whites. The next year we had a whole roster of Whites: Antonio White, Andre White, Aloysius White and Alonzo White."

The 1966 triumph by upstart Texas Western University, who in the NCAA basketball championship contest employed an all black lineup, over the all white and traditionally powerful University of Kentucky and its perceived racist coach, Adolph Rupp, is given credit by many today as a landmark in the acceptance of black athletes in the mainstream of American college sports.

In 1972, the University of Alabama and its legendary coach Paul (Bear) Bryant scheduled a home game against the University of Southern California and its stable of black superstar players. To that point in time, Bryant and Alabama had yet to suit a black player for a varsity football game and had seldom played integrated teams on its home field. On that hot September evening, USC crushed Bryant's Crimson Tide. Legend has it that after the contest, Bryant brought USC's star fullback, Sam (Bam) Cunningham into the Alabama locker room. In front of his stunned players and the media, Bryant pointed to the African American athlete who had just run roughshod over his lily white defense and announced to all, "Gentleman, this is what a football player looks like."

While Rupp, despite the cries of unfairness by his family, has gone down in lore as the wicked racist, Bryant, who although for 30 years had done nothing to break the segregated color line of southern athletic teams, is today not only given a free ride by historians, but is viewed by some as a revisionist who many claim scheduled the game with USC as a way to show his fanatical supporters that their beloved Crimson Tide could no longer compete with the best in the nation unless they integrated. Perhaps true, perhaps bull and maybe somewhere in between. Regardless, after the 1972 Alabama vs. USC game, the segregation dam was broken and the flood of black athletes onto the rosters of previously all white southern college teams became a reality.

Due to the gradual integration of southern college athletic squads, the glory days of the HBC football teams were fading. By the early 80's, as Terry Houston lugged the pigskin for the glory of Virginia State, most star black athletes from the southern states were no longer just tolerated by the southern football powers, but actively recruited.

"It is not what it once was," admits Houston. "The black communities in the south now no longer show their allegiance to the HBC teams. And why should they? Blacks in the south can now go to the state colleges and cheer for black athletes. It is an improvement, but it did doom the HBC, no denying that. The best black students and the best black athletes are now coveted by the former all white colleges. It has taken the cream right off the top. (Recruits) that use to feel fortunate to have an interest expressed by a Virginia State now will not even consider such a school when the University of Virginia or Virginia Tech expresses an interest," observed Houston. It is in many ways a scenario all too familiar to once proud inner city black high schools who have seen the "cream" attracted away to the more affluent suburban schools. Left behind are schools like Roosevelt, fighting for its very survival with a cast of characters who for whatever reason, have been abandoned by the integration movement in schools still segregated, but now only shells of what they once were.

Using Roosevelt Yearbooks as a source of historical resource, the role of race is enlightening to trace through the 80+ years of Roosevelt's existence.

Early yearbooks were often used to publicize student writing and poetry skills. More than half of the 1926 edition of the "Bwana," the first edition of the Roosevelt High School Yearbook, contains student poetry, essays and other forms of student creativity. Clubs and organizations were numerous and well staffed with eager students drawn to such diverse interests as the Ukulele Club, The Radio Club and the Indoor Girls Baseball Club. Along with the aforementioned organizations – that would be considered, at the best, "exotic" in today's schools - can also be found such time honored and contemporarily popular student groups as Student Council, National Honor Society and Band.

Prominent in these early annuals are student attempts at humor. These light hearted pages were given places of prominence throughout the 275 pages of the 1926 Bwana. Many of these efforts can be at best described as "corny" in nature. Example: "Condemned Man: Warden, I'd like to get a little exercise. Warden:

What do you want to do? Condemned Man: Skip the rope." The social acceptance of the racial prejudice of the time are also on display. In the 1926 edition, on page 227, is depicted a cartoon with the signature of "Weber." The cartoon depicts an African American, with oversized and exaggerated lips, adorned in prison stripes and running while clutching a chicken. The caption under the cartoon of the chicken thief: "A Fast Black." Other cartoons in the 1926 edition depict Amos and Andy type stereotypes of the lazy, shuffling, "yees sirr Negro," so commonly found in the media of the 1920's. On page 255 is a stereotyped caricature that today would be considered so offensive to the political correctness of the 21st century that it would draw national attention and protest, if it could ever survive the delete key of even the most negligent of school production editors. A black couple, dressed in the best depiction of the rag tag clothing of 1920's, has the following conversation: Wife: "Honey, get me some ob dat candy." Husband: "Euphrates, dat am eat-em'n weep candy."

Fast forward a decade and the 1937 RHS Annual proudly boasts of the diversity to be found in the Depression era's student body of over 2400 young men and women. "We have students representing 18 different nations (of origin of birth)," the article boasts. It can be assumed, due to city and state laws, none were of African decent.

A visit to the Yearbooks of the 1950's shows social change coming, ready or not, as the winds of integration were set to blow through a city often labeled by historians and social scientists as the nation's "most southern northern city."

The 1954 Bwana - the year of the landmark Brown v Board of Education judgment - an edict that overturned the Plessey v Ferguson decision of 1896 and the subsequent Jim Crow "separate but equal" laws that were the backbone of 60 years of segregation - contains a notice that the "students from the Negro schools, as a show of friendship," had been invited to the city wide high school Track and Field Day.

By 1956, with close inspection of the RHS annual, six lonely black faces out of over 2000 students, can be identified. They stare expressionless at the camera that records for future posterity their student class pictures. The student class section of the yearbook is the only place the image of these African American students is to be found. They do not appear in any club or athletic photos.

Surprisingly, considering that with the passage of Brown v. Board in 1954, one would expect the number of black students at Roosevelt to increase from the six found in the 1956 annual; but by 1961, only one black face can be found within the 204 pages of that year's Bwana. Standing stiffly at the end of row 3 of Miss Olson's Advisory group is one John Calvin. An exhaustive inspection of the book will detail no other documentation of Mr. Calvin's experience as a member of the student body of Roosevelt High School. Even a basic fact, such as his year in school, is lacking. Assuming he was born between the years of 1946 to 1949, a search of school and city archives gives no record of Mr. Calvin, before or after he stiffly posed with his fellow Roughriders for a picture snapped nearly 50 years ago. Nor can any record be found in school or city archives about the six trail blazing African American students who desegregated the Roughrider student body in 1956. Any of the accomplishments and triumphs of these early black students; along with disappointments and failures, has for over 50 years remained unrecorded, and has probably been lost to time.

By the mid 1970's, black students had become much more entwined into the social life at Roosevelt. Homecoming, Prom and Social Clubs - along with athletics - were no longer exclusive of black students. The late 70's - the years immediately preceding the court order busing program - seem to be, when using yearbooks as a barometer of inclusion, the most diversified in the school's history. When change did come to Roosevelt, it came swiftly. In the 1978 yearbook, on page 72, the boy's varsity basketball team's picture depicts a squad made up entirely of white athletes. On the facing page 73, the Junior Varsity squad's team picture, with one exception, shows a roster completely composed of black athletes. 1978 appears to be the demarcation year for the shift from a white majority to a black majority at RHS. By relying on the team photos found in the yearbooks as an accurate source, no white basketball player has, since 1978, suited up for the Roosevelt Roughriders Varsity team.

One city Coach would not allow PHL glory to die completely. If the Vashon Wolverines boy's basketball team and Coach Floyd Irons were going to go down, it would not be without passionate resistance. Irons never, both critics and admirers agreed, backed away from a good fight. Irons thrived on controversy.

He diligently built his boys basketball team at the north side school into a 30 year dynasty, storming to 11 state titles won along the way. From the late 1970's to 2006, Irons' take no prisoner style had made him both a revered and feared man in the circle of St. Louis area high school athletics.

Despite his many St. Louis area critics, both in the city and the county suburban high schools, Irons remained a constant and defiant voice; a man viewed by many north side residents as a local hero. Irons refused to sit by idly and watch the Vashon boy's basketball program sink to the sub mediocrity levels that had been the fate of most PHL athletic entities. His success at the poor school was nothing short of amazing, highlighted by over 800 wins. Admires and critics - and there was an abundance of both - saw Irons as either a proud and talented coach who fought for the black community, or as a bully and cheater, always ready to play the "race card" to his advantage when his methods were challenged.

"I worked for him some when I was at the "V," said Roosevelt Assistant Football Coach George Simmons, he himself a veteran of nearly 40 years of PHL service. "He was always cool with me," said Simmons. "But watch out if you crossed him."

What Simmons recalled most clearly was Irons' skills as a teacher. "I loved to watch his teams practice. Total organization and total discipline. Floyd's practices were a thing of beauty. Say what you want about the man, but he could coach. You might not like the dude, but give him his due. He could coach."

Irons' Wolverines were not only the scourge of St. Louis area high school basketball, but in time, the entire nation. By the dawn of the new century, the Wolverines were viewed as one of the top programs in the United States. In 2005, Vashon rose to the lofty perch of the USA Today's #1 ranked high school basketball team in America, an amazing accomplishment for a 21st century PHL team. While the rest of the league was a local embarrassment, Irons' teams were now known and respected nation wide. That season would prove to be a high point in Irons' 30 year iron clad control over Vashon basketball. When the subsequent fall of Irons and the "V" came, his many enemies and critics would show no mercy.

In March, 2005, with Vashon and Irons on the cusp of immortality - an undefeated national championship season - his #1 ranked club was bushwhacked in the state championship game by rural out-state power Poplar Bluff and their white superstar, future North Carolina All American, Tyler Hansbrough. Irons and Vashon would never again breathe such rarified air. Trouble for Vashon and Irons came quickly and the fall was swift and severe. By the summer of 2007, Irons' world was collapsing under the weight of a federal police investigation that would eventually lead to his imprisonment. The last proud and deviant voice of the PHL would finally be silenced.

Accusations of illegal recruiting of players who lived in other districts had dogged Irons for years. Many of his legion of supporters in the black community claimed that if Irons was recruiting, then after years of white county coaches raiding city talent under the guise of the desegregation busing program, Irons was simply reversing the tables by going to the county and illegally recruiting their black stars to move to the city and play for Vashon. As would later be learned, many didn't even bother to move to the city before they enrolled at Vashon. "You played for the "V" and Floyd, you were special," said George Simmons. "Only time I can ever remember kids lying about where they lived to get into a city school. Kids in the city lie all the time about living in the county to go to the county schools, but with Floyd, it was just the opposite. To play for Vashon was the greatest honor for a black high school basketball player in the city. That is how powerful Floyd and Vashon basketball had become. If you wore the uniform of the "V," you were a god."

In 2002, a candid as always Irons gave the Riverfront Times his take on who needed who in the St. Louis area high school athletic world and the importance of the city black athlete to the winning programs in the white county schools. "If I had 10,000 white students coming into black schools here, I can see how, football-wise, they might have helped, just in numbers. But would they have helped as much as we've helped them? Let me put it this way: They wouldn't have helped my basketball program."

Irons' cockiness during the heady days of 2002 would not last. In four years it would be another Riverfront Times expose that started the investigation that would eventually lead to his downfall and imprisonment on federal fraud and conspiracy charges, a fate - depending upon ones view of the controversial Irons - was either Greek tragedy or poetic justice.

In a stinging and critical article published in November 2006, titled *Basketball by the Book*, the Times documented one smoking gun after another that provided substantiation to what many area coaches had complained about for years: that Irons had illegally enticed talented young black basketball players who did not live in Vashon's district, to transfer to the city school and become a part of the almost cult like status his teams had attained. The lure of the "V" was strong as player after player, many from the same county district's that had been raiding city talent for 25 years, found their way to Irons' mythical program.

The RFT article first paid tribute to Irons: "The gymnasium at Vashon bears Irons' name – testament to a community icon who has been not only a coach, but a father figure to many of his players, visiting them at home and helping out financially when the need arose."

Then the RFT dropped a bomb shell. The Times claimed that it's research showed that the 2004 State Champion Vashon Wolverines had no less than seven players who were in violation of MSHSAA by-laws in regard to residence and/or recruiting. Then a following shot that registered a 10 on the Richter Scale throughout the St. Louis sports scene: "a three-month Riverfront Times investigation has revealed that Vashon apparently fielded teams with at least three ineligible players – and sometimes as many as ten – each and every season dating back to the 1998-'99 school year." The article sent shock waves through local basketball circles. Some were amazed at the depth of the deception at Vashon, and wondered how many city school administrators had been involved in a possible conspiracy, to protect Irons and Vashon over the years; while others paid tribute and expressed admiration to the apparent air tight investigation that the Times had executed; and that someone had finally showed the gumption and fortitude to stand up to the bullying Irons.

The publishing of the November, 2006 article was not the beginning of Irons' problems. That previous summer, Irons had been unrepentantly and unceremoniously fired by the St. Louis School Board from his positions of district wide Athletic Director of the PHL and the coach of the Vashon Boys Basketball team. The fallout the next day was rollicking. Then Superintendent, Greg Williams, who did not favor Irons' ouster and publically protested it, was himself fired.

The School Board claimed that an internal investigation had reveled missing funds from the Vashon basketball program totaling tens of thousands of dollars. It was also alleged that several years before, Irons had assaulted a special education student at Vashon. The Social Services investigator assigned to the case recommended that Irons be charged with a felony. But friends in high places, both in the City Prosecutors Office and the School District, had allegedly helped sweep the incident under the rug. The young man and his family had filed a civil suit against Irons and the SLPS. Days before the case was to be heard in court, the young man was found murdered. The apparent homicide has never been solved.

In 2005, the most decorated basketball coach in state history, now found himself without a team to coach, relegated by Board of Education reassignment to the role of a Junior High Social Studies Teacher. In August of 2005, Irons informed the Board he was going on extended sick leave and never did report to his junior high classroom. At the end of the 2005-2006 school year, Irons officially retired.

Irons and his large group of followers did not take the board action lightly, and their response was swift and loud. Threats of discrimination law suits, protesting and picketing at the Board of Education President's residence and threats to air revelations about "where the skeletons are hid" in the St. Louis Public School System, were publicly levied by irate Irons supporters. It was obvious Irons had friends in high places. The help of US Congressman William "Lacy" Clay" was soon at Irons' disposal. When it was first reported that Irons was under investigation and before he was removed as Vashon coach, Clay wrote to the SLPS School Board that: "I can assure you that the political leadership of this community, at all levels, will not stand by quietly while a man who has devoted his entire adult life to helping young people is treated in this intolerable manner."

Despite such threats, all efforts to save Irons' job at Vashon were to no avail. When practice began that fall, for the first time in over 30 years, the Mighty Wolverines of Vashon had a new leader; Anthony Bonner, ironically Irons' greatest Vashon player ever. The former Irons protégée, a St. Louis University record setter and National Basketball Association star, was now in charge at Vashon.

And Irons problems would soon only grow in magnitude.

That fall, it was revealed that Irons and several associates were under an FBI investigation and that the feds had subpoenaed all district correspondence involving Irons including, a seizure and search of Irons' school computer. As rumors spread about Irons legal problems, his world quickly sped out of control.

In September of 2007, Irons pled guilty to one count of mail fraud and one count of wire fraud for his role in a real estate scam. The Riverfront Times outlined Irons role in the scheme as such: "Incorporation papers filed with the Missouri Secretary of State indicate that Best of the Midwest Youth Foundation (formerly known as Best of Midwest Basketball Foundation) is operated by Michael Noll, of Chesterfield. Noll registered the nonprofit with the Secretary of State in 2004. Floyd Irons joined its board of directors in 2005, according to the organization's annual report, also filed with the Secretary of State. According to the court documents, Irons and "Doe"(an unindicted, and thus unnamed accomplice), devised a plan to purchase residential real estate at inflated prices. The pair purchased a total of three homes in 2005 and 2006 — one in Tower Grove East, one in De Mun and the third in Wildwood. The men obtained loans by submitting false paperwork in Irons' name, and with mortgage broker Mineo's assistance received a total of $120,000 in kickbacks." Soon after buying the homes, Irons and "Doe" put them up for sale. All the properties were eventually foreclosed upon when Irons and "Doe" failed to make mortgage payments.

In one 2005 transaction not involving Mineo; Irons and "Doe" used Irons' son, Altonio, as a "straw purchaser" of a brownstone "Doe" owned in Lafayette Square. In June 2005 "Doe" bought the home for $135,000. Five months later Altonio Irons purchased it from "Doe" for $167,000. Though Altonio Irons was attending the College of the Ozarks near Branson at the time, "his father submitted a false loan application stating that Altonio planned to live in the house full-time and was employed by Best of the Midwest Youth Foundation, where he was earning almost $5,000 a month. The loan was approved."

In March 2008, Irons, for his role in the scam, was sentenced to one year in Federal Prison and ordered to pay back $650,000. By state law, as a convicted felon, Irons' teaching certificate was revoked; making it impossible for him to ever coach again in a Missouri public high school. He had originally faced up to 30 years in prison and fines of up to one million dollars.

Still, Irons had one more piper to pay. He had agreed, as a part of his plea bargain to the Federal charges, to tell all he knew about illegal recruiting, both at Vashon and other St. Louis area high schools. Under court order, he met with the MSHSAA and gave testimony as to both his, and others, roles in the illegal recruiting of high school athletes. It was a day Irons critics had long hoped to see. Facing additional federal prison time- and possible charges of perjury - if not candid and truthful under oath, Irons was finally ready to "sing."

Many state coaches and school officials for years had complained that Irons and Vashon was a "sacred cow" and that the MSHSAA did not have the backbone or the political courage to investigate the city school. It was felt around the state that the MSHSAA lived in constant fear of Irons and his well known use of the "race card" defense when challenged or questioned about activities at the "V." Despite the many years of rumored recruiting violations, the feeling was that the MSHSAA did not want to endure the charges of racism which would inevitably come from Irons and his supporters, if Vashon was ever brought to task about eligibility violations.

Now, finally, the long awaited day of reckoning between Irons and the MSHSAA was at hand. The outcome of the information gleaned at this summit would leave most around the state angry at a state athletic board now viewed as refusing to investigate Vashon when they (MSHSAA) had, for years, in their possession obvious probable cause that rules were being broken on a frequent and blatant basis, by a school that had built a dynasty based on a now perceived foundation of cheating.

The real jaw dropper from the court mandated meeting with the MSHSAA was the revelation that Irons admitted paying between $25,000 and $30,000 to house, feed, provide a car and a house keeper for two 6'8 brothers, Bobby and Johnny Hill. The two, who graduated from Vashon in 2005 and 2006 respectively, had transferred to Vashon from Alton, IL High School. A follow up investigation by the media found that officials at Alton High School had traveled to Missouri at the time of the Hills leaving Alton for Vashon, and meet with MSHSAA director Becky Oakes, giving her what they felt was proof positive that Irons had broken the rules in securing the playing services of the Hills. Oakes later commented that since Alton had not filed an official complaint that there was nothing her association could do in the way of an investigation of Vashon. Alton officials subsequently claimed they were never told anything about filing a complaint. Since they were from another state, it would appear that MSHSAA by-laws would not allow for such action by the Illinois school officials.

Alton officials stated that they left the meeting with Oakes under the assumption that she had heard their complaints, saw their documenting proof, and that her organization would do a thorough investigation of the matter. As it turned out, nothing could have been farther from the truth, and Vashon continued to rack up state titles based on illegal recruiting.

The Hills' affair became a public relations nightmare for the MSHSAA, with many coaches and school officials saying "I told you so." What had been rumored and groused about for years, that the MSHSAA would nail a small rural district - which could not afford high priced litigation - to the wall for a minor violation; but would cower and look the other way when obvious violations were occurring at Vashon, many now felt had been proven as fact.

Many felt that the MSHSAA's lack of action against Vashon was rooted in a fear of charges of racism from Irons and his vocal supporters. Several years earlier, the Suburban North Athletic Directors, representing schools located in North St. Louis County, many of them with predominantly African-American enrollments and schools from which several questionable Vashon transfers had occurred; did file a recruiting complaint against Vashon. The complaint was withdrawn when a St. Louis black weekly newspaper penned an editorial accusing the Athletic Directors of racism.

Irons will remain always a controversial figure and a lightning rod for St. Louis area sports fans. Was he a proud black man who, against all odds, fought to build a basketball dynasty that gave at least a glimmer of hope to a down trodden city school system that had seen it's best students and athletes taken away for the glory of white suburban districts? Had he fought the powerful suburban districts and beat them at their own game; a man who refused to accept second best for his players, his school and his neighborhood? Or was he merely a bully, always willing to cry racism every time he was accused of not playing by the rules?

Whether Irons' methods were noble in intend, or corrupt by plan; there is no question that for years the Vashon Wolverines Basketball team stood alone as a source of pride for a success starved Public High League. The rally cry of "the V get ready to Roll," announced the arrival of the proud Wolverines and their legions of supporters and followers. Chanted with an aggressive pride, it became the symbolic chant of what many non-city residents viewed as the aggressiveness and the danger of Irons' teams and its thug supporters. But in all fairness, for a community stripped of all other sources of athletic success, Irons and his teams were the pride of the city, a last glimmer of hope. With Irons and his juggernaut teams to grasp on to, the glory days of PHL athletics still lived. However, by 2008, their leader had been publically disgraced and carted off to a Federal Prison. The PHL athletic teams were now totally adrift in a sea of inadequacy and failure.

By sheer numbers alone, the recanting of the downfall of the SLPS is distressing, the future prognosis for the St. Louis Public schools, bleak. From a high enrollment of over 115,000 in 1967, the St. Louis Public Schools by 2008 served only 23,000 students. Predictions for the next five years have that number falling to under 20,000. If this ominous prediction comes true, for the first time in anyone's memory, the district will no longer be the largest in the state. What has gone wrong?

Historically, the St. Louis Public Schools have a long glorious and storied past. The first public High School was opened in the city in 1855, among the first coeducational high schools in the United States. Upon its completion, the building was hailed as the "most lavish schoolhouse west of New York." The cost: an unheard of at the time $50,000. In 1875, renown education leader Susan Blow created the nations first Kindergarten, housed in St. Louis. The first public high school west of the Mississippi for African American students was opened in St. Louis with the construction of Sumner High School. By 1900, with a population growth fueled by the immigrant boom of the late 19th century, the St. Louis Public School system was educating close to 20,000 students.

A report filed in 2007 with the St. Louis City Information System gives a succinct look at the history of racial segregation in St. Louis, both by law and by de facto residential patterns: "blacks were relegated to their own city neighborhoods, where their children attended neighborhood schools. When housing is segregated, so too are the schools. Funding, and therefore educational quality, receded during the 1950s and 1960s as well. What had once been one of the best public school systems in the United States had plummeted. Black students especially suffered as public schools declined in a core city with a disproportionately high African-American population. Three in four students in the St. Louis Public Schools were black in 1980, while more than two in five white youngsters attended school outside the system. Public education in St. Louis came under court supervision in 1980, with the goal of desegregating St. Louis Public Schools."

The wheels of legal action in reality had begun to turn as early as 1972 when Minnie Liddell, a north St. Louis African American resident, filed a class action lawsuit on behalf of her daughter seeking "an adequate public education." She based her complaint on the 14th Amendment constitutional guarantee of equal protection under the law. According to St. Louis Magazine, "An initial ruling found in favor of the city's board of education, but that was overturned in 1980 when a panel of three judges in the 8th Circuit Court reversed the lower court, ruling that the city board of education failed to do enough to desegregate the school system even after the U.S. Supreme Court struck down the separate but equal doctrine at the public school level in Brown v. Board of Education in 1954."

The segregation of the St. Louis Public Schools is a decades old problem, one that continues to tear at the very fiber of the system, and perhaps doom its future survival. Blatantly segregated by law before the landmark Brown v. Board 1954 Supreme Court Decision, the St. Louis Public School system – after 1954 - simply meet the letter of the law post Brown v Board, still maintaining a segregated system through long established racial housing patterns; and what some saw as political gerrymandering of attendance zones to maintain the status quo of traditionally white schools on the south side. That arrangement would all come to a screeching and abrupt halt, thanks to the 1980 efforts of a Federal Judge.

Enter into the game one who would turn out to be the major player in the desegregating of the St. Louis Public Schools; Federal Judge William Hungate. A Congressman from the Missouri Ninth District from 1964 to 1977, Hungate would serve on the St. Louis Federal Court from 1977 to 1992. His view involving the racial makeup of the St. Louis Schools was described as both "revolutionary and incendiary."

By the spring of 1981, Hungate had drawn the "line in the sand." His challenge to the Suburban County Districts who were resisting any "voluntary" desegregation program was made crystal clear: come on board on your own, or deal with my terms. According to St. Louis Magazine, Hungate meant business. "(He) warned school districts in the county that if they insisted on arguing in court that their schools were not, in fact, segregated and if they were ultimately found liable, the solution could include consolidating all 23 suburban school districts and the city's school district into a single metropolitan school district, in which some white suburban students would be bused into the city."

Hungate's threat to create one large, super district, encompassing the entire city and county, if the city and county educational leaders could not come to a solution that would meet the court's mandate to integrate the area schools, sent shock waves through the wealthy suburban districts, as images of their children being bussed to the inner city added much due haste to resolving the judge's concerns. Hungate asked both sides to work for a remedy before the date of February 14, 1983, a time for which he had schedule the lawsuit to be heard. The now defunct daily paper, the Globe-Democrat – known for its conservative lean - labeled Hungate "Attila the Hungate."

According to St. Louis Magazine, in an article published in September 2007, "The suburban school districts—including parents, employees and elected school board members—did not take the news lightly. They scrambled to the negotiating table to avoid the abolition of their districts. Rather than risk disappearance, they agreed to a settlement of the desegregation suit that included the "voluntary" acceptance of some African-American students from the city."

"The successes and failures of that interdistrict transfer plan have been, and will continue to be argued ad infinitum; it turned out to be the nation's longest and most expensive school desegregation program. At its height, more than 13,000 African-American students from the city went to suburban schools. Overall, the voluntary district plan cost the state more than $1.6 billion."

"Yet after all these years and all these struggles, it would be kind to say only that the St. Louis Public Schools have a lousy image: The district has been unaccredited since June, it is run by a three-person appointed transitional board and its enrollment continues to plummet. In 1980 the city school district had 62,000 students. Today, it has fewer than 30,000, (23,000 by 2008) while the 24 suburban districts—including the county's Special School District—have slightly more than 100,000 students."

But was busing the answer; or was it a misguided attempt to right a racist wrong, that in reality destroyed not only the public schools on the white south side; but also the city's black dominated north side schools as well?

In 1993, Freeman Bosley Jr., the city's first elected African American Mayor, called for an end to the desegregation program. Bosley claimed the program had the opposite of hoped for effect; in reality he argued, forced busing had caused a mass exodus from the city school's of not only whites fleeing to the county, but also of black students busing daily to suburban schools with white dominated student bodies. Brain drain, Bosley claimed, was taking the brightest and the best of African American students away from their neighborhoods, and leaving those behind, whom for lack of means, motive or support; were simply left to flounder in an educational waste land. Destroy the neighborhood schools, Bosley said, and destroy the community. His prophetic warning was at the time heard, but unheeded.

To understand the problems of the St. Louis Public Schools, one must look closely at the post WWII demographical shifts that have taken place in the suburbs of St. Louis County. Many of the surrounding area county school districts, especially those to the north, are now experiencing their own "white flight" dilemma, 2008 style. Many white families have now fled the county schools for points farther west and north, such as the booming Fort Zumwalt, Francis Howell and Troy School Districts.

St. Louis Magazine reports, "It could be argued that it's (the voluntary program) a moot question from both a legal and a political standpoint. Legally, the desegregation case has been settled. Politically, no elected official with any instinct for survival would ever campaign to mix races, classes and incomes by taking such a drastic step. Yet as the city schools and inner-ring suburban districts (e.g., Wellston, Riverview Gardens) continue to struggle, it's important to look at the role a district's socioeconomic makeup plays in how effectively students are educated. Not surprisingly, districts that are pockets of poverty don't do as well as districts with upscale demographics. As these disparities persist, the opportunity and outcome gaps between the haves and have-nots widen."

Leveling the playing field with one "super" district by combining all area resources was seen by most county districts as a threat – legal blackmail to gain their support for Hungate's voluntary county-city busing plan. But many experts felt the one "super" district plan had merit. "A better mix of economic backgrounds leads to better overall results", says Todd Swanstrom, professor of public policy at Saint Louis University.

"Research shows if you have socioeconomically balanced schools, the experience in the classroom would be much better for the lower-income children and it would not pull down high-income children, so long as there is not a high concentration of children from poor families in any one school," Swanstrom says.

Leading local expert Lana Stein, chair of the political science department at the University of Missouri–St. Louis and the co-author of City Schools & City Politics: Institutions and Leadership in Pittsburgh, Boston and St. Louis, sees the "balkanization" of education as a contributor to the St. Louis region's lack of cohesion. When the book was published in 1999, Stein thought Pittsburgh had the best system of the three cities, although now she says Boston does. In either scenario, St. Louis comes in third.

"We have our little identities: 'I'm from Ferguson,' 'I'm from Mehlville,' whatever. It's rather parochial. If you had merged cities, you would get people looking at things in a larger scope," says Stein. "The more people are together in a naturally occurring situation; they can learn more about others and break down all the old myths and stereotypes."

The problem is compounded by the mass chaos of the different political and educational subdivisions in St. Louis County, 92 municipalities alone. The difference between the drive from wealthy Clayton to third world poor Wellston may be only a few miles in distance, but light years in tax based revenue. It would be hard to argue that the resources available to these two school district would pass any legal challenge to the doctrine of equal education for all. St. Louis Magazine's analysis is concise and poignant: "Consider Clayton and Wellston. The two municipalities are only a few miles apart geographically, but in other ways they are galaxies apart. They have separate school districts. Wellston lost its accreditation in 1994, and again in 2003. In 2006, 64.9 percent of Clayton's graduating high school class scored at or above the national average on the ACT. Of the 29 Wellston graduates who took the ACT in 2006, none scored at or above the national average."

That's not to say that all of Wellston's problems would be solved if it shared a district with Clayton. Small districts can be run well, and large districts can be run poorly. In fact, Susan Uchitelle, who served as executive director of the Voluntary Inter-district Coordinating Council, the body that administered the school desegregation program, says it's not fair to compare Wellston and Clayton. "Wellston, most unfortunately, in the past was so poorly run the kids never had a chance," she says. Varying levels of resources, according to many of the experts weighing in one the ills of segregated school in the St. Louis Metro area, compound the problems. The yoke of poverty is passed from one generation to the next in poor school districts that can not adequately educate students. This was a major factor in the de facto residential segregation that dominated St. Louis city schools after the 1954 Brown v Board decision."

"Fragmented school districts reinforce economic segregation," Swanstrom says. "They have a definite impact on housing values, which in turn segregate." In addition to the remedy of the busing of city black students to the county, the courts had a year earlier, in 1980, issued a parallel ruling that the city schools would have to use busing to create more diversified schools within its boundaries, regardless of the city-county proposed plan. In one mighty swipe, the courts demanded that busing be implemented to guarantee that each of the city's public high schools be of a racial makeup that would reflect that of the overall city population.

In August of 1980, the busses began to roll. Students from the predominantly African American neighborhoods in the North were now transported daily to the South; into the long time neighborhoods of the Irish, Italian and German Americans who for five generations had made South St. Louis their strong hold. Tight knit neighborhoods like The Hill, Bevo Mill, St. Louis Hills and Soulard, now felt they were under siege. Although not as violent as the reaction from other cities to urban busing to meet integration goals in public schools - Boston being the most famous - the South Side's reaction to forced busing was one of great amounts of hand wringing rhetoric by white parents.

By the early 1980's, "White Flight" was in full force. Many parents moved their children to the already overloaded parochial schools, which had a long and rich tradition in South St. Louis; or they simply packed up and moved to the suburbs in St. Louis County. The mass exodus from the St. Louis Public Schools was now underway. It has not slowed since, and it is not limited to just white students.

In 2006, the SLPS Board President Veronica O'Bryan and the PHL's most famous and successful coach, Vashon Boys Basketball Coach Floyd Irons; became intertwined in a headline grabbing, bitter, ugly and nasty dispute over Irons' termination by SLPS. Many felt the firing was orchestrated by O'Bryan in a power play against the then Superintendent. Despite their polarizing differences, one common denominator that each did share was how they chose to educate their own children. Neither chose the SLPS. Coach Irons' son attended a private parochial high school. Board President O'Bryan, through the voluntary desegregation program, sent her children to the suburban Clayton District.

As could well be predicted, it did not take long after the inception of the forced busing plan for the politicians to move to the forefront and posture to the whims of their constituents. In the early 80's, a young and ambitious Missouri Attorney General, John Ashcroft - destined to go on with career stops as Governor, US Senator and US Attorney General - stepped into the public spotlight. Ashcroft fought forced busing with every weapon, and at every venue available to him.

According to a report filed by the liberal think tank, People for the American Way, "Ashcroft's significant involvement with desegregation in St. Louis began around 1980, for in that year both the federal court of appeals for the Eighth Circuit and the federal district court in St. Louis found both the State of Missouri and the City school board liable for continued segregation of the public schools. The State's liability was based primarily on state legal and constitutional provisions dating back to 1865, which mandated separate schools for blacks and whites (provisions not completely repealed until 1976); the mandatory transfer of black suburban students into segregated city schools to enforce segregation; and the state's failure to take effective action to dismantle the racially dual school system and its effects. See Adams v. United States, 620 F.2d 1277, 1280-81 (8th Cir.), cert. denied, 449 U.S. 826 (1980). As the district court recognized that year, 'the State defendants stand before this Court as primary constitutional wrongdoers who have abdicated their affirmative remedial duty.' Liddell v. Board of Education of City of St. Louis, 491 F. Supp. 351, 359 (E.D. Mo. 1980), aff'd, 667 F.2d 643 (8th Cir.), cert. denied, 454 U.S. 1081, 1091 (1981)."

Enter the unique plan strongly suggested by the federal courts as a voluntary plan of cooperation between the predominantly white St. Louis County

Suburban Schools and the increasingly African American dominated St. Louis City Schools. The voluntary plan was set up to allow black students from the city to voluntarily be bussed to predominately white districts in the county. In return the city would create special "Magnet" schools, to entice white suburban students to voluntarily bus to the city. Thus sprung to life were such innovative city high schools with specific themes such as Cleveland Naval ROTC Academy, Central Visual and Performing Arts Academy, Math and Science Academy, Gateway Tech and Soldan International Studies Academy. The premise being, and the hoped for result the court sought was that black students would seize upon the opportunity to enroll in St. Louis County schools; reaping the benefits of better facilities, college preparation and extra curricular activities; while white students from the County schools would be attracted by the special and unique curriculums of the magnet schools. If the theory held and proved valid, then forced busing would not be necessary.

The projections proved to be half right. black students from the north side city schools flooded to the county schools; so much so that many county districts' had to initiate a lottery system to determine which city students would be allowed into the voluntary desegregation program. The flow from the white students in the suburbs to the city magnet schools was, at best, a trickle and a dismal failure.

By 1983, the Federal Court and Judge Hungate were growing tired of the delaying tactics of individual suburban districts; and the hindrance of state elected officials such as State Attorney Ashcroft. The stakes were ratcheted up as the court deadlines lay looming on the near horizon.

According to an historical article by the People for the American Way, Ashcroft, representing the people of the state of Missouri, was a major stumbling block to meeting court demands. "Although the district court's order had directed the parties to work out a voluntary plan to begin in 1980-81, delays continued throughout the school year. After the state finally submitted an initial plan, the judge rejected it as lacking in specifics and called on the state to submit another, but the state did not do so. The NAACP and the City Board then filed a claim for mandatory inter-district relief, based in part on the failure of the state to act. Ashcroft responded not only by opposing any such mandatory relief, but by declaring that voluntary efforts were now impossible and by asking for another delay in submitting a voluntary plan."

In a 1981 editorial, the St. Louis Post-Dispatch blasted Ashcroft:

"The logic of these arguments is mystifying...Even now, acquiescence in a voluntary program might dispense with the need for one ordered by court...As matters stand, a state that for more than a century required its schools to segregate the races now presents itself as unable to help them desegregate, even on a voluntary basis...Judge Meredith had asked the state to take the lead in developing suggestions for a voluntary program. Take the lead? The attorney general has put state leadership in reverse." — St. Louis Post-Dispatch, Feb. 1 and Feb. 4, 1981.

Shortly before the trial that many believed would be devastating to the suburban districts that were resisting the voluntary program was to begin, the City Board, the NAACP, and the suburban districts announced a tentative settlement.

Beating Hungate's zero hour by literally days, the St. Louis Public School District, the NAACP - who had entered the fray as a friend to the plaintiffs - and the St. Louis County School Districts announced an agreement based upon a "significant expansion of the city-suburb voluntary desegregation program, as well as for additional efforts to improve education in city schools to help remedy the educational vestiges of segregation." The City School Board and all 23 County School District's approved the plan. When the Federal Courts gave its stamp of approval, a loud sight of relief could be heard throughout St. Louis County.

With the courts now no longer holding the threat of consolidation over the heads of the county schools, the race for the brightest, the strongest, and best of the African American city students would begin in earnest. Predominantly black county districts were not a part of the court order voluntary plan. Districts such as Normandy, Berkeley and Wellston, already predominantly black, could not accept black transfer students from the city schools. But wealthy white districts could. In no area was the recruitment of talented black students more apparent and profoundly impactful than in athletics. The opportunity to dramatically improve a high school team, in particular the high exposure sports of boy's basketball and football, was now a possibility that left county coaches salivating.

The transfer of athletes from the city schools was immediate, and almost overnight left the teams of the once mighty Public High League woefully undermanned. At the same time, the transfer student-athletes from the city would turn programs such as Mehlville in football and Lafayette in boy's basketball, into state powers; a status built upon the talented backs of black city athletes that would last for 20 years. It was not uncommon in the 1980s and 1990s to see previously all white county districts like Clayton and Ladue starting as many as five black basketball players, all city transfer students.

By 2000, athletics at the city high schools, with a few notable exceptions such as boy's basketball at Vashon and girl's basketball at Metro, were no more than an afterthought, a stage of embarrassment for those left behind. PHL football teams, after so many years of dominant play, were now simply trying to survive, hanging on in some cases by a mere thread. Underpaid coaches, and horrific facilities (if any existed at all, a majority of city football teams had no campus facility to play home games, and in several cases, not even an on campus practice facility) were still the norm in the PHL.

By the late 1990's there seemed to be a universal understanding or resignation; depending on one's stance on the desegregation issue, that the end of the city county busing program had to be near. The system had become too expensive and too cumbersome to retain any type of educational creditability.

After 25 years, in 2005, the St. Louis desegregation case was grinding to a thudding conclusion. Even the most adamant supporters dating back to the early 1970's now were resigned to the acceptance that the program had been a huge failure, and the cost associated with it would no longer be the burden of all state tax payers and state school districts. The end was viewed as inevitable. The question was how, and when, with a frightening, "what then" question looming over everyone's head.

The millions of dollars spent on the desegregation program in St. Louis had rubbed raw political alliances within in the state Democratic party. Many out state schools- "out state" being a unique Missouri term that meant any area outside of the metropolitan areas of St. Louis and Kansas City – were suffering through very trying times. They resented what was viewed as excesses in the urban districts, all thanks to the generosity of the Federal Courts in ordering their state money now disproportionally sent to city schools and those county schools willing to accept city students.

In 1997, Jay Nixon was a young and upcoming star of the Missouri Democratic Party. The Jefferson County native had, in 1992 at the ripe old age of 36, won a heavily contested state wide election to become State Attorney General. In 2008 he would be elected Governor of Missouri.

Within six years of undertaking the office of Attorney General, Nixon would be viewed as a major player in the upcoming mid term elections of 1998. As Attorney General for the State, Nixon eagerly took upon himself the mostly popular role as the man responsible for ending what many rural Missourians viewed as the money train that had for years depleted the resources of their own community rural schools and sent it up the tracks to be wasted in St. Louis on a system, despite the huge resources delegated to it, that was a dismal failure.

In an ironic twist, as Attorney General Nixon became the point man in the fight against what many rural citizens saw as the enemy in this issue, the Federal Courts. Nixon now found himself in the same role that his Republican predecessor, John Ashcroft, had taken back in the chaotic beginning of the court ordered program two decades prior.

Many black St. Louis Democratic leaders viewed Nixon's action against continuation of the desegregation program as a blatant pandering to white rural voters, and threatened there would be consequences. With the ambitious Nixon already eyeing higher political offices, he took the threat of black voter revolt seriously. Despite Nixon's offer to spend $304,000,000 of state money to build new city schools and renovate old ones, as a means of preparing the SLPS for the return of its wayward bussed students, the peace offering did nothing to placate the outraged leaders of the city's black community.

Influential Missouri Representative William L. Clay threatened revolt within the party ranks. Clay wrote to then President Bill Clinton in November of 1997, requesting that the President not attend a fund raiser for Nixon's Senate Campaign. The President did attend the dinner, but Clay said, "I'll do what I have to do" to insure the failure of Nixon, and his own Democratic party's attempt to take back a critical US Senate seat. Nixon did have the support of one black civic leader, St. Louis Mayor Clarence Harmon. "Campaigns of this kind are emotional," Harmon said. "They don't necessarily border on anything rational."

Nixon found himself the lighting rod smack in the middle of a racially charged firestorm. It was not a politically advantageous position and the savvy and astute Nixon knew it. Protests were loud and threatened to rip apart the state

Democratic Party just as the all important mid term elections of 1998 approached. The NAACP organized protest marches against Nixon. Many of the demonstrators were life time Democrats. Their protest signs carried such slogans as: NO WAY JAY"; "Deseg Yes, Segregation No"; "WHATEVER HAPPENED TO INTEGRITY?"

And of course, the Missouri Republican Party sat back and rubbed its hands with glee. Previously, the Republican Party of Missouri had shamelessly played to the fears of white Missourians in the early 1980's. Many white families in South St. Louis at the time still sent their children to the public schools, and State Attorney Ashcroft and the Republican Party capitalized on their fear of school integration. This scare tactic allowed the Republican Party to make unprecedented inroads in the heavily union, and previously solid, Democratic area of white South St. Louis.

The anti- busing rhetoric also played well in more conservative outstate rural Missouri. The local schools and their constituents saw no need to send their hard earned school tax dollars down Interstate 70 and up Interstates 55 and 44 to the mismanaged SLPS, to counteract a segregation dilemma which was neither their doing, or concern. In 1997, sixteen years later, the Republicans could now turn the tables on Nixon and the Democrats. This time they intended to take no proactive action. State Republicans could now sit back and let Nixon's proposals to end the busing program anger the upper level leadership of black St. Louis, and watch a demographic that Nixon and the Democrats needed desperately, if they were to have any chance of unseating the popular entrenched incumbent Senator Kit Bond, slide from their grasp.

The Senatorial Election of 1998 was very predictable - Nixon was defeated by a landslide. Ten years later, in 2008, rifts between the once solid local Democratic Party, dictated and drawn along bitter racial lines, due to the St. Louis School Desegregation issue, can still be felt.

Sam Dunlap had spent over 25 years at Roosevelt High School as a coach and an athletic director until he was elevated in 2006 to the downtown position and empowered as the top district athletic administrator in charge of the PHL, replacing the dismissed and disgraced Floyd Irons. Many hard liners in the area felt that Dunlap's appointment was symbolic of the demise and the second class citizen treatment of city athletes. Said area sports personality Demetrious Johnson, the most vocal of Floyd Irons supporters, in a stinging evaluation of the PHL, "Dunlap was a racist when he was at Roosevelt and nothing has changed since he been downtown. He is there because they know as long as he is in charge the PHL, will continue to be a joke and that is what they want. The PHL programs in all sports have been dismantled by the St. Louis Public School's Board of Education. It has been done intentionally and consistently for the last 20 years. They don't want to see these city black kids have any success. It is a disgrace what has been done to the PHL and (it) was done by plan."

Since the forced exit of Irons from the PHL scene, the role of lightning rod in regard to issues of race in St. Louis high school athletics had fallen onto Johnson's broad shoulders. It is a role he does not back away from.

Johnson, in many ways, is a PHL success story. He graduated from the now closed McKinley High School in 1979, went on to a stellar career as a defensive back at the University of Missouri and was a first round draft choice of the Detroit Lions. Johnson spent seven years playing in the National Football League.

After his playing days were complete, Johnson returned to St. Louis and immersed himself in the lives of the city youth. His Demetrious Johnson Foundation has raised millions of dollars over the past 15 years for the benefit of athletics and academic enrichment programs in the city of St. Louis. Johnson is also the host of a very popular weekly radio show focusing on local high school sports.

Johnson's outspokenness has led him to be called a visionary by many, a bully and a race baiter by others. Johnson supporters and detractors are most clearly split along racial lines. Johnson is intelligent, opinionated and enjoys his celebrity status among the St. Louis area African American community.

Trying to put a label on the enigmatic Johnson can be a slippery assignment. While many black leaders in the city were leading loud and sometimes chaotic demonstrations against the 2007 State Board of Education's takeover of the St. Louis Public Schools, Johnson was one of the few black community leaders to applaud the disenfranchisement of the city voters. "Needed to happen and should have happened a long time ago," he stated in a 2008 interview. "We can't blame whites for this one, we have to blame ourselves. We let our schools be taken over by politicians, many white, who had no concern about what was best for kids. They took over the schools and intentionally created a segregated and unequal system for black kids in the city. It is nothing short of a form of apartheid. In a School District starving for solutions and resources, the SLPS has proved amazing in its ability to reject facts they deem to be inconvenient. It voted to fight the State's takeover of the district. Such denial would be amusing, if its impact upon the black community weren't so damn debilitating and if so many black parents, politicians and community leaders weren't buying into it. It's always so much easier to scream, 'blame the white man'! But, the white man didn't pull the trigger on this one and at some point in time, hopefully soon, the blacks in this town better step up, stop throwing their children's democratic legacy away and start focusing on building better schools. Push your kids to graduate – wherever you have to push!"

Johnson's suggested approach for improving the SLPS is very similar to the plan Terry Houston has instituted for the revival of Roosevelt High School. "We need to be accountable," Johnson says. "Stop using racism as an excuse for not working harder to build better schools. Stop trusting black leaders, politicians and church people simply because they are black."

Johnson backs his harsh observations with the dismal fact that city graduation rates have fallen to near 50%, while the state wide average hovers around 90%. "I understand the frustration and deep dissatisfaction people in our community feel towards public education; but, we need thinkers, not sheep. We got more than enough Judas Goats running around, bleating and leading us to the slaughter. If we do not end this blame game and start looking at ourselves and honestly appraise our self-inflicted wounds, then we create an atmosphere in which racism in its most primitive form becomes an acceptable part of the debate."

Particularly painful to Johnson is the current sorry state of PHL athletics. "Sports are what we need to keep these kids in school and build some pride and self esteem, not only for the kids, but for the community. Look how the north side of the city rallied around Floyd Irons and the Vashon basketball team. They represented a commitment to excellence that the leaders of the SLPS will not tolerate, especially when it is lead by a strong and proud black man. The leaders of St. Louis know this and that is why they have stripped the athletic programs to the bone. Under the current leadership, our kids have no chance to succeed athletically if they stay in the city and attend a PHL high school."

Johnson uses his own personal saga as proof of what a strong athletic program in the city could mean. "In 1978, our McKinley team played Sumner for the PHL title at Soldan Stadium. You could not have squeezed another soul into the bleachers that day. It was packed. It was ours against yours, McKinley South Side pride on one side, Sumner North Side pride on the other. The community was there, not just a few parents. It was a happening for our neighborhoods. Our teams brought pride to the community and I will never forget the chills of pride I felt walking onto that field that day, and having the whole community stand and show us their support. Now that Floyd Irons is gone, not one kid in the PHL can feel that type of community backing. Go to any game now, and how many fans do you see? A few parents, maybe. Gateway and Roosevelt played for the PHL title last week, and the crowd (size) on hand was what, maybe 200 people? That is embarrassing, but it shows what happens when you create an apartheid type system based on racism. It shows what happens when hopes and dreams die. Nobody cares, and our young athletes are reminded of that stark reality every time they take the court, or a field, in the PHL. They are the throw away kids who couldn't get into the private schools, not in the busing program, just stuck in the PHL."

Johnson sees the fall of the PHL as a calculated move. "This city does not want to see our educational system develop strong black males. That scares people. If a black young man is to succeed, then it needs to be because he was taken to the county and given a "white" upbringing. Look what they did to Coach Irons."

Irons and his Vashon boy's basketball team had, in 2008, been stripped of four state championships, based partly on Irons giving of financial support to two 6'8" brothers who moved into the Vashon district to play for the legendary Coach. In 2006, Irons was fired by the School Board. In 2008 he was sentenced to one year in federal prison for his unrelated role in a mortgage kick back scheme. Irons was paroled to a half way house in November of 2008, after serving six months of his sentence.

"Did you see 360 the other night?" asked Johnson, referring to the ESPN investigative television show?" A recent episode had dealt with the story of University of Missouri All-American football player Jeremy Maclin; an African American who had attended suburban Kirkwood High School. In the spring of 2009, Maclin would follow a path similar to Johnson's: he would be a first round draft choice of the NFL's Philadelphia Eagles. Maclin's early life roots were anchored in a dysfunctional family setting, intensified by a poverty ridden, minority existence. When he entered the much more affluent world of Kirkwood High School, he was befriended by a white couple who welcomed him into their home and became his unofficial guardians. They provided the emerging star athlete with physical necessities and an emotional support system - portrayed on the ESPN show - as paramount to Maclin's development as an athlete, a student, and a person.

"How is that different than what Coach (Irons) did for the Hill brothers?" Johnson asks in reference to the aid Irons had secretly - and in violation of Missouri State High School Activities Association rules – rendered to the 6'8" brothers. The MSHSAA saw Irons' actions as an illegal enticement to convince the Hills to transfer to Vashon from their Metro East hometown high school.

"When it's a white family helping a black kid, it is a heart warming story. But when it is a strong and proud black man like Floyd Irons helping black kids, then it is manipulative and evil and they say 'he's only doing it to win games.' Think those white families in Kirkwood take in a lot of black kids with no athletic ability," Johnson rhetorically asks?

The failure of the PHL, and the subsequent demise and inability of its members to compete outside of the conference is not, according to Johnson, a happenstance of fate. "The athletic programs (of the PHL) represented the last vestige of pride many of the black communities had left. I will say it again, because it needs to be said over and over, look what Floyd Irons and the Vashon Wolverines meant to the north side. People who had no kids playing, no connection to the school, not even as alums, came out to support "their" team. And the county white schools hated Irons for it," Johnson stated, in reference to the large assemblage that followed the Vashon team wherever they played.

The Vashon cheering section was, in the eyes of many whites, often rambunctious threatening. Their trademark cheer of "The V Get Ready To Roll," for nearly two glorious decades, cascaded down on many a suburban gymnasium, announcing the arrival of the proud group of surviving warriors from the north side streets of a tough city. To black residents of North St. Louis, the chant symbolized both pride and loyalty to their often beleaguered and besieged part of the city.

The swagger the Vashon fans brought to out of town gymnasiums, in particular among the legions of young black men, ages 20 to 30, who had attached themselves to Irons' juggernaut, was often viewed by leery white school administrators as a sign of danger. As one white county athletic administrator stated off the record, "When Vashon came, we always knew we had to hire extra security."

And Irons was not one to back down from a fight. Once when the student cheering section at long time Vashon rival and state powerhouse, DeSmet - an exclusive all boy's catholic school in St. Louis County - came to a Vashon contest adorned in Gorilla masks, Iron refused to have his team take the floor until the masks, which he viewed as an insensitive racial taunt, were removed.

"These city leaders could not let Floyd Irons succeed," said Johnson, in defense of his long time friend. "He did it his own way and bowed to no one. He kept hope alive in the communities of the black city residents. There will never be another Coach Irons. Those in charge will not let it happen. The closest we have now in the PHL, in terms of the positive impact he has on the lives of his players and the way he helps (them) prepare for life, is Coach Campbell at Roosevelt."

If Johnson were put in charge of PHL athletics, his first move would be radical. "The first day, I would fire all the coaches; every one of them. I would let them reapply for their jobs and I might hire back a handful, but most need to go. They are not in it for the kids. They are in it for a paycheck and that is the root of the problem. If you complain, if you question the status quo, you are gone. If you just keep your mouth shut and don't worry about how the whole system is set up to make sure PHL athletes fail, then you will be rewarded. You might even become Director of the PHL," Johnson said in a thinly veiled jab at Sam Dunlap, current District Athletic Director. "I can name one varsity boys basketball coach in the PHL who has had the same job at the same school for the last 15 years and he has sent three players of college. Three! We don't need people like that in the system."

Johnson believes that, coaching needs to be more of a calling and less of a job. "We need Coaches like Floyd Irons and DeAndre Campbell who truly care about the future of the young men on their team, and who are going to show them how to use athletics to get out of the ghetto, to break the cycle."

Johnson, know affectionately as DJ in the St. Louis African American community, sees the current state of public education in St. Louis as a runaway train of educational problems that have grown to catastrophic levels after years of roaring unimpeded down the track. His conclusion is to the point: if the SLPS is to survive, serious problems need to be addressed with extreme action, and the sooner the better. "In the last four decades, the SLPS lost 90,000 kids," Johnson says. During the 40 year span Johnson refers to, SLPS enrollment dropped from 115,000 to 25,000. "The (odds) are already stacked against a black child born into the inner city of St. Louis," Johnson points out. The bitter reality, according to Johnson, is that the school system, perhaps the last life line of hope for these children, is doing nothing to help the predicament that is the birthright of most inner city youth. "Black children in St. Louis must also deal with a school system that seems to bend over backward to fail them. I mean, we live in a society where one in every three black male children will spend time in jail."

The importance of historical perspective is not lost on Johnson. His says it is crucial if the fight to remake the St. Louis Public Schools into a functioning unit that can provide the education that the city's youth both legally and morally deserve, then the past must not be forgotten.

"Education for blacks used to be about the Emancipation Proclamation of 1863 that freed all slaves, and the 13th Amendment to the U.S. Constitution that declared slavery illegal. It used to be about the right to an education – a necessity for those freed men and women to start their new journey in life – that is so deeply enshrined in those documents", Johnson wrote in 2006. "And what about *Brown v. the Board of Education of Topeka*, which desegregated the "separate but equal" policy imposed on schools by *Plessey v. Ferguson* and other Jim Crow laws that sought to erode the rights of blacks. And remember the Bus Boycott that began in 1955 when white policemen arrested Rosa Parks for not letting a white person have her seat on a bus? Or the Freedom Rides of 1961, designed to end segregation in facilities dependent on interstate commerce?"

"We need to stop taking 150 years of educational gains for granted, suck it up and do what needs to be done, regardless of whether or not you're too young to have witnessed, or too young to remember the gruesome realities of the Civil Rights era when black kids were stoned and shot at and spit on. Our black kids are facing a much more gruesome reality, if we don't act now."

According to Johnson, black citizens, especially parents, must become vigilant overseers of the public schools. "Instead of bashing everyone over the head with black victimhood, or allowing politicians who prostitute themselves for the almighty dollar fight, we need to push our black children to graduate on time and raise their confidence and grades with one hand, while fighting against anyone or policy or program that seeks to lower their expectations, or test scores with the other. We need to fight to get our black kids qualified teachers, and then fight to get their teachers the resources they need to help our kids succeed," Johnson says.

Johnson hammers home the point that the stakes in the new millennium for a quality education are too high to not demand the best for the students of the SLPS. Johnson concludes that "a huge achievement gap does exist between our kids and those attending schools in the county, and our sole goal should be to make sure our kids are no longer part of it. So, get involved. Get motivated. Get educated on the facts. By doing so, you can help lift the black community up. We need to elevate to educate, to be vigilant, always. This is our children's life on the line. This is their future. This is our children's America in crisis."

Against the grain to the end, in the fall of 2007, Johnson gave a no holds barred assessment of the necessity of the state takeover of the SLPS. "The way blacks in this town are acting about the loss of the District's accreditation and the State takeover of the School District, which in my mind, given the abject failure of the black community to educate its own, was absolutely right and necessary - you'd think the thought they were entitled to nothing more than handouts. Weren't worthy of anything more than the master's crumbs. That they'd forgotten the sacrifice of black lives it took to even secure blacks' right to read and write. The main and simple truth is, public education in the St. Louis School District has turned into a catastrophic failure."

The state of Missouri in 1999, as part of a concession to get the courts to set a deadline for the end of the busing program, agreed to fund the inter-district transfer program for another 10 years. By 2008, that stop point was rapidly approaching.

Still, not all the spin doctors were willing to admit the busing program was a failure. The "never admit defeat" approach of the SLPS was reminiscent of a classic comment made in the hallways of Congress during the strife filled years of the Vietnam War. A Republican Senator from Vermont, George Aiken, when looking for a graceful way out of a situation that just kept turning from bad to worse, had a simple solution: "Why don't we just say we won and go home."

One member of the state government knew his history when he made this statement, based on the same simple logic as deduced by the good Senator from Vermont all those years ago: "This is an historic day for children in St. Louis and the surrounding suburbs," said Bill Lann Lee, Acting Assistant Attorney General for Civil Rights, in 1999. "This agreement ensures the continuation of highly successful magnet schools in St. Louis, small classes in other city schools, the implementation of an ambitious school improvement program in city schools, and the continuation of the nation's most successful voluntary interdistrict transfer program. This case has greatly enhanced educational opportunities for children in St. Louis." At best, a view gleamed through rose colored glasses.

The agreement touted that it would allow for continued funding of the city magnet schools. During the nearly 20 years of the court plan, over 12,000 city students had attended magnet schools. But the original lure of the plan, that white students would transfer from county schools to the city magnets to take advantage of the specialized and unique curriculum at each school, never happened. Over the life of the program, only 1200 white county students took up this voluntary option. The buses taking black kids daily to suburban schools was a caravan comparable to the evacuation of a large army, when compared to the few lonely buses carrying white suburban students to the city schools.

In all fairness, the city magnet schools could, in some ways, be labeled as successes. But many educational and community leaders of St. Louis, both white and black, would also argue that the magnet schools were killing the one hope of a reprieve for the failing city schools: the return to prominence of the SLPS neighborhood schools. Supporters of the return to neighborhood school enrollments argued that without thriving schools back up and operating, providing anchors for their communities, the neighborhoods abandoned by the shuttering of these vital social cogs were doomed to a continued apathetic demise.

Realizing that a sudden stoppage in the program would overwhelm city schools that had lost a whole generation of its best and brightest to county districts, and whose facilities were in no condition to now take back all students who lived within the city boundaries, the courts brokered a gradual wind down of the voluntary desegregation program. County schools agreed to continue to take city transfer students for a period of three years. After that, each county district would decide on its own if they would stay in the "voluntary" program. Furthermore, any student who had started high school when this three year extension expired would be allowed to finish high school at the accepting school. In essence, every county school involved in the original order would see high school transfer students from the city in its high school classrooms for at least seven more years, or until 2006. Regardless, it was now on paper that the end was near. Mr. Lee summarized through his rose colored glasses, "It is time to take the next step in our continuing effort to ensure equal educational opportunity for school children in St. Louis."

Today, the lack of confidence in the SLPS is a major hurdle faced by city leaders in their attempt at urban renewal. In an April 2008 report by the St. Louis Post Dispatch, with the catchy title of: *They Love the City, But Not the Schools*, reporter Nancy Cambria examined the quandary faced by young professional city residents. Many had bought and invested heavily in revitalized city neighborhoods while they were childless. Now, with their children reaching school age, many were giving up on the idea of city living. Their choice was between paying expensive tuition to private schools in the city, or uprooting and relocating in the suburbs for the advantage of adequate public schools. The SLPS was not an option most would even consider. "I will not play Russian roulette with my child's education," said one parent who had chosen the move to the suburbs. "My child's education is too important."

The Education advisor to St. Louis Mayor Francis Slay, Robbyn Wahby, told the Post that the Mayor was very concerned that the rebirth of many of the city's older neighborhoods would never reach its full potential without adequate public schools. "We can't continue to see this kind of growth pattern without good, affordable schools," Wahby said. One frustrated parent echoed Wahby's concerns, "The city schools are crumbling," she said. "I love the area where I live, but you've got to make sacrifices for your kids."

Steven Bingler, President of a New Orleans architectural firm that specializes in educational planning, has provided analysis on the closing of urban neighborhood schools around the nation. He states that St. Louis citizens should be concerned for the survival of their own neighborhoods. Even more importantly, he points out, "If kids can't walk to school, then their parents can't get to school either, and when parents can't participate in their child's education, in many cases that child will fail. For our most vulnerable kids, smaller places are better. People know who they are and they can stay better connected to their community," Bingler said.

By 2008, the SLPS was a figurative carcass by the side of the highway – road kill that had been picked over for the most desirable parts of the deceased - the rest left to rot in an apathetic state of educational hopelessness. The SLPS were a mess, dying a slow death of attrition and neglect.

For years, politicians throughout the state have used the SLPS to shamelessly court votes based upon irrational racial fears. Judges have used the urban students that form the constituency of the district like laboratory test mice, in a complex social experiment that created an idealistic master plan that promised educational bliss, but delivered results that have borne little academic success, while indirectly destroying block after block of city neighborhoods. At the same time, predominantly white suburban school districts, in the name of social benevolence, have taken the brightest and the best from the city schools, leaving those less blessed in academic and athletic prowess, to defend for themselves in a system that is as dismal a failure as any school district in the nation.

Bottom line: Despite the millions spent on what the courts determined to be the solution to segregated St. Louis schools, the end result is in 2008 a system much more segregated than at the start of the 1981 court ordered forced busing program.

CHAPTER 4
SUMMER

I say luck is when an opportunity comes along, and you're prepared for it.
— Denzel Washington

Volunteering is for suckers. Did you know that so called 'Volunteers' don't even get paid?
— Homer Simpson

A bone to the dog is not charity. Charity is the bone shared with the dog, when you are just as hungry as the dog.
— Jack London

Show a little faith, there is magic in the night. Hey, you ain't no beauty, but hey, you're alright.
— Bruce Springsteen

I am not dying, not anymore than any of us are at any moment. We run, hopefully as fast as we can, and then everyone must stop. We can only choose how we handle the race.
— Hugh Elliott

Football Coaches, by nature, are worriers. What is the opposition doing to get better? What are we doing to get better? Are we doing enough? The uncertainty, manifested by self doubt and questioning, can become maddening as the season draws near. With the evolution to a 12 month a year job, football coaches no longer have the luxury of an "off season". Year round weight training, quickness, and agility drills have become the norm. What at one time raised winning programs above the competition - a year round focus on improvement - is now the standard for any player or coach who has the simple goal to be competitive. 24/7 is the commitment level necessary in today's world of high school football.

As late spring turned into summer in 2008, the focus of the Roosevelt Roughriders football team was as sharp as the batting eye of the great Cardinal slugger, Albert Pujols. As the city of St. Louis gave its emotional attention to the developing Central Division pennant race between the Cardinals and their hated rival from Chicago, the Cubs, Coach Campbell and his team were on an all consuming drive to betterment. "Year round training, that is something that is changing in the PHL and we like to think we are leading the charge," said Campbell on a June Tuesday evening as he oversaw a weight training session outside of the stadium concession stand. Due to construction inside of the Roosevelt building, the team held summer weight training outside. Before the beginning and after the completion of each workout session, players would drag barbells, dumbbells and benches from inside the stand, dutifully retuning them at the conclusion of their workout.

Realizing the critical role that the development of his offensive line would play in the 2008 fortunes of the Roughriders, Campbell and the offensive linemen would gather each Saturday morning in June and July to study, and implement, an offensive play book that on a now weekly basis was growing in thickness. "Line play, both sides of the line of scrimmage, is where we have to get better," said Campbell. Those sentiments were echoed by his students of the art of blocking and tackling. "We are the key," said offensive center and line captain, Tyler Clubb. "We have to function as a unit. I make all the line calls. The time we spend together this summer is going to make our job much easier this fall. We have the backs, the quarterback and the receivers to have a great team. The pressure is on us, the line, to get better."

For many years college football coaches have flocked to the St. Louis PHL schools like an SUV to a gas pump. The PHL is a lucrative and well stocked hunting ground for skilled offensive position players – running backs and receivers. Often these future college stars toiled playing for PHL teams who were woefully inept. The word amongst the college talent scouts was out: the coaching, the facilities, the technique, the overall level of play in the city schools in abysmal, but you will find at PHL schools an abundance of the one factor that can not be coached: speed, and in the wide open style of football favored by most colleges today, speed kills.

It was not uncommon in the decades of the 80's and 90's, and up to the mid decade of the new millennium, to see outstate powers like perennial state champion Jefferson City have fewer Division I recruits on their rosters than a wasteland of a program like Roosevelt. College Coaches mined these "diamonds in the rough" at PHL schools with intensity befitting the raw talent found in city league schools. But it was also well known amongst college coaches that the position area lacking in college caliber talent in the city schools was that of linemen. The type of PHL athlete that filled the slots in the trenches fell into one of two categories: very undersized and weak, or oversized to the point of obesity. It was not uncommon in the city league to see a 145 pound guard next to a 375 pound tackle. In most instances, neither was an athlete of fitness or power. Weak and overpowered, or fat and worn out, the offensive and defensive lines of most PHL teams, come game time, became exercises in futility that negated any possibility for their teams to compete outside of the PHL.

According to Coach Campbell that is changing; line play is getting better in the PHL because of the dedication of a new group of young coaches who are willing to stress its importance; and willing to make the time commitment to condition and train athletes to the level needed to achieve success on the line of scrimmage. "We are starting to see more and more true athletes on the line," said Campbell. "It used to be in the PHL that you took your best athlete and made him your quarterback, your next three became the running backs. We didn't worry about receivers much. We had some in this league who would have been great, but the quarterbacks couldn't get the ball to them because the line couldn't block long enough to keep the pass rush off to have time to throw the ball. That is changing. College scouts are looking at our kids on the line now. The technique is there, the strength and conditioning is there. As line play improves, so do teams in the PHL." Campbell points to the number of college scouts already drooling over Roosevelt Junior Offensive and Defensive Lineman Rene Faulk.

A natural disaster of mythical proportions, the Katrina Hurricane of September 2005 set in motion a chain of events that would turn upside down the world of Rene Faulk; and greatly benefit the football talent level of the Roosevelt Roughriders in 2008. One of the tens of thousands displaced by the natural disaster, Faulk was at the time a New Orleans 8th grade student. He and his six brothers, along with his mother and father, made the migration north to St. Louis. For the Faulk clan, the chosen destination was not one of happenstance, but of connection. Rene's uncle is future Hall of Fame professional football player, and retired St. Louis Ram Running Back, Marshall Faulk.

Like many in New Orleans when Katrina hit, the Faulk family found themselves stranded. For four days the family huddled in the chaotic and dangerous environment of the New Orleans Superdome. "All we brought with us," said Rene, "was what we could carry. It was a very bad time. I still do not like to talk about it. I didn't want to move and leave all of my friends, but I had no choice. We had nothing left to go home to."

Faulk's famous football playing uncle threw the family a life line with plane tickets to St. Louis. "He got us set up," remembers Rene. "He got us up here and got us a place to live, but still we had lost everything. We were all angry. I missed my friends and my house."

Marshall Faulk, recently retired from the Rams, remains a beloved icon on the St. Louis sporting scene. His efforts for the Rams offensive juggernaut of the late 90's, nicknamed "The Greatest Show On Turf," propelled St. Louis to two Super Bowls and one World Championship.

Having an uncle who was a legendary hero in your newly chosen home town is the type of introduction to the neighborhood any teenager would treasure. Rene is no exception. "Everyone knows my Uncle Marshall. He was one of the more popular Rams. I always had tickets to the home games and a lot of people from school knew who I was because of Marshall. They all thought I could get them tickets to all the games."

The road to big time college football recruit continues to be long and winding for the younger Faulk, lined with academic pitfalls and behavioral demons he continues to battle. He has none of the small and quick attributes of his diminutive Uncle. Rene stands 6'2 and weighs 310 pounds. His ankles are massive, supporting a powerful, if still somewhat soft body. The small size of his feet - size 9 - makes the youngster appear to be constantly off balance as he runs. Aptly named "Man-Child" by Assistant Coach Darren West, Faulk has only been involved in organized football for three years. "I never played in New Orleans," Faulk informs a visiting coach.

Faulk is candid in discussing both his past academic shortfalls and his lack of ambition for a college education. "If I can't play football, I am not going to college," he states in a matter of fact way. "If football don't work out, I will go with my daddy and work construction. That is what I love to do. I never have liked school." Compounding Faulk's frustration was the destruction of his school records in the aftermath of Katrina. "I got put back in as a 8th grader when I got here," he recalls. "I didn't like that. I was too old and too big to be in junior high, but that is where I was stuck."

Faulk has only recently begun to develop his football skills. His academic standing is even more of a work in progress. The RHS Coaching staff gives glowing accounts of his potential as a player.

"He has great feet," says Coach Campbell.

"He moves like a big cat," chimes in Offensive Line Coach Darren West.

According to Campbell, the University of Missouri became smitten with Faulk at an instructional camp in the Spring of 2008. "They felt he was the best lineman they had seen in the Class of 2010. "Man-Child" can do it, but he has to become a complete player. He still takes off too many plays, but when that big ole dude decides he is not going to be stopped, well, he doesn't get stopped."

Faulk's overall appearance is not that of a finely tuned athlete. "I'm still too soft," Rene self evaluates, "but I am getting stronger and quicker. I am eating better and losing baby fat. I can now bench twice the weight (290 lbs.) that I could when I started lifting with the team last year," Faulk states. "Rene is powerful but he is not yet strong," is Coach Campbell's assessment of Faulk's strength development. "He has such great natural talent, such a great blood line. He moves so well for a man of his size. He is truly a Man-Child. His upside is scary, man, I am telling you, and he has the potential to be a big time recruit. It is all up to him," says Campbell.

Line Coach West is a constant driving force for Faulk. Rene's physical conditioning, or in the coach's view his lack of conditioning, is a constant source of torment for West.

"'Man-Child.' you won that one (play) and you might win the next one," West declares in the middle of pre-season one on one blocking drills. "But you know what, by the 4th play, you will quit, because you are tired. So you see "Man-Child," we going to just keep right on bringing it to you, until you quit and then we got you. Your big ass might as well get off the field by the fifth play cause dude, you'll be doubled over sucking wind."

Discipline on and off the football field, or more accurately lack of discipline, has been an issue that has followed Rene for as long as he can remember. "I use to like to fight. It got me in a lot of trouble." Faulk is another of the athletes that took advantage of the transfer rule to play for Roosevelt his sophomore season (2007). That year he attended Logos High School, a special school within the SLPS for students with behavioral problems, a sort of "alternative" school for the child who does not function well in the traditional school setting. According to Faulk, he has been diagnosed as a disabled student due to behavioral disorders. He was allowed to play football at Roosevelt because Logos has no football team and Roosevelt is his neighborhood school. According to Rene, he spent his first few years in St. Louis in special education classrooms.

In January of 2008 Faulk transferred to Roosevelt full time, but much to his disapproval and disappointment, he was assigned to a special education self contained classroom. During the summer preceding his Junior year, Faulk shared plans for him to transfer into a regular classroom setting when school opened in August, 2008. "I didn't like school in St. Louis until I got onto the football team at Roosevelt. Being on the team I now have a lot of good friends in my teammates." Faulk told the St. Louis Post Dispatch in September of 2008, "(Football) helped me to trust people. When I first got here, I didn't trust anybody. I found players on my team and we became friends, in and out of school. In practice and out of practice. It helped me a lot."

Faulk will often approach a stranger with caution. An initial perception is that he is quiet to the point of being sullen. As the 2008 season wore on, the positive transformation of Faulk was obvious to those associated with the Roughrider program. His practice punctuality improved as the season progressed. From all indications, his academic standing was also on the rise. But it was on the football field that Faulk's talents were undeniable; "scary" as Coach Campbell would say. Any trained observer with a good eye for football talent could give testimonial to the talent of Faulk. When focused and motivated, he was the best player in the city.

In late September, 2008 Roosevelt would play Gateway Tech and its star player, defensive end Sheldon Richardson. The week before the game, Richardson, listed at 6'3" and 280 lbs. and possessing a blazing 40 yard dash time of 4.45 seconds was ranked by the national scouting service, Rivals.com, as the 4th best high school football player in the nation. Such lofty acclaim needs to be repeated for emphasis, **the fourth best high school football player in the nation**. Richardson had scholarship offers from all the nation's top college football programs. Eventually, after committing and un-committing to the University of Missouri at least twice, Richardson in February of 2009 signed a grant in aid with the instate Tigers.

The Gateway star began the September 2008 game against Roosevelt at the right defensive end position for the Jaguars. He was lined up one on one with Roosevelt's left offensive tackle, Rene Faulk. The highly touted Richardson, with his combination of speed, strength and size - the fourth best player in the entire nation - through his pass rush alone, should dominate a spread offense such as employed by Roosevelt. Richardson did dominate –eventually - when his coaches astutely moved him to the opposite side of the field and away from Rene Faulk. While lined up over Faulk, man to man, Richardson was not a factor. Faulk completely neutralized him, both on the pass and the run. Richardson was under the total control of the motivated (for this day at least) "Man-Child."

Richardson may well have been the 4th best player in the nation, but on this particular day, as anyone willing to objectively view the game film will attest to he was, at best, only the second best lineman on the Gateway Stadium field.

Faulk has an almost uncanny facial resemblance to the former Heavyweight Boxing Champion of the World, Sonny Liston. Much like Faulk, Liston was born and spent his early years in the deep south, the 24th of his father's 25 children. Liston moved to St. Louis when he was 14 years old to escape the abusive father.

When relocating to the city, Liston did not have an outlet like high school football to give his life structure. It didn't take long for the brooding Liston to find trouble in St. Louis. In 1950, at the age of 18, having pled guilty to several robberies, Liston was sent to the Missouri State Penitentiary in Jefferson City. While in prison, Liston took up the sport of boxing. In later years, Liston often credited his discovery of the sport with saving his life.

Paroled in 1952, Liston had a meteorically quick rise to the top of the boxing world, first winning the amateur national Golden Gloves title, then turning professional later that same year. Liston began his long climb to the Heavyweight Champion of the World, finally winning the belt in 1962 with a knockout of Floyd Patterson. During his boxing ascent, Liston once again ran afoul of the law. In a case that drew much criticism for what many felt was a trumped up charge, Liston was sent back to prison in 1956, drawing a six month sentence after a conviction for assaulting a police officer.

For a champion who never did gain the favor of the nation's sports fans, Liston will mostly be remembered not for the championship bout he won, but for the two he lost; both to the legendary Muhammad Ali. Still known by his birth name of Cassius Clay when he took the belt from Liston in Miami, FL in February of 1964, Ali was the antithesis of Liston. Ali was photogenic, glib with a quote, and craved the media spot light. Middle class white America saw Ali as "uppity." In contrast, Liston was a brooding giant, possessing terrifying physical strength. Mean and surly, Liston scared middle class white America with the fierce and brutal beatings he administered to opponents in the ring. While Ali, with his mouth and self promoting pronouncement of "I am the Greatest," was irradiating, Liston, to contemporary white America at the apex of the nation's Civil Right's Movement, was down right terrifying.

The title bout in Miami was stopped in the 7th round when Liston, a 7-1 favorite over Ali, refused to answer the bell. Many observers and gamblers felt that the fight was fixed.

Even more controversial was the rematch in March 1965, when the new champion, now known as Muhammad Ali after his conversion earlier that year to Islam, knocked out Liston in the first round. The fight held in Lewiston, ME, is still to this day controversial.

The Ali punch that dropped Liston to the canvas has gone down in boxing lore as the "phantom" punch. The photo of Ali attempting to land a right hook that appears to miss its mark, Liston's chin, by at least a foot, and Liston's subsequent fall to the canvas like a mob informant into the East River, is one of the more famous sports photos in history. Most felt for certain that Liston, long rumored to be under the control of organized crime, had once again taken a dive in a fixed heavyweight title bout.

There is a great - albeit little known – story about the first Miami Liston and Ali title fight. Ali was just beginning to burst upon the American sports scene; and had found a stage to build a self persona that would in due time culturally dwarf that of any other sports personality of the era. Since his arrival in Miami, Ali had crowed long and loud to the media about Liston's deficiencies, in particular his lack of intelligence and less than pleasant physical appearance. Ali called Liston a gorilla. It was a different era in regard to political correctness. His public hogging of the spotlight was, for Ali, the first in a long line of clever and orchestrated media staged events, launching the engaging young man on a path to fulfilling his self prophecy of "I am the greatest." But it was all an act, carefully choreographed for a nation that didn't quite know how to take the loud upstart "Negro;" but was now hanging on every outrageous media comment he made. It was an Ali spectacle at its best, an event the world over the next decade would come to know well.

One evening when out on the town and, unbeknownst to Ali, he and his followers entered a Miami Night Club already occupied by Liston, seated alone and unrecognized in a far back dark corner of the smoke filled bar. After Ali was seated, Liston rose - perhaps he had decided to not wait until the approaching night of the fight to quiet the insulting upstart challenger - and walked unseen and unnoticed toward Ali's table. Upon arrival, Liston placed his hand on Ali's shoulder. This was not a staged for the news cameras confrontation between the loud photogenic Ali and the hulking champion. Several such recent encounters in Miami in the days leading up to the fight had already achieved the publicity that Ali's backers so coveted. No, on this night, it was simply two men who didn't like each other that now, due to a chance encounter, were upon a possible violent collision course.

As Ali turned to face Liston, he was startled to recognize the former convict and reputed mob muscle man. Observers claim the look of terror on Ali's face, not knowing the intentions of Liston, was one of pure genuine fright, something they had never seen before, or would ever see again from Ali. Fortunately, Liston was not in a fighting mood that evening. He simple told Ali, "keep talking little man," turned, and walked away. For once, it was reported, Ali was speechless.

Liston's boxing career ended when his life did. On January 5, 1970, his wife found him dead in his Las Vegas home. It was believed he had been deceased between 6 to 8 days when the body was discovered. The official cause of death is listed as heart failure. However many conspiracy theorists feel that Liston died as he lived, violently. Needle marks were found on his arms, leading to speculation of a heroin overdose. Liston had a very well known fear of needles and if he did die of an overdose of the illegal drug, then the theory was he was shot up against his will by underworld connections who wanted Liston silenced once and for all. It is believed that Liston was 38 years old at the time of his death, although no one could ever verify, for certain, his age through legal documentation.

Upon initial impression, Faulk appears to possess many of the same traits that so scared white America in regard to Liston: very black skin on a huge body that portrays frightful and powerful natural strength, facial expressions that seldom give off a glimpse of a happy or content individual, all tied together with a quiet nature that can easily be misperceived as a form of anti-social sullenness. The enigmatic Faulk will prove to be the most difficult of the mainstays amongst the Roughriders to label. The youngster with the star power relative idolized on the local sports scene admits he has few close friends.

As the 2008 season progressed, Faulk would begin to come out of his shell, both as a person and as a football player. By season's end, Campbell will be pleased with the development of the "Man-Child." "He became more of a leader, more of a stand up kind of team mate," Campbell observed, after the 2008 season's conclusion.

Campbell continued, "Rene is finally starting to realize his potential, that he does have a bright future. This is a kid who came to us with no self esteem, a kid who settled all disputes with his fists. To be honest with you, when he came here from New Orleans, "Man-Child" was not the type of kid you wanted in your school, or living next door to you in the neighborhood. His size alone scares a lot of people. But inside, there is a good kid, he just didn't know how to express (himself) except with the only (attribute) he felt he had, his strength and size. He has a reputation as a guy not to mess with. Football gives him a more acceptable way to use his natural size and strength in a way that will get him positive social status. Football here at Roosevelt, I really feel, has turned this young man's life around. I am proud of "Man-Child" and what he is becoming, both as a football player and as a young African American male, who now realizes he can live a good and productive life. He doesn't have to be a punk or a gang banger."

Faulk also credits football and the discipline instilled by Coach Campbell as motivating factors that have dramatically improved his personal future outlook and level of ambition. "I now want to play college football. I never even thought about college before I came to Roosevelt, but I can't do that (go to college) if I am in trouble. I have got to straighten up. Football use to mean nothing to me, now it is a big part of my life. Our coaches are so determined. All we think about is how to get better. To be a good football player and on the team here, I know I have to make my grades and not get in trouble. We are going to win the state championship and I am going to be a part of it. I am a changed person. I don't fight anymore and I keep my cool. If there is trouble, I used to get in the middle of it as fast as I could. Now I go the other way. I am a football player at Roosevelt and that means no trouble, or you don't play."

You cannot tell the story of the revitalization of high school football in the St. Louis City schools without giving due props to the grass roots, feel good story of a volunteer group know as PHL, Inc.

We live in a skeptical world. The late comedian Lenny Bruce once said, "The only anonymous giver is the guy who knocks up your daughter." Despite the infamous 1960's off-color comedian's sarcasm, his intended message is transparent. No one does anything for nothing, everyone has an ulterior motive and a hidden agenda.

Well, maybe not.

Approach any PHL high school football coach or administrator and ask, "name me who has done the most good for the St. Louis public school kids who play high school football," and the answer will be unanimous: PHL, Inc. Thom Kuhn and Charlie Tallman are two of the founding members of the non profit group. The two unlikely benefactors are major cogs in a multi million dollar construction company, Millstone and Bangert, Inc. Kuhn is the CEO of the firm that specializes in large scale government projects, most notably, bridge and road construction. Some of their recent gigs include the runways and taxiway paving of the Denver and St. Louis airports.

With their firm located in St. Charles County, a locale about as removed from the inner city of St. Louis as one can get, makes the duo of Kuhn and Tallman the most unlikely of saviors for inner city Public High League athletes. The distance in miles – twenty two – from the campus of Roosevelt High School to the firm's St. Charles County office, in no way equates the figurative distance between the two environments. St. Charles County and its inhabitants are light years removed from the daily inner city grind of Roosevelt High School students. The almost "third world" existence of their neighborhood holds no relative comparison to the wide open and beautifully landscaped and spacious terrain found a few miles to the west in the fast growing and prosperous St. Charles County. Despite no apparent reason for a connection between the two, over the years from 2005-2008, Kuhn and Tallman have given birth to, and nurtured, a grass roots organization that has raised more than $1.5 million for the benefit of woefully underfunded and neglected inner city public high school athletes, most notably, high school football players. Coach Campbell, head football coach of Roosevelt, refers to the duo as "our Angels."

In October 2004, Tom Wheatley of the St. Louis Post-Dispatch wrote a two part series depicting the wretched and dangerous conditions that PHL football teams had to endure. His writings detailed playing fields that had not seen grass since the original George Bush administration, with ground as hard as a concrete parking lot. According to Wheatley, practice and game equipment was often outdated and broken, and of insufficient numbers – players forced to share helmets during practices and games. Accompanying the woeful lack of facilities were daily challenges no high school athlete should have to endure. Example: To find sufficient space for practice, football players at Vashon High School walked one mile from their on campus dressing room to a city park, a daily jaunt that took them through some of the most hotly contested gang turf in the city.

Taking the name *PHL, Inc.*, the group's original mission was basic: to grow grass on city football fields. From this humble beginning objective flourished an organization given across the board credit for helping revitalize the city's long dormant high school football programs.

Kuhn, Tallman, and their fellow *PHL, Inc.* members, have somehow managed to take their good intentions and maneuver their way through the land where good ideas go to die - otherwise known as the upper echelons of the St. Louis Public School System. They have cultivated and brought to harvest the rarest of results in modern day urban public education, a program that really helps kids. Breaking through the gridlock that had stifled and frustrated to the point of surrender, many a previous potential beneficiary of the failing and flailing SLPS, is seen by many as a more amazing accomplishment than growing grass on once barren athletic fields. *PHL, Inc.* allowed neither red tape, nor apathy, to forestall its mission.

Sitting in their company board room in April 2008, Kuhn and Tallman agreed to discuss the formation and the growth of *PHL, Inc*; squeezing a busy morning schedule that would also include meetings with representatives from an architectural firm to compile bid proposals on a 3 million dollar bridge building project, along with a meeting with Nike officials to secure grant money to help construction improvements at Gateway Technical High School's track, and to buy playing shoes for members of PHL girl's soccer teams. The old maxim that if you want something done right, assign the task to someone who is busy, is a perfect fit for both Kuhn and Tallman.

How did you get so much done so fast when those with good ideas before you could never get past the planning stages with SLPS, is the first question many ask the *PHL, Inc.* leaders. "We just knew a few of the right people," says Kuhn. "In November of 2004, we began discussions that led to the formation of *PHL, Inc.* We graded our first field (at Vashon High) in February of 2005. It took us two days to complete the grading," is Kuhn's summation of the time frame needed to go from good idea to tangible results. "Once they saw what we could do, we got a lot of support from SLPS."

Self deprecating in nature, and looking nothing like the prototype corporate executive, Kuhn possesses a huge body that encompasses an even larger personality. When talking to associates of Kuhn, one quickly deduces that most who know Kuhn, like him. He does not dress or act the part of the successful businessman. When discussing deals involving contracts that can run into the tens of millions of dollars, with men and women who control huge amounts of the heartland's money and capital, Kuhn's preferred attire is khaki slacks and pullover shirts, with an occasional collared shirt - preferably Hawaiian - thrown in for good measure. Friends say Brooks Brothers is not his style. Getting the job done is.

Kuhn's physical size is an immediate attention grabber. A fair guess of height would be some where in the 6'5" range, an estimation of his weight, a few biscuits shy of 300 lbs. Kuhn has the look of a football player who simply ran out of eligibility and was forced, against his will, to hang up his helmet and reluctantly search for a job in the real world. But when asked his own football playing background, his answer creates another enigmatic image for a man who for the past three years has given so much of himself, so that others can play the game of football: "I played a little flag football in college intramurals. That is about the extent of my football playing experience."

Kuhn's easy going manner and unassuming nature allow him to, with ease, downplay any attempt to give notice and credit for the accomplishments of *PHL, Inc*. "At first we wanted no publicity," Kuhn says. "We needed to make sure that we could get grass to grow. We didn't want to look like fools." Kuhn is a bottom line guy and, despite the easy going nature he exudes upon first encounter; it doesn't take long to detect a Tony Baretta quality about him. Like Barretta, the no nonsense tough guy NYC copy on the TV series bearing the same name who wouldn't hesitate to toss the rule book out the window if that is what it took to bring the bad guys to justice, Kuhn will do what it takes to get the job done. In this case, providing PHL athletes and coaches the facilities they deserve.

Tallman is the perfect sidekick to Kuhn. He could be straight from central casting as the strong, silent type of leading man, so popular in the B movies of the 1950's. Associates claim his business sense, ability to stay on task and meet deadlines, are perfect balances to Kuhn's "it's not the destination but the journey" cavalier approach. Tallman is efficient, as opposed to Kuhn's effervescence, and guarded in choosing his words to answer even the simplest of questions.

Those who know Tallman say he is a man of calculated responses and proactive preparation. He oozes a quiet confidence that begets a calmness which is essential and a valuable tool in the intense dog eat dog board rooms of the high dollar construction industry; where he and Kuhn have so successfully found their niche. The distinct talents that each brings to the table is a lethal combination. "A deadly duo" was the descriptor used by former Soldan High School Head Football Coach and current Roosevelt High School Principal, Terry Houston to describe Kuhn and Tallman.*PHL Inc.'s* circumventing of the notorious upper level administration of the SLPS and the producing of results in such a short time span has become the lore of legend amongst observers of the often stumbling and bumbling SLPS. "The people at the top of SLPS have not held us back" said Kuhn. "At first, they were skeptical. 'Who are these guys and what do they want' was never said outright, but it was easy to see they were skeptical of our motives. You could read the body language."

Tallman is more blunt in his summation of the formation of *PHL, Inc.* "We read Wheatley's articles in the Post. A number of concerned people had called Wheatley, including us, wanting to do something to help. Names were (exchanged) and we got together about a month after the articles were written. We have a charity golf tournament that we were running and we were looking for a new beneficiary. But first, we wanted to (validate) the problem. So we drove around to the four fields - we called them lakes - that at the time the PHL was using for varsity football games."

Kuhn picks up the story; "They (the fields) were even worse than we imagined. It (the day of the tour) was your typical St. Louis crappy November day. It had been raining for about a week. We walked around all four fields and when (we) were done, we didn't even need to wipe our shoes to come inside. Despite all the rain, the playing fields were so hard - like concrete - you didn't have to worry about mud."

As each layer of facility and field inadequacy was peeled back, new and additional problems became visible. "Some of these fields had gone years without proper maintenance," said Tallman. "And it wasn't just the fields. The bleachers at all four fields were literally falling down. They needed to be replaced, if for no other reason than safety. If we had stuff that unsafe on our job site, OSHA would hit us with a big fine."

With a mission statement of "repair, replace, purchase, improve and build athletic facilities" for the benefit of St. Louis public school athletes, in early 2005, *PHL, Inc.* came to life, rolled up its collective sleeves and went to work. The group set its initial sights on the city's four woefully maintained football game facilities. The fields at Southwest (CVPA), Roosevelt, Gateway Tech and Soldan would be given complete facelifts. Leveling and grading of the playing surfaces, new grass planted, new goal posts and automated sprinkling systems, along with bleacher repair, was the master plan presented to SLPS.

Despite the dire need for these improvements, an initial apathetic response from the SLPS, almost doomed PHL, Inc before it even got off the drawing board. When the district was first approached, Kuhn and his supporters were met with unexpected hesitancy from the upper level administration of SLPS. The district administration wanted any funds raised by PHL, Inc to be placed in the coffers of SLPS. PHL, Inc. balked at such an arrangement, insistent that any money raised would go directly to the refurbishing and reconstructing the district's woeful athletic venues, and would be controlled by PHL, Inc. The District turned down the offer. "We were told flat out, 'you can't do it,'" recalls Kuhn.

The genius of Kuhn, Tallman and the other members of *PHL, Inc* was the tenacious belief in their goal and their refusal to accept "no" for an answer. "We deal with government agencies and officials all the time in our (construction) business," explained Kuhn. "You just keep moving forward. You just stay the course, no matter the number or severity of the obstacles that jump in your face. Giving up, for us, was never an option. What we wanted to (accomplish), and once we saw that the conditions Wheatley described were, in all reality, worse than we expected, the goal was too important to not keep pushing. Kids, no matter where they live, deserve better than what the PHL kids were getting."

Kuhn continued, "We knew the right people to call and, three days later, we were told, 'okay, if you want to try, go ahead.' On February 8 2005, we turned dirt." Still, it took several more meetings with high level district officials to gain their full support of the project, but once tangible results could be seen, the local communities rallied around the cause.

"We had several more early meetings with top officials in the district," recalls Kuhn, "and they were very polite, but we got a lot of head nodding and body language that said, 'sure, we've heard this kind of thing before.' But after our first project at Vashon (the building of a football practice field) was done in two days, the attitude (of SLPS) changed." Kuhn points out repeatedly that since the initial reluctance of the school district, support from the district wide administration has been unwavering. He pays special kudos to Chief of Operations Deanna Anderson and Roger Cayce, along with Coordinators of Athletics Sam Dunlap and Dave Cook. "We don't spend a dime on overhead. We don't spend a dime on administrative costs. Every penny we raise goes directly into the field improvement projects," Kuhn proudly points out.

According to Tallman, the gratitude of the local citizens was an unexpected plus, a boost to the group's morale, and removed any anxiety that the efforts of *PHL, Inc.* would be wiped out by vandalism. "A lot of people said, 'you can build it, but in no time it will be tore up.' I will tell you that anywhere we have gone, the local citizens, many of them elderly with no children in the school, have come out of the woodwork to support us. A big problem on paint days is, we get way more volunteers from the neighborhoods than we need. We just buy more paint brushes. We want the neighborhood residents to 'touch' the project. This gives them ownership and gives them pride in what is happening at their local school. For this program to work, we have to have the support of the people in the neighborhoods, and we have gotten it beyond any of our original expectations. On paint days, they come from far and wide. These people (in the inner city) are human beings just like you find anywhere else. They want nice neighborhoods and schools."

"There is an older lady who lives near Vashon, she has grandkids in the school, and she has come out literally since the day we started our first project there," said Kuhn. "She let us know that it was the first time in recent memory that anyone had done something to help fix up her community and that she would personally keep an eye on things. We encouraged her to call the police if she saw any (suspicious) activities. She told us she didn't need the police. Besides, she said it takes them 45 minutes to respond from the sub station that was only two blocks away. What she had been doing, if she saw a problem, was to bring a baseball bat and her husbands shot gun with her to investigate. We would never encourage something like that, but she meant it. That story has repeated itself everywhere we have had a project. The success we have had is because of the grass roots neighborhood level (support) we have had."

After the initial positive and promising start of *PHL, Inc.* became knowledge throughout the metro area, support began to pick up momentum at an inexorable pace. Wide ranging public praise poured in, along with offers to help. Even veterans of years of battles within the SLPS joined the ranks of *PHL, Inc* volunteers. Retired Vashon Principal Cozy Marks, who spent 40 years working in the district, and is currently the head of the influential Vashon Alumni Association, was so impressed with the intentions of *PHL, Inc.* that he became a member of the Board of Directors. "I think it's a godsend," Marks told the St. Louis Post Dispatch in 2005. "It's something that is sorely needed for the city. It's shown the community what can be done when people are truly interested in the success of young people. One of the things that needed to be restored in our district is confidence. Morale bottomed out. There was nothing there. Everyone is so happy with what these guys have done for the city schools. Folks in the community are beginning to take more ownership in their schools and teams, and encouraging others to participate."

Eventually, PHL, Inc.'s Board of Directors grew to include along with Kuhn, Tallman and Marks; Mike Clark (Businessman), Dan Dierdorf (retired hall of fame NFL player and current national broadcaster), Jim Hanifan (former NFL Head Coach), Rick Veatch (Businessman),Keith Wortman (retired NFL player)), Bob Wallace (St.Louis Rams), Bill Jones (Anheuser-Busch) and Steven Esparza (The Home Depot).

First year PHL, Inc. projects included: the above mentioned new practice field with an irrigation system on a vacant lot at the Vashon High School campus, re-grading, re-planting and repairing an irrigation system on the fields at Gateway Institute of Technology, Soldan International Studies High Schools and Roosevelt High School. The installation of new goalposts and player benches at Vashon, Gateway, Soldan and Roosevelt High Schools. The re-painting of fences, stadiums, and bleachers at Soldan and Roosevelt, the fences and ticket booths, press box and concession stand at Gateway Institute of Technology and the fences at Cleveland High School. The installation of safety handrails on steps at Roosevelt High School. The re-paving with asphalt the deteriorated area in front of the Roosevelt concession stand. The removal of unsafe bleachers at Roosevelt and the Planting of five Bradford Pear trees on the grounds of the Soldan stadium.

When the first football season (2005) after the *PHL, Inc.* improvements rolled around, the upsurge in participants and interest in the long dormant Public High League football programs drew the immediate notice of the St. Louis Sports community. "It definitely brings an excitement for the program, for the school and for our community," Vashon coach Reggie Ferguson in 2005 told the St. Louis Post Dispatch. He also noted the community pride in the improvements. "I'm really blown away by the neighborhood. They love the improvements. Neighbors may see a difference in the fields. Players can feel it." In 2005, Gateway Tech players also noted the changes. "Last year it was concrete," said Jeremiah Kinealy. "Now, it's a pillow. Last year, you'd make a tackle and slide over rocks," said Jamal Ahmed. "The middle of the field was pretty much jagged rocks, and we had sprinklers sticking up, too. You'd get cuts and bruises."

In 2005, Roosevelt lineman Josh Lane bemoaned the prior conditions at RHS Stadium. "It was like bricks every time we hit the ground last year. Unless it rained. If you wanted to take a bath, then just play in that big old mud bowl we had."

Coach Campbell of the Roughriders tells a good story of his playing days at Cleveland High School in the early 90's. "My Junior year," Campbell said in a 2008 interview, "we played right here at Roosevelt. I got tackled and fell on a rock that ripped open my arm and it took 25 stitches to close the wound." To prove his point, Campbell raises his right shirt sleeve to exhibit a seven inch scar on his forearm. "Everyday, I walk around with a reminder of what playing on the turf at Roosevelt, before PHL, Inc; used to be like."

With the new practice field at Vashon ready for the start of 2005 summer camp, the issue of safety was now not a concern. No longer would the Vashon football players have to endure the previously mentioned mile walk to Chambers Park to practice, a stroll that was life threatening each time it was made. As Vashon player Jerry Brown told the Post Dispatch, "It's less of a risk now. We don't have to walk through two 'hoods'. We don't have to worry about getting hurt wearing the wrong color shirt." Hitting the ground to avoid gun fire was a regular experience for Wolverine players on their way to the Park. "It's a whole lot more peaceful here (the new practice field)," said Vashon player DeVaughn Reece "You get a better workout instead of watching your back. When you catch a pass, you can worry about getting hit and not about getting shot."

Within a year of PHL, Inc.'s inception, praise from high sources began to echo down. St. Louis City Mayor Francis Slay – often at odds with, and a vocal critic of SLPS, in letter to PHL, Inc. dated October 2005 jumped on the speeding bandwagon. "Many organizations have ideas – your group put your ideas into action. It was my pleasure to visit Soldan High School in August to see the improvements you have made. It was just as you had planed, rocks, trash and debris had been removed from the fields, holes were filled; the field was seeded, striped and ready for play."

In a September 2006 Press Release, SLPS District Athletic Director Dave Cook said: "Their (*PHL, Inc.*) goal has remained the same for nearly two years, and that is to improve the conditions of our fields for the students who play sports."

Then Superintendent of the SLPS, Dr. Diana Bourisaw, chimed in with praise: "We are grateful for what *PHL, Inc.* is doing for our district and community," said Bourisaw. "Our plans are to continue to work with *PHL, Inc.* until all of our facilities are where they should be."

Forthcoming from Board of Alderman James Shrewsberry was this November of 2006 memo to *PHL, Inc*: "Thank you for inviting me to Vashon High School last week. I am very impressed with your good work and your efforts of behalf of the St. Louis Public Schools. I'm more than happy to assist you in any way possible."

The St. Louis Post-Dispatch also took notice. On March 5 2005, the Post did a follow up story on the progress of a program that had been inspired by its own reporting. "A remarkable, grass roots effort has sprung up on the dusty, barren playing fields of the city's Public High League. An extraordinary group of ordinary citizens responded to Post-Dispatch sports reporter Tom Wheatley's articles about the terrible condition of the city high schools' athletic fields.......forming *PHL Inc.*, a group of volunteers with the moxie and the means to help. It's an inspiring model of how good things can happen in the face of apathy, neglect and red tape."

In the spring of 2008, Kuhn was proud to announce a grant through a partnership with the city's National Football League franchise, the Rams, that had exciting possibilities. "It's a $200,000 matching grant for the conversion of Tandy Park in North St. Louis into a multi-use facility with artificial turf, a walking track, sprinting chute, bleachers, pavilions, concession stand and a bunch of other amenities," said Kuhn. "The facility will be right in front of Sumner High School. Sumner now has no outdoor facilities. The football, baseball and soccer teams practice in the park. (They) have state-champion sprinters from the past few years practicing in the school halls. It is one of the poorest sections of town." Commitments had been secured from area businesses for labor and materials. The biggest and most ambitious project yet undertaken by *PHL, Inc*, it was hoped, would be a shot in the arm to one of the city's least developed, and most poverty ridden areas.

For the opening of the 2007 season, *PHL, Inc.* and the Rams hit upon another innovative idea that proved to be a morale boosting home run for the city high school football teams. The group arranged with the Rams to allow league teams to scrimmage each other in the Rams domed stadium the Saturday morning before the start of the regular high school season. "That costs the Rams some money, but it was so well received we hope to do it again this August," Tallman said in the spring of 2008. "The turnout was amazing. Some schools filled a whole cheering section with supporters. The kids were thrilled."

So were the coaches. Sumner Coach Sorrell Harvey told the Post Dispatch, "Oh, man, the kids can't believe it, even the coaches are excited." Vashon coach Reggie Ferguson added, "I'm going to have to buy a new coaching outfit for this deal, a new hat or something."

Tallman and Kuhn's years of hard lobbying of the Rams was beginning to pay off. Many would rhetorically ask in a sarcastic tone, "what took so long?"

In 2006, the impressive list of improvements continued to grow. At the Central Visual and Performing Arts Academy (CVPA, the former Southwest High School) the field was re-graded and the sprinkler system (which had not run since 1992) was repaired and put in working order. Fescue sod was laid on the playing field. The stadium bleachers were repaired and painted. For the first time in years, bleachers on both sides of the CVPA field were usable. At Vashon, an in-ground sprinkler system was installed. A practice/P.E. field was graded and seeded. A fence around the perimeter (3,000 +/- linear feet) of the athletic complex was installed. Beaumont High School had its field graded and fescue sod put in place. A new sprinkler system was also installed. New goalposts, player benches and a scoreboard were purchased and installed. Roosevelt High School's concession stand was given a new roof. Labor intensive turf maintenance programs were begun at Vashon, Gateway, Roosevelt, Beaumont, CVPA and Soldan. Stadiums and bleachers were painted at CVPA, Gateway, Roosevelt and Soldan. Negotiations with a national corporation were begun on a deal to supply new scoreboards to the district. The arrangement would cost the district nothing, while creating income for the district within five years or less.

By 2007, the improvements to PHL facilities were continuing at a head spinning pace. Track repairs were completed and a new press box constructed at Gateway. A new asphalt entrance was laid at CVPA, along with bathroom upgrades. Decorative block walls and erosion repairs at CVPA's stadium were completed. New sprinkler systems were installed at CVPA, Gateway and Roosevelt. Stadium cracks were sealed, and locker room repairs at Soldan were completed. A new high school on the city's north side, to be known as Northwest Academy, also drew the resources of PHL, Inc. The Home Depot, the Rams and a national charitable organization called KaBOOM! and its supporters spent a month preparing the field and installing a state-of-the-art sprinkler system. In one day, volunteers from The Home Depot, Northwest, the Rams and PHL, Inc. - led by Rams wide receiver Isaac Bruce - installed the field's new turf and did numerous other improvement projects. Painting was also completed in time for the start of the 2007 season's pre season practice, at Roosevelt, CVPA, Gateway, Soldan and Northwest .

As of the spring of 2008, PHL, Inc continued to provide all of the maintenance and upkeep, with the exception of mowing, for all football fields in the PHL. "The district has outsourced the mowing to a private company. That has gone well," said Kuhn. "It frees up our crews to do other things. After a few problems early on, (the fields) are now mowed correctly." Over the years, PHL, Inc. has spent more than $150,000 on equipment ranging from football uniforms, pads and helmets, to cheerleader uniforms, wrestling shoes, basketballs, volleyballs, track uniforms, girls soccer uniforms and weight training equipment.

"Why did it get this bad?" Kuhn says he is often asked. "We don't know and we don't care," is his curt response. "All we are concerned with is remedying the problem. Look, if the district was able to take care of things on their own, it would have never gotten so bad in the first place." Tallman confers and continues: "They (SLPS) are not all of a sudden going to have the resources to take care of the improved fields. Athletic fields are high maintenance. We knew that going in. We are committed to the long term upkeep of these facilities. For two years, every time there was a game (football or boys and girls soccer) held on one of the fields we upgraded, we send our people, on our dime, out that day to get the fields ready. At times we had as many as three crews doing nothing three days a week but striping fields. Every striper the district owns is right back there in our warehouse. We still take care of the maintenance on all the stripers, keeping them running right."

Kuhn points out that their day to day maintenance responsibilities are progressively being delegated. "Nike has taken over the striping at Soldan. Coach Campbell does his own at Roosevelt – another reason we love the guy. Slowly, the schools are taking on that role. How long can we keep doing this? The original thought was five years and we'd bow out of the daily upkeep and turn it over to SLPS. Now we know that is not going to happen, it is only two years away. How much longer will we stay? However long it takes, it takes."

So where does *PHL, Inc* go from here? "Our eventual goal," explains Tallman, "is to set up an endowment fund to take care of upkeep and maintenance. We have made it very clear from the beginning that the fields are not 'ours', they belong to SLPS. However, letting them fall back into the state of the conditions of 2004, is not an option. It is going to take a lot of money, but a self supporting endowment is our future goal."

Can a comparison of *PHL, Inc.'s* growing involvement in the day to day responsibility of maintaining the SLPS's athletic fields be made to President George W. Bush's 2008 dilemma in Iraq? Was *PHL, Inc.*, a good idea born of noble intentions to eradicate a problem, one whose initial conquering took much less time and resources than expected, but now is bogged down in a perpetual state of commitment that seems to be never ending? "Never thought of it like that," chuckled Kuhn. "Look, we made it clear from the beginning that we did not want to take over, we just wanted to help." Kuhn follows with a statement that in 2008 would sound empathetic to the ears of George W. Bush: "someday, we have to back away. We are businessmen with a business to run. Our hope is that the people at SLPS can eventually, with the help of the endowment fund that Charlie mentioned, handle this on their own." How close is that day? "It's not here yet," says Kuhn. "You have to understand that the entire budget this year for the 13 high school athletic programs of city schools is 1.1 million dollars. Of that amount, over $950,000 will go to salaries. That leaves $7500 per school, for everything else. All sports, all needs. I don't know where all their (SLPS) money goes. We don't get into that. Bottom line, there is no money for PHL athletes. We are trying to fill that void."

Kuhn and Tallman point proudly to the before and after photos they have compiled of the different playing venues where *PHL, Inc.* has worked its magic. The color photos are striking, the improvements startling. Three ring binders contain photo after photo of the wretched "before" state of conditions of PHL fields, depicting rutted and uneven weed infested fields. The numerous "after" photos leap from the page and graphically show that *PHL, Inc.* makeovers have, time and again, produced thick green carpets of grass, replacing the rock hard, pot holed fields of embarrassments that a generation of PHL players had to endure.

For years, non-PHL area high schools had refused to schedule, on two year home and away contracts, non-district football games with PHL teams. They would only play if the PHL team was willing to travel to their superior facilities. In district contests, where the state activities association mandated two year home and away arrangements, the non-PHL schools cried long and hard to the state association about the horrible conditions at PHL "home" sites. But now, Kuhn can point proudly to 2006, when Chaminade, the exclusive and expensive all boys boarding school in St. Louis County, voluntarily scheduled an away game at a PHL site. In 2008, the schedule for the first Saturday in September shows traditional out-state powers Columbia Hickman and Jefferson City Helias traveling to the city to play a double header at Gateway Tech's revamped stadium, with PHL member schools Vashon and Gateway, respectfully, providing the opposition. On the same afternoon, St. Louis County's Eureka High School - whose football team has, for over 20 years, benefited from infused talents of city athletes attending Eureka under the voluntary desegregation program - will travel to play at Roosevelt. "Five years ago, there was not enough money in the bank to get teams of this caliber and tradition to play a game of their own free will at a PHL facility," says Kuhn.

The ripple effect of good spawned by PHL, Inc's efforts is hard to calculate. How many of the hundreds of additional young men, whose numbers have swollen the ranks of PHL football rosters since the improved facilities have been available, have stayed in school for only the chance to play football? How many will graduate and become productive citizens because of a diploma that might otherwise have been neglected if not for the football carrot at the end of the educational stick? "We hope this program can become a template for other large urban city school systems," says Tallman. "That someone in Detroit or New York or Chicago can hear about what has happened in St. Louis and replicate it in their city."

Kuhn's "down home, aw shucks" summation of the first three years of PHL, Inc: "Hey, there'll be issues no matter what you do. It's been an adventure, but it's been a good adventure."

In the spring of 2008, three years since the inception of PHL, Inc., morale, along with school and community support for Public High League football was, at a 30 year high water mark. Participation rates had doubled at all city public high schools, even tripling at some - all proof positive of a quote attributed to the ironically named movie, Field of Dreams: "If you build it, they will come."

Some men spend a lifetime amassing "things." There is no denying that these peerless paragons of power cut a wide swath of influence in the short time allotted each of us on this earth. But in the end, the legacy we leave is not what we own, but what we give. In his book *How Full Is Your Bucket*, Author Tom Rath theorizes that we each possess a figurative bucket and dipper. Through daily interaction with others, we are constantly depleting or replenishing the bucket of those we come into contact with. If we choose to interact in a positive and supportive way, says Rath, we then help fill the bucket of our fellow man, and at the same time replenish our own bucket, leading to a contented life of fulfillment and satisfaction.

In Tom Rath's world, Thom Kuhn, Charlie Tallman and the other volunteers of PHL, Inc., have buckets that are overflowing. Their unbridled, no strings attached philanthropy, has given the teenage football players of the St. Louis, MO Public High League a brief reprise from the daily grind of coming of age in a harsh and unforgiving city. In a culture where most inner city youth are forced to grow up much too fast, *PHL, Inc.* has provided a gift whose value is beyond measure: the chance to be forever young - suspended Peter Pan style - in a perpetual state of youthful exuberance and celebration. Due to the generosity of strangers, the athletes of the Public High League now play on athletic fields of grass so green it hurts your eyes, so soft you never want to leave. "Man," says

Roosevelt quarterback Arlando Bailey, "I just want to stay right here, right now, and play football forever."

Football is a game that can trace its origins to the English sport of rugby. Tight formations and brutal force were the traits needed to be successful in the late 19th century early days of American Football. As the game evolved, offenses began to spread out with the invention and legalization of the forward pass in 1905, leading to an emphasis placed on speed, quickness and deception.

A very predictable pattern in coaching developed over the history of the sport; high school football coaches are almost always several years behind their college counterparts as they emulated the newest and most successful innovations being put on Saturday afternoon display at the great collegiate stadiums around the nation.

In the early years of the 20th century, legendary coach Pop Warner, with his star player at Carlisle Indian School, Jim Thorpe, developed and fine tuned the single wing formation. The name for the formation was derived by the alignment of the four backs, with the tailback five yards directly behind the center and the other three backs aligned in a wing between the guard and end line positions. The center would directly snap the ball to the tailback who had the option to pass, run or hand the ball off to one of the other three backs. Fakes and deception were critical to keeping the defense off balance.

In the 1920's, Notre Dame, under the leadership of Knute Rockne, took the single wing principles of timing and deception and developed what became known as the Notre Dame Box Shift. The four backs would be put into movement slightly ahead of the snap of the ball, and the precision of the backfield shifts made the offense almost impossible to stop. So effective were the Irish with their shift, that overmatched opponents demanded rule changes to counteract the offense's deadly efficiency. Much as the three second and goaltending rules were implemented in basketball to off set the domination of Wilt Chamberlin in the 1950's, the rules of 1920's football were changed to do what no defense could, stymie Rockne's Notre Dame Box Shift. A rule was adopted that made it mandatory that backs must be set for at least one second before the ball is snapped. With a later modification that allows for one back to be in motion parallel to the line of scrimmage before the snap, this same rule is still on the books today.

In the 1930's, the next major formation innovation was developed by University of Chicago, and later Stanford University head coach, Clark Shaughnessy, considered the father of the T Formation. Shaughnessy brought the quarterback up under center to take the snap directly from the center. A rule change in 1933 helped the popularity of the T-formation. A forward pass could now be thrown anywhere behind the line of scrimmage, instead of only between the ends as had been the previous rule. By 1953, the last team in the NFL to run the Single Wing, the Pittsburgh Steelers, had converted to the T formation.

In the late 1960's, the University of Texas introduced the wishbone formation. The "Bone" moved the fullback up from the T formation, to only a yard behind the quarterback. The signal calling QB now would have the option of handing the ball to the fullback on a quick dive play, run the ball himself around end, or pitch to a trailing halfback. This "triple option" proved lethal for nearly twenty years. By the early 1970's, almost all of the great active coaches of the college game had embraced the wishbone. Bear Bryant at Alabama, Darrell Royal of Texas, Woody Hayes at Ohio State and Lou Holtz at first, Arkansas, and later at the University of Notre Dame; won numerous national championships riding to glory and riches upon the triple option wishbone offense.

Limitations, more so than weaknesses, of the wishbone eventually were identified by defensive coaches. The wishbone quarterback would take a terrible beating as he would be hit by the defensive end every time he slid down the line of scrimmage to execute the option play. In theory, the defensive end was the man that the quarterback would "option," and was always left unblocked, allowed a free and unabated shot at the quarterback on every option play. Another major detraction of the wishbone was that the forward pass was almost a non existent weapon in a team's offensive arsenal, and therefore made it very difficult for a team to come back from a large deficit. Wishbone quarterbacks were chosen more for their running ability than passing skills. The wishbone also was a high risk offense that would result in a large number of fumbles, making developing consistency and ball control on offense an allusive accomplishment. By the mid 1990's, the wishbone had all but disappeared from the college football landscape.

The wishbone is also the one and only major college offensive development, due to the beating the Quarterback took, that did not catch on in the NFL.

The latest in-vogue formation to ripple down to the high school level from the collegiate ranks is the spread offense, an off-shoot of the NFL's West Coast Offense, perfected in the late 80's and early 90's by Bill Walsh and the San Francisco 49ers. Quarterback Joe Montana, a low draft pick and bench warmer for most of his college career at Notre Dame, hitched a ride on the West Coast offense express, riding it all the way to the Pro Football Hall of Fame in Canton, OH.

The strategy the spread is based on evolves around a series of short, high percentage passes. The quarterback is given great latitude in "reading" the defense, both before and after the snap of the ball, making quick decisions based upon defensive responses to offensive formations and the pass patterns being run by receivers.

The spread is most often initiated from the shotgun formation, moving the quarterback out from under center, back five to seven yards off the line of scrimmage, allowing for a long and direct snap from the center. The shotgun, by moving the QB away from the line of scrimmage, allowed the quarterback of less stature – Montana stood barely 6 foot tall – to be more effective through improved sight lines in seeing over large onrushing linemen. Football historians are quick to point out the similarities between the spread and the 1920's single wing formation.

Trickle down has always been the process for innovation amongst high school football coaches. Going back to the early days of the last century, all the way through today's wide open passing games, trends that take hold in college require about five years before showing up on the high school level. This is very apparent in 2008 as high school after high school began deploying the spread offense. The Roosevelt Roughriders are no exception.

Throughout the Spring and Summer of 2008, the Roughrider's offensive skill players - quarterbacks, running backs and receivers - spent countless hours honing their intricate pass patterns and reads, essential for the success of the spread offense. The change is 180 degrees from the previous run oriented style favored by Coach Campbell, a running back in his own playing days.

It was obvious in the early summer days of 2008, the transformation of Campbell to a pass first mentality, would not be an easy one. He would declare that with the talents of Bailey at quarterback, Carter at running back; along with the stable of outstanding speedy and athletic receivers that the Roosevelt arsenal owned, the spread, with its emphasis on speed, was the natural offense for the Roughriders.

Another caveat that Campbell was quick to seize upon during the off season, as he tried to convince others, and himself, of the wisdom of adopting the spread was that his undersized offensive line would now depend more upon speed and quickness, as opposed to size and strength, which was so paramount to the success of the more physical running game. Emphasis on the athletic ability of the offensive line, something PHL linemen had often before been short of, would help alleviate the decades old Achilles heel of city league teams: offensive line play.

However, it was often difficult to determine, in the summer of 2008, when listening to Campbell preach the wondrous potential of the spread, who he was trying hardest to win over - the listener or himself. One morning he would proclaim, "we will throw it 70% of the time. We will be unstoppable." By afternoon, the percentage had fallen to "probably 50% run, 50% pass. We got to keep the balance." By the evening, the scales had tipped back to "60% run, 40% pass" with the promise of, "we will establish the run first, then when we do go to the spread, it will open up our passing schemes because the defense will have to respect our running game."

Quarterback Arlando Bailey's intelligence and his new found off season devotion to studying the art of playing quarterback in the spread, weighed heavily on the mind of Campbell as he wrestled with his personal commitment to this new wide open philosophy of offensive football. Bailey, who throughout his playing career, had been told numerous times that he did not have a big time quarterback's stature and should consider a move to running back or the line, embraced the spread as a way to break the mold of the prototypical 6'4" drop back passer. Bailey was quick to point out that he was the same height - 5'10 - as the University of Missouri's 2008 Heisman Trophy candidate; quarterback Chase Daniels. In 2007, Daniels had used the spread offense to lead the long suffering Missouri program to unexpected heights and to the cusp of a National Championship, a laughable thought only a few years earlier.

Bailey saw in the new offensive system the stage he needed to prove wrong all those past naysayers who questioned if quarterback was his natural position. "I love the spread," proclaimed Bailey in the summer of 2008. "It lets me do all the things I am good at. I can read the defense, I can make quick decisions, and I can take what the defense gives us."

Campbell reinforced the thoughts of Bailey. "The spread is made for CBC (Bailey). He is like a coach on the field. We can not only go to the spread, we can also go to the no huddle. That will help us when we see the county schools and all the large rosters they have. With the spread, we are always on the attack. We don't huddle between plays. We don't allow the defense time for situational substitutions. They may have 80 players and we may only have 40, but they can only get 11 on the field at a time and, if we go with the No Huddle, it limits their ability to use those big rosters through situational substitutions. It also helps our linemen. Our smaller linemen can now compete with the bigger lines we see in the county. Quickness is now as important as brute strength. We will now zone block more. You don't have to over power the guy across from you, you just have to contain him."

Coach Campbell had a rare chance in late July to stop, catch his breath and reflect on the condition of his football team. He appeared to finally be content with his team's progress as the summer drew to a close. Dressed in his normal summer attire of nylon shorts and tee shirt, seated beneath a shade tree behind the east end zone at Roughrider Stadium, he eagerly discussed with a visitor his perception of where his team stood. The offense had consistently developed over the summer in its emergence into the complexities of the spread offense. His defense was once again loaded with lean and aggressive athletes. The commitment to the program by his core group of 30 players left him pleased. At this point in time, he stated that his coaches and players had done everything within their power to prepare for the upcoming season. For one of the few times over the summer, Campbell had a content look upon his face. It was a state of calm that was short lived.

Campbell was asked if he had a kicker on his roster. The visitor even injected that the road to the state playoffs could easily come down to a made or missed field goal or extra point. Campbell's demeanor immediately went into coaching mode, his mind now back into a perpetual state of worry. "CBC can kick if we need him to. I am sure we (have) some other guys out there, I just don't know yet." Campbell's eyes clearly sent the message: "did you have to bring this up when I was just starting to relax?" His mind now totally engaged on improving his football team, Campbell retrieved a nugget from his memory, "there is a kid who talked to me last spring…yeah, an African kid, plays on the soccer team here. He said he wants to play on the team. Maybe he can kick."

Racial quirks in terms of athletic prowess in the United States are an interesting social phenomena to break down. For example, African Americans dominate the rosters of the National Basketball Association. Why? Are there genetic factors at work that give black athletes physical advantages that are paramount to success in basketball? Is there a scientific backing to the presumption that "White men can't jump?" Or is the advantage social in root? Why have so many Caucasian players from Europe been so successful in the NBA, when their racial kin from the United States are today almost totally absent from the upper level college and professional basketball ranks?

Or, go to an integrated and racially diverse high school track meet anywhere in the USA, and you will find the sprints dominated by black athletes, while the vast majority of participants in the distance races are white. Why? Are blacks genetically deficient in terms of the aerobic capacity and the oxygen delivery system needed for top flight distance running? But watch any Olympic distance race and the front runners are dominated by the African nations, in particular, Kenya and Ethiopia. Why have American black athletes not found the same level of success in distance running in this country?

In the USA, kicking a football has become almost the total domain of white athletes. In college football, a black placekicker or punter is as rare as a white defensive corner back. Now that the quarterback position has been integrated, the lone position in football left to be total devoid of black athletes, is that of the kicker. Even historically black colleges like Grambling often will have only one or two white members on the team, most often kickers.

African-American place kickers in the National Football league have been rare. George Mingo, a high school drop out from Akron, OH, who mastered football in the military, became the first in 1960, when he played for the Denver Broncos. As opposed to today's kickers, who are specialists and do nothing but kick; Mingo was also an accomplished wide receiver. Few have followed the path Mingo blazed. A list of Black Place Kickers to have adorned National Football League rosters is a short one: Aherb Travenio: San Diego (1964-65). Obed Ariri: Tampa Bay (1984), Washington (1987). Donald Egwebuike: Tampa Bay (1985-89), Minnesota (1990). Cedric Oglesby: Arizona (2001).

The only two to make significant contributions to their teams were Ariri and Egwebuike. Both were Nigerians who were recruited to Clemson University to play soccer. Ariri actually taught Egwebuike to kick a football. After a record setting year with Tampa Bay in 1984, in an ironic twist, the mentor Ariri was replaced on the Bucs roster by the his pupil, Egwebuike.

Ariri's short career was, for all purposes, finished. Today, he drives a cab in Tampa, FL. Egwebuike, after several seasons with the Bucs, became caught up in an international drug sting. He was arrested and accused of attempting to smuggle cocaine into the United States. The Bucs placed him on waivers. He was later cleared of the drug charges, but the stigma remained. After a short second chance with Minnesota, he too drifted off into football oblivion.

In 2007, for the entire season, Roosevelt attempted only 14 point after touchdown kicks. A puny total of 6 were successful, all made by graduated senior Michael Johnson. On the other 17 occasions that Roosevelt hit pay dirt that season they attempted a two point conversion. The Roughriders have not attempted a field goal in over three years.

For the entire season of 2007, PHL teams connected on only two successful field goal attempts, both kicked by James Latimore of Gateway Tech. Both three pointers came in the same game against Beaumont. In the other 112 contests that PHL teams were involved in, not one successful field goal occurred. With kicking such an important phase of the game, having no one on the roster capable of successfully kicking the ball through the uprights, puts a team at a marked disadvantage before the game even begins.

When playing each other, the lack of kickers in the PHL is a wash, with neither team having a disadvantage or advantage. But when city teams step out of the PHL, conference members find themselves once again not on an equal playing field with their county and private school rivals, most of whom have at least competent kickers on their rosters. Responsibility for this disadvantage falls squarely at the feet (no pun intended) of the PHL Coaches. "We don't stress it (kicking)," admitted Campbell. "I never kicked. I know nothing about it." Obviously, a PHL team with an accomplished kicker would find themselves at a distinct competitive advantage within the PHL. On a July afternoon, Coach Campbell searched his memory desperately trying to recall the name of the young man from Africa who wanted to trade his soccer cleats for football spikes.

Mohammad Dukly was serious about coming out for the Roosevelt football team. The junior had watched the game as a fan since immigrating to the United States at the age of 14. "We have the NFL channel at home so I have seen a lot of games, Dukly states in broken English highlighted by a heavy West African accent. Dukly's native language is Mandingo, a common language of most West African nations. He says his English has improved markedly since moving to St. Louis and enrolling at Roosevelt in November of 2007.

Dukly is a native of the West African nation of Liberia. In 1996, when Mohammad was two years old, his entire extended family fled during the nation's rapidly deepening civil war. The family settled into refugee camps in the neighboring nation of Guinea. For the next 12 years, along with tens of thousands of other Liberian nationals, the family shuffled between refuge camps in the Guinea capital city of Conakry. "It was not a good life," says Mohammad. "We always had to move. We lived in tents. It was very hard."

In 2004, Dukly's family moved to Virginia to become reunited with an older sister, Ciata. The older sibling had come to the USA to attend college, subsequently married, and hence could now qualify as a sponsor for her family. Dukly and his family entered the USA under the Federal Government's Refugee program.

After two years in Virginia, Dukly's parents decided to return to Liberia. Not wanting to leave the United States, Mohammad made the decision to relocate to St. Louis and live with his father's brother. The family consisted of his uncle and his wife, Rasytou, and their seven month old daughter. Mohammad's brother, 17 year old Fabloe, also made the move to St. Louis and, along with Mohammad, enrolled at Roosevelt High School. Mohammad's twin brother, Moris, chose to stay in Virginia.

Mohammad's uncle, upon his move to the Gateway City, had settled into a south side St. Louis neighborhood predominated by African immigrants. The uncle worked hard to establish his stake in the American dream. Working full time while attending college at night in Chicago, he earned a bachelor's degree in Social Work, eventually moving to St. Louis and obtaining a job as a counselor with the Missouri Department of Mental Health. With a solid middle class income, he had the resources to support his wife, infant daughter and two teenage nephews in a fashion that was the envy of many in the Liberian enclave that had developed in the Tower Grove Park area.

Dukly found acclimation to American high school life in Virginia to be at first a struggle. The language barrier was immense and a formidable obstacle. Watching hours of American television, he says, was a helpful tool in becoming more proficient in the English language. Academic work that was often confusing to him, as well as a limited social awareness of American customs, frustrated the young man who takes his education very seriously. "Education is the reason I wanted to stay in this county and not go back to Africa with my parents. I can have a much better life here. There is no opportunity in the refugee camps back in Guinea and because of the civil war in Liberia, it is too dangerous for someone my age to go back to my home country. In no time, one side or the other would force me to fight for them. I am at the age that they like to take boys and turn them into soldiers. If I had stayed, by the time I was 12, I would have been killing people or I would have been killed myself. I like it much better here at Roosevelt."

Mohammad Dukly brought a much different perspective in his view of the life of a teenage student than most of his Roosevelt classmates. Although the environment around Roosevelt could be harsh, in no way did it compare to what Mohammad had left behind in Africa. "If I can get a good education in the United States, then I can find a good paying job and send money back to help my family in Africa. I have to study very hard. My whole life depends on my education," said the 16 year old.

Muhammad had never kicked a football before July 2008. His first attempts were comical to his new teammates. His kicks were of such a low trajectory, that the center and offensive linemen set up to block for him, expressed an urgent desire to protect their manhood. "Dude going to hit me in the nuts kicking like that," was the exasperation of fear expressed by one lineman. Much to the hooting delight of the players on the sideline, the entire line would collapse to the ground when the thud of foot meeting leather was heard. A flustered and embarrassed Dukly soon learned that the art of kicking a football is much different than kicking a soccer ball. On his first attempts, Mohammad would sprint to the ball, kicking it with his instep and driving the ball in a line drive, the perfect soccer kick. He soon learned that getting lift under the football, and getting the ball aloft quickly, with good height, was the key in not having his kicks blocked – by either the hard rushing defensive line, or the back sides of his blockers on the offensive line.

After several practice sessions, Mohammad had learned to make his approach to the kick in a compact two step stride. Right, Left, Kick; he would repeat silently to himself as he lined up a practice kick. Working with a live holder and center were also keys to his development. Quarterback Bailey – having lost his incumbent job as kicker – became the team's new holder. Mississippi Sanford, in further testament to his all around football skills, was the team's deep snapper. Within several days, both players – holding the lofty status as senior leaders - could see the improvement in the young man from Africa, and realized he could be an important cog in the Roosevelt offense.

Dukly became a constant and lonely figure at the far end of the practice field, as he daily worked alone on perfecting his new found kicking skills. Within two weeks, he was gaining accuracy and distance to his kicks, successful up to a range of 45 yards. When the team would conduct live kicking drills during the early stages of daily practice sessions, Mohammad would, on occasion, exhibit his nervousness, too eager to impress his new teammates and coaches. At other times, considering his lack of experience and practice at kicking an American football, his performance was inspiring hope in the coaches that the football gods had dropped an unexpected offensive gift into their laps. During two a days at the end of the summer, on an live extra point attempt, Dukly struck the ball square in the "sweet spot," driving it not only through the uprights 20 yards away, but also over the restraining wall at the east end of the stadium and onto

Gravois Road, a good 30 additional yards beyond the goal posts. The players and the coaches stood with mouths open in awe as the ball rose in trajectory and carried onto the busy thoroughfare. As his teammate's acceptance grew, so did Dukly's confidence in his kicking skills.

A recent addition to the high school summer football training regimen is the growth of 7 on 7 passing leagues. Similar to informal summer basketball leagues and competition camps, the organized setting of the events offer coaches the opportunity to work with their skilled players - four backs and two ends – in simulated competitive game situations, against defenses composed of another schools linebackers and defensive backs – in reality six offensive players against seven defenders. Pads and helmets are not worn. An offensive player is downed upon touch. Rushing the quarterback is not allowed. Neither is running the football past the line of scrimmage. The snap is simulated by the ball being placed on a stool, the quarterback snatching the ball to signal the start of the play. If the team employees a "shot gun" formation, the ball will be spiraled back to the quarterback, simulating the five yard snap from center.

Rules vary from league to league, but the quarterback has a set time to throw the ball, usually four to five seconds, or the defense is credited with a sack and the ball is downed at that spot. The field is normally shortened to 50 yards and it is not unusual to see two games, involving four different schools, going on simultaneously at opposite ends of the field. All offensive drives start on the 50 yard line. The offense has four downs to make twenty yards – by crossing the 30 yard line. Once the initial first down is achieved, the offense faces a goal to go situation, with four downs to score, regardless of where the ball was spotted after the initial first down. The scenario sounds much like a game of touch football, but the demeanor of the players, observed by chastising and demanding coaches, is of a much more serious tone than Sunday afternoon touch games played in the back yard.

With linemen totally excluded from play, both on offense and defense, it is center stage for skilled position players to show their passing and receiving skills. PHL teams feasted on county teams during these summer pick up games, proof once again of the dominance of county teams in the area of line play. Remove the respective five linemen on each side of the line of scrimmage, and speed became the dominant trait for success in 7 on 7 games. Thriving on this maximizing of their team's inherent offensive strength - receivers and backs with speed and good hands, accompanied by a quarterback with more than adequate skills when given time to throw the ball - Roosevelt took these summer games with a seriousness lacking amongst their county and private school rivals.

"We get a lot of good out of seven on seven scrimmages," said Coach Campbell. "It shows what kind of skill-player talent we have. With us going more to the spread (offense) this year, it also gives us a lot of reps to work on our receiver's routes and our quarterback reads. It gives us a chance to get our kids thinking football. Go by the playgrounds in the summer and see how many kids are playing pick up basketball. The playgrounds are packed with summer basketball players. There are also numerous leagues in the summer for basketball players. A basketball coach knows that summer is a very important time to develop kids. It is also time for them to get (the basketball player) exposure. AAU has done that and most college basketball coaches recruit more in the summer than they do in the season. (Much to the chagrin of high school basketball coaches, in many cases the AAU summer team coach becomes the main adult of contact for a college in hopes of recruiting a talented high school hoopster). Seven on 7 has done that same thing for football. You can see a lot of players in one site. We go to Forest Park every summer for the Demetrious Johnson 7 on 7 Tournament. There will be 30 schools there from all over the St. Louis area, east and west side. 7 on 7s (games) are a very important time for our team development and a highlight for our summer training program. Our kids love it."

On Tuesday evenings in June and July, Roosevelt hosted a loosely organized seven on seven league. The structure was rag tag, at best, and it was seldom known - often no more than a guess prior to the starting time - how many schools would attend on any particular Tuesday evening. Yet the atmosphere was always one of excitement, almost carnival like in fun and energy, as and energized mood of anticipation settled around Roughrider Stadium each summer Tuesday evening.

Much like the neighborhood playground was to summer basketball, Roosevelt High Roughrider Stadium had become the St. Louis area's football enthusiasts favorite 7 on 7 venue. Parents, girl friends, former players, neighborhood hangers-ons, and even an occasional fan from outside the area who simply wanted a late summer dose of high school football, all knew that in the summer of 2008, Roosevelt was the place to be on summer Tuesday evenings.

Most of Roosevelt's linemen would stick around after the team's weight lifting session in their summer temporary weight "room" – outside the stadium concession stand - but they were simply spectators, offering support and encouragement. Conversely, the skilled position players basked in the limelight, and their pre game demeanor showed just such.

On one particular late July evening, the buzz was ratcheted up a notch more than normal, when word was passed that the traditional area county powerhouse, the Mehlville Panthers, were on their way up from South St. Louis County to test the 7 on 7 waters at Roosevelt High. As many Roughrider fan would be quick to point out, it was not a long journey for many of the Mehlville players, since for over 20 years the Panther dynasty had been built upon the fleet footed desegregation city kids who rode the bus south each day to attend Mehlville High School. Since the early 80's, many city coaches had groused about the cozy relationship between Mehlville Coaches and the leaders at the city's Mathews-Dickey Boys and Girls Clubs. While it would have been illegal to coerce an athlete to attend a school strictly because of athletic influences, most knew the pattern had been too long standing to simply credit random luck. A junior high age black city athlete who showed football potential in the Boys Club's highly organized youth football league, had a good chance of ending up at Mehlville High School. Few area football enthusiasts believed that the year after year talent haul of Mehlville was just happenstance. "They (city athletes) start staying home and Mehlville takes a lot of ass kickings playing with their own home grown talent," miffed one PHL coach in the summer of 2008.

As speculated, and much to the delight of the 100 or so spectators gathered at Roughrider Stadium, Mehlville did show on this particular weather perfect evening. The racial make up of their contingent from Mehlville was interesting. Four white coaches and ten athletes; nine black and one white, made up the South County team's entry. The Mehlville school district is over 93% white. A safe assumption was that most of the backs and receivers wearing the Mehlville green practice jerseys would lay the heads that evening on pillows in domiciles located within the city limits of St. Louis; many within walking distance of Roosevelt High School. Such arrangements always left PHL Coaches like Campbell dreaming of "what if." It also made a victory over such carpet bagging teams very sweet, even in a non descript, and meaningless, Summer 7 on 7 League contest.

The body language and the tension that Mehlville's arrival generated on the RHS sideline was indicative of the special meaning for the RHS coaches and players for this seemingly meaningless pick up game. "I am fired up. We need to make a statement tonight," said Coach Campbell, loudly and to no one in particular, as his players stretched around him. Running Back Antonio Carter pawed at the ground nervously as he stretched from a seated position within the semi circle of his teammates. The normally poker faced quarterback, Arlando Bailey, also showed signs of anxiousness. "Man, you talk too much. Go somewhere else and be silly," Bailey admonished Rene "Man-Child" Faulk, his loud and clowning teammate. Since Faulk and his line mates would not play that evening, Faulk had not the sense of urgency of Bailey. The scolded lineman bade a quick retreat back to lifting weights at the concession stand.

On the first play from scrimmage, Mehlville's quarterback, a left handed African American, rolled to his left and fired a perfectly thrown 40 yard spiral to a streaking receiver who, upon securing the pass, would stride untouched into the Roughrider end zone. It was as if the collective wind, built up throughout a promising and productive off season, had been instantly taken out of the Roosevelt sails. It might be only a summer pick up game that had no meaning outside of personal pride, but the confidence factor associated with a good performance by Roosevelt, staged against Mehlville - the traditional bully and raider of city league talent - was something this team needed badly.

In the flash of one pass play, the Roosevelt swagger was gone. All the boasting now appeared as only a poorly veiled attempt to convince themselves that they could compete on the same level as a state power like Mehlville. Nothing more than false bravado, now suddenly exposed for its worthlessness. And this was 7 on 7. What happens when the line is factored in? The doubt was ominously evident in the eyes of the team in red jerseys How quickly doubt had taken over the sideline was both amazing and troubling to Roosevelt supporters.

Assistant Coach Darren Wade, in charge of the defense, went into immediate damage control. He made no attempt to conceal his passion or his displeasure. "Heads up, right now," he commanded. "You scared, then get out. I'll find me someone who is not scared." Several Roosevelt defensive backs argued and bickered amongst themselves, in an animated discussion as to who had blown the coverage responsible for allowing the easy touchdown pass.

As Wade circled the defensive wagons on the sideline, Arlando Bailey and the offense took to the field. Under the rules of 7 on 7, a touchdown is worth 7 points. An interception credits the defensive team with three points. After Bailey's first pass attempt, the Riders were down 10-0, an ignominious start for a team who had wanted to "make a statement." A look at the body language of the veteran Mehlville coaches was one of a confident group who had seen this same scenario play out in countless City vs. County battles over the last 20 years. Once again on the offense, it took the visitors only two plays to make their next first down. The third play of the series saw a wide open green clad receiver drop a perfectly thrown pass, with no red Roosevelt jersey within 10 yards, negating what would have been an easy touchdown. After this unforced error by the offense, on the next play RHS middle linebacker George Bell somehow became invisible to the previous unshakeable and highly efficient Mehlville QB who now laid a pass right into the chest of the Roosevelt linebacker. Bell held on for the interception. Mehlville 10, Roosevelt 3.

Bailey and the offense, upon retaking the field after the Mehlville turnover, wasted no time in scoring. Two swing passes to Running Back Antonio Carter moved the ball into the red zone. Bailey, on a roll out to his left, found a streaking Quadricous - better known by all as Mississippi - Sanford cutting across the grain in the back of the end zone. Bailey's laser shot, impressively thrown on the run, found its mark. Suddenly the slate stood Mehlville 10, Roosevelt 10.

Just as suddenly, the swagger was back in the strut of the team in red. Coach Campbell showed no restraint in praising Bailey as he left the field. Bailey had run the spread offense to perfection. He had "read" the defense and followed the proper "check downs" as he looked to find an open receiver in a predetermined progressive order. Sanford had been Bailey's fourth option on the particular route that resulted in the Touchdown, but had been the correct choice. "Take what they give you. All day, dude, we can do this all day. Way to use your head CBC," praised Campbell.

On Mehlville's next possession another wide open green clad receiver streaked down the RHS side line. The QB spotted him instantly, and lofted a soft pass down the left sideline in an attempt to lead his receiver and allow him to catch the pass in full stride as he crossed the goal line. So confident was the receiver of an impending touchdown catch that he let out a hoot - a loud mocking cry of "yoooo" - as he broke into the open along the Roosevelt sideline.

What the Mehlville QB did not see was that Roosevelt was in a "Cover 2" defense, the two defensive safeties each taking one deep half of the field. The distance a long pass to the end zone would have to travel would allow for the ample and sufficient time needed for the safety to see the pass thrown and then break on the ball in the direction it was thrown. The sideline receiver was not really open. The Mehlville offense had failed to read the defense and had been duped into throwing the pass right where the defense wanted it thrown. The RHS safety, Sanford, made the easy interception.

The Mehlville receiver who had "hooted" for the pass that led to the interception, found himself in the unfavorable position of the vicinity of the RHS sideline. The Riders let him have it, serenading him with mocking "hoots" of their own. The swagger was back, indeed.

The scrimmage ended with Roosevelt on the winning side of a 27-20 score. Did the outcome have any validity or relevance to any prognosis of how the two teams would fare in a full contact 11 on 11 regular season game: probably not. What the outcome did accomplish for Coach Campbell and his athletes was a validation that their hard work in the offseason was paying off. "Last year, we would have quit. Not this year," Campbell stated as he praised his players in a 50 yard line team meeting at the completion of the scrimmage. "We are taking it to another level this year, baby," Campbell crowed. His pronouncement was met with hearty agreement from his players.

As the sun set over Roughrider Stadium on this hot July evening, there was a strong feeling of accomplishment amongst the home team partisans. The players had worked hard and now they had seen deductive and real proof - albeit in only a modified non-descript summer scrimmage - that they were making real progress. Both players and coaches knew it would be a major stretch to claim after a win in a 7 on 7 scrimmage that they could now compete on the lofty level of a county powerhouse like Mehlville. The jury would remain out until Roosevelt could show, in a real game, that its improved play in the trenches on both sides of the line of scrimmage had moved them to the legitimate rank of area contender. All knew that many future obstacles lie in the long road ahead with much hard work remaining to be done.

But for one summer night, at least, it didn't matter. The coaches would allow the players to bask in their earned success. They would, for a brief time, take the same luxury for themselves. The world of the Roosevelt Roughriders was now, for the time being at least, spinning in greased grooves. A comforting and empowering aura permeated the humid summer dusk air. The false bravado of previous years was now giving way to a quiet optimism, fueled by the giddiness of a triumph over a long time boogie man foe from the County.

Let tomorrow bring what it may, but this night was one for the books.

As July turned into August, DeAndre Campbell appeared to be a man in dire need of a vacation. The problem was, his work load would soon explode in the number of hours required of him, and the pace would not slacken at any time over the course of the next three months.

At a time when 24 hours a day was not sufficient to complete all tasks now demanded of Campbell, a vacation was out of the question.

Campbell was a man pulled in many directions. The bags under his eyes, testament to not enough sleep, the edge in his voice a clue to the intense pressure he could now feel taking over his life. Football season was here, and ready or not, the season opening game opponent, county powerhouse Eureka High School, was poised ominously on the horizon. Campbell was also now walking with a distinct limp and had developed a nagging cough he couldn't seem to shake.

Summer Football Camp with its torturous two a day practices, once a right of passage for a high school football team, has all but disappeared from the landscape of prep football regimens. A high school football coach in the past could almost always count on at least two weeks, perhaps as much as four, of total focus in the pre season to prepare his team for the upcoming season. The period would take place from the time a state association would allow for the start of official practice –sometime from early to the middle of August – until the start of the school year, normally around Labor Day.

Today, with many high schools starting the fall term as early as the middle of August, and with most coaches under contract to attend mandatory teacher's meetings for at least one week prior to the opening of the school term; no time remains on the August calendar for pre-season high school football camps. Old timers bemoan this loss of a venue to forge the skills of not only football, but also to instill toughness and togetherness that would help a team develop the fighting spirit so paramount to meeting the challenges of the upcoming season. "We use to weed them out during two a days," lamented long time PHL Coach and Roosevelt Assistant George Simmons. "If they were still on the team when school started, that meant they survived two a days and were real players."

During summer two a days, or training camp as it was sometimes referred to, football became a 24/7 commitment from players and coaches alike. Many teams, in an attempt to eliminate all outside distractions: girl friends, over protective parents, part time jobs, cars and other such youthful pursuits, would load their would be teenage warriors on buses and take their team to a remote location to hold camp. The prevailing thought was, the more Spartan the facilities and location, the better.

In order to instill discipline through long torturous practices, in 1954 Coach Paul "Bear" Bryant took his first Texas A&M Aggies team to the desolate locale of Junction, Texas. Lore has it that Bryant transported over 150 athletes to Junction on five buses. Two weeks later, only one bus - so the story goes - was needed to transport the 30 survivors back to campus. The group that persevered became legendary, immortalized through books such as _The Junction Boys_ by Jim Dent, which was later turned into a hit made for TV movie by the same name.

Jack Pardee grew up in a west Texas town so small the local high school did not have enough boys enrolled to play regular 11 man football. The local team competed against other such small ranching towns with the same numbers problem in a mutant form of the game known as 6 man football. (Small schools in Northwest MO play a similar game, but with 8 players to a side.) Pardee went on to a long time career as an All-Pro NFL linebacker with the Washington Redskins, eventually becoming the head coach of the DC based team.

Pardee was one of the 30 who survived Bryant's 1954 camp. He later told ESPN.go: "What Coach Bryant did was build a foundation. We developed a trust in each other. Having survived Junction, we knew our teammates would give all they had. It's a team sport, and we learned to depend on each other. You see those players today who make a tackle and beat their chest? They would only do that once for Coach Bryant. Coach Bryant's major theme was 'Don't be a quitter.' He drummed into us that we can't quit on ourselves, our teammates, our family and our friends. He said it's easy to play in the first quarter, but how will you play in the fourth quarter? Junction was all about preparing for the fourth quarter."

The Movie *Remember the Titans* also glorified the important role that "two a days" play in forming team chemistry and bonding. The setting is the volatile year of 1971, amidst the desegregation of the Alexander, VA public school system. When the town's black high school is closed and its students moved to previously all white TC Williams High School, the town began to look all too similar like one more battleground for the school racial desegregations wars so common in the South in the 1960s and 1970s. Adding fuel to the racially charged fire is the demotion to assistant coaching status of TC Williams popular and successful white coach, Bill Yoast. He is replaced by a black man, Herman Boone. The story, documented by Gary Allen Howard in his book *Remember the Titans*, details how Boone made the decision, which would prove to be a stroke of genius; to take his divided team for a one week football camp stay at Gettysburg College in Pennsylvania.

The popular movie version of the book was given a "Hollywood" makeover to embellish some of the more dramatic scenes depicted. For instance, in the movie Coach Boone tells his integrated Titans that every other team they will play in 1971 will be all white. In reality, every team TC Williams faced that season represented an integrated school. However, the scene where Coach Boone integrated the buses before departing for the week long camp at Gettysburg, did occur. Boone later told ESPN.com that, "I forced them on each other. I forced them to learn each other's culture. I forced them to be a part of each other's lives."

Most involved with that magical season agree that the seven days they were forced to live together around the clock, while enduring three a day practices under the boiling August sun, was paramount to a team that dominated the competition on the way to a 13-0 record, a state championship and an end of the season number two national ranking. The real 1971 TC Williams team was much more dominant than the movie portrays. The state title game was a 27-0 blow out of Andrew Lewis High School, not the nail biter that required last minute heroics displayed on the part of TC Williams to "snatch victory from the jaws of defeat." The Titans were so dominant in 1971, that they pitched shutouts on defense in nine of their 13 contests, and never allowed over 16 points in any single game.

A more ominous page in the annals of high school football camps and summer two a days is the nightmarish story of Bellmore-Merrick High School, located in Long Island, NY. The upper middle class school's football team had a long and proud tradition of excellence and winning. The team's lofty status, along with deep rooted tradition and community pride, would all came tumbling down in scandal, victim of some serious crimes that occurred during the team's 1995 summer camp.

After returning from the week long camp, felony criminal hazing allegations surfaced. Charges were made that while at the out of town site, younger players were initiated onto the team through a series of barbaric and illegal hazing rituals. Stories of freshmen sodomized with a baseball bat by varsity players set off an outcry that eventually led to the cancellation of the team's season, the firing of the coaches, and criminal charges against three senior players. This type of potential liability, coupled with the early openings of schools for the fall term, has made two a days, especially overnight camps held out of town, an endangered species in the world of high school football.

Summer camp for Coach Campbell and the 2008 Roughriders would consist of one week, starting on August 11. The Roughriders would practice from 8 am to 11 am each morning, take a one hour lunch break, and be back on the field in the afternoon from Noon until 2:30 pm. School would begin the following Monday, August 18. Since most players did not live in the immediate area of the school and rode public transportation to get to practice, the one hour lunch break left few options for the mid day reprise from the August heat. Most players and coaches would bring their lunch with them, brown bagging it. Others would find refuge in the air conditioned home of Arlando Bailey, right across the street from Roosevelt High School.

"It is hard", said Coach Campbell, "to get in everything we want to get in. Ideally, we would like to practice early in the morning and late in the evening to avoid the heat. We would use the afternoons for film and meetings. That isn't going to happen here. We have no way to feed the kids. No way to transport them twice a day and many of our kids still have to work in the evening. Hey man, this is the PHL, we do what we have to do to survive. We are used to things not being ideal. As a matter of fact, it would probably throw off our whole rhythm if things were simple and easy."

Football practice for Missouri high schools officially began on August 11, 2008. Most teams though had been going full bore all summer, flying under the radar screen of the Missouri State High School Activity Association (MSHSAA) rule book by holding only "voluntary" workouts. Mandatory practice would begin on the second Monday of August. The state did enforce a short duration "dead period" from the first of August until the official start of practice. By rule, during this 11 day period, coaches were allowed no contact with their athletes. The short break was an opportunity that several coaches had used to get away from the grind. A late summer family outing to the lake was a common diversion. Assistant Coach Darren Wade had gotten married and honeymooned in Mexico.

The team would have only one full week of extended summer practice time without the distraction of school. In addition, another restriction was imposed by MSHSAA rules: the first two days of football practice must be conducted without any form of full contact drills. Helmets and shoulder pads were allowed, but shorts had to be worn by athletes those first two days. The Roughriders had not been in full pads since concluding the 2007 season the previous November. Through the endless hours of spring and summer toil and drills - weight lifting, agility drills, 7 on 7 passing league, conditioning drills - which the team had endured over the last 9 months, none had been executed in full pads. That would now change. It was time to play "real football."

Every high school football player and coach in the state knew the significance of the third day of practice, the pads went on and the hitting began. Despite all of the high tech and complicated offenses and defenses that the creative imaginations of coaches could conjure up for the modern game, football still remains a simple endeavor. As veteran and venerable Roughrider Assistant Coach George Simmons had stated, "it is still all about blocking and tackling." Players knew that come Day 3 of summer camp, all the talk would stop. Months of chest puffing bravado, of how hard a player could hit - "they call me the Sandman, when I hit you, you are put to sleep," boosted one Roosevelt player at a summer weight lifting session - would now have to be backed up with action. It was Alpha Male time, macho behavior at its best; or maybe worst, depending on one's point of view. But it was also high school football at its essence. Players with a mean streak and a desire - even an enjoyment - of contact were a necessary component of any successful team. The bottom line: football has, and always will be, a violent sport.

As the players gathered around Coach Campbell at the conclusion of the second day of practice, he reminded them to be at the field the next morning by 7 am, in order to be issued the remainder of their equipment, and to be "padded up" and ready to begin the workout by 8 am. The announcement of the beginning of full contact practices was greeted by the team with the obligatory cheer. The question as to how many of these teenagers were relishing the opportunity for full contact the next day, compared to how many were terrified with the thought, but trying to put up a brave front in the face of their teammates; would soon be answered.

Or, maybe it wouldn't.

On Wednesday morning, August 13, the first day the state rules allowed for full contact, the Roughriders were still in shorts. The day before, someone at Roosevelt had concluded that it would be a good time to paint the floor around the football equipment room. The paint would not dry for at least another 24 hours, delaying the issuing of full pads for at least one more day. Campbell's 7 am announcement of the delay was met with anguish by the players. For some, the delay was disappointing. For others, despite their public testament to their displeasure, it was time to take a long sigh of relief, a 24 hour reprieve.

The Missouri State High School Activities Association allows for teams to play 10 football games before the playoff single elimination tournament begins. The first seven games are used as a warm up for the district portion of the schedule, which occurs during the last three weeks of the regular season. The first seven games, while having no bearing on the outcome of who qualifies for the state playoffs, often are still meaningful games as they feature conference matchups and many long time geographical rivalries. Roosevelt would only play nine games in 2008. They would have no game the first week of the season, Labor Day weekend.

Originally Campbell thought the PHL had lined up a game for the Roughriders with a school in Memphis, TN. "We were going to travel down there, but then all kinds of problems, including money, began to pop up," said Campbell when explaining the hole in the front end of his 2008 schedule. "We'd like to have a game, but we are not. We will just have to make the best of it. The Jamboree will be very important to us this year," said Campbell.

Preseason football jamborees are a rather new innovation to Missouri high school football. In the late 1990's, the MSHSAA decided to allow teams, the weekend before the regular season began, to scrimmage other schools under modified conditions; a sort of high school version of an NFL pre season game. Special teams and kicking were not allowed. Score would not be kept. Each team would be allowed a pre determined number of snaps on both offense and defense. Play would occur on only one end of the field. Four teams would be involved, with simultaneous action occurring on both ends of the field.

Helping contribute to the almost carnival like atmosphere found at most jamborees was the allowing of coaches to be on the field with their teams. Referees also used the jamborees as a pre season exhibition game to get themselves ready for the upcoming season, and to break in new officials at the varsity level. It was a time of learning for everyone. On most occasions, the crowds were surprisingly large, sometimes numbering as high as for a regular season game. Everyone was anxious to see how the home team looked and what to expect in the looming regular season. Coaches and fans alike were not that interested in winning or losing at a jamboree, since no score was kept, it was often a moot point. Jamborees were about teaching and learning; preparation for the upcoming games that would be "played for keeps" – a sort of dress rehearsal before opening night.

Often times the jamborees served as the final evaluation for the coaches to determine who would be the team's starters and backups. For all involved, the stakes were high. Despite the lack of interest in a game score, jamborees were taken as serious encounters by coaches and players alike. The scrimmages signified the end of the pre-season and the dawning of a new year of high school football. Plus, it was nice to be able to hit someone who was not a teammate or a friend.

The Roughriders were scheduled to participate in a three team jamboree (the PHL could not find a 4th team that would travel to the city) at Gateway High School on August 23, the Saturday before the regular season opener for every high school team in the St. Louis area but Roosevelt. The players and coaches spent the previous week in practice expressing their excitement about the upcoming opportunity to lay pads on someone besides their teammates. The previous year's jamboree had been a monumental event for the PHL. All ten teams, thanks to the efforts of PHL, Inc., had participated in a four hour long extravaganza at the home of the NFL's Rams, the 66,000 seat Edward Jones Dome. Because of the Rams having scheduled an exhibition game for themselves on August 23 of 2008, the Dome was not an option. Gateway Tech's field, the only one in the city with lights, would have to do.

By the second week of practice, it was obvious from the on field fights at practice that the Roughriders needed to start hitting someone besides themselves. The team, players and coaches both, had become "chippy;" skirmishes between team mates were now common place. With the opening game against Eureka still over two weeks away, the Saturday jamboree was on everyone's mind.

Finally, on the 10th day of practice, Campbell ordered the first all out scrimmage of the year. The only restriction ordered by Campbell was that quarterback Arlando Bailey was strictly off limits. Bailey wore a red vest over his jersey to further denote that he was "out of season" to any aggressive head hunter on the defensive side of the line of scrimmage. Pity the poor defender who failed to heed Coach Campbell's warning: "You hit my quarterback and I will run your ass till you drop. You'll be doing up downs till I get tired," Campbell warned his defense before the scrimmage began. As Campbell well knew, losing Bailey to an injury would derail the hopes and dreams of a breakthrough season. If Bailey was going to go down with an injury, Coach Campbell intended to make sure it would not be inflicted by one of his own teammates.

Legendary Michigan State University Coach Duffy Daugherty, who built a national power house in East Lansing in the 1950's and 1960's, was once asked by a young reporter if football was a contact sport. His response: "No young man, ballroom dancing is a contact sport, football is a collision sport."

At the Wednesday afternoon practice, seventy two hours before the Jamboree, Coach Campbell held the first live scrimmage of the year. Football coaches must reach a balance in practice sessions between the need to have live hitting - both blocking and tackling, the two basic fundamentals of football - and the avoidance of injures due to such scrimmages.

The transformation of junior lineman Rene Faulk, once the "collisions" started amongst the Roughriders, was, to say the least, startling. The 6'3, 310 lb Faulk, much hyped by the coaching staff for his potential for future college stardom, had not been impressive in early season non-contact drills. He often appeared disinterested and unmotivated. He drew constant criticism from coaches and teammates alike for his lack of practice hustle. He was often the last man on the field to start practice. "Man-Child," screamed Line Coach Darren West during a pre season practice, "I hope you are not walking to my station. I hope your big ass is jogging, because I about had enough."

But when the ball was snapped for the first live scrimmage play of the season, it became immediately apparent that the moniker "Man-Child" had been aptly earned. Faulk's effort was 100%, his play vicious. On the first full contact play of the day, seeing Faulk coming down the line of scrimmage as a pulling tackle, leading a sweep for running back Antonio Carter, had to be terrifying to 175 lb. defensive cornerback Charles Banks. The sophomore defender was often praised by the coaching staff for his fearless play. Banks was viewed as an up and coming star. For the moment though, the only stars in Banks' world were the ones swimming in front of his eyeballs after he had been run over by the "Man-Child."

Faulk's play for the first 15 minutes of the scrimmage was awe inspiring. On some plays, he would block as many as three defenders - one at the line of scrimmage and several more down field, as he ran interference for long runs from scrimmage by Carter and fellow running back Quadricous Sanford. For the first time all season, Roosevelt was playing real football, and for the first time all season, Rene Faulk was performing like a real football player.

A 5 foot 4 inch dynamo, senior running back Antonio Carter listens to the National Anthem minutes before the start of his final game as a Roughrider. For anyone who witnessed the diminutive Carter lug the pigskin, his dogged determination left an indelible and inspiring impression.

Senior receiver Quadricous Sanford sprints into the end zone. However, in what could be the season's recap in a single picture, the touchdown is nullified by the block in the back documented to the right.

On a picture perfect fall Saturday afternoon on the green grass of Roughrider Stadium, Antonio Carter sweeps the left side of the line, headed for the end zone. Carter lived for just such moments. For three hours each Saturday, the senior Running Back did what he loved – and for an all too short interlude, his world spun in greased grooves.

Junior Placekicker Muhammad Dukly shows perfect form, booting a field goal out of the hold of Arlando Bailey. An African native, Dukly never failed to count his blessing for the chance to play football for the Roughriders as opposed to the life of a child soldier, his probable destiny had he remained in his native homeland

With Miller Career Academy providing the opposition, Senior Quadricous Sanford looks back for a long pass. Sanford, the most decorated of the 2008 Roughriders, answered to the nickname of "Mississippi", in tribute to his home state.

Senior Quarterback Arlando Bailey: the quiet but quintessential leader. Known as CBC, Bailey was a rarity amongst his peers, standing out not only on the gridiron, but also in the classroom.

Head Coach DeAndre Campbell gives a pre-game hands on demonstration in pass blocking to his star pupil, junior lineman Rene Faulk. Always passionate about his role as a leader of young men, Campbell's motivational style could take on a stinging edge.

With no locker room to call their own, halftime finds the Roughriders - sans shade, water, and restroom facilities - sprawled on the ground in full torment of the hot September afternoon Sun.

"Mississippi" heads unimpeded down the sideline.

The dynamic duo of RHS football: Assistant Coach Darren West (left) and Head Coach DeAndre Campbell. West, extremely popular with his players despite his demanding coaching style, was a stand up comic waiting to be discovered. Campbell not only accepted the disadvantages inherent with coaching at an inner city school, but embraced them to be worn as a Badge of Honor. Campbell viewed his work at Roosevelt as not a job, but a calling; an attitude all too lacking though out most of the Public High League.

The Head Roughrider: Principal Terry Houston. The praise for the efforts of Houston in the turnaround of Roosevelt High School came from far and wide. The acclaim was well deserved.

Different Worlds: Roosevelt Homecoming Past and Present.

When sufficiently motivated, the Man Child proved to be aptly named.

"One more time, you got to give it to me just one more time!"
In the 4th quarter against Career Academy, with the game and the PHL title on the line, Coach Campbell implores his offense.

"Sometime" Defensive Coordinator and Assistant Coach Darren Wade provides instruction to one of his defensive backs.

Another long run - another penalty flag.

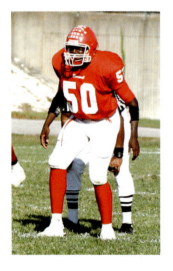

Roosevelt High School's "Renaissance Man," George Bell. Unshakeable and immensely likeable; glib and witty to the point of sometimes insolence - a hard hitting linebacker and self proclaimed underrated kick returner.

Having given up the Penthouse of high school football stardom under the Friday Night Lights of South Paola, MS, for the Outhouse of anonymity and apathy of the PHL; Quadricus Sanford's parting remarks are telltale: "No regrets, man. I loved playing football at Roosevelt High School."

Assistant Coach Darren West

A group that never lost its enthusiasm, the RHS cheerleaders fire up a less than capacity cheering section.

A much maligned group: the Offensive Line

The Red Wave: Against the back drop of Roughrider Stadium, behind a wall of blockers, Antonio Carter advances the ball up the field.

"A Band of Brothers" after the Gateway Tech game.

But with no warning, after 15 minutes of brutally dominant offensive line play, the "Man- Child" morphed back into Rene: the disinterested and out of shape underachiever that drove his coaches crazy. As if a light switch had been thrown, Faulk was done for the day. He now walked back to the huddle, was the last man off the line at the snap of the ball, and seldom got more than a couple of strides down the field. Out of shape, or just an exhaustion of all his bent up hostility for the day? The coaches wished they knew the answer, and thus the key to unlocking the vast football potential held by the enigmatic Faulk.

The play of the offensive line in the scrimmage was duly noted by Campbell as a success. As he often stated in the off season, Roosevelt would go as far in the upcoming season as their offensive line would carry them. "We did a great job of getting to the second level (the defensive back field) and making blocks," said Campbell in a post practice evaluation of the line play. "Our linemen are so smart this year. George Bell and Tyler Clubb, you won't find two smarter kids in this high school. And Mummy (6'4, 285 lb Sr. Tackle, Maurice Jones), 25 on the ACT. And, "Man-Child", he may not be a great student in school, but he is smart when he wants to be. And did I not tell you, he will flat out knock people on their ass. He is going to be something, and you haven't even seen him yet on the defensive line. He is unmovable. He is still not in shape, but he is a lot better than he was last year. It is just a matter of time. I am telling you, he will be playing big time college football in a couple of years. We just got to get him to stop taking plays off."

The word from the Central Administrative Offices of the SLPS came at noon on Friday, in the form of an e-mail that arrived in Coach Campbell's school account. The communiqué was short and to the point: "Due to the possibility of rain tomorrow, the football jamboree you were scheduled to participate in has been canceled."

The news to Campbell was frustrating, to his players it was dispiriting. To a causal observer it was asinine. Cancel a scrimmage 30 hours in advance because of a chance of rain? Do so without consulting the people effected most by the decision, in essence no collaboration with those on the front lines? Could such a decision not have waited until Saturday afternoon when the severity of potential storms could have been more accurately assessed? Not in the Alice in Wonderland world where the St. Louis Public School System resides.

"This hurts bad since we do not have a game the first week," said Campbell. "Any other year we could have adjusted. But without a first game we will go into the Eureka game playing a team that has not only had their jamboree, but also has played a game. It's not fair to our kids, but we're going to have to deal with it," Campbell stated in resignation.

Later, at Friday's practice, Campbell did his best to lessen the disappointment of his players. "At least Eureka will not get a chance to scout us. We will see them twice before we play them. All they will have on us is last year's film, and that will not include the spread offense. We can really catch them by surprise." The players were not buying the attempted positive spin by Coach Campbell of the disappointing news. The Friday afternoon practice, dampened by the deflating earlier announcement of the deep sixing of the jamboree, was by any generous assessment, dispirited.

Friday evening's weather was post card perfect. Saturday morning broke the same, not a cloud in the sky. The temperature and humidity remained low through the day. By Saturday evening, for August in St. Louis, the weather was as pleasant as anyone could want. It rained not a drop all weekend.

CHAPTER 5
THE REGULAR SEASON

I say luck is when an opportunity comes along, and you're prepared for it.
— *Denzel Washington*

Volunteering is for suckers. Did you know that so called 'Volunteers' don't even get paid?
— *Homer Simpson*

A bone to the dog is not charity. Charity is the bone shared with the dog, when you are just as hungry as the dog.
— *Jack London*

September 6, 2008, 1:30 pm; the Eureka Wildcats vs. the Roosevelt Roughriders. The season opener at Roughrider Stadium was finally at hand.

By 8 am, Roosevelt senior running back Antonio Carter was well into his game day preparation. He had risen early from a restless sleep and secured one last final check on his game day gear. Everything was in place. Everything was ready. Adorned in his white game jersey - he and his teammates would change to their red home jerseys after the completion of their on field warm up and prior to the game's opening kickoff - Carter lowered his head and began the trek up Gravois Blvd., equipment bag slung over his shoulder, his head down and his long dreadlocks bobbing to his stride, rap music blaring through the ear phones of his walkman. Carter would join his teammates for a 9 am team breakfast to be served in the school cafeteria. Early in the afternoon, his father would follow the same path to Roughrider Stadium. He would be Carter's only relative in attendance for the game.

Since the disappointing conclusion to the 2007 season, opening day 2008 had been burned into the collective conciseness of everyone involved with the Roosevelt football program. The Eureka Wildcats would provide a stiff early season test. The long time suburban power house was a unanimous favorite to win the always strong Suburban South Conference. They would travel to the city with 14 starters returning from a 9-1 club, earning them a pre-season ranking of third in the St. Louis Metro area. If Roosevelt could compete with this juggernaut, then all would know that their dreams of a deep playoff run in November was well grounded in reality.

Coach Campbell had talked incessantly all spring and summer about the importance of the season opening Eureka game. "We have to show we can play with the big boys from the county. We might as well find out right away," was Campbell's rationale for scheduling such a stiff first game. "Are we worried about a poor performance by our guys? If it happens, we will deal with it."

Per Campbell's request, his squad's 2008 schedule had seen the competitive bar raised to a considerable new height. Gone were PHL patsies Cleveland and Soldan, replaced on the schedule by the now cursed first week bye and Eureka. PHL rivals Career Academy, Vashon and Gateway Tech, were all viewed as improved teams and none would be a guaranteed mid season win. Lurking at

Chapter 5: The Regular Season

the back end of the schedule were this year's district foes, all strong programs expecting solid performances in 2008: Webster Groves, Chaminade and Vianney. It was highly possible, if fate broke the wrong direction, that Roosevelt could have a much stronger team in 2008, but a lesser final tally than the 6-4 mark of 2007.

Some within the inner circles of the Roosevelt program questioned the wisdom of scheduling Eureka as an opener. If the Roughriders did lay an egg in the season's first contest, would the rest of the season be in peril? The players, to a man, had bought into Campbell's demands for total commitment to the football program. They had immersed themselves into a torturous off season conditioning program. Would player confidence erode with the realization that despite all of their off season preparation, Roosevelt was still not at the level of the county powers? Would team morale then collapse? Would the program return to the pre-Campbell days of lackadaisical commitment and expectations? Campbell had worked obsessively over three years to eliminate just such an attitude. Could all the coaches and players efforts be for naught if his early season gamble backfired?

"We will play well. We will compete with Eureka. Our kids, our coaches, our fans, the whole St. Louis area will know that Roosevelt is for real after the Eureka game," said a confident Campbell, the week before the opener. "We have worked too hard, and have improved too much. We need this kind of first game test."

Campbell's body language and voice tone left no doubt that he was sincere in his belief that his team was up to the test Eureka would present. Campbell was gambling that everyone else would suddenly realize what he now so confidently knew. "I am around these guys everyday. I know where we are. I would bet my life right now that we are ready," said Campbell. Perhaps his offer for such a wager was an exaggeration. While maybe not risking his own life, Campbell was, in the eyes of many, by putting so much emphasis on an early season game that meant nothing in regard to the conference or district standings - risking his whole season on the outcome of one game.

Eureka had won it's season opener on the road, a listless 12-7 victory over a projected middle of the road Lafayette squad. The game was marred by many of the problems one would expect from a first game. Campbell and his assistants, while still concerned about not having played a game of their own the first weekend of the season- compounded by the cancelation of their jamboree - had taken advantage of the opportunity to scout Eureka in both their jamboree and season opener. "They have not seen us," Campbell said. "We have seen them twice. We have to take advantage of that, because we know we are at a disadvantage without the jamboree or a real game under our belts."

The RHS staff had video taped both Eureka encounters – the Jamboree and the Lafayette game - and had labored long hours breaking down the tapes to detect tendencies and weakness in the Wildcat's schemes. An 8 hour film marathon at Coach Campbell's house the day after the Eureka vs. Lafayette game – Labor Day Saturday - had produced a game plan the coaches felt good about. "We have a good game plan," stated Assistant Coach Simmons on Labor Day afternoon, as the team assembled to begin game week preparations. "We'd better have a good one," he said. "We gave (up) a holiday weekend to put it together." The task now was to teach the strategy to the players in a short period of time. As the RHS Coaching staff knew, the greatest strategy in the world was worthless without the player's ability to execute it crisply and effectively under the strain of live game conditions.

At the Labor Day afternoon practice, Coach Campbell and his staff began the task of transforming their game plan from paper into game field execution. The 40 odd players and coaches were cramped into Coach Campbell's basement classroom for an afternoon film session, starring the Eureka Wildcats. The subterranean room also served as the site for the RHS In-School Suspension Program, headed by Campbell.

The late summer afternoon heat was stifling, the uncomfortable environment inside the class room compounded by the lack of air conditioning and 40 husky young bodies, some in full football gear that had not had a recent laundering, crammed into an area designed for 25. Once the 20 odd desks were taken, the rest of the team and coaches either sat on the floor or leaned against the cement walls. Campbell sat directly in front of a 36 inch television set anchored to a rolling cart. He provided non-stop commentary as his remote control device ran one play after another, over and over. A common request throughout the session

Chapter 5: The Regular Season

came from Coach West in the back of the darkened room, "Coach, run that back again. Now look, see what I am talking about?"

The attention of the players was, unlike many times in the off season, totally focused on the TV screen and the verbal instruction provided by Campbell and West. It was teaching at its finest. Time after time the players in unison would immediately snap off the right answer in response to a scenario based upon a question asked by Campbell or West. "If they show either twins or trips to the wide side, we in Smoke or Crash," quizzed Campbell? In unison the players answered correctly, "Crash."

The knowledge and the grasp the players had on the questions thrown at them, in a jargon that would be foreign to any non-football person who had happened to stumble upon the film session, was impressive. A visitor could speculate if any better teaching and student retention of educational material took place in the building during the regular school day.

"George Bell, we say 3-1, what are we really in," Campbell asks. "44, Coach," Bell answers correctly and without hesitation. "See the back, watch number 14, they going to run behind him every time, EVERY TIME," Coach West repeats for emphasis. "He blocks and he blocks well. That is why they go to his side 90% of the time. We got to bust him every play, keep him on the line of scrimmage, jam him, he can't hurt us if he can't get of the line," exhorts West. "They line up in twins to his side, would do we do?" Campbell asks, "Run Bear," the players respond. "We do and they will try and go Jet, what do we call, George?" "Nebraska", Bell answers. "Correct," says Campbell, "and his ass got nowhere to go, they will throw it right to us and we take it back to the house."

From the look on Campbell's face, he is pleased with how his players have handled the game plan quiz. Even the notoriously and self labeled non interested student, Rene Faulk, eagerly watches and listens with total attention. Coach Campbell replays three times a favorite Eureka play - a fullback draw run from the spread formation. It was Eureka's most productive offensive play against Lafayette and is run through a hole in the defensive line that on Saturday will be anchored by the 310 pound Faulk. "Man-Child," Coach Campbell declares, "when the back hits that hole on Saturday, your big ass going to be right there waiting for him." Faulk grins and nods his head in the affirmative.

After an hour and 15 minutes, the players depart the film session for the practice field. Viewing Eureka in action has lifted the spirits and the confidence level of the team.

"I am tired of losing to these county teams," running back Antonio Carter says, as he and his teammates go through their pre practice stretching routine. "The quarterback has no arm. They are not that fast. I am tired of losing to these county schools," Carter repeats.

The coaches attempt to build on the team's growing confidence level, "We should score 14 points off of their turnovers," says Coach West. "They can not pass. The QB's arm is weak. He throws an out, we jump the route and into the end zone we go. 14 points is what I want or I will be disappointed! And that don't even include the points the offense going to score." But West delivers a warning; verbalizing to the players the coaches concerns of what could go wrong. "We can't let them hide the ball. We got to get it away from them. They will control the clock on you if you let them. They did that to Lafayette. Kept the ball almost the whole third quarter. We have got to make plays on defense. Force them into second and long, and third and long. On defense, we must force them to throw. They will run the ball right up our ass, all game long, if we let them. We have got to get the ball into the hands of our offense."

At the end of the spirited Monday holiday practice, Coach Campbell gathers his players around him at midfield. "Take a knee," he directs. "Fellows, we are here. It is game week. GAME WEEK. All the hard work we have done. All spring. All summer. Now its time to make it pay off. We have a better football team than Eureka. We have better football players than Eureka. I don't care what the rankings say. We have better athletes, and we execute better. We block and tackle better. We pass and catch better. We are a better football team. But fellows, here is the question: are we disciplined? Will we not jump offsides? Will we watch the ball instead of listening to the QB cadence? Will we avoid the killer 15 yard penalties; the late hits (and) the unsportsmanlike conduct penalties? Or, are we just another sloppy ass, undisciplined team from the PHL that all the county schools laugh at? Saturday, dudes, we got a chance to answer those questions, to send a message (throughout) the St. Louis area that Roosevelt is for real. That Roosevelt is disciplined. That this year, brother, Roosevelt does not beat themselves. That when you come to our field, you come to our neighborhood, you had better get ready to get your ass kicked by a very good, DISCI-PLINED football team."

As the first game of the season approached, Mohammad Dukly, the Liberian refugee place kicker, was a developing weapon for the Roughriders. He spent each day at one end of the practice field, by himself, perfecting his new found place kicking skills. Three weeks earlier, when Dukly first approached the coaches about their need for a kicker, he was viewed by Campbell as a curiosity. Dukly had never kicked a football in his life. His unexpected progress, in the eyes of the coaches, now made him a legitimate offensive threat. Once he had mastered the technique of kicking a football for height and distance, as opposed to kicking a soccer ball on a line drive - his accuracy became deadly. The coaching staff now expressed confidence in his ability to kick field goals of up to 40 yards.

In the PHL, where few teams could claim even the woeful success rate on extra point kicks of 50%, the field goal was a forgotten part of the game. Football rules allow for five methods to score points - a touchdown, a safety, a kicked field goal, a point after touchdown conversion kick and a point after touchdown two point conversion run/pass. Two of the five require kicking. For one team to have these scoring methods at its' beckoning, when the other team did not, was an advantage of game winning magnitude. With a field goal kicker, a PHL team had a distinct advantage, comparable to allowing one baseball team four outs, while the other team received only the customary three. The advantage would not guarantee victory, but it certainly slanted the odds to the side of the team with a kicker.

Dukly was also a devout Muslim. Within the Roosevelt student body was a growing group of West African refugees, such as Dukly, who were practicing Muslims. The young kicker was always subconscious, but dutiful, about walking away from the player lead pre-game prayer, standing alone and away from his huddled Christian team mates.

Labor Day, September 1, not only marked the traditional end of summer in America, but around the world the beginning of the Muslim holy month of Ramadan. Followers believed the time of Ramadan to be the month in which the Qur'an was revealed to Angel Gabriel, who later revealed it to the Prophet Muhammad For thirty days, devout followers would refrain from eating or drinking between the hours of dawn and sunset. To the true believers, fasting was a way to cleanse and purify the body. Dukly and his family took this form of religious sacrifice very seriously. It was not open to compromise.

Between 5 am and 8 pm, Dukly would take no bodily nourishment, neither food nor liquid. For an athlete such as Mohammad, practicing in the late summer heat and humidity of St. Louis, dehydration became a real concern, along with dizziness and weakness.

"Ramadan, what is that? Do you know what it is?" a perplexed Coach Campbell inquired of an assistant coach. On Wednesday prior to the Eureka game, Mohammad informed Campbell that he would probably be light headed and weak during afternoon practices for the next month. His place kicking skills would obviously be affected by such physical problems. After being informed of his kicker's self imposed fast, Campbell shook his head in disbelief. "What next?" he asked an assistant coach.

In less than 48 hours, his team would open its season against the third ranked team in the Metro area. Before the first game snap of the 2008 season had been made, Campbell had dealt with being the only team in the area to not play a game on the opening weekend, having the team's Jamboree canceled due to a phantom thunderstorm that never materialized; and now, the realization that his new found secret weapon's effectiveness would be in question, thanks to a self imposed religious fast. With a whimsical shaking of his head, Campbell summed up the life of a head football coach in the PHL. "Nobody ever said this job was going to be easy."

There may be a record documented somewhere of a worse high school football practice, but it is hard to fathom any session in the history of the sport being more of a disaster and exercise in futility than what the Roosevelt Roughriders endured on the day before their season opening contest with Eureka.

The Friday academic day had ended after lunch. A school wide dance during the last two class hours was scheduled. Because of security concerns, many urban high schools had adopted a policy of holding traditional dances during the school day as a way to monitor and control who attends such functions. Despite the unorthodox arrangement, the students looked forward to these social events. Classroom attendance was always high the day of a dance. Students were required to be in attendance the entire day to be given access to the after lunch event. A looming opening day football contest did nothing to stem the raging teen age hormones that were revved up by the afternoon dance. "See me dance with her," bragged one player during the Friday afternoon pre practice stretching period. "She may be a teacher, but man, she is hot."

After two hours of active socializing, the football players were not in a focused frame of mind for the final practice before the season opener. It did not take long for the coaches to realize that the attention on the task at hand – important game day organizational tasks, such as reviews of what players were on different special teams – was very lacking. A mid week downpour, remnants of a tropical hurricane in the Gulf of Mexico that had worked its way inland up the Mississippi River, had left the Roosevelt game field turf a soft and muddy mess. Due to the rain, Thursday's practice had consisted of indoor film sessions, but no on field work; raising the level of importance for a sharp and organized practice on Friday. Compounding the lax atmosphere was Coach Campbell's unexplained absence. One of the many hats that Campbell wore at RHS included that of groundskeeper at the Roosevelt Stadium. He had spent the entire day Friday mowing and striping the game field in preparation for Saturday's contest. The job was made more difficult by the muddy conditions. With so many details involving his team that needed to be addressed, Campbell's stress level on Friday was raised to an exasperating level by the added chores of field preparation. He was sure that the coaching staff at Eureka had no such responsibilities placed on their collective plates. He knew that their focus was squarely on preparing their squad for tomorrow's game, not on maintenance details.

With Campbell's absence, assistant coaches Wade and West attempted to rope in the young athlete's attention to focus on the task at hand, preparing for a contest less than 24 hours away with the area's third ranked team. They were having little success. The frustration level of the assistants was glaringly apparent, a blow up from one or both was imminent. Instruction was interrupted on more than one occasion with profanity laced tirades from the coaches at the unmotivated athletes. "I will kick your ass right off this football team," threatened West, midway through the practice. "I don't care who you are. This is shit! I want your attention and I want it now or we will run hills the rest of this practice." West's darkening mood was exasperated by the failure of the team to place the right 11 players on the field when he called for the punt return squad. The coaching staff had devoted a large amount of pre-season practice time to organizing the special teams. They had stressed constantly to their players the importance of special teams – kickoff, kickoff return, punting, punt return and field goal teams. The Eureka game would, in due time, painfully drive home the wisdom of the coach's pleadings, efforts at the present that were falling on the deaf ears of their athletes.

At 5:00 pm, Campbell was finally on the practice field. His clothes were soaked, plastered with mud and white paint, testament to the long day he had put in preparing the field. His pent up stress had reduced his patience to the analogous level of a man on death row. After watching several missed offensive assignments during a walkthrough of plays that had been rehearsed hundreds of times since last summer, Campbell finally blew. He ordered the entire squad to the "Hill;" a steep grassy incline behind the visiting team's bleachers, on the south side of the Stadium. As Coach Simmons put air in his whistle, the players were required to come out of a three point stance and sprint up to the top of the rise, turn around and sprint back down the hill, at which time they would resume a three point stance, awaiting Simmons's next whistle that would propel them up the hill again. After several repetitions of the punishment drill, Campbell noticed quarterback Arlando Bailey limping badly. "CBC, you hurt?" Campbell inquired, almost in an apologetic and pleading voice. "I'll make it," Bailey shot back through clenched teeth. One more trip, with the quarterback limping up the hill, brought a sharp whistle from Campbell, signaling the end of the punishment session. Campbell suddenly realized this form of punishment the day before a game may not have been such a good idea, perhaps costing him the opening game services of his most indispensable player.

Coaches and players alike, departed the aborted practice with moods gloomier than the overcast and misty Friday night weather.

Chapter 5: The Regular Season

Game day was, at long last, at hand for the Roosevelt Roughriders. Any American male who has padded up for the big game can attest that there is no feeling quite like the electric environment that dominates a football team gathered as a unit to endure the final agonizingly slow minutes prior to taking the field for the season's opening kickoff. The air is charged with anticipation and dread, permeated with fear and excitement, individual confidence and fearful doubts dominate the private thoughts of each young athlete. The eerie silence is unnerving. The hard work is done, now the time has arrived to strap on the pads and place your manhood on the line. Your town, family and school pride travels with you into battle. It is up to you and your teammates to protect your turf, your home neighborhood. The enemy - in this case, attired in purple and white jerseys - has arrived at the city gates.

Outfitted in full red and white battle gear, each Roosevelt player sits alone with their individual thoughts. They are ready to jump into fox holes with their teammates, prepared for the test they have pondered since the end of the last season, nine months prior. Hopefully, for most of these boys, it is as close to the experience of storming the beaches at Normandy that they will ever encounter, the pregame quiet serving as their own personal figurative boat ride across the English Channel.

An exception to the seriousness of the mood was Mohammad Dukly, the Liberian born placekicker, who in a few short minutes would play in the first live football game he will have ever seen. He appears almost bored. Dukly leans against a brick exterior wall behind his teammates, calmly tossing from one hand to the other the kicking tee he keeps with him at all times. "It is only a game," he says when asked if he is nervous. "I want to play because it will be fun." His view is tempered by a past far from relevant to his American born teammates. Dukly is a young man who from birth knew nothing but civil war and refugee camps in his native African homeland of Liberia, and later his adopted country of Guinea. His life had been one of daily survival in refuge camps always overloaded to the brim with the casualties caused by an endless civil war. At the age of 12, he and his family fled to America. "If I was home in Liberia right now, I would have been a soldier for the last four years," Dukly observed. "Or (I) would be dead now. Or (I) would have killed many boys my age so that I could live. I would rather be here playing football. This is fun."

The kicker Dukly made a tackle on the first live football play he ever saw. Unfortunately, for both he and the Roughriders, it was 50 yards downfield; and his tackle was more of a collision of self defense necessitated by his inability to avoid the breakaway Eureka kick returner. Regardless of Dukly's intent, his effort did save a touchdown. It was an ominous start to the 2008 season. Six plays later, Eureka was in the end zone, and with the subsequent conversation kick, owned a 7-0 lead before most of the late arriving Roosevelt crowd had found their seats.

Just as Coach West had prophesized the day before, poor special teams play would doom Roosevelt in the season opener. Eureka would survive a third quarter scare and pull away for a 24-7 victory. The second of the visitor's touchdowns could also be placed squarely on the shoulders of the kickoff team. After the Rider's defensive back Dashaun Moss returned his second of three interceptions on the day for a 37 yard touchdown, his listless teammates suddenly seemed to have life. Dukly drilled the extra point dead center of the uprights and half way through the third quarter, the Eureka lead stood at only 10-7. The charge of momentum that had electrified the home team and its followers, dissipated as suddenly as it had arrived. Eureka returned the kickoff following Moss's touchdown 65 yards, all the way to the Roosevelt 24 yard line. Four running plays later, the visitors were again in the Roosevelt end zone. Staked now to a 17-7 lead, Eureka entrusted the game's outcome to its ball control offense again, just as Coach West had warned in the Monday film session. Behind its' massive offensive line, Eureka ran play after play straight into the line, controlling the ball and running the clock. As West had stated on Monday, "we can't score if we don't get the offense the ball." After Eureka secured the mid third quarter 10 point advantage, the victor of the game was never again in doubt.

Roughrider frustration mounted on the sidelines as the contest ground down to its disappointing conclusion. Communication between the coaches and players had noticeably broken down. By the 4th quarter, defensive coordinator Darren Wade was still calling defensive alignments from the sidelines. He would use hand signals to communicate to the defense. The players were to then look down at their wrist bands to determine their assignments for that play. On Eureka's last drive, not one defensive player could be viewed checking their wrist band in response to Wade's verbal and visual sideline cues. The players were simply freelancing, doing whatever they felt like, "wherever and whenever the spirit moves you," as Wade would tell the team after the game. Eureka took advantage of the opposition's confusion by methodically going on two long drives and eating up most of the 4th quarter clock, negating any thoughts of a late Roosevelt comeback. With five minutes left in the game, a disgusted and dispirited Campbell told Wade, "save your breath. The lazy asses are not even looking at their wrist bands."

"We practice like crap and then we play like crap," was quarterback Arlando Bailey's post game assessment of his team's opening performance. "I never found a rhythm throwing the ball," he stated, diplomatically ignoring the multiple dropped balls by his normally dependable pass receivers. "We moved the ball until we got in the red zone, then we would do something dumb and it would be 3rd and 20. We have got to get it together."

Quadricous Sanford also professed a sense of urgency brought on by the realization that he would never again play a season opening high school football game. Showing a release of pent up frustration after the game; he broke loose with a tirade aimed at those teammates still malingering 20 minutes after the game's conclusion. "It is crazy man. We got so many good players and we get beat like this? We got to get it together. I don't care about all the yards I got today. We got beat. I am a senior. We can't keep playing like this. Guys need to get serious in practice. We got to get it together, NOW. We got to."

A subdued Coach Campbell addressed his team's performance in a post game interview. "Special teams sucked. We kickoff twice and they run it down our throats twice and (they) score on short drives. One was to start the game and there goes all the pregame momentum we had built. The second comes after Dashaun gives us life (with an interception return for a touchdown). Two key points of the game turn against us because we can not cover kickoffs. Then they kick off to us five times, and three times we get 15 yard holding penalties and start drives inside of our 15 yard line. Their third touchdown was when we went to sleep on the punt return and let them convert a 4th down fake punt. They scored on that drive as well. I thought our defense played well. They were on the field at least 2/3 of the game. The offense gave them (the defense) no help. Eureka had short fields to operate on all day. We just never could get our offense going. Why? I don't know, but I will by Monday."

All spring and summer the coaching staff had preached the importance of offensive line play. Campbell's after game assessment of the opening day play by his lineman in the trenches: "C+. We have work to do. We never could run the ball and CBC (Quarterback Arlando Bailey) never seemed to have enough time to throw. The offense was not clicking today. We'll need to break down the game film, and address these problems come Monday."

When speaking to the team after the game, Campbell attempted to put a positive spin on the just concluded contest. As he gathered his team around him in the west end zone, Campbell stressed all the football his team had left to play in the 2008 season. "Last year, we would have quit after so many bad breaks. We didn't today. We hit them hard on defense all day. They will know when they wake up in the morning that Roosevelt will hit you. But we played with no confidence on offense today. We dominated 7 on 7 all summer and we come out here today and we drop passes, we make tentative reads, we run patterns like we are scared, we break no long runs. I don't get it. What is the problem? We will look at the film and we will figure out what is going on. These guys (Eureka) are opposite our district. We could very well see them in the first round of the state playoffs. That needs to be our goal right now. We have got two months to get better and to earn another chance to play these guys. How bad do you want it? We will find out on Monday."

Statistically, the game had been much closer than the final score would indicate. One ominous conclusion that jumped out from the post game stat sheet was that the vaunted Roosevelt rushing game had been held in check. Highly regarded running back Antonio Carter gained only 58 yards on nine carries. But Bailey, despite throwing three interceptions, completed 12 passes for 308 yards - a sparkling 25 yard per catch average. Quadricous Sanford caught five passes for a career high of 192 yards. Still, the most significant offensive statistic was the lack of an offensive score by the Roughriders. At least five catchable balls were dropped by Bailey's receivers. Nonetheless, by game's end, the grousing from the Roosevelt stands in regard to Bailey's performance could be clearly heard on the home team sideline by coaches and players alike. Bailey had still not won over all the Roughrider faithful. The effects of having replaced a popular "neighborhood guy" in last year's quarterback battle, perhaps, would make his acceptance amongst some of his peers a near impossibility. "Screw 'em," was Campbell's post game response to the restless faithful. "He (Bailey) was sitting on his ass all day because we never picked up their blitz. We work for a month on the flash down (blocking) technique when we recognized the blitz. We get out there today and our offensive line looks like they have no clue of what we are saying. CBC (Bailey) is fine. Next year, he will be on a football scholarship somewhere, getting an education, making something of himself, and those jokers," Campbell gestures with his right hand to the stands, "will still be sitting up there running their mouths."

A large sun soaked crowd had attended the season opening game. The Eureka grandstand, on the south side of the stadium, was filled to capacity. The Roosevelt section, across the field, was the viewing site for a surprisingly good number of Roughrider supporters: parents, classmates and interested community members. Principal Houston took pride in the growing following Coach Campbell and his team was beginning to draw. "It means we are doing some things right," Houston said. "Sports can foster pride in a school, and also in a community. We have worked hard to make Roosevelt a viable part of the community. Look around today and see the white faces that are here to support our team. They are neighborhood people with no kids here, but they like the direction the school is heading and what more viable and visible way to show that support than being here today to cheer on our kids. That just didn't happen, it is something we have worked hard at, cultivated, and babied it along. It is great to see so many white faces in the crowd. We all wear red today. We are all Roughriders."

As had been the practice for years at Roughrider Stadium, a large group - mostly young men between the ages of 18 to 30 - watched the game from the Gravois Avenue sidewalk overlooking the east end zone. The view was good and the spectators "on the fence" could avoid the required $4 admission charge levied upon those fans entering the Stadium gates. Bottles in brown paper bags were a common companion of those "on the fence." Rap music, blaring from parked car stereos, added to the festive mood of the crowd. It was inner city tailgating at its best.

The Public High League, as was standard policy for each game, had sent a healthy contingent of security personnel to monitor the event. The security detachment was in the wrong spot - as usual - all huddled together by the concession stand, when a second half fight broke out in the Roosevelt cheering section. The ensuing uproar caused such a commotion as to momentarily halt the game, as players, officials, and coaches all watched two young male combatants wail away at each other with fists swinging wildly. The two fighters, while seldom landing a punch of any consequence, were loudly cheered on by groups of teenage supporters. With the large student section of spectators drawn to the fight like an SUV to a gas pump, several adults in the vicinity attempted to separate the fighters. While the security officers moved ever so slowly into the fray, Roosevelt Principal Terry Houston maneuvered nimbly and quickly through the crowd to lend his presence to the would be peace keepers already on the scene. After the two young men were separated, and after they exchanged the obligatory threats to each other; "you a dead motherfucker when I see you again" - both were escorted by security personnel from the stadium and the game resumed.

Since coming to Roosevelt, Houston had spent a considerable amount of his time and energy in an attempt to reshape the public persona of Roosevelt High School. It had become his passion, some would say an obsession. Houston had visited with countless community leaders to inform them about the good that was happening in his school. He had lectured his students repeatedly, some would say repetitively, about the importance of public perceptions, never missing an opportunity to drive home his point: Roosevelt High School is a safe place to earn an excellent high school education. In his mind's eye, he saw not only the rebirth of a school, but an entire neighborhood. Now, several young thugs, in a matter of minutes, had done more harm to Houston's dream than he wished to acknowledge.

After peace was restored and the hooligans banned from the stadium, Houston learned from an assistant principal that neither troublemaker was a Roosevelt student. A police inquiry established that the altercation was rooted in a gang dispute that did not involve Houston's RHS students. Of course, the entire episode was conducted in full view of the Eureka crowd. Houston could only imagine the stereotyping conversations that would take place on Monday morning during suburban office coffee breaks: "We had to go to the city and play Roosevelt and they had a gang riot in the stands. Those city schools are dangerous and out of control. Thank God they can't afford lights or we would have to go down there at night."

The day had started just as Houston had scripted it, using the football game as a stage to showcase the talents of the Roosevelt student body. RHS students were in attendance in healthy numbers. They followed the game intently, cheering on each good play by their red jersey clad class mates. The cheerleaders were organized and precise, in constant motion and providing high levels of energy to the Roosevelt crowd. The Marine ROTC Color Guard, made up of Roosevelt students, impressively displayed the school, state and national flags during the pre game national anthem. (In December it was announced that the Marine Corp had chosen the Roosevelt ROTC chapter to present the colors at President elect Barack Obama's January, 2009 inauguration).

But once the fight took center stage, the feel good aura that permeated the game's festivities disappeared as quickly as last year's tax return. One step forward, two steps back.

To add insult to injury, by Monday morning Houston had learned that one of the fighters was a Roosevelt dropout. The other young man was identified as an area resident, who ironically was enrolled in the voluntary desegregation program. He attended Eureka High School.

As Coach Campbell had predicted after the game on Saturday, the game film indeed did tell the story, and it was not one that Campbell enjoyed as he replayed, over and over all day Sunday, the video tape of the opening game loss. With each repeat, his anger grew, his frustration boiling over. By Monday afternoon, he was ready to tear into what he now saw as his underachieving team, a squad that had not given him the opening game effort he had hoped for.

At 3:00 pm on a hot early September Monday afternoon, the Roughriders gathered on the aged concrete blocked steps to the west of the home team bleachers. The walkway led up the hill from the field to the high school building. For years, this spot had become the traditional setting for the football team picture. A trip to the archives of the Roosevelt High School library, and a search of over 80 years of RHS yearbooks, showed how the demographics - the hair styles and the ethnic and racial make up of the RHS gridiron heroes - had changed since

1925. But one factor of each picture was constant: the location of the concrete steps.

No pictures would be taken on this day, the Monday after the Eureka game. Instead, soul searching and a passionate ass chewing from the coaches was the agenda at hand. Coaches Campbell and West had the sermon well prepared. "We will not win a game this year, gentleman, if we play on the offensive line again like we did on Saturday," Campbell began his address to an unusually quiet group of young men. "If you watched that film and saw what I saw, it would make you sick." Campbell's initial post game grade on Saturday of "C+" for the performance of his offensive line had been downgraded by Monday to "shit."

The first player Campbell intended to call out in front of his teammates was the enigmatic Rene Faulk. The only problem with that plan was Faulk's unexplained absence from the meeting. "Man-Child," was an embarrassment on Saturday," Campbell said. "And now he is not even here. He blocked nobody all day. All he did was stand around and let people run around his big fat ass and now he can't even show up for practice," said an angry Campbell.

Coach West continued with the stinging dissecting assessment of the offensive line's play, "Mental breakdowns, mental lapses, no fight, no fire," West lectured in a voice rising in volume and emotion. "Sumner will kick your ass on Saturday, if we do not get some things straightened out. And I mean right now. They (Sumner) won 62-0 on Saturday. 62-0! Think they don't want to kick your ass this Saturday? Think they don't want to pay you back for the last two years? Think (former RHS) Coach Harvey doesn't want to pay you back for the last two years. Coach Campbell and I talked about this all last night. We are going to find some people who will block. I don't care how big you are, your ass is going to the bench and I will start pulling linebackers, ends, defensive backs, kickers, whoever I can find that will go on that field with some fire and some drive, because none of you offensive linemen had any of that on Saturday. I want guys out there who play like Rottweilers who haven't eaten for nine days. I want hungry players and I am going to find them."

Coach West, well known amongst the players for his impassionate pleas that tug at their collective pride, was just warming up. It was the absolute worse timing possible for the late arriving Rene Faulk. When West spotted Faulk, 30 minutes late for practice, attempting to slide undetected – always a difficult task for the 6 foot three inch 310 pound 16 year old - into the top row of seats, he unloaded both barrels of his disgust upon the huge junior lineman. "Man-Child," you finally make it! So good of you to join us my friend! And "Man-Child," that was a great article (Faulk had recently been featured in a local publication on high school football). Be sure and bring it with you to read on Saturday, when your lazy ass is sitting on the bench, because that is exactly where you are going to be. You are a bullshit practice player and because of that you are a bullshit game player. And that is our fault, us coaches, for letting you get away with it and it is going to stop, dude, it is going to stop. You got to make a decision right now, "Man-Child," either get with it right now or turn your shit in. I mean turn it in right now. You got a way out, man. You can chuck it and walk away right now. I will not look down on you if you quit." West shrugs his huge shoulders, spreads his hands palms up and grins to reinforce the sincerity of his offer. "I still like you, "Man-Child," and I will still shoot the bull with you. Will not hold it (quitting) against you, I promise. But I will never again watch you play football like I watched you Saturday, Your performance absolutely sucked this past game. You didn't quit. Dude, you never started!"

As West pauses to catch his breath, Campbell jumps back in. "This is the most talent I have had on a team in nine years, and I have had some good teams. But I am telling you dudes, you are close to being a complete flop. All the talking we've done, means nothing now, we need to buck up dudes, and right now. We will not win a game if we do not improve this week in practice."

"Seniors, raise your hands," West orders. "Now look around. Have you guys been leaders? I don't think so. Well let me clue you in. This Saturday, THE WAR IS ON. It is on, fellows. You bet your ass it is. Sumner is going to bring it. And Roosevelt better bring it too, or your senior year is going to be the biggest flop you have ever experienced. It's your call, dudes." West grins one last time for emphasis and begins his slow walk to the practice field.

By Tuesday, the Roosevelt football program, which only a few short weeks prior had appeared a steady sea going vessel, had now hit an iceberg and was sinking fast. As the after school practice session began, the attention span of the athletes was, at best, minimal. Their on field practice performance, worse. With the practice session less than halfway completed, Coach Campbell banished the entire team, sending them home and canceling the rest of the week's varsity practices. "Get out. I am through," said a clearly frustrated Campbell. "I don't want to see any of you until next Monday. I will take the JV over to play Sumner on Saturday. Right now, I don't want you on my football team. We have no leadership. You don't care, so why should I? Get out!"

As the varsity squad slowly trudged its' way to the locker room, chief mumbles among the players were inquires as to Campbell's seriousness. Was he for real? Would he throw away an all important and winnable conference game with Sumner? Or was the banishment just a ploy to get their attention? Opinions varied, from the upset "piss on him, I am tired of him fucking with my head" attitudes of a few disgruntled seniors, to the now panic stricken majority who saw all of their hopes and dreams of a memorable senior season swirling rapidly down the drain. "Fuck you, man; you don't care and that is why we are the team we are right now," was the angry and confrontational response from one senior who questioned the will to win of the complainers. A team that had spent the off season dreaming grandiose visions of state titles, was now knocking squarely on the door of disaster. Could things get much worse?

By Wednesday, Campbell was in damage control mode. He spent a good part of the school day in small group soul searching discussions with team leaders. "George Bell," Campbell inquired of the intelligent and introspective senior, "what is going on? This is bullshit, man. We got too much talent with this team. You know Kansas State called me today. They are coming to the Gateway Tech game. Will we even still have a team by then? You seniors have got to turn this thing around. We have got to get this righted, and immediately."

Bell inquired as to Campbell's intention to follow through with his pronouncement of the previous evening that the varsity was banned from the field until next Monday; with the JV providing the Roosevelt entry for Saturday's game with Sumner. When Campbell confirmed that this was still his intention, Bell proposed instead a player's only meeting in the locker room after school. It was the senior captain's hope, he told Campbell, to lay it on the line to his comrades, that this was a team at a crossroads. The 2008 season was hanging by a thread. It was time to clear the air.

"We are not a family, George, because we have no senior leadership right now," Campbell said. "It is falling apart man. We can't have another practice like last night. If we do, I am through with you guys. You want a chance to straighten this out? Ok, you got it. But I am telling you George, this is it. We turn it around right now, or I go with the JV, and to hell with the scouts from K-State."

True to his word, Bell organized a player's only meeting to be held Wednesday afternoon. The varsity players met at 3 pm in their cramped downstairs locker room. Whatever was said, it launched a noticeable different attitude, a refocused football team that conducted on Wednesday, the team's best practice in at least two weeks. "We just was honest with each other and tried to talk about how we needed to come together as a team," confided Quadricous Sanford. "We want to win so bad, we are going to overcome this. We still believe in each other and that is all, right now, that matters. Coaches don't want to coach us, fine, we will coach ourselves. We're alright. You will see on Saturday."

Winning makes a multitude of sins disappear. The air is cleared, rifts are bridged and past bones of contention are buried. The Roosevelt Roughriders needed a win in the most desperate of ways in their week two encounter against the dangerous Sumner Bulldogs. The game was not pretty, and it did not go completely as it had been scripted by the RHS coaches, but it was a win nonetheless, a 21-0 shutout.

Roosevelt took control early as they scored two first quarter touchdowns. The first score came as the climax of a drive that began with the game's opening kickoff. The Roughriders marched the length of the field, buoyed by a balanced running and passing attack. Arlando Bailey scored the first offensive TD of the season with a 5 yard quarterback keeper. The second touchdown came less than four minutes later, as Roosevelt converted a Sumner turnover- a Charles (Smoke) Weatherspoon pass interception - into a Bailey to Antonio Carter 15 yard touchdown pass. Carter, as he did throughout the day, broke several Bulldog tackles as he scampered into the end zone. Mohammad Dukly converted both point after touchdown kicks, as the Roughriders appeared to be poised for a possible rout of their PHL opponent.

"Feels just like last year," Bailey told the coaches as he left the field after the second score. Bailey and his teammates executed their spread offense to perfection in the first 8 minutes of the game, despite operating into the teeth of a blustery 15-25 mile an hour wind. The offense, for the first time all season, looked unstoppable. The Sumner defense was on its heels, with no apparent response to the balanced run/pass Roosevelt offense. On the far sideline, the Sumner coaches could be seen shaking their heads. This game had the look of a lopsided Roosevelt win and one long afternoon for the north side Sumner Bulldogs.

But as suddenly as Roosevelt had caught offensive fire, their productivity fizzled. Bailey and the offense moved the ball consistently the remainder of the half, but first an interception, followed by a Bailey fumble on the Sumner two yard line that derailed two deep drives into the enemy's red zone. On the third offensive drive of the second quarter; Campbell called on his developing secret weapon, kicker Muhammad Dukly, to try the first field goal of his career, from an unheard of distance in the PHL, 47 yards. With the wind at his back in warm-ups, Dukly had blasted two rocket shots through the goal posts from a distance of 50 yards. As the Roughriders lined up for the field goal attempt, the side judged refused to allow Roosevelt to sub in the ball that Dukly preferred to kick with. The kick fell 2 yards short.

The low point of the game for Roosevelt came in the first five minutes of the second half. Sumner had won the pre game coin toss and had deferred to the second half. Their choice to take the ball to begin the third quarter left Roosevelt with the option of taking the increasingly strong wind in the third quarter in an attempt to place the game out of reach; or to go into the wind the third quarter, banking on the defense repeating its strong first half performance, giving Roosevelt the advantage in the 4th quarter. Roosevelt chose the wind for the third quarter with the hope of a quick knock out punch. The aggressive strategy almost blew up in the Roughriders face.

After the wind aided kickoff from Dukly sailed through the end zone, Sumner started the first drive of the second half from its own 20 yard line. For the first time in the game, the Bulldogs executed their offense to perfection, and thus generated the worst case scenario for Roosevelt. By keeping the ball on the ground

Chapter 5: The Regular Season

and driving the length of the field, Sumner ate up over one half of the third quarter, negating any attempt by the Roosevelt offense to use the third quarter wind to their advantage. On a 4th and goal from the 13 yard line, the Sumner offense put the finishing touches on an impressive drive with a circus catch in the right hand corner of the end zone by a leaping Bulldog receiver. The apparent touchdown would cut the Roosevelt lead in half. The momentum of the contest had made a marked shift to the direction of the team in the maroon jerseys. The joy of the north side school however, was short lived. A holding penalty negated the touchdown and the drive stalled.

The reprieve pumped new life into the Roosevelt offense. In their best drive of the day, after taking over on the Sumner 26 yard line, Bailey led the offense on a 74 yard, 8 play excursion into the Bulldog end zone. The touchdown scoring play came on a third and long as Antonio Carter found pay dirt for the second time in the game, his first rushing touchdown of the season. Carter's 25 yard jaunt featured several broken tackles and highlighted the lethal combination of speed, balance and power that made Carter one of the most feared running backs in the PHL. Dukly added the extra point kick for a now comfortable 21 point lead.

Sumner entered the red zone one more time late in the game, threatening the Roughrider's defensive shutout. Rivalries within a team, based on one's alliance to either the offense or defense, are a common concern and rift creator on many football teams. Due to so many Roosevelt players going both ways – playing both offense and defense – the offensive/defensive rivalry within this team was more of one between RHS coaches than the Roughrider players.

By the Sumner contest, the second game of the season, it was still unclear who the team's defensive coordinator was. At various time over the summer and through pre season practice, Coach Campbell had referred to both Coach West and Coach Wade as defensive coordinator. On several other occasions he had referred to himself as the head defensive coach. Coach Darren Wade had called most of the defensive signals during the Sumner game and desperately wanted to see his unit's stellar performance rewarded with the ultimate tribute to any football defense, a complete game shutout of the opposition.

With less than two minutes to go in the 4th quarter, the Roughriders faced a fourth down at their own 40 yard line. A decent punt, buoyed by a shifting strong wind, would have pushed Sumner deep into its own end of the field and negated any reasonable chance at a score in the games waning minutes. Much to the demonstrative agitation of Coach Wade, Campbell made the surprisingly unorthodox decision to go on fourth down. An incomplete pass turned the ball over to Sumner, only 40 yards from the Roosevelt end zone, and with a strong wind at the Bulldogs backs. To add to Wade's darkening mood, Campbell also sent in the second team defense.

It is accepted protocol in football, that after the game's outcome has been obviously decided, you do not embarrass an overmatched opponent by continuing to rack up points by the use of your first string offensive personnel. Defense, however, is another matter. Almost all teams when faced with the opportunity to gain a shutout, will deploy their first string defense until the game's conclusion. Wade's consternation steamed from what he saw as a lack of his input into the late game substitution decision, coupled with his anger over what he perceived as Campbell's lack of appreciation of the defense's efforts in shutting out the Sumner offense, a unit that had scored 62 points the previous Saturday. By deciding not to punt on 4th down, Wade felt that the head coach was not showing support for what Wade and the defense viewed as a noble goal, a shut out. "I can't handle this anymore," Wade confided to a friend on the sidelines. He had now positioned himself at the opposite end of the bench area, as far away from his defense and the rest of the coaching staff as he could. Wade's chosen area of stance spoke to his displeasure with the events that had transpired in the games waning moments. "They don't want to listen to me, fine. I don't want to coach."

Ultimately Roosevelt's second team defense proved up to the challenge and kept the Bulldogs out of the end zone. The Roughriders had earned a hard fought, and much needed, 21-0 win over a dangerous Sumner squad.

From a spectator's view, the game had appeared to be sloppily played on both sides. However, the final game statistics showed a solid, if not spectacular Roosevelt effort. Bailey completed 18 of 24 passes for 308 yards, an eye popping average of 17.1 yards per reception. He threw for one touchdown and had one pass intercepted. Antonio Carter was workmanlike, with his day's effort of 18 carries for 125 yards and two touchdowns. Quadricous Sanford had an outstanding game on both offense and defense. He finished the day with six catches for 120 yards, one rushing attempt for 35 yards, a 35 yard kick off return, setting the tone to start the game, and propel Roosevelt to its early first touchdown. On defense Sanford was also a star, recording an interception and a soon to be disputed six defensive tackles.

For the day, the Roughriders showed the type of offensive balance – 24 passes, 26 rushes – that Coach Campbell had dreamed of in the off season. The resulting 509 yards of total offense was a figure that would be sufficient to win most games on the RHS schedule.

Although his offensive skills garnered him the most publicity, it was Sanford's performance as a defensive back that excited college coaches. His ability to close on the football from his defensive safety position caught the eye of any talent scout viewing a Roughrider game tape. Sanford was relentless in his pursuit of the football. As one coach waxed poetically to the defensive closing speed of the talented young South Paola, Mississippi transplant, "Only Cinderella's step sisters get to the ball faster than Q."

Statistics also played a role in the day's last bit of drama. As the Roughriders gathered their gear from the makeshift meeting site in the grassy area behind their bench at Soldan Tiger Stadium, Sanford was seen jawing with a young assistant coach who had kept the statistical tackle sheet for the game. "Come on man, I know I had more tackles than that. What game you watching?" Sanford pleaded. The young coach was more than willing to stand his ground and assertively meet the challenge to his authoritative role by the young star player, only several years his junior. "Get out my face man, you got what you earned. The tackles are correct," the animated young coach yelled at Sanford.

Campbell witnessed only the end of the encounter and he instinctively chose to verbally confront his young assistant. "Man why you always in someone's face," Campbell scolded the assistant coach. "You suppose to be my boy and every time I look around you challenging someone. Now it's "Mississippi." Man you been watching too much of that Tupoc shit on TV. Drop all that." The younger coach was steadfast in his refusal to relent - to the star player or to the head coach. "The stats is right, coach. "Mississippi" got all he had coming, and then he is up in my face and you taking his side. I don't need this," said the young coach, tossing his clipboard in the air, slinging his arms wildly for emphasis and storming towards the exit gate. "Hey man," Campbell said, "now don't go away mad. Get back here, man, we got to all get along."

The young assistant accepted Campbell's peace offering, reversed his field and returned to confront his former coach and current boss. "I just trying to do my job, Coach Campbell," he said in an almost whisper. "I know you are" said the head coach, in a now soothing tone to the young man who only several years prior had played for Campbell during his stint as an assistant coach at Beaumont. "You still my boy, but man you got to tone it down. Drop all that gangster act. We got a long season still to go."

The assistant nodded his head while gathering from the Soldan Stadium turf his discarded clip board and its contested statistical data. "But I am telling you, "Mississippi" got all he got coming, and that I ain't going to change it." In a calm voice, Campbell reassured the young coach, "Nobody asking you to dude, now let's get to the bus and get out of here."

The young first year coach then began his second exit from the field, at a much slower pace than the original tract, feeling he had maintained some semblance of status by not backing down to either the star senior player or the head coach.

One could only wonder what the mood within the Roosevelt program would be at this time if the game's outcome had been reversed.

The third game of the regular season would be the long anticipated encounter between the two pre-season PHL top picks, the Roosevelt Roughriders and the Gateway Tech Jaguars. Gateway was coming off what one St. Louis area paper was calling "the biggest PHL win in years," a thrilling 14-7 victory over outstate powerhouse Jackson. A strong rivalry existed between the two PHL rivals. Gateway was viewed by many at Roosevelt as the recipient of favoritism by the downtown SLPS administration. Gateway was a magnet school and was often held up to public view by school leaders as an example of an urban school success story. Admission to Gateway was dependent upon a merit entrance test. The student body included black and white students from throughout the city, and a number of white students from St. Louis County, all drawn to Gateway by the school's award winning technology based curriculum. Money, some at Roosevelt complained, seemed to flow much freer to a magnet school like Gateway, than to a neighborhood school like Roosevelt.

The rivalry between the two football teams, both coaches and players, was also deeply rooted in the dislike each felt for the other. "Gateway got all the talent, how often we heard that?" Campbell asked his team the Monday before the game. He then alluded to the team's two marquee athletes: "They got Pearson and they got Richardson; and they both too good to go to some half ass neighborhood school like Roosevelt. How often we heard that? But remember, they have never beat us on the football field and they are not going to on Saturday, and you know why?" Campbell asked his team. Not waiting for an answer to his own question, Campbell told his assembled squad, "because we will be more disciplined than them."

The start of practice time at Roosevelt was always in a state of flux. The set announced time for most days was simply; "after school." Players would show up anywhere from 2:45 to 3:20. The late arrivers, from the view of an outsider, never seemed to be in a hurry - no sense of a pressing urgency to be on the field for the stretching exercises that signaled the beginning of practice. It was not uncommon for coaches and players alike to come wandering onto the practice field after the majority of the group had already begun the day's organized schedule. For some, like Rene Faulk (at least early in the season), it was more of a surprise for him to be on time for practice than it was for him to be tardy.

Getting his players to be punctual in their responsibilities as members of his team was a problem that Campbell acknowledged, but took a pragmatic view of. Arriving in time for the start of practice was a challenge for both Roosevelt players and coaches alike. In many of the nations top high school programs, football was the number one responsibility in a young player's life. Short of the funeral of an immediate family member, an athlete never had a legitimate reason to miss practice. Not true at inner city schools like Roosevelt. All of the Roughriders assistant coaches taught at schools other than Roosevelt. The top two varsity assistants, Coaches Wade and West, were employed as full time teachers at city school Beaumont High and the county school district of Brentwood, respectively. Both coaches were often at the mercy of their own building administrators who made professional demands upon their time, with little regard to the impending practice schedule of the Roosevelt Roughriders football team. Wade was indeed a coaching nomad. He coached football at Roosevelt, was the head track and field coach at his home district, Brentwood, and was the head varsity girl's basketball coach at the all inner city Catholic high school Cardinal Ritter Prep. (In March of 2009, Wade's Lady Lion cagers, a team with no history of success and an average record in 2009, made a Cinderella run to a Class 3 Missouri State Championship, winning the title game by one point on a last second free throw.) Even Head Coach Campbell would often find himself with conflicting responsibilities outside of his duties as head football coach, tearing him away from his team at the most inconvenient of times.

Compounding the problem was that inner city players were subjugated to the demands of everyday survival that were standard for poor urban kids – jobs, constant relocation to the homes of various relatives, the obligations of parenthood – but not conducive to building a championship level high school football program. A real concern for where their next meal would come from was the stark reality of survival for many of the Roosevelt athletes. Football was a brief distraction, a much welcomed interlude, from the very real issues of everyday poverty. Many of the players, to the constant frustration of the coaches, treated football as just such: a distraction.

By Tuesday of the Gateway Tech game week, the developing soap opera that was becoming "Team Roosevelt" was back in full production. Campbell was forced to spend the first 15 minutes of practice playing peace keeper between Senior Tyler Clubb and a junior defensive back. As customary, the players started the day's practice routine with a two lap jog around the field's 1/2 mile track. Clubb had been tardy and did his warm up run after the rest of the team had completed the task. The underclassman had noted that Tyler had only jogged one lap before joining his fellow linemen in a blocking drill. "Tyler, run your other fucking lap," the underclassman had called out loud enough for everyone to hear. This unwelcomed order enraged Clubb at what he considered a form of disrespect shown him by his younger teammate. In anger, Clubb removed his helmet and informed his challenger: "You are no captain and you are no senior, you don't tell me what to do. I got to take no disrespect bullshit from you." The underclassman, faced with the option of losing face before the entire team and being shown up by Clubb, a white upperclassman at that, held his ground. "You no better that anyone else here. Run your fucking laps like me. Now you showing me disrespect," said the junior.

Coach Campbell arrived at practice in the middle of the confrontation, not privy to the circumstances that had ignited what was turning into a very combustible situation, immediately took charge. "Tyler, you need to run your laps," Campbell said calmly.

"I don't need him telling me shit," said Clubb. "I don't respect him because he has done nothing to earn my respect. I respect my seniors and they can tell me to run and I will run. But not him," Clubb gestured angrily with his helmet still in hand at his adversary.

"Tyler," Campbell said in a still calm voice, "I am telling you, run your laps."

Clubb, one of the most committed and devoted members of the team, made the snap judgment that enough was enough. "I don't need this shit and I am out of here." Now brisk with anger, Tyler began to walk off the field in a defiant show of insubordination, in effect, quitting the team. Several of Clubb's senior friends and teammates ran after him, pleading with him that he was making a fatal and regrettable mistake.

Halfway up the stairs from the practice field to the locker room, Clubb's shoulders noticeably sank. His decision making ability now perhaps more rational, he returned with his teammates to the practice field, and completed the day's work, after running his one owed lap.

At the conclusion of practice, Campbell addressed Clubb's pre-practice mutiny. It was Campbell once again playing an ever increasing role - team psychologist. "Guys, we got to get along. We talk all the time about family. What was this bullshit at the start of practice all about?" Campbell then allowed each of the participants to voice their opinion. Several team leaders then gave their take on the issue of "respect" and who had disciplinary authority on the team and who did not. "Guys, do what the captains say," Campbell advised. "If you don't think it is fair, for the good of the team, do it anyway and then bring it to my or any of the coach's attention. Fellows, it is called following the chain of command, and it is how things work in the real world."

Despite the rocky start, the practice had gone well and Campbell was pleased. His post practice mood rubbed off on his players. Tensions that had built to breakable levels over the past several weeks seemed to loosen. Jokes were cracked freely among the players and coaches.

During the after practice talk, Coach West stressed the importance of "families" talking with each other to work out their problems. Prior to ending the day's practice and dismissing the team, Campbell called Clubb, Stephen Banta - the team's other white member - and quarterback Arlando Bailey to the front. "Guys, these are our three Caucasian teammates; we got to be nice to them." The inclusion of the African American Bailey, who lived with white foster parents and who eschewed the conventional urban dress and language of his black teammates; brought a roar of laughter from the team, with Bailey perhaps laughing the loudest. The Roosevelt Soap Opera was still in production but the storm of discontent between the coaches and players, while maybe not having yet completely passed, seemed to have at least hit a lull.

On Friday, before practice, Campbell lectured his athletes about their expected behavior at that evening's Beaumont vs. Career Academy game. The two conference schools were scheduled to play under the lights at Gateway's Field, the evening before the Gateway vs. Roosevelt matchup. The Roughriders, as a show of team unity, had plans to attend the Friday game at Gateway en mass.

Campbell warned his players, "You go over there tonight, remember you are representing Roosevelt High School. You are representing me and Mr. Houston. You are representing your families and everyone who cares about you. I want you all in your red shirts. I want you looking and acting like a team. No sagging. No running your mouth. No 'nigger this and nigger that.' You act up and everyone says that is just the way they are at Roosevelt. I will hear about it and so will Mr. Houston. You know Gateway's players will be there. You know they will be talking shit. You stay disciplined and on Saturday, when the game is over, you just point to the scoreboard. That will shut them up. They have great players, but they have no discipline. That is why we will win, and it starts with your behavior over there this evening."

At Saturday morning's pregame breakfast, several players reported to Campbell, with pride, that they had followed his advice to the letter. One of Gateway's star players, who had just recently received a full scholarship offer from the University of Miami had, according to the Roosevelt players, made repeated attempts to cause a confrontation. The Roughriders told Campbell that they had ignored such loud taunts as "fuck Roosevelt and fuck Campbell too. They coming to my house tomorrow." Tomorrow was now here - and as Campbell had told his players the night before, the scoreboard would have the ultimate and final word.

Gateway Tech Stadium was considered the crown jewel of the PHL's football facilities. It was the only public facility in the city that had both a legal sized usable running track and lights. The district administration several weeks prior had refused to let Roosevelt hold its pre-season jamboree at the Gateway field because of the chance of rain. The downtown office had canceled the event 24 hours in advance on a weekend that saw not a drop of rainfall. With such pampering of the turf, one would expect to find a playing surface of an immaculate green carpet of well maintained grass. In reality, the field was a mess. It was obvious that Gateway had used it for a practice field, regardless of the weather. The center of the field, the area between the hash marks and the 20 yard lines, was barren, uneven and hard. The people at PHL, Inc., who had funneled a large amount of money into the field, would not have been happy if they could now witness the negligent care provided for their investment. As one Roosevelt assistant coach stated while inspecting the field before the team began its pre game warm up, "They canceled our Jamboree to save this? What a bunch of shit. Nothing they (the district administration) do makes any fucking sense."

The game started for Roosevelt with an offensive bang, as the Roughriders drove the length of the field on its first offensive possession, hitting pay dirt on a 20 yard touchdown pass from Bailey to Sanford. It was the beginning of what to this point in his Roosevelt career, would be Bailey's most productive day. For the first time all season, Dukly missed the extra point, pulling his kick wide left. Roosevelt 6, Gateway 0.

Gateway wasted no time in tying the score. On the home team's second play from scrimmage, after Dukly had booted the kick off into the end zone, sophomore running back sensation Anthony Pierson took a pitchout to the short side of the field, sprinted to his left, broke several tackles at the line of scrimmage and dashed untouched 79 yards into the end zone. Gateway also missed their conversion kick and with less than four minutes elapsed on the scoreboard clock; each team had already tallied a touchdown.

Due to the easy touchdown run of Pearson, the Roosevelt defensive coaches made several early personnel changes, moving smaller but quicker athletes into the defensive end positions. On their next offensive possession, Gateway continued to try and run around the ends. When this strategy met with futility, the Gateway coaches elected to try to attack the talented Roosevelt pass defenders, which proved to be a big mistake as Sanford, George Bell and Charles (Smoke) Weatherspoon each picked off a pass to stifle a Gateway offense that found little first half success after Pierson's early long touchdown run.

The Roosevelt offense, although not proficient to an extreme, did move the ball consistently in the first half, especially through the air. With 10:08 left in the second quarter, Kicker Dukly notched his first career field goal, a 27 yard effort, into the wind to put the Riders on top, 9-6. After a punt from each squad, Bailey and the Roosevelt aerial attack broke loose again. The emerging senior quarterback found Robert Scott sprinting away from a Gateway defensive back down the left sideline. Scott never broke stride as he hauled in the perfect tight spiraling pass and sprinted into the east end zone with a 65 yard TD reception. Roosevelt, after a failed two point conversion attempt, now held a 15-6 half time lead.

Once again, at halftime, Campbell was not happy with the play of his offensive line, again reading them the riot act. "We are not blocking shit," was his cut to the bone assessment of the unit's first half performance. Coach West seconded his point. "Terrible. We cannot run the ball if you are just going to lean on people. We have got to make contact and drive. We have got to get a helmet on their second line people (linebackers and defensive backs)." Campbell sensed the frustration of his running back, Antonio Carter, who had been held to 24 first half rushing yards. Carter had been overshadowed by Pierson, the talented sophomore Jaguar. Carter's pride was wounded. He viewed himself as the best back in the league and he knew that his paltry first half rushing total had left him in Pierson's shadow. Carter had hoped for a break out game, using the notoriety from his duel with Pearson to jump start the college interest in his future services. Campbell came to his embattled star's aid. "Antonio is working his ass off out there. He is hitting, he is clawing, he is laying it all out, and you lazy asses will not block for him. I will say it again, and I have said it at least one hundred times, this team will go only as far as our offensive line will take us." Wrapping up on a positive note, Campbell said, "You are doing a great job pass blocking. We need to see that same effort when we run block."

Campbell's irritation with the performance of the offensive line was rooted in his fondness for Carter, and the effort the senior brought to the field each Saturday. Nobody ran the ball with more effort, with more reckless abandon, than the 140 pound Carter. He would think nothing of lowering his head to take on a tackler twice his size. Carter did not go down easy. A defender who did not "wrap up" the Roosevelt back, would see Carter pinball off the tackler and continue plowing up field. On one play in the second quarter of the Gateway game, Carter took a pitchout to his right and was met in his own backfield by two Gateway defenders. Carter split both men, but one blue clad defender did manage to reach out and dislodge Carter's helmet as he spun away from the contact. Carrying the ball in his right arm, Carter somehow reached out with his left hand to instinctively catch his head gear as it fell from his head and before it struck the ground. Without breaking stride and with a look of disdain in his wide eyes, Carter tossed his helmet to the side, without hesitation, discarding the vital piece of equipment, in favor of continuing his attack into the Gateway secondary. It was an emphatic display of courage and desire by the undersized back, aptly described by one rival PHL coach as having "more guts than a fish market."

The five man officiating crew of the Roosevelt vs. Gateway contest enforced an unheard of 31 penalties against the two teams - 17 on Gateway and 14 on Roosevelt. Four offsetting penalties (flags on each team on the same play) were nullified by rule and not enforced. Roosevelt declined three Gateway infractions and the home team did the same on two other Roosevelt fouls. All told, the officiating crew detected and called 44 penalties in the 48 minute contest. Campbell's post game take after reviewing the film: "The officiating probably hurt us less than it did them" – his squad saw 100 yards in penalties marched off against them, while Gateway suffered to the tune of 154 yards – "but how many big plays did we lose to holding penalties? It is scary to think how many yards Mississippi (Quadricous Sanford) would have had on (punt) returns if he doesn't have those two called back (one a 70 yard punt return for a score). From looking at the film, I would say at least half of those holding penalties, on each team, should not have been called."

An RHS assistant coach saw racial overtones as an interesting dynamic for the game arbitrated by four white and one black official. "You get these white crews (of officials) down here and they show up before the game worried about a riot. They think 'Oh no, this is Gateway and Roosevelt. These kids are all in gangs. We have got to get this game under control or we will have a gang fight.' So they go overboard and throw a flag on every play. They ruined the game. They didn't cheat anybody and it might have even been subconscious on their part, but they ruined the game. If this had been two white county teams playing the exact same game, those jokers would not have thrown 1/3 of the flags they did on Saturday."

As proof of the coach's point, one need look no further than the game's first play from scrimmage. Roughrider offensive center, Tyler Clubb (ironically the only white player on the field regularly for each team), and his counterpart across the line of scrimmage - Gateway's defensive nose guard - were locked in a pile up. The official threw his flag and declared offsetting multiple fouls against each player. The man in stripes then admonished both teams in a loud voice, "I see any more of that from either one of you and you will be sitting on the sideline. And that goes for everyone else. We will not put up with any rough play today." An astounded Clubb, when he came to the bench at the end of the drive, expressed a confused and dumbfounded reaction as to the intent of the official's lecture. "I didn't do a damn thing. I just blocked him. I never said a word, I just waited for him to get off of me and the guy (official) throws a flag and jumps in my face. I have no idea why he called that penalty on me."

Later in the first half, sophomore defensive back Charles Banks caught a punt on his own forty yard line, broke several tackles as he raced down the near side of the field; neatly pivoted away from a would be sideline tackler at the Gateway 30 yard line, reversed direction and sprinted to the center of the field. Not breaking stride, Banks subsequently careened off of two final Gateway defenders and ran the last 20 yards untouched into the end zone. It was an electrifying 60 yard return that showcased the athletic ability of Banks. The play was called back due to another holding penalty (imagine that), but still the play had brought some energy to the previously quiet small contingent of Roosevelt rooters. After the score, as Banks ran to the sideline and before he realized that his spectacular return would be nullified by a penalty, the sophomore was greeted by teammate Quadricous Sanford and the two gave their best impression of an NFL version of the jump and bump celebration. The head official sprinted to the Roosevelt sideline, pulling Roughriders from his path until he reached Banks, grabbed the young man from behind by the shoulder pads, spun him around and informed him sternly, that "if I see that crap again it will cost you 15 yards. This isn't the NFL and you are not on TV, yet. Do you hear me?" Banks meekly nodded his head.

After the game, a Roughrider assistant broke down his view on the racial makeup of an officiating crew, the teams involved in the contest and the way the officials would inevitably call the game. "If you got an all black team and you are playing an all white team, you want white officials. The 'guilty conscious' kicks in. They will always call more penalties on them than us. Guaranteed. It is like Glory Road," - a reference to the famous NCAA basketball final in 1966 where an unheralded Texas Western University, with an unheard of for the era five black starters, upset an all white southern powerhouse Kentucky team. The contest was officiated by two white referees. The championship match was destined to echo throughout history for its social significance. Many observers felt that the two men in stripes that evening were under intense pressure to show the world they were not prejudiced against the black athletes of Texas Western; and subconsciously favored the upstarts to prove their color blindness. This type of reverse discrimination has been hotly disputed for years in debates on the dynamics of race and athletic competition. The RHS assistant coach concluded, "If your team is all black, you want all white officials. But if both teams are black and the officials are white, it will rain penalty flags all day."

Before sending his team back out onto the Gateway field for the second half, Coach Campbell lectured his men that the next 24 minutes of play would be a benchmark assessment of the 2008 Roosevelt Roughriders. "They are ranked 10th in the area. We are picked with them as one and two in the PHL. They have already this season beaten some top state wide teams. They have what many say are the best two players in the PHL. Well dudes, let me tell you something, we are better than them. We have better players, better athletes. We have better offensive and defensive (schemes). We have worked harder than them. There is no reason why we should not dominate this football team in the second half. We will know a lot more about what type of team we have when this second half is over. How bad do you want it?"

The Roughriders took their head coach's half time challenge to heart. After Gateway had cut the halftime lead to a slim margin of 3 points, with a third quarter Pierson touchdown scamper of 35 yards, for the first time all season, RHS showed the tenacity to finish off a good opponent; just the characteristic Campbell had asked his team at halftime to display. The offense continued to attack with a balanced run/pass onslaught. The defense buckled down on the corners and denied Pearson any more breakaway runs. Despite the continued shower of yellow penalty flags that seemed to fall on nearly every play, Roosevelt took control of the game and pulled away to a convincing 29-12 win. Two long 4th quarter drives lead to touchdowns, climaxed with a Bailey 15 yard pass to Sanford and an Antonio Carter 5 yard run. Roosevelt had gone on the road and showed the fortitude to dominate a good football team in the second half.

Bailey finished the game with another 300 yard + passing effort. His 19 for 33, 2 TD pass effort was marred only by the 3 interceptions he threw. Despite playing one fewer game than most all other QBs in the metro area, the release of the weekend's cumulative stats would show that Bailey's over 900 yard season total placed him well on top of the area passing charts.

Sanford had a monster day on offense, an effort that would propel him to the honor of Metro Area player of the week. He held on to nine of Bailey throws for 112 yards and returned seven kicks for a whopping total of 180 yards.

Running Back Antonio Carter was once again the odd man left out of the offensive statistical bonanza. He was held to a season low 38 yards on 13 carries, a dismal average of less than three yards per effort. Carter was noticeably downcast after the game. When given the opportunity by a teammate to criticize Coach Campbell's play calling, he deferred. Despite his diplomacy, it was obvious the senior was concerned about his lack of performance and how it would affect his college football aspirations. "It just didn't happen for me today. Just the way it was," Carter answered in a voice barely above a whisper as he walked off the Gateway field. "It will get better. It has to. I am a senior. No college going to want a back getting only 50 yards a game."

"Get your head up Dawg," Sanford instructed Carter as the two walked off the Gateway Field. "Your turn coming, you know it and so do we all."

"When?" asked Carter.

After the game – in what would prove to be arguably the best performance of the season by the Riders - Campbell praised his team but cautioned against a premature celebration. "This win is nice. It is a neighborhood win. You seniors never lost to Gateway, and they have had some good teams the last three years. We are in control now of the PHL race. But guys, that is not what we want. We have got to stay focused on districts. We want to go to state. Our mind right now is on what we need to do to get better. To get good enough to beat the district teams: Webster Groves, Chaminade and Vianney. We have got to get better on the offensive line. We can't live by the pass like we did today. We have got to be able to run the football. You cannot win championships if you cannot run the ball. We have got to be disciplined. This was a PHL game today, and although we beat a good team, you know what they are saying out there in the county, 'Roosevelt is still just another undisciplined PHL team full of thugs. Half asses that are too lazy and too undisciplined to beat the county teams.' We got a chance to prove them wrong. But we only got four weeks to get to that level, cause dudes, we ain't there yet."

The night previous to the Gateway game, the national TV Network ESPN had carried, live, the interstate high school football contest between the reigning large school Mississippi state champion, South Paola; and perennial Florida national power Apopka High. In recent years, such national broadcasts of high profile high school games have become commonplace on ESPN. The South Paola/Apopka game promised to be one of the best. South Paola owned the nation's longest current winning streak, 78 games, entering the showdown. Incredibly, the Tigers had not lost a game since the state championship contest in 2002. The current seniors on the 2008 team were in 5th grade the last time the Batesville, MS school tasted defeat on the gridiron. An interested observer of the contest was arguably Roosevelt's best player, Quadricous (Mississippi) Sanford.

Sanford had attended the South Paola schools his entire life before moving to St. Louis the summer before his sophomore year. He played in the South Paola football program during his junior high days and as a freshman, spending the summer before his sophomore year immersed in the off season training program of the Mississippi powerhouse. A late summer decision, agreed upon by both Quadricous and his parents, had sent him north to St. Louis to live with his grandmother. His enrollment at Roosevelt and his subsequent addition to the Roughrider team was an unexpected housewarming gift for the new RHS head football coach, DeAndre Campbell.

Sanford has no qualms about discussing the monster that has become South Paola football. "First class. The town really comes together. There is still a lot of racial stuff in Mississippi. Especially in the Delta. (Batesville is located in North Mississippi, 60 miles south of downtown Memphis, an area that saw many of the South's more violent episodes during the 60's Civil Rights Movement). But on Friday night, everyone, the whole town, whites and blacks, come together," said Sanford.

South Paola's student body is predominately black - 48%, compared to 46% white and 6% "other," mostly students of Hispanic decent. The quality of the equipment and facilities of the South Paola's program dwarfs the imagination of anything a member of the Roughriders would experience during their careers in the PHL.

"I started in 7th grade," reminisced Sanford. "From that point on at our school, football was everything. We worked year round. In junior high, we ran the same offenses and defenses that the high school varsity ran."

The regimentation and the precision of the program at the Mississippi school were stark in contrast to what Roosevelt players would experience. With the constant movement in student residency, most Roosevelt athletes would never acquire the sense of ownership and school loyalty grounded in the roots of long term attendance in one school system. All of the main ingredients that made up the 2008 edition of the Roughriders - Bailey, Faulk, Carter, Bell, along with Sanford, had seen numerous moves throughout their educational sojourn. The only exception to this nomadic routine was ironically the teams lone white senior, Tyler Clubb. Tyler had attended the St. Louis Public Schools since entering kindergarten, 13 years prior.

Sanford is vague about why he left the only town he had ever lived in, just as he was ready to walk in the front door of one of the biggest mansions in high school football. "It was best for me. Coming to St. Louis was the best hope I had for getting to my potential as a person. It was hard," he says. "But I needed to get away. It was for the best. If I wanted to get to college and achieve to my academic potential, I needed to get away. I spent the summer before my sophomore year working out in Mississippi, planning on making the varsity squad. But at the end of the summer, my parents and I agreed that it would be best if I moved to St. Louis to live with my grandma."

Over the course of his senior year, even though asked repeatedly about his abrupt move to St. Louis, Sanford would never give a specific reason for the change, remaining mum to all questions. The mystery of his transfer cast an enigmatic shadow over the otherwise openly friendly Sanford, a sort of closely guarded personal secret. Head Coach Campbell chose not to push the issue with Sanford. "I am just glad he is here," said Campbell. "He can flat out play and we would be hard pressed to replace him."

South Paola - whose 2008 roster contained three of Sanford's first cousins - plays its home games in a new multi million dollar athletic complex; complete with such glitzy accessories as a new artificial playing surface, a video re-play scoreboard, a state of the art training room, a well equipped strength training area and a spacious and well furnished locker room. In contrast, Sanford and his Roosevelt teammates dressed for home games in a cramped locker room so small that after putting on enough essentials to meet modesty standards, most Roosevelt players would take the bulk of their pads and uniforms outside and finish dressing in the school parking lot. For home games, the locker room's limited size would not allow for the whole squad to assemble together. The RHS coaches would conduct both pre-game and halftime sessions in a grassy and shady area to the north of the stadium, adjacent to the west side of the school. Any need for the use of a restroom was facilitated by the well placed bushes that lined the lower level of the school building. While Sanford's former friends and team mates in Mississippi conducted pre game and half time meetings with their coaches in posh climate controlled modern meeting rooms, Sanford's environment at Roosevelt was much more primitive. During pre-game and halftime sessions at Roughrider Stadium, when nature called, Sanford simply arose from his seat under a shade tree and relieved himself in the bushes next to the school.

To an outsider, the lack of expectations of both players and coaches in the PHL, in regard to facilities, was eye opening. Surprisingly, the coaches and players seldom complained about the wretched conditions they worked daily in. But to an outside observer, the lack of concern for better game and facility organization on the part of the district's administration was galling.

One coach, when pushed about the pathetic conditions endured by PHL members, gave a succinct declaration, with nothing more than a shrug of the shoulders: "the people running the PHL don't give a shit."

Aging PHL scoreboards that were constructed to give the down and distance for each play, would seldom have that capability utilized. If one was to believe the scoreboard's information, every play from scrimmage in the PHL is first and 10. The chain gang and those who manned it were an ongoing adventure at PHL football games. In many established high school football programs, it was viewed as a privilege to operate the first down chains on game night. Many schools have the same three or four community members man the chain crew year after year. In the PHL, without exception, the chain gang consisted of three junior varsity players, drafted by the home team's varsity coach. These conscripts would make anyone within ear shot aware that they did not want this "honor." Their job performance would most often reflect their lack of interest. Frustrated referees were in constant conflict with these youths to not move the chains until signaled to. It was also hard to operate the first down sticks in a timely and accurate manner, when one of your hands is in a constant commitment to holding up your oversized pants.

Before the onslaught of soccer style place kickers into American football, a movement that showed itself in the late 1960's, then flourishing in the 70's and 80's, every football team had a kicker who would boot the ball with his toe. In contrast to a soccer style technique where the kicker would strike the ball with their instep, this old school form of kicking was known as "Straight On" or American style place kicking.

To aid the "toe" kicker's consistency, accuracy and distance - the three most important characteristics of a successful football kick - the "kicking shoe" was

Chapter 5: The Regular Season 231

developed. The foot gear came with an enlarged squared toe area. It was also molded to have the toe area bent into an upward angle, thus stimulating the locking of the ankle when the ball was struck by the kicker's toe. This feature gives the ball good trajectory when kicked. The special shoe also gave the kicker a much larger area to "strike" the "sweet spot" of the ball when kicking.

The squared toe kicking shoe, once a staple found in the equipment bag of every football team, by 2008, had gone the way of the Polaroid snap shot and the slide rule; victims of new and improved ways of doing things.

With the disappearance from the football landscape of the toe kicker – Mark Mosley of the Washington Redskins in the late 80's was the last productive practicing professional of this style – most high school football players today have witnessed no other form of kicking a football than the sidewinder.

Roosevelt players were encouraged by the coaching staff to get to the practice field early if they wanted to work of special team skills: punting, kicking, long snapping and place kick holding. With the exception of place kicker and former soccer player Mohammad Dukly, who spent each practice session working solely on his kicking skills, all other specialists on the squad were also position players and had no time, other than the brief pre-practice time slot, during the after school practices to perfect these special skills.

One athlete who displayed a strong placekicking leg during these pre practice workouts was sophomore Reggie Curry, a practitioner of the old style toe kicking. Curry was nicknamed, for no known reason that any player or coach could offer, "Animal." He was a starting defensive and offensive lineman on the JV squad, but saw no varsity playing time.

One veteran coach had suggested buying Reggie a squared toed kicking shoe. "What" asked Coach Campbell? When the special piece of equipment was explained to Campbell, he continued to profess bewilderment. "Never heard of such a thing. Is it legal?" A quick survey of the other assistant coaches turned up a solid lack of any familiarity with a square toed kicking shoe.

The exception amongst the assistants, of course, was the nearly 40 year veteran of PHL football, Coach George Simmons. "Sure I know what it is. All kickers used them back in the old days," said Simmons. "Do what you got to do," a still disbelieving Campbell responded to the request to find such a shoe.

An extensive search was begun for the special shoe. First, calls were made to local sporting goods dealers. Store employees under the age of 40 had never heard of a kicking shoe, let alone ever sold any. "Is this a joke?" inquired one young clerk. Fearing he was being set up by his friends to be the butt of a practical prank - a snipe hunt sort of trickery - the young man was not going to bite.

"No kicking shoe, no, but we do have those special high tech batting glasses for hitting a baseball. They just came out and we got them on the shelves this morning. Makes a baseball look as big as a beach ball. Soon everyone in the big leagues will be wearing them. Can I interest you in a pair?"

Older dealers were not as flippant. "Sure I remember the square toed shoe, but I haven't sold one in years," reported one.

Finally, with the aid of the internet and E-Bay, a size 12 right footed square toe kicking shoe for sale was located in California. Within 10 days, it was placed on the right foot of Roosevelt sophomore Reggie "Animal" Curry.

Curry's first attempt with his new shoe, watched by a skeptical coaching staff, was squibbed badly off the side of his foot, driven on a low line drive flight pattern 20 yards wide of its intended target, the Roosevelt Stadium's east goal posts. His second kick, 25 yards from the uprights, took off like a missile. It orbited end over end to a height of at least 35 feet in the air as it cleared the goal post cross bar, continued to rise in an arc that would pass over the running track, over the 15 foot retaining wall behind the east end zone, over a school bus parked by the side of the road and halfway into the four lane, and busy, Gravois Road. The accompanying sound of "thud," when the ball was launched from Curry's right foot, gave added impact and drama to the startling unexpected performance.

Longtime baseball men say that a very few select hitters in the long history of the game, when making contact with a baseball's "sweet spot," could create a distinctive sound of horsehide striking wood that once heard, cannot be forgotten. The distinctive sound alone, tells the listener that the ball is leaving the park. Old timers say that Babe Ruth and Stan Musial belonged to this exclusive club. The same is said about current Cardinal superstar Albert Pujols.

"Hear that, hear that," said Coach West after witnessing Curry kick. "It sounded like the frigging ball was going to explode!" Curry's kick covered at least 55 yards in the air.

"Are you sure that thing (shoe) is legal?" Campbell asked for the second time.

Along with the opened mouth coaching staff, witnessing the event was a suddenly interested, and vulnerable, Mohammad Dukly. As the varsity wandered out to begin practice, news of "the kick" had spread amongst the older players. "Animal kicked one over the fucking bus," one senior lineman informed another as they stretched in preparation for the day's practice.

"Let me see that shoe," an unconvinced senior inquired of Curry, who was clearly basking in his new found celebrity.

"Looks like something Frankenstein would wear," assessed a second upperclassman. "Old school, dude, old school," another laughed.

"And it's legal," said Campbell, still shaking his head.

The usually unflappable Dukly followed Curry's kicking show with his worst practice of the year. During the 5 minute period devoted to the field goal unit, with the entire team and coaching staff in observation, he pulled three consecutive 35 yard field goal attempts wide to the right. Competition for Dukly, deemed after the previous game by his head coach as the best kicker in the PHL, had come suddenly and unexpectedly. The young African blew off in his typical caviler manner, the threat to his throne. "I not worry. "Animal" has no accuracy. Not like me. And soon as Ramadan is over (in 8 days), I will get my strength back. He just B team kicker. You will see."

Was Mohammad - before practice the reigning king of the PHL kicking core - now only the second best kicker on his own team? The possibilities lead to a great deal of good natured razzing from his teammates. Dukly failed to see the humor as he trotted back to his corner of the practice field to finish his solo, and lonely, practice kicking regimen.

Roosevelt's opponent in week four of the 2008 season would be the Beaumont Yellow Jackets, a team fighting through a miserable season. The previous Friday evening, with many of the Roosevelt players in attendance, Beaumont had fallen behind by halftime to a previously winless Miller Career Academy team, by the blowout margin of 45-0. Campbell did not try to con his players during the week prior to the Beaumont game with fearful stories of the danger that Beaumont could provide on Saturday to an overconfident team of Roughriders. "They are having a tough year," Campbell told his players on Monday. "They can't beat us, but they can make us regress if we don't stay focused. We have got to get better each week. Forget about Beaumont. We need to be ready for districts, and we can't do that if we have a crappy week of practice, simply because we know Beaumont can't beat us."

Campbell's honest approach seemed to work. After a workmanlike week of practice, the Roughriders dominated the overmatched opponent, winning by a final score of 46-0. After scoring on their first four possessions to claim a 27-0 first quarter lead, Campbell put his offense into ground mode, throwing a season low 12 passes for the game, only two after the first quarter. The RHS mentor also held out several starters to let them heal some lingering pains from the hard hitting Gateway game of the previous week. So dominant was the Roosevelt offensive attack that for, the entire game, the Roughriders were never forced to punt.

The lopsided matchup did allow Campbell the opportunity to pad the stats of the previous week's neglected star, running back Antonio Carter. Against Beaumont, the senior rushed 12 times for 112 yards. The current season's new emphasis on the spread offense had limited Carter's rushing attempts and had thus diminished what he had pinned his college hopes on: a breakout senior season. Where he had over the summer dreamed of a "two dime," or 2000 yard season he now was on a pace that put him in danger of falling below his junior year production level of slightly over 900 yards.

For many of the senior class of Roughriders, the only route they could visualize for a life beyond the city ghetto they now called home was a college football scholarship. However, the athletes knew that a full ride scholarship was a much sought after prize and only those with the glitziest of individual stats would catch the eye of the college talent scouts.

The statistical dilemma presented to Campbell had been forged by his own doing. Emphasis on individual statistics can destroy the heart and the soul of a team by creating jealousy and selfishness within its ranks. But players knew that without eye popping individual statistics, they would go unnoticed by college scouts. Campbell often used the dreams of a college football career and the ensuing scholarship that came with it, as a motivating factor for his inner city athletes. Campbell would also use the football aspirations of his players as a means to drive home the importance of maintaining a solid academic record. "Without the grades, you going to end up at SU – Shit University," he often reminded his players.

Too much emphasis on personal stats, as Campbell well knew, could serve as a death knoll for his team. It was his job to walk the teetering and often blurry line between the motivation that individual recognition brought, and the sacrifice for the good of the unit that, if withheld by jealous teammates, would doom his ambitious post season plans for his current crop of Roughriders.

Quarterback Bailey had been limited by Campbell's play calling to only 12 pass attempts against Beaumont. The emphasis on pumping up Carter's lethargic production via the run had caused Bailey to relinquish his spot at the top of the area passing charts.

Quadricous Sanford caught a season low three passes against the Yellow Jackets, necessitating his fall from the top of the area receiving statistics. It was a potential problem both players, and coaches were aware of it, even if reluctant to verbally address. "I am not worried about (stats)," said Bailey on the Monday after the Beaumont game. "I completed nine of twelve, so my percentage stayed up. Besides, my arm was sore, I needed the rest. As long as we win, I am fine."

Although noble in cause, Bailey's "one for all, all for one" pronouncements were hard to take at face value. He was, after all, still a teenager with big dreams fueled by, and validated through the eyes of, college recruiters by personal achievements. Several more "run first, pass second" game plans executed by Coach Campbell would leave the senior signal caller in his own state of athletic adrift, in jeopardy of finding himself odd man out in the race with his teammates for college football scholarships.

If faced with such a scenario, what would Bailey's reaction be? "I wouldn't be happy," he responded honestly. "Getting a college scholarship is why I have dedicated myself like I have for the last year. It drives me, drives everything I do, every decision on and off the field I make. Yes, I want very much to win, but I want even more to go to college."

Coach Campbell recognized that using a college scholarship as a motivating tool for improvement was a two sided sword. "Our players know that the harder they work, the more little things they do to make us a winner, then the more I will reward them by promoting them with college coaches. Sure, the scouts are going to look at stats, but they are also going to ask me, 'what kind of a kid is he? How coachable is he? What kind of a student is he? What kind of a citizen is he?' The kids have to understand that talent is only a part of it. Once they get to college, everyone has talent. Everyone had great high school stats. What sets the kid who gets to play in college over the one who does not is attitude. Our players know I will not lie to a college coach. If one of our kids has a 'me first' attitude, I will tell the coach that. College coaches know I will be honest with them about a player's attitude. If I am not, then that would risk my creditability with them, and would hurt our future players. I will not do that."

Campbell would often use both, past failures and successes, to hammer home his "team first" message to his players. During the week of preparation for the Vashon game, he told his defense: "You don't pursue to the ball, you don't fly down field to the ball, and then colleges will not want you. They want you to play fast and furious, snap to whistle. They want hitters, and when they look at the film of you, it will not lie. Have you heard Marquise got an offer from Michigan State this week? (Marquise Wallace was a 250 pound lineman who had graduated from Roosevelt in May 2008. Due to being a non academic NCAA qualifier, he was playing his freshman year of college football at Coffeyville Community College in Kansas). You know what got him that ride? The Chaminade game last year. I am talking Big Ten here guys, Michigan State! I am not talking about Shit University. The coaches at Michigan State loved his pursuit, the way he flew to the ball on every play. They couldn't care less how many tackles or sacks he had playing against high school boys. They want to see the film, man, and that film don't lie, guys. You want to play at the next level, you better fly to that ball."

The win over Beaumont was bittersweet for Roosevelt assistant coach Darren West, a Beaumont graduate, Class of 1991. West had left a legacy of success as a student at the near north side school. He graduated as the senior class president, the school's valedictorian and the captain of the Yellow Jackets 1990 PHL champion football team.

After high school graduation, West headed to the small town of Marshall, MO. The central Missouri enclave was home to Missouri Valley College, of whose football team West became a member. While suiting up with the Vikings, West became a teammate to fellow PHL alum, one year his junior, Cleveland Naval ROTC Academy grad DeAndre Campbell.

After three years at the outstate school, homesick and with a growing family to support, West returned to St. Louis and eventually, in 1996, earned his Bachelor's Degree in Education from his hometown's Harris-Stowe College. West's wife, Holly, also a Beaumont graduate, is an Administrator for the SLPS. The couple have three children, ages 20, 12 and 9.

West, much to the unhappiness of both he and Campbell, had been given a late summer transfer from Roosevelt back to Beaumont for the 2008-2009 school year. As the new school year began, the personable West was struggling to implement an In School Suspension (ISS) program at Beaumont. The program is a tool, and an option, for the school administration to use as a discipline resource in lieu of an Out of School Suspension (OSS). Depending on the severity and the type of infraction, wayward students are given book work and assignments by their regular class room teacher, to be done in the ISS room, all under the supervision of a monitor, who at Beaumont was now Coach West. The setting is to be Spartan, with the facilitator serving more of a role of overseer as opposed to mentor. Common thought among those who run high school buildings is that ISS is meant to be punishment and students should view it in that light. This, however, was not the way West chose to approach his job. His mentoring, "full speed ahead" style with students had already landed him in the doghouse of the Beaumont administration.

West described the late summer maneuvering that had led to his reluctant move form Roosevelt to Beaumont: "Coach Campbell and I both had ISS the last two years at Roosevelt, and we loved it. I was able to work with troubled kids every day, a chance to show them a better way, a path to success and not an endless cycle of failure. That (failure) is all some of these kids have ever known, both in and out of school, nothing but failure. Also, at Roosevelt, I was in the same building with my players every day. That is important to me. I am just not a football coach, I am a leader, and I want to be a mentor to these kids. I want to show them that you can come out of a PHL school and still make something of yourself. Last year, I was part of the family at Roosevelt. Maybe we did too good of a job with ISS there, because the other high school Principals began to say to the downtown people, 'hey, we want ISS in our school as well.' So here I am, back home," West chuckled.

The week of the Beaumont vs. Roosevelt battle, West found himself the target of some good natured ribbing by several Beaumont players. But, according to West, it was all minor. "These kids are smart enough here at Beaumont to know we are going to kick their butts come Saturday. Nothing they can do about that and they know it is coming. They don't want to say much because they know I am going right back to my boys at Roosevelt and tell them every bit of smack these dudes say. Believe me, they don't want to rile up "Man-Child" or "Mummy," West said with a laugh. In other words, don't tug on Superman's cape.

In his non air conditioned second floor class room, on a hot and sticky late summer afternoon, West, with his voice volume set at its usual booming level, lectured the six male students assigned to that day's ISS. Several minutes earlier a female student, unhappy with the uncomfortable level of heat in the room, and not satisfied that her behavior had warranted the ISS sentence imposed by a Beaumont assistant principal, simply stood up and walked out of the room. West was unfazed. "Hey, you want to go, go," he told those remaining in the ISS room. "I am not tackling anybody. But you need to understand that there are always going to be consequences for you actions. It is called accountability, and most of you have never been held accountable. That is why you end up in here. That is why you don't graduate, can't find a job and end up in prison. Dudes, we got to break the cycle. We are killing ourselves. As young black men, you got more of a chance to end up in prison than you do to go to college. Think about that. That is sad. But listen man, how can I teach Calculus to you when it takes the first 25 minutes of a 45 minute class to get you to settle down? You done blew over 50% of the opportunity - your opportunity - to learn that hour. How you going to get into college like that? You are not. If you want to compete out there with those white kids in the suburbs, with your home boys who ride the bus to the suburbs everyday to go to high school, then you got to clean up your attitude. You not hurting Old Coach West being a fool. You are only hurting yourself - and that makes you a fool."

Within minutes of the AWOL student leaving his watch, West was summoned to the hallway outside of his classroom by two Beaumont Assistant Principals; one male, one female; both African American.

"Did you allow a student to leave your room?" inquired the female administrator.

"Nope," said West, in a tone invoking no concern or panic, and not disrespectful or flippant.

"Did you try and stop him?" asked the male administrator, recognizing that West was simply semantically tap dancing around a rhetorical question.

"It was a her," West corrected, "and I am not stopping anyone that wants to leave. I will not lay a hand on a student. Not smart to do, and I will not do it."

For no apparent reason, the female administrator turned and walked away, evidently either satisfied with the resolution or frustrated in having no other angle to question the coach's decision. The male assistant principal, half of West's size and several years the coach's junior in age, chose to go into an assertive administrative mode. "You have got to develop some strategies to help these kids understand that they cannot just walk out of your room. We can't start this. We have children in the office that teachers said you sent back to class after I placed them in ISS."

West remained calm and answered in his best reassuring voice that his intent was not insubordination, but that his procedure on how his ISS classroom would function was firm and not open to debate, "I can't take more than six (students) at a time in here. This (ISS) can't just be a dumping ground for any kid that a teacher is fed up with. You want strategies, fine. I will sit down with you and we will develop some. The bottom line is, the only way ISS will work is for the kids to realize they are getting a break by not being suspended. If they want OSS (Out of School Suspension), they are going to find a way to get it. And like I said, I ain't tackling anyone who decides they are leaving."

West closed his summation with one of his patented shoulder shrugs with arms stretched wide and palms raised to the sky, as if to say to his supervisor, "dude, it is what it is."

The young assistant principal started to respond, paused in mid flight, lapsed into several seconds of thought; then turned and retreated. Outfitted in a stylish $400 suit, he chose not to continue this philosophical battle of wits with the engaging West - adorned in his ever present wind suit warm up - over the proper function of an ISS program in the modern urban high school setting. Instead, he turned on his heels and returned to the safety and order of his end of the hallway administrative office. West returned to his captive ISS audience, now numbering six and holding.

A constant source of frustration for Coach Campbell was the seemly endless problem of getting players and coaches to practice on time. The frustration continued during the Friday practice before the Vashon game. "Where is "Man-Child?" Campbell inquired as the team when through its pre practice stretching.

No one knew the whereabouts of Faulk. Coach West pulled out his cell phone and began punching numbers in an attempt to locate the wayward junior lineman.

"That is bull shit, "Man-Child," West screamed into the phone. "Your mommy don't need you to go to that meeting. You got more damn meetings to go to than anyone I have ever seen. Study meetings, community meetings, AIDS awareness meetings. Dude you are the king of meetings. When do football kick in with you?"

West disconnected the call without waiting for an answer and replaced the phone into his pocket.

Campbell continued the roll call. "Where is Tyler and Carves?"

Both senior lineman were students at Central Visual and Performing Arts Academy and rode the after school activity bus the mile route down Arsenal Street each day to Roosevelt.

"They missed the bus coach, they walking over," offered one player.

"Well isn't that great," said Campbell. "I tell you what they were doing, messing with some girls after school over at CVPA, I bet you; and now they worry about getting here with us. It's 3:40, they got out of school at 2:18, and they still not here." Campbell spit out the last few words while shaking his head in disgust.

As was common practice during such heart to heart talks, when Campbell began to tire and lose steam, Coach West took over.

"Seniors. These guys are our seniors and they can't get here? How bad did they want to get here? We got no hope guys. Every year we talk the talk after the season, and then when we get to the (new) season, we fall back into the same old habits. Remember after last year? You guys go to Coach Campbell's room and watch film and you talk big, 'Oh look at the seniors, look at so and so, he don't block, he not in shape, wait till next year, I will be different.' So we get you in the weight room all winter and spring. We take you to camps, we bring you up here on weekends, all summer, and we play 7 on 7 all over the damn area to give you a chance to back up your talk. When it gets down to time to start playing, you go back into the same old half ass patterns that the seniors before you followed. I don't see any difference right now with you guys. I really don't, and if it don't change soon, I won't see any difference in district results either. I am getting really tired of these meetings, guys. Real tired. We got to lead the friggin PHL in team meetings."

The inter personal dynamics amongst the interaction of the coaching staff of the Roughriders made it often hard for an outsider to accurately gauge the motives and the mood of the staff, especially Campbell. For one familiar to the dogmatic, almost sterile interaction between coaches and players in non-inner city programs, the practice sessions at Roosevelt seemed to be at times teetering on almost total chaos and rebellion. Coach Campbell would often use sarcasm in instructing his players. Certain established seniors, in particular Arlando Bailey and George Bell, were not afraid to fire right back at Campbell and the coaches with the same biting edge that the coaches used to communicate with the athletes.

Even more unconventional, from a suburban frame of reference, was the dialogue between the coaches themselves. Often, with the players serving as an audience of witnesses, Campbell and defensive coordinator Darren Wade would engage in at least two on the field arguments per practice. Often the debate would center on the proper and most effective tactics that should be employed by the defense. Campbell and Wade's discussions would quickly reach a very loud decibel level. Such adversarial exchanges between a head coach and a subservient assistant at a non-city school would have quickly become the talk of the school, if not the whole community. At an inner city school, as Wade would later attest, "It's just the way we do business. Nobody takes it personal. We just give our opinion. We are used to fighting for something when we feel we are right. It is not a sign of discontent among the staff, we all know Campbell is in charge."

With the coaches sending conflicting directives to the players, it was a common sight during practice for the whole defensive unit to look to the sidelines with confused shrugs of their shoulders as they were not sure which coach's directions they were to follow. It was not unusual for the staff's loud and emotional exchanges to shut down practice for as long as five minutes of on field coaching debates, before a compromise could be reached, and they could be given unified instructions. This truce and united front between Wade and Campbell would seldom hold for more than several plays, when the next animated discussion between the two would be in full swing.

For an outsider, it was often hard to know when a coach or player was serious with an on field outburst. Was one witnessing true anger or just mischievous clowning?

At one midseason practice session, Campbell yelled across the field at an assistant who was sitting on a sideline bench, "Think you could get off you ass and maybe do something today?"

The assistant, in full view of the team, shot back, "Like what?"

Campbell in a loud and frustrated voice, halted practice and commanded that the entire coaching staff meet with him in the middle of the field for an impromptu mid practice coaches conference. With his staff gathered around him, and out of ear shot of the players, Campbell asked, "Remember that bird that was here all last year, our lucky bird? Where has he been? That is what we are missing. Should we shut down practice and have the team go look for our lucky bird?" Campbell asked in a mockingly sincere tone.

"No Coach," said Coach West. "I heard the bird got in the desegregation program and now rides the bus to Eureka."

The players, sequestered out of hearing range of Campbell's discussion with his staff, assumed the assistants were catching the wrath of the lately often unhappy and dissatisfied head coach.

Vashon presented an interesting challenge to Roosevelt. The Wolverines had become the 2008 Jekyll and Hyde team of the PHL. Observers never knew from day to day, week to week, which team would show up, the squad who had played a strong out of state private school power - Jefferson City Helias - to a stand still, or the team the week before who had turned in a more PHL type performance, trailing 35-0 by halftime of the SLUH game.

For the 2008 season, Vashon Coach Reginald Ferguson had installed the spread offense, which was more than adequately led by his quarterbacking son, Raynell. The younger Ferguson had spent the previous season as the starting signal caller for Suburban North county power Hazelwood Central (who in late November would be crowned the 2008 large school Missouri State Champion). His availability for the Wolverines, due to transfer eligibility requirements, had been in question all the way to the start of pre-season camp. The Missouri State Activities Association finally, just before the season opener, cleared the young quarterback to play for his dad's team.

The younger Ferguson was known as a dual offensive threat, he could pass when the need arose; but his strength was as a running quarterback. The Roosevelt defense would have to contain him in the pocket on every play. Coach Wade's defensive plan was to have middle linebacker George Bell shadow Ferguson each and every time the ball was snapped.

Roosevelt jumped ahead on the scoreboard following a first quarter circus touchdown catch by Robert Scott. The ensuing extra point put the Roughriders on top, 7-0. After a fumble recovery by the Roughrider defense at mid field, the Roosevelt offense sputtered. Such offensive futility after a quick start was becoming a familiar game day pattern for Campbell's team, initial text book precession of offensive execution, followed by an inexplicable loss of focus. Inevitably, the floundering offense would be plagued by metal mistakes, missed assignments, penalties and turnovers. On this particularly beautiful Saturday fall afternoon, the opposition capitalized and Vashon used good field position following an interception and a fumble recovery to put together two short field drives for touchdowns, taking a 12-7 lead with 4:37 remaining in the first half.

"What the fuck is going on out here," asked Roosevelt senior, Tyler Clubb, after the visitors had taken the lead. "No fucking pride. They are sticking it up our ass and telling us to like it, and we just roll over for them. Well, fuck that. From here on, I am doing my thing. It will not be my fault if we lose to this sorry ass team. I might get kicked out, but this one won't be my bad," Clubb raged to his teammates on the RHS sideline.

On this day though, the Roughriders responded to first half adversity with a solid drive of their own. Fueled by two timely 4th down conversions, with 23 seconds left in the half, the offense found itself with a first and goal at the Vashon 11 yard line.

First and goal on the 11 yard line, the official announced. What, asked a confused Roosevelt sideline? Shouldn't it be a first and 10 from the 11 yard line? No explained an official to Campbell. "The field is not marked correctly. We used the first down sticks and it is only 7 yards from the 10 yard line to the goal line. So even though you are on the 11, it is really the 8." For the frustrated Campbell it was just another head shaking example of the everyday Alice in Wonderland logic one must accept to keep ones sanity in the PHL.

After two fade route passes into the right corner of the end zone, intended for Harold Brown, fell incomplete, Campbell called time out. Eight seconds showed on the scoreboard clock. "Take the three," urged assistant coach Wade. "The way we are playing, we need something (positive) to go into half time with."

Campbell responded, "it's only third down."

Wade called after Campbell as the head coach walked away from the bench, onto the game field and to the Roughrider offensive huddle, "we are out of time outs."

Campbell, showing the frustration that had built in him as he had watched his high powered offense stifled three times in the red zone already - Roosevelt had not punted, and would not until midway through the 4th quarter - shot back at Wade, "I know we are out of time outs, you've told me twice now." Wade threw his hands up in disgust, "then make sure they know. We need the sure three," Wade yelled at Campbell.

Campbell's plan was to attempt one quick third down pass play into the end zone. He was wagering that if unsuccessful, there would still be a second or two left on the first half clock. Campbell's whole strategy hinged on the pass being either a touchdown or incomplete, thus stopping the clock. He would then send in Dukly and the field goal team for the chip shot kick. Wade's concern was that if a running play was unsuccessful; and if the ball carrier was tackled in the field of play, and with no timeouts at Roosevelt's disposal, the clock would run out and the half would expire before a field goal kick could be attempted. Also, Wade had informed Campbell, since Roosevelt had now used its last time out, it was critical that Bailey not be sacked attempting to pass, or time would expire with no field goal attempt forth coming. Wade wanted Campbell to emphasize that to quarterback Bailey. His concerns would prove to be well founded.

The crossing route pass pattern that Campbell called for the third down play, did not develop quickly enough. Bailey made a critical mistake by holding onto the ball instead of throwing it away for an incompletion. As Wade had feared, Bailey was sacked in the backfield by the blitzing Vashon defense.

If Bailey had simply thrown the pass away, the clock would have stopped and Roosevelt could have kicked the field goal. Wade was beside himself over the goof that he had tried in vain seconds earlier to warn Campbell about. All Wade had gotten for his efforts was the ire of Campbell.

"Why didn't he (Bailey) throw it away? I tried to tell (Campbell) we had no more time outs, I tried, but he said he knew. Then why didn't he tell CBC (Bailey)?" asked a frustrated Wade as the coaches walked off the field.

As the team gathered under the shade trees on the west side of the school building for its halftime conference, frustration amongst the players began to spill out. The coaches had not yet made it over to the meeting area, and it was now "players only" time to vent.

"You ain't blocking shit, and don't try and tell me you are," said running back Antonio Carter. "I am busting my ass out there and you guys on the line ain't hitting shit." It was a rare outburst of emotion from the normally restrained Carter.

Senior center Tyler Clubb took exception to the line being called out by Carter. "I am busting my ass. You can't blame the line this time. They got too many (defenders) in the box. We can't keep trying to run up the gut. They got more people in the box than we do. Maybe if the receivers and backs could catch the fucking ball, they might take some of those guys out of there."

Bailey threw in his opinion as the shouting between teammates grew to a level that was now audible to the coaching staff still crossing the game field. "We are playing stupid," said Bailey, although it was not clear if he was including in his assessment his own mental lapse of taking a sack and allowing the clock to run out to end the half. "Ain't any of you acting like you want to win this game. This is Vashon! They are not even as good as Sumner and here we are losing at halftime."

Campbell and the coaches had now reached the site of the team's half time summit. "Take a knee," Campbell instructed in a low key tone of voice. "Fellows, only person beating Roosevelt right now is Roosevelt. We need to settle down. We are going to be alright and we are going to win this game. Just relax. We need to make a couple of adjustments and then we will be fine."

Coach West handed the head coach a small erasable white board. Campbell and his assistants spent the remainder of the 15 minute intermission calmly drawing diagrams on the board, showing the now quiet group of young men the strategic changes in the game plan that needed to be implemented to ensure a productive second half.

The players seemed to be taken back by the calm halftime approach of the normally emotional Campbell. Whether by design or by chance, the low key approach chosen by Campbell would prove to be the right tonic for what ailed

Chapter 5: The Regular Season

the team. The Roughriders departed the shady area in a much more cohesive and workmanlike frame of mind.

"Time to go to work," said Quadricous Sanford, as he pulled himself up off the ground and followed his teammates back onto the field of play.

The 3rd quarter continued as an exercise in futility for the Roughriders. On all three offensive possessions they drove the ball into the red zone – inside of the Vashon 20 yard line – but all three possessions ended with no points tallied to the Roosevelt side of the scoreboard. Twice, Roosevelt was derailed on downs. Each time Campbell eschewed field goal attempts in favor of attempting a 4th down conversion. The third Roughrider drive of the half was quashed by a fumble on the Vashon 14 yard line.

As the 4th quarter began, the Roosevelt sideline, while not in panic, showed concern. The game was unfolding as almost a duplicate of last year's dispiriting loss to Vashon, a defeat that cost Roosevelt the PHL title. Throughout the week, Campbell had warned his players repeatedly to remember how they felt after the 2007 loss. He pleaded with them not to take the talented Vashon contingent lightly.

With 9 minutes left in the contest, Roosevelt finally caught a break. Vashon was still clinging to their halftime lead of 12-7. Punting into a strengthening breeze, the Wolverine's kicker managed only an 8 yard effort. Roosevelt took possession on the visitor's 44 yard line.

"Now or never, offense," Bailey barked to his teammates as he strapped on his helmet and took the field to lead a team that knew all too well how devastating a loss to Vashon would be.

The PHL title, an accolade that Campbell had often scoffed at throughout the summer and pre-season, suddenly took on an importance for both coaches and players. "PHL, right now," said Campbell as his struggling offense took the field. "How bad do you want it?"

On the first two plays of the critical drive, Bailey completed passes, one to each sideline, followed by a swing pass to Sanford who caught the ball five yards downfield. The senior broke numerous Wolverine arm tackles, turning the short swing pass into a huge twenty five yard gain. Roosevelt was now poised on the Vashon one yard line, first and goal.

The most obvious weakness of the high octane spread offense is its ineffectiveness inside the opposition's 20 yard line. By the nature of the spread, a large area of the field is required to maximize the distance the defense has to cover. The spread, as its name would indicate, needs space to operate. But with only 11 yards to work with - the one yard to the goal line, and the attached 10 yard end zone- Campbell's options were now limited. The spread is not a smash mouth, three yards and a cloud of dust power type offense. Roosevelt had few plays in its repertoire that would take Bailey from the shot gun formation and place him under center, the formation preferred by power running teams. Of the few options in the RHS playbook for red zone situations, most required a pitch and a run around one of the ends.

Not wanting to use his only remaining timeout, Campbell took one step onto the field and called to his team a new play for the team playbook, one they had not practiced. "CBC, get under center. Get in behind "Man-Child" and push."

Of course, the Vashon defenders were also in earshot of the instructions from Campbell. Vashon had to steal no signals on this particular play to know its opponent's intentions. Bailey was stopped cold.

"CBC, same thing. "Man-Child," we got to push," called out Simmons for the second down attempt from the Vashon one yard line.

Same play, same result.

In desperation Campbell went back to the spread. The play signaled in from the sideline called for a handoff to Carter up the middle. Although conservative within the philosophy of the spread, the play was risky when run from the goal line because Carter would line up seven yards behind the line of scrimmage. The line would have to hold their blocks for a longer count than would be required for a simple power play initiated with the quarterback located under center. The formation also took several would be blockers out of the backfield by placing them as wide receivers, in essence, spectators.

Unfortunately for the home team, the success of Campbell's call would never be known. Center Tyler Clubb picked a very inopportune time to make his first bad shotgun snap of the day. The ball sailed high and wide. A leaping Bailey managed to get his left hand on the errant snap and bat the ball to the ground where he summarily fell on it. From first and goal from the one yard line to fourth and goal from the six yard line, the Roosevelt offense was headed in the wrong direction. The PHL title, and perhaps the whole season, now hung in the balance, predicated on the next critical play from scrimmage.

Despite the high flying offenses of the past few years that have turned football games at all levels into track meets in shoulder pads - with final scores that resemble basketball games - football is still considered a macho game. The true test of a team's toughness is on the goal line. With the game defining play now at hand, Vashon, pitted against a heavily favorite team on the road, had been faced with the daunting task of stopping an opponent four times from the one yard line. What seemed an impossibility three plays before, now looked like a certainty. The manhood of the Roughriders appeared to have been taken from them by a team that refused to allow its own goal line to be penetrated. The disgust on the Roosevelt side of the field - players, coaches and supporters - gave the situation a hopeless feel. The swagger was gone.

Campbell called his final timeout.

"We do it now, or we don't get it done. This is the game," Campbell told his assembled offense.

The critical play called by Campbell would be a pass: a crossing pattern into the end zone. The play's success would hinge on Bailey's ability to read the Vashon defense and make a split second decision as to which receiver was open. He chose senior Harold Bailey, and he chose wisely. Brown secured the pass between two defenders and fell to the ground three yards into the end zone. The two point conversion pass failed. Roosevelt, a team that had been totally outplayed for almost three quarters, now clung to a precarious one point lead, 13-12. The defense needed to hold the line for six minutes and the Roughriders would have stolen a much needed win in a critical PHL game.

Vashon, on this day, would not go away without a final fight. One final offensive volley lobbed at an exhausted Roughrider defense still remained on the Wolverine's agenda. Ferguson, on alternating short passes to the flats, and swivel hipped broken field runs, marched the Wolverines inside of the Rider 20 yard line. From the fringes of the red zone, Ferguson twice fired passes to the left corner of the Roosevelt end zone. Both times Ferguson badly overthrew wide open receivers. Roosevelt had twice dodged a potentially lethal bullet. The collective wind being sucked out of the Roosevelt side of the field was literally audible.

The Roosevelt coaches, with no timeouts at their disposal, were in desperate voice as they tried to instruct the defensive backs as to the proper coverage scheme. Chaos prevailed.

The drive stalled as a harried Ferguson, under pressure from one of the few pass rushes Roosevelt had mustered on the day, threw a 4th down pass far short of its intended target. Roosevelt took possession of the ball on their own 8 yard line. Vashon's lack of either an accurate passer of a competent field goal kicker, had come to the rescue of the Roosevelt team. But, as Coach Campbell pointed out to Bailey and the offense as they took the field, with three minutes on the game clock and a full contingent of Vashon time outs left to its disposal, the game's outcome was still very much in doubt.

Campbell chose to keep the ball on the ground, hoping at best to attain at least two first downs and eat up the remaining time left in the game, or at worse, to force Vashon to use their three timeouts to conserve the remaining clock. Three consecutive running plays exhausted the supply of Vashon timeouts, but netted only two yards. On 4th down, junior punter Robert Scott dropped back into the shadow of his own goal posts to attempt his first punt of the day. Punting was not considered a strong suit of the special team's play of Roosevelt, but in the clutch, Scott came through. With the help of the wind at his back, he booted a low, end over end line drive, which went over the head of the Vashon return man and was downed, after a long roll, inside the visitor's 20 yard line. The resulting 74 yard punt, by almost 25 yards the longest of Scott's career, came at the most opportune of times for the staggering Roughriders.

Without a timeout, Vashon was forced to the air. After registering a first down, an errant Ferguson pass created a new hero in a red uniform, junior linebacker Timothy "Rudy" Banta. With less than two minutes to play, Banta tracked down and intercepted Ferguson's desperate throw. To ice the win, with 45 seconds remaining in the game, Sanford scampered 31 yards to paydirt, sealing a 19-12 Roosevelt win.

Due to Banta's resemblance to the character in the feel good movie that told the story of an undersized walk-on who realized his dream of playing for the Notre Dame Fighting Irish, Banta had been affectingly nicknamed by Coach West, "Rudy." Banta rarely saw playing time. He was however, a player that the coaches grew to know they could count on. One of only two white players on the varsity roster, Banta was often held up by Coach West as a model defender. "Rudy is disciplined. Rudy is consistent. Rudy does what we ask Rudy to do. That is why Rudy is always in the right place at the right time."

Banta was also not afraid to lay a hit on an opponent. His choir boy looks, small stature and white skin, in games filled with much larger black players, made for astonishment from opponents when Banta would fearlessly throw his body into the fray. Throughout the season, when calling for Rudy to enter the contest, Coach West would bark out, "I need my hard hitting Caucasian. Rudy get in there."

Banta's increased playing time in the Vashon game was due to starting linebacker Dashaun Moss sitting out most of the week's practices with a sore shoulder. The insertion of the undersized linebacker was a move the Roosevelt cheering section had been calling for all year. Drawn more by his hard hitting play on special teams than the novelty of his pale skin, Rudy had become a crowd favorite of the mostly African-American Roosevelt cheering section. It had become common throughout the early games of the season to hear the chant "we want Rudy, we want Rudy," cascading down from the stands behind the Roosevelt bench.

After the game, when speaking to the press, Campbell paid Banta his due, "Rudy got the reps in practice this week. We have a lot of confidence in him. We told him, 'drop and see the QB's eyes.' He made a big play when we really needed one."

A beaming Banta, while accepting numerous post-game high fives from his teammates, could hardly conceal his excitement. Normally reserved and quiet, Banta summed up his day and "Rudy" like moment: "Just to get to play in a big game like this, it makes all the work worth it. I couldn't be happier. I am glad I got the chance to help out today."

As Vashon Coach Ferguson gathered his disappointed team for a post game talk, he immediately drove home the story line of the day, "We gave that one away. We outplayed them all day and then we gave it away at the end."

It would be hard for even the most ardent Roughrider supporter to disagree with Ferguson's summation of the day's game: Roosevelt had been lucky. Although a fine runner, on this particular day, the younger Ferguson's lack of passing accuracy doomed Vashon. On the last drive into Roughrider territory alone, he had failed on three occasions to connect in the end zone with a wide open receiver. Swap jerseys on the respective quarterbacks, and even with the subpar day Arlando Bailey had throwing the ball, Vashon wins by at least two touchdowns.

As the dust settled on the 6th weekend of the high school season, several developments caught the attention of the Roosevelt team. Miller Career Academy had upset Gateway Academy, setting up a showdown at Roosevelt the next Saturday, with the winner claiming sole title to the PHL crown. The game would be the last PHL tilt on the schedule and the last game before district play would begin. The game would also be Roosevelt's homecoming.

Perhaps a more ominous sign for a team who had declared from the beginning that the PHL crown was not at the top of their season goals - that only a district title and post season play would validate their season - was the strong weekend of play by the three district foes Roosevelt would do battle with. Chaminade ran its' record to 5-1 with a surprising victory over one of the area's traditional powers, DeSmet, by a convincing score of 42-25. Webster Groves dominated its game with Parkway West, the team who the previous week had knocked Eureka from the ranks of the undefeated, racing to a 21-0 half time lead. Eureka was the team who had handily defeated Roosevelt back in week one. The last district foe on the Roughrider's schedule, Vianney, saw their record drop to 4-2, as they lost a wild shootout to St. Louis University High School, 63-32. SLUH had earlier defeated Vashon handily after taking a huge 35-0 halftime lead. The pass happy Vianney team had put the ball in the air 51 times, throwing for 397 yards, in the SLUH game alone.

After reviewing the poor pass coverage demonstrated by Roosevelt in the Vashon game, Campbell knew that all three district opponents would attempt to victimize a secondary that had survived the Vashon challenge only due to the inability of the Wolverines to deliver the ball into the arms of open receivers. "Come district," said Campbell, "if we don't start to lock down back there, those (passes) will be touchdowns. We had better be able to score from the one yard line on first and goal."

But first, for the senior class of Roughriders, there remained one last non district game, one last PHL game, and one last homecoming game.

Chapter 5: The Regular Season

The tradition of the homecoming football game is long and deeply embedded in the social culture of the American high school. The first homecomings took place at universities and, after several years, trickled down to the high school level. Along with the spring prom, the most important date on the high school social calendar has become homecoming. Even high schools that are too small to field football teams will during the winter hold homecoming festivities at basketball games; often referring to the event as a "court warming."

Several universities lay claim as the originator of the homecoming tradition. Two Midwest rivals, the University of Missouri and the University of Illinois, both self tout themselves as the university to have sponsored the first campus wide homecoming celebration. Mizzou has solidified its claim with endorsements by such a wide range of sources as the NCAA, the TV game show Jeopardy and the popular board game Trivial Pursuit. The first homecoming game is documented as the Missouri vs. Kansas game held on the Columbia, MO campus in 1911, although some claim the origins of homecomings can be traced back as far as 1891. As the tradition began to catch on in the nation's high schools, such staples as a bon fire, pep rally, parade and homecoming dance where added to the festivities. Royalty, in the form of a school wide King and Queen, were crowned either at the dance following the game; or at halftime. Every little girl in the USA grows up with the aspirations and dreams of someday being chosen as the fairest in the school: Homecoming Queen.

Roosevelt High School has had a long history of celebrating homecoming. The Bwana - the school yearbook - is well documented with recordings of the homecoming festivities since at least 1930. Older alumni say that the tradition of homecoming has, over the years, begun to wane at the south side school. Yet, several members of the Roosevelt High School Alumni Association have reached out to grasp on to a sort of line of re-connection, thrown to them my current Roosevelt High School principal Terry Houston. These alums, many in their 70's and 80's, are once again immersing themselves in the school. Two dozen chose the 2008 homecoming game as a time to revisit their alma mater.

"We need this link to the past," said Houston at halftime of the 2008 homecoming football game. "They (RHS alumni) are an active organization, but they no longer felt connected to the school. They met to reminisce, but really knew nothing of what was transpiring at their old school. When I met with the Officers of their group, they were all elderly or middle aged and living in the county and the suburbs (Houston didn't add, but he could have, they are all white). Their meetings were all about reunions and not about the present. Having them here today is great for our kids and lets them know that Roosevelt has a long tradition," Houston said in references to the alumni association members seated in the bleachers for the homecoming game. "We are getting them back into the Roosevelt family. We are asking them to come in and volunteer to help today's students. They are a great untapped resource. Not only can these older alumni help with things like tutoring and one on one reading help, but they also let our current students connect with the great history we have here at Roosevelt. Old and young, we are all part of the Roosevelt family. Forty, fifty years from now, and God willing we still have a Roosevelt High School, I would hope today's students would want to come back and give back like we are asking the alumni to do now."

One alumnus in attendance at the game, but not in the bleachers, was 80 year old Robert Wardel. The St. Louis County resident, class of 1947, was decked out in his Roosevelt letter sweater, the same costume he had worn as head Roughrider cheerleader, over 60 years previous.

Wardel spent the time before the 2008 homecoming game teaching the current corps of RHS cheerleaders some of the renditions he had recited three generations before. It was obvious that Wardel was enjoying the attention. It was surprising; however, to witness the sincere interest the half dozen African American teenage girls had in listening to stories told by a white man over 60 years their elder, and from a world they had no connection to.

"We had big crowds back then," Wardel told the youngsters. "It was our job to get the fans organized. We were not only supporting the players on the field, we were also competing against the cheerleaders and the fans from the other school. We always wanted Roosevelt to have the best cheering section."

After the game, Werdel pledged to Principal Houston that he would donate $500 towards the cost of new uniforms for the school's cheerleaders.

It was, to say the least, a very strange conference championship celebration.

Coach Campbell's team had just defeated their visiting PHL rival, Miller Career Academy, 26-14. The victory sealed an undefeated PHL championship run for Roosevelt. The Roughriders had made one last statement that they were in 2008 the clear choice as the dominant force in PHL football.

As had become their trademark, Roosevelt sprinted out of the blocks to open the game on the fly, racing to a 14-0 lead six minutes into the game. Antonio Carter capped the first TD drive with a one yard plunge into the end zone. After a three and out by the Career Academy Phoenix, quarterback Arlando Bailey connected with Quadricous Sanford for a 65 yard, pass and run touchdown. But, like a broken record, the Roughriders did not sustain their early level of play. After the quick start, the offense became mired in a slew of turnovers, missed assignments and dropped passes, allowing an overmatched opponent to remain in contention and put a second half scare into the Roughriders.

A telltale statistic from the game was that Roosevelt was only able to convert on 3 of 11 third down opportunities. What frustrated Coach Campbell and his staff, particularly offensive line coach Darren West, was the team's season long inability to score consistently when in the red zone. West warned this deficiency would come back to haunt Roosevelt when district play began the next week. "I am calling you out, every one of you offensive linemen, in front of this whole team," West said after the Career Academy game. "We are not tough enough. We get four downs inside the 10 and we have to score. We have got to be able to run the ball down their ass when we get it inside the 20. We have to punch them in the mouth and run right over them and you have not shown me you can do that. Come 4th quarter today, and this team is within one touchdown of us, one play! Think about it dudes. Think we aren't going to see a much more dominant bunch next week?"

The statistics for the game, from Roosevelt's standards, were not bad. The offensive balance was again good. Led by Carter, the team had rushed for 177 yards. Bailey had passed for 220. Sanford had returned a punt for over 50 yards and, for once, the special team kick coverage units had more than held their own. The defense was again rock solid and had sacked the Career Academy quarterbacks five times. This did little to appease Campbell and his desire to get his team's focus on the future and away from past PHL triumphs.

Campbell's post game comments to the press were reserved. He told a reporter after the game: "We cannot compete in our district if we play like we did today. Too many mental mistakes. We have never been concerned about winning the PHL. Taking nothing away from the PHL, but we been there, done that. We want to come out of districts and get into post season play and that will not happen if we don't put together three strong games the next three weeks."

After his obligatory comments to the Press, Campbell made sure the privacy of his team's meeting area was secure. He gathered his team around him in the grassy area to the east of the old school, his team's "outdoor" locker room. Before speaking to his squad, the coach asked that the area be cleared of non essential personnel. "I want everyone not a player or coach to please leave," requested Campbell. Assorted students, family members and other team supporters who had gathered for what they felt would be a team celebration of a PHL title; amongst quizzical nods to each other, heeded the coach's request and left the area.

Campbell then turned his full attention to his assembled troops. He was direct and to the point, holding back nothing.

"We will not win another game this year if we play like we did today. I am sick from watching this. You want to celebrate? What? A championship of a half assed league like the PHL? We need to realize right now that we are through with playing PHL teams. That part of the schedule is done. From now on we play the big boys, the county schools and the private schools. And they will whip your sorry asses all over the field come the next three Saturdays if we don't get some discipline. Penalties, missed assignments, lack of finishing plays, (not) wrapping up tackles. We (will) not beat Webster Groves next week if we put out the kind of shitty effort I saw out there today. You know why? You want to know? Ok, I will lay it on the line to you. Because they (the private schools and county schools) have got all the good players that the city had to offer. They came in and skimmed the cream right (off) the top. They took the stars, and all they left for the half ass ghetto schools like Roosevelt is what they didn't want, and who is that: ITS YOU GUYS. Look around this group. They didn't want you guys and you know it. If you had been a star in the JFL (Junior Football League) when you were in junior high, if you had been smart enough, if your parents had enough money, you wouldn't be at Roosevelt, you would be at Webster Groves, Chaminade or Vianney. Well dude, guess who we going to play the next three weeks? You got it, Webster, Chaminade and Vianney. And you know who else they don't want? Us; me and the rest of your coaches. We the throwaways as well. 'Let'em rot at Roosevelt,' they say. Think about that as you celebrate your PHL title."

Was Campbell's tirade to his team, a group who had just won a conference title, a calculated move to motivate his athletes? For a year Campbell had told his team that they had "bigger fish to fry" than what would be found in the waters of the PHL. He had incessantly pleaded with his team to separate themselves from the other PHL schools that were viewed as an easy mark when they ventured from the friendly confines of the city league. Or was he truly concerned that his team had not progressed to the point of taking "our game to the next level," a credo he had preached time and again for the last twelve months?

If Campbell knew, he wasn't saying. After his brief remarks to his still quiet and assembled team, he walked to his pickup truck, got in and drove off.

CHAPTER 6
THE DISTRICTS

There is nothing like returning to a place that remains unchanged to find the ways in which you yourself have altered.

— Nelson Mandela

Before you begin a thing, remind yourself that difficulties and delays quite impossible to foresee are ahead. If you could see them clearly, naturally you could do a great deal to get rid of them but you can't. You can only see one thing clearly and that is your goal. Form a mental vision of that and cling to it through thick and thin.

— Kathleen Norris

Reality is merely an illusion, albeit a very persistent one.

— Albert Einstein

Success isn't permanent, and failure isn't fatal.

— Mike Ditka

That is why athletics are important. They demonstrate the scope of human possibility, which is limitless. The inconceivable is conceived, and then it is accomplished.

— Brian Glanville

The timing could have not been worse, the result more devastating and final. On the eve of the beginning of district play, roadblocks to the post season success the Roughriders had dreamed of for a year, were suddenly raised to what seemed insurmountable heights.

With the district playoffs looming, the Roughriders suffered through a week of one catastrophe after another, in preparing for the opener against a powerful Webster Groves team. Roosevelt had failed, back in the season's first game in September against county power Eureka, to prove to the doubters that they had the mettle to throw off the yoke of years of PHL frustration and compete with the non-PHL powers. They had endured many off field setbacks as they rode undefeated, but often joyless, through their Public High League schedule. It was, as Coach Campbell told his team at the Monday practice, the time to put up or shut up.

Practices the week of the Webster game did not go well. The coaches were on edge. The players sensed it, and the atmosphere at practice was often confrontational. Several times during the week Coach Campbell once again, openly at practice, questioned the defensive game plan. The plan's architect, Coach Wade, attempted on Monday afternoon to implement with the players their responsibilities in throttling the powerful and explosive Webster Groves offense. As Wade labored, Campbell twice stopped the instruction and made spontaneous changes to the schemes and player assignments. "Why we in cover two," Campbell questioned on Tuesday. "No man, we got to change that, got to," Campbell said, shaking his head. Wade continued his work with his defensive unit in apparent total disregard for his boss's concerns. The karma hovering over Roughrider nation, at the most critical time of the season, was not good.

On Thursday, came more bad news. During a tackling drill, Quadricus Sanford suffered a severe high ankle sprain. The timing left many of the players questioning the purpose of a contact drill only two days before the district opener. "Nobody tackles on Thursday, fucking nobody," groused one player on Friday morning when word spread that the popular "Mississippi," arguably the team's best player, might not be available for action on Saturday.

Sanford's value to Roosevelt was unquestioned. He led the team in receiving, a statistical category that found him ranked third in the entire St. Louis area. He was also the team's safety on defense, using his foot speed and aggressive play to bolster a strong defense that had played well in the final weeks of the PHL schedule. At the conclusion of the season, Sanford's value on defense would be recognized as he was named as a first team Class 5 all-state defensive back. Sanford was also the long snapper on the punting and field goal teams, returned kickoffs and punts, and was a "gunner, " running down field to cover kickoffs and punts. Seldom during a game did he ever leave the playing field. Replacing such a productive athlete on the eve of a critical contest would be difficult, and the prospect did not help the increasing shaky confidence level of the team.

Sanford, unlike many of his senior teammates, and a few assistant coaches, refused to second guess Coach Campbell's decision to employ the unorthodox tackling drill so late in the season and so close to a big game. "Just bad luck, all the way around, no doubt about it. Who could have guessed our fat quarterback would have fallen on me. Right, cuz?" Sanford said at Friday's practice, well within ear shot of quarterback Arlando Bailey, whose practice tumble had injured Sanford's ankle.

All week, in his basement classroom, Campbell had reviewed films with his team of the Vashon and Career Academy games, bemoaning what he felt was a poor job of tackling by his defense. "If you don't wrap, dude; if you don't drive with your legs when you make contact, them big backs at Webster and Chaminade (Roosevelt's second district foe) will run over our skinny asses," Campbell told his team on Wednesday.

By Thursday, he had stewed enough. Late in the season or not, Campbell decided to address the problem head on. Practice on Thursday began with a tacking drill. Within five minutes, Sanford was down on the ground, writhing in pain. By Friday morning, he could not walk without the aid of crutches.

Campbell had intended to spend Friday morning transporting Sanford to the doctor for treatment on his ankle, hoping for some sort of miracle he knew was highly unlikely - that somehow Sanford would answer the bell on Saturday afternoon. By 9:00 am, when seeing Sanford's severe limp, Campbell had to face the stark reality that the star player would not be in uniform for the next day's game. Could things get much worse? By 10 am, the Coach had his answer. Yes they could, much worse.

Campbell was contacted by Principal Terry Houston and informed that a serious eligibility problem had arisen. Sophomore defensive back Charles Banks, whose hard hitting style and abundance of athletic ability had moved Campbell to label his as a rising star with a college Division I scholarship within his reach, was declared ineligible. Banks did not attend Roosevelt High School. He was enrolled in a north side charter school, Career Construction Center. Each day after school he would ride the city bus from Career Construction to Roosevelt and football practice. The next morning, he would board the same city bus for the return trip to the north side and "Triple C," as the charter school was known.

Banks' strange migration to the Roughriders was in line with his multiple teammates who also did not attend Roosevelt, but were allowed to play for the school since their SLPS magnet schools did not offer football. Central Visual and Performing Arts Academy was the main contributor of talented players suiting up for Roosevelt. This mercenary arrangement was approved by the State Activates Association (MSHSAA), and Campbell was more than willing to have the talented players from the magnet schools in his program. However, Banks' situation hinged on one major difference from his teammates who attended CVPA: he did not attend an SLPS school. Based on his residency - he lived with his grandmother only several blocks from Roosevelt - his neighborhood school was Roosevelt. If he had chosen to attend one of the SLPS magnet schools, and that school did not offer football, then he could have, within the rules, played on Roosevelt's team. Career Construction Center however, was not a magnet school and not even a part of the SLPS. CCC was a charter school.

The charter school movement was a new phenomenon to public education. Charter schools operate under a mucky set of rules and regulations that the courts in 2008 were still trying to sort out. Charter schools could apply for sanctions under the law that would make them eligible for state and local tax revenue, yet they were not accountable to either SLPS or the State of Missouri's Department of Education. Supporters claimed that eliminating the autocratic red tape and removing the control of the incompetents who ran the SLPS, would allow the self proclaimed visionaries who ran the charter schools to better educate urban students. From the charter school movement in the St. Louis area alone, came both horror stories of fraud, and subsistent levels of education, along with uplifting stories of urban education success.

Many St. Louis leaders, most notably Mayor Francis Slay - no friend of the SLPS - held beliefs that the charter schools were the last hope for any semblance of a tax payer supported school system that could provide a free and appropriate education to the urban poor in the city of St. Louis. Others, in particular the still powerful teacher's union, saw charters as the final nail in the coffin of the St. Louis Public School System. The charter movement was hitting full stride precisely at a time when the community, due to the recent state takeover of the SLPS, had lost all local control over the education of their young. As students poured out of the SLPS and into the private, county and charter schools - lured by the hope of glowing promises of a real education - the public schools sank deeper into despair.

The exodus took not only students, but also much needed state aid that now would follow the students to their chosen charter or county public school. The critics of this system pointed out it was just another tool to maintain a separate and unequal educational system, saddled on the backs of the real losers, the poor black inner city students who remained in the SLPS.

Charles Banks cared nothing about the political and ideological struggles over the charter schools movement. He just wanted to play football for the Roosevelt Roughriders. He knew Coach Campbell wanted him on his team and he knew that football might be his only way to college. He did not understand the system which now told him he could not play for the remainder of the season, and perhaps never again at Roosevelt.

By Friday afternoon, the reality that his season was over, and the real possibility that he may never again pull on his red jersey and take the field for Roosevelt, was beginning to set in with Banks. "Coach Campbell came to talk to me at my junior high in 8th grade," recalled Banks. "He told me I could come to Roosevelt and be a big part of some great teams. I love playing here. I can't imagine not ever playing again. But what I want to know is why? I just did what I was told to do. I don't know nothing about any rules. I went to Triple C last year and it was cool for me to play here at Roosevelt. I played the whole year and no problems. I been here this whole season (this year) and no problems. I got nothing to hide, so why now do we lose the PHL? It's all my fault," Banks stated, choking back tears.

At 2:30 on Friday afternoon, the day before the start of the district season that his team had prepared - albeit sometimes inconsistently - for since last January, Campbell held a closed door meeting with his team. Instead of a reviewing the game plan for the next day's big challenge that a very good Webster Groves team would provide, Campbell instead told the assembled group of young men- his young men – that they would have to forfeit the five consecutive PHL games that they had won. With one swoop of the eligibility sword, the Roughriders record was reduced from 5-1 to 0-6. In addition, the six games they had won in 2007, with Banks on the roster, would also be forfeited. From a current respectable mark of 11-5 to a winless 0-16, was the legacy that history would record for the current group of seniors. For all of their effort and dedication, it seemed to a man in the Roosevelt family, the cruelest of fates.

As the players emerged from the meeting in Campbell's room on Friday afternoon, it was obvious many had been crying. Campbell was immediately whisked off by Houston to a meeting with district higher ups. The SLPS administration, due much to the lingering after effects of the Vashon basketball eligibility scandal, went into immediate damage control mode. Vashon and its iconic coach, Floyd Irons, had recently been stripped of four state basketball titles. The high powered and nationally ranked PHL roundball program had fallen suddenly from grace, due to their blatant and intentional disregard for eligibility rules. After the Irons debacle, district officials had made it clear that no longer would the district look away, nor tolerate lax enforcement of state eligibility rules. Building principals were, hence forward, responsible, and would be held accountable for the athletes in their school being in alignment with state association residence standards. Houston and Campbell both took this edict from their bosses seriously. Both knew this was serious, that because of this snafu, their respective careers could suffer adverse and permanent damage.

The bad news had spread throughout the school on Friday afternoon and into the community by that evening. Although the problem had been discovered before the first district game, and Banks would be held out for the rest of the season; the forfeit of the PHL title did not sit well with most at Roosevelt. The question now became, who is to blame?

Many in the Roosevelt family continued to support Coach Campbell and Principal Houston. An honest mistake had been made, they acknowledged, but that one misstep should not negate all the good that had been done at RHS in general, and specifically within the school's winning football program, seemed to be the consensus of community public opinion. "They (the players) live in the Roosevelt district, but attend a charter school and not a magnet school. That's where the confusion (comes from). The school self reported itself, and not after being found out. This is not a matter akin to Floyd Irons recruiting players. This was an honest mistake by honest people and it's a shame MSHSAA didn't take that into consideration. Shame on them," posted one supporter on a local internet chat room.

But not all were so inclined to give those in charge at RHS a free pass. "The rule is very clear. The following should be removed: the head football coach for doing it, the school AD for not checking the team players list, and district AD for not checking the list that the school AD turned in. Roosevelt did not report the violation, but another PHL school (did)," was a statement found on an area high school football message board. The blogger was, of course, anonymous.

Public opinion was not a concern for Campbell on this difficult Friday afternoon, rallying his dispirited team was. After the afternoon practice, in his basement classroom, he again addressed his assembled team. "There is nothing we can do about this now. They say that we are not PHL champs. We know better. They will say we had to cheat to win. We know better. We are family so we hurt for Charles. Charles is a great football player. Charles will be fine. Charles has two more years to play high school ball. He will prove himself. But we got to go on now without him, without our brother. That is what we are most upset about. CA (Career Academy) turned us in (a rumor later substantiated). You know it. I know it. We can deal with that at the right time, but not now. Some of you going over to Gateway to their game tonight, I hear. Well let me tell you something, you go over there tonight acting the fool, you will do nothing but make matters much worse. Much worse. Show some class. Show some pride. They can slap us around all they want, but they can't take (our) pride. They can't take our spirit. You are accountable for your actions. You want to do something for Charles? Then let's get ready for Webster."

Despite Campbell's attempts to rally his troops by focusing on the important battle looming the next day, that afternoon's practice had been the worst of the season. Campbell was not in attendance until late in the session, as he was ordered "downtown" for further meetings with district officials. Coach West, as Campbell's replacement, was as dispirited as his team.

"Why we even here, man?" West asked the team 30 minutes into the practice. "You wasting my time. We have no focus?"

The players did not respond well to West's urgings. As the skies darkened in anticipation of a late afternoon shower, the structure and discipline of this once promising team of young athletes fell apart. In the middle of a special team walk-through, and after another in a long list of mental mistakes and missed assignments that had dominated the practice, West ordered the team "to the hill," for punishment running.

Several team leaders balked. "What the fuck for," was heard from a group standing on the sidelines. "I ain't running no more," stated one bold senior, not attempting to keep his comments from earshot of the coaches. "I am tired of this shit. All we do is work and all we do is get shit on. It happens every time. EVERY FUCKING TIME! This is Roosevelt. This is the way it will always be. Running hills ain't going to make no difference. No matter what we do, no matter how hard we try, we get fucked and I am tired of it. Nobody stands up for us."

With mutiny in the ranks, West wisely shifted gears. "Once more, one more screw up and we going to the hill," was his face saving attempt at staving off an imminent mutiny. As all successful leaders learn, sometimes discretion in the heat of battle, is the better part of valor.

In its usual and now predictable fashion, Roosevelt opened the game with a sustained and impressive drive to take a 6-0 lead. The extra point attempt was blocked. The drive was flawless. It was also the only points Roosevelt would score in the crucial district opener. The 74 yard march was climaxed with an Arlando Bailey to Robert Scott 6 yard touchdown pass.

Four turnovers would doom the Roughriders this afternoon against the talented Webster Groves Statesmen. Too many special team mistakes would also lead to the decisive loss. Webster Groves, on the other hand, managed to play the entire four quarters without a turnover.

On Webster's first possession of the game, the visitors methodically marched down the field to re-take the lead. Quarterback Marquis Clemons found the end zone on the first play of the second quarter, with a four yard run. The conversion kick was good and the Statesmen held a 7-6 lead.

Webster Groves employed a two quarterback system in their precise drive. They would utilize this strategy throughout the game as one signal-caller, Marquis Clemons, provided the ground game, while the second QB, Derrick Dilworth, sustained several critical drives with timely passes. For the game, statistics would show the effectiveness of the duo quarterbacking system. Dilworth led the team in passing with 215 yards, earned with 9 completions in 13 attempts. Clemons, effectively executing the option play, was the Statesman's leading ground gainer, with 35 yards on 9 attempts.

Midway through the second quarter, on only Webster's second possession of the opening half, they needed only two plays to penetrate the Roughrider end zone. Two passes, both to wideout Josh Thomas, covered the 55 yards needed to reach paydirt. A strong defensive stand by Roosevelt as the second quarter concluded, gave the team a small amount of momentum, as they headed to the halftime break, trailing only 14-6.

At halftime, Campbell was calm. "We are ok. We are in this game. They have not stopped us on offense yet. We have stopped ourselves. Get our assignments on their blitzes straightened out, and we are going to score. We can run the ball if you hold your blocks. The passing game is there. But we have to protect the QB. CBC can't throw if he is lying on his ass and he is getting hit way too much. Give him time to throw and he will pick them apart. Defense: Great job! Great job! That was a big stop at the end. Keep hitting them. Stay disciplined. Stay away from the silly penalties and we can win this game. We do and we are in the district driver's seat. We are that close dudes, to taking it to the next level."

Campbell's final caution to his team proved to be deadly accurate. "We get the ball first. We have got to have a good return. Then we got to take care of the ball. We cannot afford any turnovers, I mean none. They are too good to give them a leg up. TAKE CARE OF THE BALL."

On the first second half play from scrimmage, on an end around run, Roosevelt fumbled. Webster Groves recovered on the Roosevelt 34 yard line. Four plays later, Webster Groves scored to take a two touchdown lead.

"Offense, over here," Campbell ordered his team as the Riders prepared to return the ensuing kickoff. "We have got to put it in the end zone. We have to do it now. We cannot let this game get away. This is it. You want to win this game, we need to score on this possession."

The offense never got the chance to meet Campbell's challenge, as disaster struck for the second time in the first three minutes of the second half.

Roosevelt fumbled the ensuing kickoff, which Webster Groves recovered on the Roosevelt 26 yard line. On the first play from scrimmage after the turnover, Jeramy Harris hauled in a perfectly thrown pass from Dilworth for another Statesmen touchdown. For all practical purposes, the game was now over. From a one score deficit at halftime, Roosevelt had dug itself a 22 point crater, while snapping the ball from the offensive line of scrimmage only once.

Statistically, the Roosevelt final tallies were impressive to the point of being mistaken for totals of the winner of a typical high school football game. The offense once again pushed the 300 yard mark for total offense. The pass/run balance was again good. Antonio Carter had rushed 13 times for 92 yards. Bailey, running effectively for the first time all season had added 61 yards on only 4 carries. He had also, despite the absence of his favorite receiver, the injured Sanford, completed 10 of 18 passes for 123 yards, with one touchdown and no interceptions. However, the costly fumbles, coupled with once again an inability to score in the red zone, made the final statistics misleading.

"How many frigging times we get in the red zone (inside the opponents 20 yard line) and can't score," were the post game comments lamented by Offensive Line Coach West. "I put it on the line's shoulders. We got to get the ball in the end zone when we get down there." West then repeated one of the most often heard phrases during the 2008 Roughrider season. "This team goes only as far as the offensive line takes us. And today, dude, our line was shit in the red zone."

As the deficit on the scoreboard piled up on the home team, so did injuries. Quadricous Sanford, still hobbled from the ill timed high ankle sprain injury at Thursday's practice, made a valiant attempt to answer the bell, but failed. "I can't cut," Sanford told Campbell after the game's first series. "It's too sore. I can't run routes on offense and I can't cover on defense," said Sanford. "Then what can you do?" asked a desperate Campbell. He and Sanford both knew the answer to the rhetorical question. The area's third leading receiver and the team's best defensive back and kick returner, spent the majority of the rest of the game on the sidelines.

Midway through the fourth quarter, with the game's outcome decided, and the Roughriders committed to passing on each play, the Webster Groves defense, as described after the game by Coach Simmons, "pinned their ears back and brought the house on each play."

The pass rush from the visitors made for numerous open hits on the Roosevelt quarterback. Bailey, finally, midway through the 4th quarter, succumbed to a vicious helmet to helmet blow and was knocked unconscious. After several tense moments, the still groggy senior was led to the sidelines. He would spend the next five days nursing a sore neck and a persistent headache. Still, he was cognizant enough to declare to his teammates before leaving the field, "I'll play next week. I got to. It's districts."

Campbell's comments after the game to his team were brief. His body language and voice left no doubt as to his disappointment over the events of the past 24 hours. "We still got a chance, men," he began his post game remarks to his dispirited followers. "We can still go. Top two make it this year. We got to win the last two. But first we got to get healed up. Be at practice on Monday, we got a lot of work to do, but we still got a chance."

Monday arrived with a renewed sense of urgency amongst the Roughrider faithful. Coach Campbell had the look of a man who had spent the entire weekend reviewing game film. His cough, which had been ever present since the first week of the season, had deepened and increased in frequency.

"Rest," Campbell responded in mock disgust to an inquiry as to his health in general, and specifically to both the quantity and quality of his rest over the weekend. "I got no time for rest. There will be enough for that after the season. Right now, we still have a chance. Last year it would have taken a miracle to get us into the playoffs after Chaminade beat us. This year, all we got to do is take care of our own business and we are in. I still believe, man. This is a good team, and we can get it done. But we have to quit beating ourselves."

The physical toll taken by the hard hitting game with Webster Groves was on full display at Monday's practice. Quarterback Bailey, the one irreplaceable cog in the Roosevelt offensive machine, observed practice in street clothes, adorned with a large pair of what he claimed were high dollar designer sunglasses. His teammates showed him no mercy. "Look like our fat ass quarterback going to have to rest for a while," taunted center Tyler Clubb as the team gathered on the field for Monday's practice.

"Maybe if you would block some, I could stand up during the game and maybe we could win," Bailey responded to the good natured jab from Clubb. "That nose guard whipped your sorry white ass all over the field Saturday," Bailey continued.

"Whipped my ass?" Clubb asked in disbelief. "Whipped my ass? He didn't hurt me none. Look at me. I'm not hurt. I'm not wearing Tom Cruise sunglasses. You were the one whose fat ass was flopping around on the field. You don't see no dollar store sunglasses on me, do you?"

Clubb's fellow linemen, smelling blood in the water, and not willing to bypass a chance to put the star quarterback in his place, joined in. "That motherfucker laid your ass out. Pow! I mean laid you out cold. Put you to sleep!"

Rene Faulk, whose practice punctuality had shown marked improvement as the season progressed, was now glad to be an early practice arrival, and had Bailey dead in his sights. "Hey cuz, who's this," Faulk asked his laughing teammates, as he threw himself on to the ground, rolling and flailing his arms in mock caricature of Saturday's performance by the injured Bailey.

Several other linemen then gave their best impersonation of Bailey's Saturday demise. Realizing discretion is the better part of valor, Bailey made a quick retreat with one last verbal volley to save face. "You sorry asses learn to block, maybe I will play Saturday. You saw what happened when Mississippi played quarterback. Without me, you got no chance," Bailey said, removing his sunglasses and striking a Hollywood type pose to the chagrin of his teammates.

"Take your fat, hurt ass down there with the kickers, CBC," one lineman responded. "Any motherfucker can throw the ball. You throw too many to the wrong team, anyway."

Any fear that the Roughriders would fold after the initial district disappointment and simply decide to mail in the remainder of the season was quickly absolved by the spirited practice held on Monday. Campbell had predicted such. "These kids are tough. They are used to hard times. They will not quit and they like to play football. You will see, they will bounce back on Monday," Campbell had accurately predicted to a confidant after the Webster game.

With spirits intact, the most pressing problem now facing Roosevelt were injuries. Quadricous Sanford, so obviously ineffective against Webster, continued to hobble on his injured ankle. "I just couldn't go on Saturday," said Sanford," and they (Webster) knew it. They just backed off of me. If I was able to run, I'd have blown em up. I couldn't push and I couldn't cut."

Campbell realized, that next to Bailey, Sanford was the key to his high powered offense. "We have got to get Mississippi ready for Saturday. No practice for him this week and lots of ice. That is all we can do. Hey, this is Roosevelt. This is the PHL. We got none of that fancy stuff: whirlpools and machines for rehab. But we do have an ice bucket and we have got (to get) Mississippi back to 100%. His ankle will be in ice all week and then we just to have to hope for the best."

Bailey's injury status was more uncertain, and more of a potential danger. "We don't take chances with head injuries," Campbell told his assembled team at Monday's practice. "We can't just stick CBC's head in a bucket of ice all week," Campbell said.

"Ain't got a bucket big enough for his head, anyway," wisecracked a teammate, unable to resist and pass on the obvious soft lobbed set up from the head coach.

Bailey had been diagnosed with a mild concussion, perhaps compounded by whiplash. His foster parents, Ron and Cathy, had taken him to the emergency room at a local hospital on Saturday evening. The prognosis had been guarded, but good. "I just have to be careful this week," Bailey said outside the earshot of his unsympathetic teammates. "I have had a headache ever since I got hit. But it is getting better. I will play. No way to stop me now. We got to get these last two or that it is it. We are done. No way am I sitting out."

Several other varsity seniors would also be held out of Monday's practice, due to a myriad of bumps and bruises suffered in the Webster game. Luckily, none would be severe enough to remove them from the active roster for the upcoming Chaminade game. With the junior varsity players dismissed after the now conclusion of their season, the number of players suited for the day's practice had hit a dangerously low mark of 23. "We barely got enough to practice," said Coach West, as he surveyed the team during pre practice stretching.

"Where is Calvin?" West called out to the team when his pre practice inventory of his linemen showed that one was not accounted for.

"He got to go see his social security lady today, coach," responded one player.

"Why?," asked West.

"His mom died, coach," was the short response, and final word, on the subject of the absent lineman.

At the conclusion of Monday's practice, Campbell gathered the team in the west end zone. Campbell, despite his confident testament to the willingness of his players to soldier on; had been concerned about the day's practice. To his relief, the practice had gone well. Campbell addressed his battered team: "Men, we will fight through all of this. It has been a tough couple of weeks. The forfeits, the injuries, losing a district game, none of us wanted any of that to happen. But it did. It is over, dudes. We got to go on from here. We can still get to the playoffs, get to the Dome. But we got no more room for mistakes. We got to play the perfect game the next two weeks."

As if on cue, Coach West stepped in front of Campbell. "Coach we got too many guys hurt. That is all I see on Saturday, guys sitting on the bench with their heads down, hurt. I go to Mummy in the 4th quarter and I say, 'Mummy, can you go;' and he says 'I ttthink soooo Coach.' West draws out the enunciation in a mocking stuttering portrayal of his lineman, all to the howling laughter of the players.

West is a talented mimicker, a ruthless and dead on impersonator of the unique characteristics of each player. Several times during the course of the season, he had introduced levity through comic imitation into a grim situation; a move that never failed to raise the morale of both players and coaches. West's timing was always impeccable. He now sensed that the team, after a week and a half of one disappointment after another, needed to lighten its collective mood. West puts his talents to work - as Improv Night at The Club Roosevelt was now in full swing.

"Mummy, where is Mummy," called out West. "Here is the Mummy. Have you ever seen the old Flintstones cartoons, when Fred would go bowling? Big ole fat Fred - just like the Mummy - would come up real fast like he is just going to throw the piss out of that ball. Then, when he gets close to the line, he just tip toes and throws it in the gutter, real sissified. Well, that is just like the Mummy going to block. He comes on like a son of a bitch to make a block. Them Webster guys must have thought 'who is this big scary black son of a bitch coming at me like he is going to take my head off.' But when the Mummy gets to the point of contact, the time to hit, he just like Fred, he starts to tip toe."

The sight of the 300+ pound, highly animated coach, doing his best replication of a ballerina, brings down the house.

West spends the next 15 minutes going up and down the line of Roughriders. No one is spared his biting humor. West is the one responsible for the nicknames given most every player on the team: Man-Child, Wild Thing, Mississippi, CBC, Mummy, Cat in the Hat; all labeling monikers dreamed up by the rich imagination and creativity of the mind of West. He shows no mercy on the assembled Roughriders. By the end of West's act, several players and coaches are laughing so hard that they are lying prone on the ground.

"It is good to have some fun," Campbell tells his team as he prepares to dismiss them at the end of the afternoon's practice. "Lord knows, after the last several days, we need it."

Soccer is a sport with very deep and passionate St. Louis roots. In particular, the south side, with its many European immigrant communities and neighborhoods - Irish (Dogtown), Italian (The Hill), German (Dutchtown) and Polish - has produced some of the nation's greatest players. In the first half of the previous century, when the rest of the nation had an almost non existent interest in the sport, soccer in St. Louis flourished. At one time, when white students were still a common part of the student make up of the SLPS, PHL teams on the south side of the city - Roosevelt, Cleveland and Southwest - would field teams competitive with the Catholic school powers of the area. That day, like last weeks flowers, is a long ago and dead memory.

Even the legions of critics of the PHL had to admit that, since the demise of Floyd Irons and his Vashon Boys basketball teams, the PHL does now practice equality. No argument there. All sports are now treated with equal apathy. In the fall of 2008, the soccer coaches of the PHL took their complaints and grievances to the press. The St. Louis Suburban Journal ran an article titled *The Pitch is Ditched*, in which reporter Ron Clements documented the abysmal condition of PHL soccer facilitates.

Finding suitable fields for the PHL soccer teams - boys in the fall, girls in the spring- was an ongoing problem. The PHL coaches, rather uncharacteristically, had collectively spoken of their displeasure. Most teams had been relegated for practices to city parks where no goals existed, and the area for play was not of sufficient size to mimic a real game.

As one PHL coach told Clements, "You can't teach the nuts and bolts of the game on an unmarked field. The goalies don't know how far to come out of the box, and the other players can't learn their positioning. I'd like them to show that they're not going to put us on a crappy field, and not write us off. We've got some good, quick kids, who deserve a chance to shine."

The four football fields in the possession of the PHL – located on the campuses of Roosevelt, Soldan, CVPA and Gateway - were "forbidden" for use by the soccer teams, relegated strictly for football use only. Several soccer coaches and athletic directors questioned the use of the Roosevelt field as a practice venue by the Roughrider football team. PHL, Inc., they pointed out had invested a great deal of money in the Roosevelt Stadium field, and with daily practices held upon it, by midseason the turf was barren in many high traffic areas.

Roosevelt soccer coach Jim Grimaud, in his 10th year at the helm of the school's soccer team, admitted that his team's banishment from the field, for games or practice, was a sore point. Still, Grimaud refused to comment directly for the Journal's story. Instead of making the 1/2 mile hike to Tower Grove Park and a larger area for practice, the Roosevelt soccer team would often use a small patch of grass, approximately 20 yards wide and 25 yards long, located to the east of the school building.

The job of PR on the complaints of the PHL Soccer Coaches fell into the lap of one Patrick Wallace, the Executive Director of Communications for SLPS. He attempted to take the diplomatic approach. "It'd be great if we had enough fields, but it comes down to availability. And we select fields for how we feel it best fits the needs of our students."

Wallace summed up the dilemma of insufficient space and facilities with the following comment, one that could be etched in stone above the door of every SLPS classroom, gymnasium and library: "I understand the coach's complaints. They just want the best for their players, just like every teacher wants the best classroom for their kids. We just have to make due with what we have," Wallace said, leaving unanswered the one burning question no PHL or SLPS administrator, although often asked, would ever address: Why?

The good aura that had been felt at the conclusion of Monday's practice, did not last. On Tuesday, Campbell's frustration level was back up. He was not pleased with the lack of focus shown by his players. One hour into the session, Campbell was drilling his offensive line. "We need to widen our splits against Chaminade," he instructed. "We need to spread them out. We have got to use our speed. We have got to create some (running) lanes for Antonio. We have got to be able to run the ball. We can't throw every down and let them just tee off on CBC like (Webster) did. That got him hurt last week. That can't happen again," Campbell said.

"Coach," spoke up center Tyler Clubb, "I can't get there (to his blocking assignment) if the guard split is that wide."

Campbell whirled towards the senior lineman in an obvious show of contempt for Clubb's lack of acceptance of the coach's decision. "What? What?" Campbell said in a loud voice to Clubb.

"I said, I can't get there if the splits are that wide," Clubb repeated.

"Then Tyler, get your ass off the line. George, you play center. Tyler doesn't think he can do what I ask, then fine, I will find someone who can," said Campbell.

With his teammates for an audience, Clubb was not about to back down from his insubordinate stance. "Fine. I don't need this shit." Clubb removed his head gear, turned, and walked off the field and in the direction of the locker room.

Despite Campbell's often stated personal like for his senior center, he showed no acknowledgement to the mutiny. Campbell, turning his back as Clubb exited the field, had, with decisive swiftness, replaced Clubb with fellow senior George Bell. "George, we are going to widen our splits. You have still got to get to your block," Campbell instructed Bell, the recipient of a battle field promotion and the new starting offensive center of the Roosevelt Roughriders.

"Can you do it?" Campbell asked. "I will get there coach," responded Bell.

Arlando Bailey had conveniently built into his daily class schedule a first hour study hall. Bailey was an infamous non-morning person, and often would sleep in during first hour, making the short walk from his house across Wyoming Street to Roosevelt in time for his second hour class.

One of the reasons Bailey had given for jumping ship at the prestigious private school CBC, after his sophomore year, was that he balked at rising at 5 am each morning to make the 45 minute one way commute to the suburban school. As the season progressed, Campbell made it clear to Bailey that he wanted him to check into study hall on time, and then report to the coach's room for film study during first hour.

Tyler Clubb knew right where Bailey would be at 8 am the day after his separation from the team. Clubb was surely aware that by calling Bailey on his cell phone at the right time, Coach Campbell would be sitting next to Bailey. When Campbell was informed by Bailey that his caller ID showed that Clubb was calling the quarterback, Campbell grabbed the phone from Bailey. "Tyler," Campbell barked into the phone's mouth piece, "you have your ass to practice on time this afternoon or tomorrow morning I am coming over to CVPA to find your white ass and I am going to embarrass both of us."

Campbell hung up the phone with a mischievous grin. "He'll be there," predicted Campbell. "Tyler has done this before. Tyler just wants to feel wanted, but don't we all?"

That afternoon, at the anointed time, Clubb was in his spot in the Pit as the team began its pre-practice stretching.

Charles Murphy teaches multi media at Roosevelt High School. His class room is a virtual warehouse of high tech computer and media equipment. Located in the basement level of the old school building, on what is known as the "0" floor, Murphy teaches four classes daily, full of Roosevelt students eager to tackle the exciting and ever expanding world of mass media.

"You want to talk to a great teacher, go talk to Mr. Murph," advised one RHS administrator. "Mr. Murphy is the best," crowed one senior student as she detailed how Murphy had not only turned her on to the great possibilities of a future career in mass media, but had also taken the pragmatic role, of helping her to inquire, apply, and fund a college education that would begin in the Fall of 09.

"Mr. Murphy, he is one of the good ones. He cares, but he also knows," said one fellow RHS faculty member, giving kudos to Murphy for not only his sincere interest in his students, but also for the practical skills he teaches and the follow up - and follow through - of placing students in internships and colleges where their interests could flourish into a good career.

Murphy has followed a less traveled road to Roosevelt High School. He graduated from the Catholic all boys St. Mary's High School on the city's south side in 1963. At a time when most St. Louis schools, both private and public, were still segregated by race, Murphy found himself as the only African American student at St. Mary's.

After high school graduation, Murphy spent 12 years as a brother in a Catholic religious order in San Antonio, TX. He returned to his hometown of St. Louis in the mid 70's. After drifting through several unfulfilling careers, he settled on teaching. He has been in his current role at Roosevelt for 11 years. "I came as a science teacher and then 11 years ago the principal at the time asked me if I would be interested in taking over the school's TV station. And I have been here ever since."

Extremely popular with his students, Murphy, also an accomplished musician; exudes a type of timeless "cool." Small and wirily built with a stylish mini dreadlock look for a hair style, accentuated by a beard of just the right level of "scruffiness;" Murphy states his age as "64, soon to be 65." His admission stuns a visitor who would not have guessed Murphy to be a day over the age of 40. "I believe in these kids and that is what keeps me young," is how he explains his personal fountain of youth.

Several campaign style buttons adorn Murphy's work shirt. One in particular highlights Murphy's belief in the impact he has on the young students of Roosevelt: "The Young Are Not The Problem, They Are The Solution," the button proclaims. "I wear this every day," Murphy says, pointing to the button. "That phrase keeps me coming back here everyday. I believe in the power of education. Knowledge is power. I try empowering my students."

Murphy's view of the future is refreshingly upbeat for a man who has been on the front lines of the urban education battle for so long. "The world is their future," he states. "What a great time to be young. The possibilities are endless. In this day and age, you can be whatever your talents allow you to be. It wasn't always like that. Not when I was young. We had limits placed on us. I was always one who broke through limits. Tell me I can't do it, and that made me want to try even harder. Now, for these kids, it is different. I watched the inauguration (of President Obama) on TV last month. What a great time to be an American. I want my kids to have hope. Without hope we have nothing. I never though I would see the day a man of color would sit in the White House. But it happened, and it gives hope to young people. Not just African American young people, but all young people. Everyone can dream, but with a dream must also come desire. The desire to get the job done, no matter what it takes, no matter how many obstacles jump in your way. The path to a dream is never an easy road, but it is a worthwhile path to follow. We, as educators, must help the young clear that path of society's obstacles. That is especially true for young people of color. I try to do that everyday. There is no greater enjoyment or sense of accomplishment than that which comes with impacting a child's life. It keeps me young, forever young, you might say."

What would prove to be the final home game for the RHS seniors would be played at Roughrider field on a beautiful late October afternoon. The sun shone bright and by game time, the temperature was pushing 60 degrees.

The game began as almost every Roosevelt game that fall had, with Roosevelt putting a solid opening possession drive into the opponent's end zone. After stifling the vaunted Chaminade run game on the Red Devils first possession, Roosevelt marched the ball 70 yards down the field in a mistake free, eight play drive, culminated by a five yard Antonia Carter touchdown run. With 8 minutes gone in the game, the Roughriders, as had become their custom, owned an early lead. "We can beat these guys. We are better than they are. We can block them on offense and we can tackle them on defense," a fiery Coach Campbell told his troops as they gathered on the sideline to prepare for the ensuing kickoff. Maybe, just maybe, this would be the day that all the potential of his team would come together.

"My legs feel good today," Arlando Bailey announced to Campbell on the sideline. "They have nobody in the box to watch me when I drop back. They are not even concerned about me running the ball. If we can get some downfield blocks, I can run all day."

Campbell's observation of the opening drive was concurrent with the quarterback's. "They know you can throw, CBC. Now show them you can run. They can't stop us. We only can stop ourselves," an obviously pumped and confident Campbell warned.

It took Chaminade and their star sophomore running back Rob Standard only 64 seconds to answer Roosevelt's opening score. After a kickoff return to near midfield, which once again left Coach West on the sidelines to wail away at the ineptness of the Roosevelt kick off coverage team, it took Standard only two running plays to get the ball into the end zone. His touchdown gallop into the east end zone, followed two costly 15 yard penalties on the Roughriders, infractions that would loom as an ominous precursor for the home team's fortunes on this beautiful fall day.

Standard was a star on the rise, a swift and powerful back that was already drawing much college Division I recruiting interest. He would finish the year with a whopping rushing total of 2350 yards and 29 touchdowns. He averaged, on the season, a monstrous 8-1/2 yards per rushing attempt. The previous week, in a district opening loss to Vianney, Standard carried the ball 45 times for a near state record 468 yards; a ghoulish 10+ yards per carry average. Vianney had edged Chaminade in one of the wilder games in the annals of St. Louis high school football; 57-54, scoring the winning points on a touchdown pass with 50 seconds left in the game.

It was not lost on Roosevelt and the other PHL teams that it was rumored that Standard was one of their own, a city resident and a graduate of the city elementary schools. "Think he's paying his own way," asked one Roosevelt coach in reference to the $17,000 + annual tuition charged to attend Chaminade. "Think he would be there if he was a little short, fat black kid that played the tuba in the band?"

Chaminade was quickly emerging as an area athletic power, boosted by several African American students with national caliber athletic ability. In March 2009, the Red Devils would be crowned large school state basketball champions, a team bolstered by a starting lineup that included four African Americans - none of whom were "little short black kids from the city who play the tuba in the band."

As Roosevelt was the home team in the Chaminade encounter, the Officials had been assigned by the PHL. Under MSHSAA rules, for regular season and district matchups, the home team contracted the officials and the visiting team had the right to approve of the selected crew. PHL Director Sam Dunlap, a white man with 28 years experience in the PHL, who had earlier been lambasted by Demetrious Johnson as a racist, was present at the contest. The five man officiating crew was all white.

"Don't Dunlap know any fucking black officials," groused one Roughrider assistant coach before the game. "This shit happens every year. Just watch. When we get to districts, we get fucked and we get fucked by guys the PHL hires. Unbelievable. Just watch."

The pattern the Roughrider offense had fallen into - a flawless opening drive to a score, followed by a long offensive hibernation - had become infuriating to Campbell. An early good drive resulting in a score would be followed by a long stretch of offensive football suicide, with Roosevelt continuously shooting themselves in the foot. Turnovers, untimely penalties, missed blocks and dropped passes- after having been teased by the early offense success - was maddening to the head coach.

By this late point in the season, Campbell was frustratingly searching for any rhyme or reason to his team's inconsistency. However, today did appear to be different. The Roughriders also moved the ball well on their second drive, but a 15 yard holding penalty called on RHS's Rene Faulk in front of the Chaminade bench, nullified a long run into Chaminade territory by Antonio Carter, forcing the Riders to punt.

"I ain't holding," an exasperated Faulk told Coach West when he reached the sidelines. "That dude cutting me on every play. I told the official and all he did was laugh. I'm telling you, I am getting tired of it. This shit happens every week, every damn week we get screwed by the officials. I ain't taking it today," said an angry "Man-Child."

After the penalty had killed the home team's second drive and the Roughriders had punted, the defense appeared to have stopped Standard well short of a first down on a third down play in Chaminade territory. As Coach Campbell called for the punt return team to take the field, a flag - a very late penalty flag - flew into the pileup on the Chaminade sideline. The call: late hit on Roosevelt. First down Chaminade.

"That is bullshit," screamed Campbell, halfway onto the field, at the officials. "You guys do this to us every year when we get to the districts. It's bullshit." Two minutes later Standard had his second TD yard run of the day and the visitors had claimed their first lead, 14-7.

But on this day, Roosevelt still had some fight in them. The offense, aided by two long Bailey scrambling runs, marched into the Chaminade end of the field. Another holding penalty on third down pushed the Riders back onto their heels, facing a third and long. Bailey then hit Harold Brown with a perfect strike between two Red Devil defensive backs at the Chaminade five yard line. Brown had used his 6'3" height to all its advantage to make the circus grab. First and goal Roosevelt, five yards to the tying score.

On first down, Bailey rolled to his right looking for Quadricus Sanford to break into the open in the corner of the end zone. When the outside linebacker chose to drop into pass coverage and double team Sanford, Bailey saw the opening created by the retreating defender, tucked the ball under his right arm and headed for the end zone. He was met at the goal line by the Chaminade middle linebacker whose helmet to ball hit dislodged the pig skin and created a mad scramble for the fumble in the Roosevelt end zone. In perhaps the most crucial play of the entire season, Senior center Tyler Clubb dove onto the ball for what as he would say later was, "the first touchdown of my career."

The ensuing obligatory pile up followed, as it always does when the football is fumbled, amongst a mix of linemen from both teams. It was clear to everyone - Clubb's parents in the stands, along with several visiting coaches from Vianney that were scouting the game- that Clubb had recovered the ball. Clubb later related that he was pulled up by his shoulder pads by one official who told him to let go of the ball and unwind from the pile of players. Clubb did as he was told and relinquished the ball. It was quickly gobbled up by an opportunistic Chamindae player.

After a short huddle, the officials rewarded the ball to Chaminade and negated what had appeared to be a tying score by the Roughriders. The officials signaled Chaminade ball on their own 20 yard line.

The official's explanation when confronted twenty yards onto the field by a livid Campbell was, "when we unpiled them, Coach, Chaminade had the ball," ignoring the fact that Clubb had been ordered by the official to let go of the ball and that everyone in the stands, including two rival coaches; clearly saw Clubb fall on the fumble for a Roosevelt touchdown.

Chaminade drove the length of the field against a dispirited Roosevelt defensive unit to add a late field goal to take a 17-7 lead into halftime. Roosevelt, after clearly outplaying the visitors for a majority of the half, now trailed by 10 points. Crucial penalties, and the robbery of an obvious touchdown, left the Riders in a defeatist mood as they gathered in their outdoor "dressing room" on the west side of the school.

The halftime collective mood of the Roosevelt players was an almost serial acceptance of their fate. No anger. No fire. No desire to right a wrong. Just resignation that this is what happens when you are from Roosevelt and you play a non-PHL team in a meaningful game. "Well, we getting fucked again," one senior said to no one in particular, as he lay in the grass awaiting the coaches' assessment of the first half.

"They will not let us win. It happens every year. It ain't even worth getting mad about. It's just the PHL for you," was senior lineman George Bell's philosophical assessment of his team's fate on what would be his final game at Roughrider Field.

"Guys, we just got to be better than them. That is just the way it is. We have got to overcome the calls. We should have expected it," Campbell told his assembled players. "We can still win this game, but we got to be so much better than them that they have to let us win. We can still do it."

The tone in Campbell's urgings, despite his words to the contrary, left no doubt in his player's minds that he knew their season was over. There would be no playoffs, no trip to the Dome. The final half of this game and the season's final game next week, would be a simple matter of playing for pride.

Chaminade nailed down the outcome of this day's contest with two unanswered touchdowns in the third quarter. Standard, the Red Devils star sophomore running back, showed the type of obvious talent that would project many to predict for him a highly decorated college career, and a long and profitable career playing future Sundays in the NFL. He was that good. Speed to burn; fluid, balanced, relentless, and courageous; Standard would finish the game with a workmanlike 217 yards. No argument from anyone on the Roosevelt sideline that the talented sophomore had all the markings of a future star.

The officiating reached almost the bizarre stage as the game wound down to its conclusion. In the third quarter, Roosevelt made a defensive substitution. As the player who was removed sprinted to the Roosevelt sideline, Chaminade put the ball in play. The side judge on the Roosevelt side of the field ruled that the player had made it across the boundary before the ball was snapped. Incredibly, the line judge on the **opposite** side of the field, in front of the Chaminade bench, threw a penalty flag and charged Roosevelt with a violation for having too many men on the field.

Once again, Campbell was beside himself with the near sideline official, the only one he could get to. "You are standing right here and you say he is off and the other guy is 50 yards across the field and he throws a flag. Explain that?"

The sheepish official could only muster up, "I can't," for a response.

"In 40 years of football, I never seen that call," said Coach George Simmons after the game. "Funny stuff happens in the PHL."

Campbell was reduced to the point of simply shaking his head in mock resignation to his team's fate at the hands of this particular officiating crew. Chaminade, on the day, would be whistled for only five penalties; three of the infractions coming in the games closing minutes of the 4th quarter, long after the contest's outcome had been decided. Roosevelt Assistant Coach Darren Wade found that, in itself, insulting. "Call a few penalties now," he yelled, "Make it look a little fairer. Chicken shits," was Wade's summation of the end of the game efforts by the officials.

The most troubling aspect of the officiating occurred midway through the 4th quarter. Rene Faulk had warned in the first half that he was tired of getting "chopped" – an illegal maneuver where the defensive linemen dive at the lower legs of a pulling offensive linemen. Faulk had previously warned both the Roosevelt coaches and the official that he would retaliate if the officials would not call a penalty on the offending Chaminade offense linemen.

In the fourth quarter, Faulk made good on his promise. After once again being chop blocked, the enraged "Man-Child," after the play had ended, grabbed the offending Chaminade lineman by the shoulder pads. The official, the same who had taken the obvious touchdown away from Roosevelt in the first half, reacted immediately and flagged Faulk for unsportsmanlike conduct. Campbell pulled the seething "Man-Child" from the game before he could further erupt. Faulk flung his helmet to the ground in disgust as he went to the bench. "I told him to stop. I told the officials to make it stop. That fucker been cutting me all day. I just finally had enough," said a clearly frustrated and angry Faulk, as he slumped on the sideline bench, his game day now over.

After the offense stalled and the unit's players came to the Roosevelt sideline, center Tyler Clubb related what had occurred during the dead ball following Faulk's departure. "The ref that took the touchdown away from me came up to me after the play when "Man-Child" went off and he told me 'you got to get control of these guys. You are the only one that these **animals** will listen to.'"

The official choosing Clubb - the only white player Roosevelt had on the field - to make this disparaging remark was not viewed as insignificant by assistant coach Simmons.

"Shit like that happens all the time down here. They (officials) come in here with a set notion that our kids are bad kids. We don't get a fair shake. Think they could get away with saying that about Chaminade kids, calling them animals?" asked Coach Simmons.

It was pointed out later, and again, by a second Roosevelt assistant coach that the PHL had hired the officials. "Watch during timeouts. Each of the two side judges is assigned to monitor the bench on their side of the field. Watch during the next time out and tell me who they watching and who they not watching."

His point was made strikingly clear during the break between the third and fourth quarters. The official assigned to the Chaminade bench made no eye contact with the private school coach instructing his huddled team, nor did he get within 15 yards of their meeting. Conversely, on the home team sideline, the official stationed himself within five yards of the Roosevelt huddle, standing erect with his hands behind his back, similar to a prison guard monitoring the day room on visiting day, on ready alert to any barbaric attacks that might arise from Campbell's instruction to his dispirited team of young black athletes.

Earlier in the game, the same official had cautioned assistant coach West about negative comments he had made during a time out to his defensive players in regard to the officiating.

"Why is he listening to what I tell my players during a time out?" stated West. "It is one thing to be a poor (official) and make a bad call. It is altogether different to come in here and have already made a determination about our kids. Calling them 'animals' is not cool. And that is not the first time something like this has happened with a white PHL crew. We had a situation a couple of years ago where parents were coming out of the stands because of names one official had called our kids. I think it was a Beaumont game. It's not right, but it keeps happening."

After the 38-13 loss, Campbell gathered his team for a depressing post game assessment. The "dream" was now officially dead. There would be no post season play; no trip to the Dome.

"It's tough guys," Campbell began. "We had high dreams, we worked hard. It just didn't work out. Now we got to decide where we go from here. We still have one chance left to prove we are a better team than what we have showed these last two weeks. I tell you one thing, I still got to make that (college recruiting) film for you. I still got to talk to the recruiters for you. How you respond next week, and not just in the game, but all week in practice, is going to be what determines what I have to say about you. Are you a bullshitter that just talks the talk and then runs when things get tough? Or are you a stand up (guy) who takes the bad things that happen and bounces back? Next week we are talking about a character test. I will be here Monday ready to give the same effort I would if we were playing for the state championship instead of a (meaningless) game. I know the coaches will do the same. We will prepare you, that I promise. The question is, what will you guys do? We will see next week."

Late in the afternoon, after the players, fans and parents had departed, the coaches gathered in a sort of reverse post game tailgating party to discuss what had gone wrong. Seated on overturned empty five gallon buckets and Coach Simmons's pickup truck tailgate, with raw game time nerves now calmed by a few beers, the coaches became philosophical.

"We just are not there," Coach West said shaking his head. "And I don't know why. We just kill ourselves. We have good kids. They work hard. We have good coaches. We work hard. But somehow, someway, every year something goes wrong and we just fold. Halftime, we were done. No fight. You could see it in their eyes. I don't have the answer. I wish I did. I'd share it with the whole PHL and we'd all be kicking ass, cause I'm telling you dude, we got the players. We just ain't got the game. Not yet, anyway."

Physically, the football field at Vianney High School was only a 15 minute drive down Highway 44 from the Roosevelt campus. In sociological terms, it might as well have been on the far side of the moon. A manicured turf grass field, smooth as any PGA putting green, was surrounded by a rubberized all surface 8-Lane running track. The entire complex was illuminated by a professional lighting system. It would be the only experience the Roughriders would have in 2008 with the uniquely American phenomena of "Friday Night Lights."

Vianney entered the game, because of their previous week's win over Webster Groves, already assured of winning the district crown. Webster Groves and Chaminade would meet the same evening, with the winner claiming the other spot in the Class 5 state playoffs. Roosevelt was the only one of the four to enter the final weekend with only pride to play for.

Practices during the week had gone surprisingly well and Campbell was pleased. The players were on time and the effort during practices was as spirited as any time during the year. "Our kids have shown me something this week. It is more than just about winning and losing. They like the game. They wouldn't have shown up with the positive attitude they did this week, if they didn't," said Campbell.

Was the mood of the team relaxed because the coaching staff had approached the week with a more relaxed attitude? Were the players enjoying the game again because the pressure of winning the district and advancing to state play was now out of reach? Now that the destination was unreachable, were the Roughriders, for the first time all year, allowed to enjoy what was left of the journey? "Maybe," said Coach Campbell, after a moment's hesitation to reflect. "I hope we didn't take the fun out of it for them. We have to have goals, but we need to have fun as well. We have to have pride and we have to push for the highest level possible. But I am proud of these kids, despite our failures on the field. We are going to get more into college this year than ever before. And that is what determines how successful we really are, not just wins and losses; district and state titles."

For the first time all season, Campbell gave his pre game talk to his team prior to the Vianney game inside of a real locker room. His speech sounded eerily like a post game one, an end of the season bid of farewell.

"Guys, we have had a good year and this is a good team, but it is time for goodbyes," Campbell said. "We didn't always show the best performance we are capable of on the field, but I am proud of each and every one of you. We have got this thing turned around and we owe a lot to our seniors. I know there were times when (I) was hard on you guys, but I look at each and every one of you as part of my family. I will get you into good schools. I promise I will do that for each and every one of you. I want to see you make something of your lives, and you can. I want you to make me proud, make Mr. Houston proud, make our assistant coaches proud, and make your parents proud. Show that Roosevelt High School can turn out good kids, not just thugs and gang bangers. I love every one of you seniors and I want to say with all sincerity, thank you."

There was still one last game to play.

As fall 2008 turned to winter, with all the items of peril facing the St. Louis Public School System, the most pressing issue was the most basic necessity of any educational system: students, or more accurately in the case of the SLPS, the lack of students. Parents continued to pull their children from the SLPS at a head spinning rate.

By December 2008, the district was claiming an enrollment figure of 26,000 students. Source at the SLPS downtown office admitted that the enrollment numbers given to the public were almost certainly inflated. "Less than 22,000 would be more like it. Maybe less than 20,000," said one Central Office District employee who requested anonymity.

In the glory days of the SLPS, student enrollment was a problem on the opposite side of the spectrum: a swelling enrollment that threw the district into a building frenzy, a desperate attempt to keep pace with a skyrocketing enrollment, growth attributed to the last vestiges of the Post War Baby Boom. SLPS enrollment peaked in the mid 1960's with a head count of 125,000+ students.

Now in 2008, enrollment had declined over the 40 year span by the incredible total of over 100,000 students, or a 400% decrease. For reasons obvious to even the most incompetent school administrator, declining student enrollment is a financial train wreck for a school district. School funding in Missouri is doled out to each district by the use of a complicated formula that dispense local, state and federal dollars to the more than 500 state wide districts. The one common component of the formula, regardless of the source of the revenue, was student enrollment; or more specifically- student attendance. In simplest of terms, the more students in attendance each day, the greater amount of government financial aid given to the District.

By late 2008, the SLPS and its newly appointed school board, had dug in its administrative heels; ready to endure what would be the most emotional public onslaught the appointed members were yet to face; the announcement of which of as many as 20 neighborhood schools would be shuttered by the time classes began in August, 2009. This painful and emotional event had become almost a yearly spring ritual for the SLPS. The district had closed 28 buildings the previous year, starting the current school year (2008-09) with 89 operational school student attendance buildings. Another 20 closing should reduce over a short period - two years - the total number of buildings in operation as student education centers by nearly 40%.

With each school closing, came another nail in the coffin of urban neighborhoods desperately attempting to hold on to a sense of community. An operational and thriving neighborhood school was referred to by many social and urban scholars as the "anchors" of inner city communities. The appointed SLPS board knew that local patrons would not stand by ideally as their neighborhood schools were mothballed and its students bussed to schools outside of the area. Citizens were demanding a life line from the school board, not the abandonment of their neighborhood they knew a school closing would bring.

"If they close your school, you might as well move too," said Roosevelt High School assistant football coach George Simmons; a veteran SLPS employee of nearly 40 years. "Cause your neighborhood will not be worth living in. It has happened on the north part of the city and it has happened in the south part of the city."

According to Simmons, who had witnessed, as a student in the mid 60's, a thriving and vibrant SLPS, a more holistic view by school leaders would be a wise approach. Simmons observed that when a school closed, it did not take long for the gangs to move in. "Go look at all the closed schools and drive through the neighborhoods. Look at the markings; look at the gang graffiti on the walls of the buildings. Look at all the young people standing on the corners, just loitering waiting for trouble to find them. It's no good. Soon you will see other signs; the tennis shoe thrown over the telephone wires," Simmons said in referral to the universal gang sign that drugs are available for sale at that location.

"Drive by a school that is still open, and look for the same signs and they are not nearly as easy to find," Simmons continued. "Close the school, the bad guys take over, and the neighborhood dies. Repeat this over and over each spring and the city just continues to die with the dying schools. You can't separate the two. When the school dies, so does the neighborhood. Every school closing causes the SLPS to die as well, one empty school at a time. We cannot afford to keep closing our schools. We have got to improve the city schools to the point that (students) will want to go to school there."

The elected Board first, and then the politically appointed Board that followed the state decertification of the SLPS, did find common ground upon one conclusion. Where long time city residents like Simmons claimed that the local communities could not afford for the SLPS to continue to close neighborhood schools; officials of the SLPS had for the past decade deduced that polar opposite conclusion – under attended schools must be closed.

The average SLPS district building in 2008 was functioning with at a student capacity rate of fewer than 60%. School officials claimed that this was not sound economic practice for a district that entered the 2008-2009 school year with a $13,000,000 budget shortfall. In justifying the school closing, Board members pointed out that savings would be substantial as consolidating buildings would lead to administrative, building maintenance and daily operating expenses reduced at significant financial savings to the SLPS.

To prepare itself for what it saw as a tough, but inevitable decision, in the Fall of 2008, the Special Appointed Board hired a consultant group from Olympia, WA that specialized in the study of the economic operations of school buildings. The company, MGT of America, Inc., was hired with a price tag of $625,000, and given the mission to evaluate each of the 89 attendance centers operated by the SLPS.

The consulting firm would throughout the fall of 2008, gather its supporting data and would report to the Board its findings and recommendations. Part of its data gathering process would be a series of public meetings to gain the insights of interested parties and patrons; incorporating the community's thoughts and concerns into its justification for its hit list of what buildings would be closed for the 2009-2010 school year.

The price tag for the consulting firm's efforts of over one half of a million dollars, by a district so strapped for cash, raised more than a few eyebrows. "Just what we needed," stated one taxpayer at one of the input gathering public meetings held in December 2008, "another study. We got money for another study, but not for fixing up our buildings," the woman declared to the loud applause of many of the approximate 50 interested persons seated in the Roosevelt High School Auditorium.

Another in attendance at Roosevelt that cold December evening who was unimpressed with the approach of the MGT of America, Inc. presentation was

Dr. Rebecca Rogers, an Associate Professor of Literacy Education at the University of Missouri - St. Louis. On several occasions during the public comment section of the program, Rogers asked the presenters from MGT pointed and cutting questions. Of particular, her ire was raised by the agenda of the meeting. Those in attendance were asked to answer a series of questions in regard to the facility and logistical operations of the current buildings in use by the SLPS. The data gathered from the public in this manner, attendees were told, would then be incorporated into the final report and recommendations made by the consulting firm to the Appointed Board of Education. Officials stressed that this process should assure those in attendance of a sense of ownership in MGT of America, Inc findings. Rogers - a critic of the state take over of the schools and the accompanying disenfranchisement of the local citizens - found irony in the fact that while the people's right to elected representation had been stripped away; they were now being asked - in what she felt was a rigged and patronizing fashion - for their input.

"This was a very tightly planned and structured meeting," Rogers explained after the evening's program had been completed. "We were not asked what we thought or what issues interested us. It was all done for us. The questions were set up in such a way that the outcome will be what the Appointed Board now in control wants; more school closings. I find it insulting to be 'led' this way."

Rogers saw a great deal of transparency in the actions of a survey she felt was structured in such a way as to give validity to a predetermined agenda favored by the Special Appointed Board. Rogers also pointed out that an inquiring look into past performance of the Board's recently chosen Superintendent, Dr. Kelvin Adams, formerly a lead School Administrator of the New Orleans, LA Public Schools, would show that he was a proponent of the Charter Schools movement.

"Look closely at his (new Superintendent Adams') role in New Orleans," Rogers would state at the conclusion of the meeting. "He was not a friend of the public schools, he was a champion of the charter school movement. We don't need profit charter schools, we need well funded neighborhood schools. We need schools that are run by the people living in the local communities, the same people who are sending their children to be educated in the(se) local schools. Locals have a vested interest in seeing a (good) high performing neighborhood school more so than some outsiders appointed by a Governor 150 miles away, or local politicians with their own agendas."

In a letter to the St. Louis Post Dispatch, which Rogers wrote after attending the public hearing at Roosevelt, she elaborated on her concerns: "the pseudo-science of the group survey, and the tightly structured small group discussions following the survey, replaces an engaged dialogue about issues that matter most to citizens. What was clear in the small group discussions is that parents and community members do not want any more charter schools and do not want existing schools to be closed. Those points, though, were not on the survey. Parents should not have to rank in order, the importance between lead-free schools and quality learning spaces. We deserve both."

Rogers verbalized the threat most feared by advocates of a strong local school system in the city of St. Louis, charter schools. St. Louis Mayor Francis Slay had become a strong proponent of the development of charter schools in the inner city, and had encouraged the nation's charter school leaders to investigate what he felt was a limitless and potentially lucrative market in the city of St. Louis. Slay, the powerful white mayor, had become a polarizing factor in the deteriorating racial climate within the city. Never good, racial divide, both black and white city leaders agreed, had widened during the first term in office of Mayor Slay. Racially sensitive nerves in the city had, by winter 2008, become rubbed to the point of raw.

Many saw Slay's supporting of charter schools as another lightly veiled move by him to fan the flames of racial unrest in the city, and thus strengthening his grip on the support of the powerful and predominantly white city labor and trade unions. Others claimed nothing but the opposite was true, that Slay's attempts to work with the black controlled elected school board had gotten nowhere and charter schools were the city's last hope to provide an adequate education for its' children of color.

Controversial since they first appeared on the nation's educational landscape early in the decade of the 1990's, charter schools were run by private individuals, absent of state regulations and rules. They could also be run for profit. Despite no government direct oversight, charter schools were entitled to the same levels of state financial aid, as were the public school districts. For every child enrolled in a charter school in the city, the level of aid that would have gone to the child's SLPS school, was now transferred to the charter school that had enrolled the child. The process created further financial drain upon the already strained coffers of the SLPS.

Many, however, saw such criticism of charters as unfounded in reality and lacking in proof, pointing out that any plan supported by Slay was an automatic red flag to the city's black leadership. Many in Slay's camp saw this as a knee jerk reaction from the black community lacking in any factual support. But many blacks saw the charter school movement in the city to have Slay's political fingerprints all over it. The makeup of the three members of the special appointed board that now legally controlled the SLPS was also deep in politics and shallow in education.

By state law, the three panel members of the SAB had each achieved their seats by the way of different political maneuvers. Chairman Rick Sullivan was appointed by Missouri Governor Matt Blunt. Richard Gaines' selection was made by Lewis Reed, president of the St. Louis City Board of Aldermen. The third member, Melanie Adams was fingered by Mayor Slay.

The Mayor had seen the SLSP elected school board make what he considered a dramatic and troubling transformation in the mid term elections of 2006. His hand picked slate of candidates, who prior to the 2006 election had held a majority of the board seats, found themselves unceremoniously uprooted and kicked to the curb by a slate of candidates whose power base lie in the predominantly black neighborhoods of north St. Louis.

Many black city political leaders saw the take over by the State Department of Education as a Slay orchestrated end run around the democratic process in favor of a Slay hand picked board - appointed by special interests – that blatantly ignored any opposition voiced in the best interest of black city school children.

Publically, Slay's stance was that the SLPS was a miserable failure, and he was frustrated with the continued lack of progress in propping up the district's abysmal test scores. The very real threat of the decertification of the city schools, Slay claimed, left him no choice but to seek drastic changes in the way St. Louis children were educated in the public schools.

The Mayor held a news conference in 2007 to announce that he would begin aggressively recruiting charter schools to set up operations in the city of St. Louis. Slay promised to provide incentives to entice these for profit educational endeavors. All the while critics claimed, Slay's actions were conducted with his full realization that charter schools would pull even more students from the rolls of the

SLPS, and provide perhaps the final nail in the coffin of a once proud and effective school system.

Slay claimed that the school system was beyond repair, that too many of the city's young people had already been denied their right to an appropriate, free and adequate education. The Mayor claimed that any more effort to work within the frame work of the SLPS was a folly the city could no longer afford. According to Slay, drastic problems called for drastic measures.

Many black city leaders saw Slay's actions as further proof that his concerns were not with the children enrolled in city schools, but with political control of the tax payer dollars set aside for education, a position of leverage he had lost at the ballot box with the recent defeats of his slate of incumbent candidates. Slay's actions, the critics claimed, was another attack on the rights of the majority of black parents who sent their children to the SLPS.

As critics and community activists repeatedly pointed out, charter schools are not held accountable by the democratic process of voters electing local community members to make school policy decisions. Instead, the continuing decline in enrollment, and the subsequent loss of educational dollars that would follow the charter movement, made it almost impossible for the city schools to raise performance standards and ward off a state takeover - a move that would put the control of the schools back into the hands of Slay and his cronies. This would be, claimed black city leaders, an abomination to the democratic process and entrenched deeper the minority white control of the city in general - and the educational system in particular.

The educational gauntlet had now been dropped by Slay and his white power base on the south side, whose own families had long ago abandoned the SLPS, in stark opposition to black civic leaders in the north who desperately wanted to prop up city school student enrollment – hopeful of maintaining and keeping their surviving neighborhood schools open. In a best case scenario, the north side leaders cast an anticipative eye to the some day resurrection of the many shuttered city schools on the north side, casualties of the past decade's declining enrollment.

Despite the loud and chaotic protests that followed the state takeover in the spring of 2007, several deterring black city education leaders supported the charter movement, and the potential benefits for black school children. "Traditional advocates of civil rights claim that charter schools are but another opportunity for whites to escape from the public school system and gain advantage for their children at taxpayers' expense," says Dr. Tomiko Brown-Nagin, an African American and a faculty member at Washington University in St. Louis. "This criticism overlooks the astounding fact, however, that most charter schools have been established in poor, minority neighborhoods and are attended disproportionately by poor, minority students — those whose schools and neighborhoods have been untouched by *Brown v. Board of Education*," Brown-Nagin said in thoughts posted in 2008 on a Washington University web site.

Brown-Nagin cites a study compiled in 2003 by The Civil Rights Project at Harvard University. The study documented that minorities made up only 41 percent of students in public schools nationwide, but the student body makeup of charter schools showed a 57 percent minority rate. The Harvard research also found the disparity of African-Americans to be even more out of sync with national figures. According to the research cited by the study, black majority enrollment was found in only 17 percent of public schools in the USA, but a statistically significant 33% of charter schools.

"This striking fact should inform our views about the nature and purposes of alternative educational spaces such as charter schools," wrote Brown-Nagin, in a published essay in the Duke Journal of Law entitled <u>Toward a Pragmatic Understanding of Status-Consciousness</u>: *The Case of Deregulated Education*.

Regardless of the political rhetoric that was bantered about so freely in the chaos of the spring of 2007, the SLPS take over by the Missouri State Department of Education became reality. The naysayers of the action continued to complain of disenfranchisement and racist intent, demanding the retention of a system that by any quantitative measure had to be deemed a complete and colossal failure. On the opposite sideline, those in charge of the takeover continued their rigid and uncompromising stand.

Against this divisive background, in 2008 the SLPS hired its sixth Superintendent in five years, and commissioned yet another in an endless line of studies, at the tidy clip to the taxpayers of $625,000 to help the appointed school board determine which of the remaining city schools would be shuttered. School officials used the district's tally sheet bottom line to justify their righteous pledges of fiscal accountability, no matter how painful, to justify more school closings. What had for the past several years become a sad spring ritual in St. Louis was once again placed into motion: city students preparing to be uprooted from their familiar neighborhood schools and transferred to new schools in distant and unfamiliar neighborhoods.

On February 5, 2009, MGM, Inc. released to the Board of Education and to the public its recommendations. The swathe, as most had suspected, fell in a wide arc. It was recommended to the Special Appointed Board of Education that the district either close or "repurpose" 29 of the district's remaining 85 functioning school buildings. This nearly 30% reduction in operating schools, the consulting group claimed, would save the cash strapped district over 22 million dollars per year, if their plan was fully implemented. The changes would be phased in over a five year period.

Surprisingly to some, the recommendations spared all of the district's neighborhood high schools: Roosevelt, Sumner, Vashon and Beaumont. Rumors of Sumner being on the hit list had surfaced several weeks before the official report was released. The first all black high school west of the Mississippi, Sumner was viewed as a valued treasure by the north St. Louis black community. Despite its staggering decrease in enrollment and the poor condition of its physical plant, black leaders made it very clear that Sumner would not be closed without a long and unpleasant battle from the city's north side occupants.

"This will not happen at Sumner like it did at Cleveland," offered one veteran SLPS employee, in reference to the closing of Cleveland High School three years before. At one time the pride of white south side residents, Cleveland had long ago fallen into disfavor with white parents, who stopped sending their offspring to "the Castle" - as Cleveland was affectionately known - after the start of forced busing in the early 80's. The strong emotional ties to Sumner were explained by a North Side resident who requested anonymity: "People on the north side still feel an owed allegiance to Sumner High School. Many of their alums still live in the neighborhood. It is not like Cleveland, where most of their alum no longer live in the city, they all out in west county. They gave up on the city. They still like to talk about the old days with fond memories, but they don't care about the neighborhood anymore."

Not true at Sumner, who had at its disposal a strong and organized alumni and booster group. With claim to such famous grads as Arthur Ashe, Dick

Gregory and Chuck Berry, Sumner would not be closed without a fight. "We will go to any means necessary to save that school," 4th Ward Alderman Samuel Moore told the St. Louis Post Dispatch in December of 2008. "To even think about taking away the history of that building is unacceptable, and I want to let you know I have a dog in the fight." Such warnings evidently were heard, as both Beaumont and Sumner, two north side neighborhood schools rumored for mothballs, were spared.

While Sumner supporters could point with historical pride to the role the institution played in the black heritage of the city, accomplishments at the school in 2008 were sorely lacking and held no standing for the chest swelling community pride its supporters had hammered home in their fight to save the school. When the historical rose colored glasses were removed, the true picture of today's Sumner High School came into sharp focus; and the view was indeed, a bleak one. With a stated capacity of 1500, the school in the Spring of 2009 housed only 615 students.

When evaluating Sumner High School, district leaders pointed out, educational quality was even more of a concern than enrollment quantity. While the state average drop out rate hovered just over 4%, Sumner's dropout rate was an astronomical 42% - two percentage points higher than the graduation rate of the school. On state wide standardized achievement tests, the performance of Sumner students was beyond even abysmal. Statewide, students achieved at the proficient rate of 39.2 percent in reading, 35.2 percent in math and 47.6 percent in science. Sumner's percentage of students at or above the proficiency rate was 6.2 percent, 5 percent and 3.6 percent, respectfully.

Public response upon the proposals release was, as predicted, not favorable. The Special Board of Education held two public hearings to gather community input. The first was held to a standing room only crowd in the Roosevelt auditorium. Over 400 people packed the room to overflow. 80 constituents waited patiently to address the board. It took over three hours for everyone to have their say.

The boisterous crowd stretched out of the hallway and into the foyer at the front of the building. To a person, the speakers made impassioned pleas for the survival of their schools. Patrons, teachers, parents and students boasted of the positive accomplishments of each doomed building, validating their comments with statistics of improved test scores, safer schools and better teaching and administrative teams. Was anyone listening? The three Board members present assured the audience they were, and that no decisions would be made until all community input could be documented, studied and evaluated. The reaction from the concerned patrons, as they left the meeting, was one of mixed resignation.

"Why pay $625,000 to someone if you are not going to do as the say?" asked one mother. "It is just going to happen. We can come down here and vent, and maybe make us feel like we have done at least all we could, but in the long run we got no say. Our schools will continue to close, our neighborhoods will continue to die and, in a few years, we will bring somebody else from the outside, pay them a lot of money and we will do another study. Nobody listens to us because the politicians want to see the schools fail and bring in the charters. Everyone on the north side knows this. Numbers, charts, budgets, I don't care about none of that. I care about my kids and their future. And closing my child's school hurts my child."

Once again, repeatedly, the same complaint was raised by the mostly African American crowd in attendance, that Mayor Slay was behind the school closings and once again he and the white power brokers on the south side of the city had disenfranchised the majority black voters.

"All they care about is destroying our schools," complained one of the evening's many speakers, who saw collusion and conspiracy in the findings of MGM. "They were paid a lot of money to come in here and say what Slay and the others want to hear, that our schools are dying," complained another. Several attendees questioned how the board, after paying MGM nearly 2/3 of a million dollars, could now objectively look at the recommendations with truly inquiring eyes.

"They want to take away the 'public' from the public schools," theorized still another disgruntled citizen. "This is all about taking education out of the control of the local people and turning it over to a bunch of outsiders who are here only to make money. They don't care what happens to our kids, our neighborhoods or our futures. It is all about making money," she added once more, for emphasis.

Privatization of the public schools through the charter school movement was the only hope, the Mayor's shrills would repeatedly proclaim over the next several weeks. The system was beyond repair was their message.

True, was the immediate response from those who were scratching and clawing in a desperate attempt to maintain some local control over public education in the city of St. Louis; but only because of the Mayor's systematic neglect through design that was intended to bring about the collapse of the SLPS.

An overflow crowd of spectators at a PHL game is about as common as a white cornerback in the NFL, but the Roosevelt crowd at Vianney set a new low standard. As the ball was teed up by the Vianney kicker to start the game, the south bleachers behind the Roosevelt bench were occupied by seven Roosevelt fans; all parents. The Roosevelt cheerleaders, as they had been all year, were out in full voice and full number. Despite their best efforts this cool fall evening, the red clad cheerleaders could raise not a sound from the crowd. In due time, just as they did at most games, they collectively – figuratively and literally - turned their backs to the crowd, and their cheering routines became a self gratifying experience in youthful energy. Even if no one noticed, they were still quite good, their routines perfected by hours and hours of after school practice.

As they did every week, the Roosevelt offense took the opening drive down the field in a flawless display of the spread offense. Mixing the slashing running of Antonio Carter, with the pinpoint passing of Arlando Bailey, the Roughriders marched 71 yards in just nine plays to reach paydirt. Mohammed Dukly added the extra point and the Roughriders, with less than six minutes gone in the first quarter, had a 7-0 lead.

No penalties, crisp blocking and flawless execution. The performance, however, as it had been all season, was nothing more than a tease, a preliminary act for a team that would soon find ways to self destruct. It was both maddening and predictable. Roosevelt would take the field and produce a masterful drive to open the game. So much talent, coupled with a glimpse of what could have been, was pure torture to the red clad supporters. The fleeting visions of a disciplined unit that would, at times shine above the numerous mistake filled ugly minutes of bad football the Riders would each week inevitably display, showed Campbell and his coaches what was possible with a roster of PHL castoffs.

"We just got to learn to sustain," Campbell would say after the season. "It is not that we can't execute, because at times we look unstoppable on offense. But then, just like that, we start in with the same old half ass bullshit: penalties, missed blocks, turnovers, poor decisions....it's there, man its there. I can see it. For (a few) minutes we can play with anybody in the state. I am serious, man. If you had one drive and could pick any team in the state, I'd take us. But we don't sustain."

After the opening offensive drive to stake the Riders to an early lead, Roosevelt was whistled for a hard to believe six defensive offsides penalties in the first half alone. Coach West was beside himself. "All you have to do is look at the frigging ball," he screamed after another hard count by the Vianney quarterback had drawn one of his defensive linemen across the neutral zone.

"Don't even listen to his count. He is getting you to jump with his voice. That is bullshit," West told the team. "We practice (this) every day. Just look at the ball. When it moves, you move."

Coach Campbell would, in disgust, at halftime label the six offsides penalties as, "just another example of a halfass PHL team that does not have the discipline to play with the county teams."

By halftime, the Roughriders trailed, 41-15. Campbell's only comment to his solemn team during the intermission was, "it's character time right now, men. How you play the last 24 minutes of this game is going to determine how you remember your high school career. Many of you will never play another down of football after these 24 minutes. Think about that."

The second half would prove to be perhaps the highlight of the season. Roosevelt somehow managed to regroup and outscore in the second half the district champion Vianney Griffins by a count of 27-21. Even though his team could not overcome a disastrous second quarter, and pulled no closer than the final score of 62-42, the spirit displayed by both the coaches and the players, in a hopeless cause, was inspiring and perhaps confusing.

With absolutely nothing tangible or concrete left to play for in those final 24 minutes - playoff hopes had disappeared after last week's loss - even a morale saving win to close out the season was now out of reach. But fight on the team did. Case in point: Campbell took his last time out with 12 seconds left in the game in an attempt to score one more meaningless touchdown.

The second half banter on the sidelines among the players was at a season high, and so was the fun factor. Senior linebacker George Bell scored the last touchdown of the 2008 season with an improbable 35 yard interception return. As a winded Bell returned to the sidelines he was greeted with high fives by his teammates and disparaging remarks about his less than suave body frame. "Didn't know your fat ass could run that fast," one assistant coach told Bell.

"Been misused my whole career," the honor roll student stated in mock disgust. "Should have been a tailback and should have been running back kicks. You coaches screwed me, man. Favoritism. Antonio ain't got nothing on me," Bell proclaimed with a high pitched laugh as he left the field after his unlikely jaunt to paydirt. Bell would never again step on the field as a high school football player. "Well, heck," Bell said, "how many dudes score their only touchdown on their last play?"

As the final seconds ticked off the clock on a team whose official record would be recorded for history as 0-9, a team that had only weeks before dreamed of playoff and state championship glory, to only have their collective hearts ripped out by a runaway train wreck of one catastrophe after another, the senior linemen lofted the water cooler to give Coach West an unexpected season ending drenching. From the observable behavior on the team's respective sidelines - without a glance at the scoreboard - an uninformed spectator would have surmised that the white clad jerseys were headed for the playoffs and the team in black was playing out the string on a disappointing season. In reality, the opposite was true.

One last duty remained for Campbell in his role as head coach of the 2008 Roosevelt Roughriders football team, the taking of the team picture. With no yearbook at Roosevelt for the last seven years, the long tradition of taking the Roosevelt team picture on the stadium steps had died with the last edition of The Bwana. Now the group shot to record, for prosperity, the image of this clan of Roughriders, would be taken on the field of the opposition. Campbell gathered his team at the 50 yard line to organize the shot. His last words to the assembled group: "This one is going up in the hallway, so no gang signs, you hear me?" And thus ended a strange season of inner city high school football.

CHAPTER 7
THE POST SEASON

Defeat is not the worst of failures. Not to have tried is the true failure.
— George E. Woodberry

But there is suffering in life, and there are defeats. No one can avoid them. But it's better to lose some of the battles in the struggles for your dreams than to be defeated without ever knowing what you're fighting for.
— Paulo Coelho

"The defeats and victories of the fellows at the top aren't always defeats and victories for the fellows at the bottom.
— Bertolt Brecht

The difference of race is one of the reasons why I fear war may always exist; because race implies difference, difference implies superiority, and superiority leads to pre dominance.
— Benjamin Disraeli

When viewed in the brutal frankness of historical record, the final 2008 season win- loss tally of the Roosevelt Roughriders football team jumps off the page in an honest, but unflattering way: 0-9. The legacy of a team that entered the season with such high and grandiose expectations – a trip to the dome and a state championship – had been brutally waylaid in a despondent fashion no one would have believed possible during the heady spring and summer months of preparation. As Coach Campbell liked to point out, the on field record of the team showed five wins and four setbacks, played against as challenging a schedule as undertaken by any PHL team in recent memory. But in reality - technicality or not - the PHL title that had been won on the field in an undefeated fashion by a team dominated by a deep, talented and dedicated senior class, was cruelly snatched away by an ambiguous eligibility ruling that the players neither understood, nor ever accepted.

As Coach Campbell had told his players during the last week of practice as they prepared to play what they knew was a meaningless final contest, "on the field, everyone knows who won the PHL. That is what you are going to remember 20 years from now. Not some rule about what kind of school someone goes to. You won the PHL and everyone in the city knows it. You hold your heads up high. You earned it. In 2008, Roosevelt is the football class of the PHL. Don't ever forget that, and don't ever let anyone try and tell you different."

Still, a season that had begun with such heady and lofty expectations during an offseason that had started the previous January, had staggered by November, to a frustrating and sputtering end.

During a post season interview, Campbell tried to give some perspective and clarity to the year. Clearly frustrated as the season wore on, now two weeks after the season's conclusion Campbell's vision was more focused on the big picture. The persistent cough that had nagged at the coach since August, was now gone. The dreary look of a man under too much stress had been replaced by a coach who was obviously bolstered with renewed energy. "Look, the main thing is we are going to get these kids into college. We are working real hard on that right now. We are losing some great kids and I feel bad for the seniors, but they are ok. I was really proud of how we played the last game at Vianney," said Campbell.

The effort given throughout the final week of practice preparing for a meaningless final game was in many ways a sign of validation to Campbell. "Our kids didn't quit. They played hard. No matter how much shit they had heaped upon them, they never quit. We still make way too many mistakes. We still are not as disciplined as I would like, but we have made so much progress here – as a football team, as a school, as a family. I am proud to be at Roosevelt High School."

With the end of every season comes the inevitable self evaluation each coach puts him or herself through. The long hours, the low pay, and the stress and frustration created by the attempt to develop perfection from imperfect teenagers, all factors a coach must consider when answering the question: is it worth it? "I have thought a lot about my future the last two weeks," Campbell said. "I am here (at Roosevelt) for the long run, however long that may be."

But what about the big picture, what about Campbell's future? By casting his lot with the bumbling SLPS and the PHL, was Campbell simply steering a hopelessly rudderless ship headed inexorably to a symbolic final wreck? Could the SLPS survive much longer and what resources would be available for future Roughriders? "I can't control any of that. I don't even bother worrying about the PHL or the SLPS," said Campbell. "I am a football coach. All I can do is coach these kids - fight for them - the best way I know how. As long as the doors at Roosevelt are open for students, I want to be the football coach here. We are about so much more than winning and losing, so much more than just football."

Titling at windmills? Perhaps, but by staying the course with a system that desperately needed coaches like him, when he had the pedigree to pursue much better paying jobs outside the city, Campbell was making an emphatic statement that paid testament to his personal belief system. "I will not quit on these kids because they never quit on me. They had a lot of chances to chuck the whole thing this year. Lots of times, and who could have blamed them. Did you see how we practiced before the Vianney game, when we knew we were not going anywhere? Did you see how we played that last game? We fought to the very last play. That tells me we are doing some good things here. We are just a work in progress and you can't measure what we do simply by wins and losses. But listen, that don't mean we can't win here. We will win. It is just going to take a lot more time and a lot more work. But we will win."

The Roughriders of 2008 were a resilient bunch, but they were also, in many ways, a cast of tragic characters. Running Back Antonio Carter, and his senior year performance, was arguably the most disappointing in a season full of disappointments. Carter had only, several months prior, dreamed of a campaign that would produce, in his words, "two dimes," or 2,000 rushing yards. A combination of injuries, spotty blocking by an inconsistent and enigmatic offensive line, a pass happy offense, and just all around bad luck, had limited the 5'4" 140 lb. senior running back to a final season total of 829 yards - or less than one half of his hoped for haul. Regardless of not reaching his high pre-season goals, Carter's efforts still produced some impressive stats for his senior season. His average per rush was over six yards a carry, a figure that would have been more than adequate in a march to 2000 yards - if he had registered 30 carries a game, as did most of the area's leading rushers. Carter's rushing attempts totaled only 132 carries for the year, or less than 15 a game. He did find the end zone on ten occasions, twice the number of his nearest teammate, Quadricous Sanford.

"It was a frustrating year," the quiet Carter confided on a cold January, 2009 morning.

Of all the prominent Roosevelt players, Carter was the hardest to get to know. He was quiet to the point of painfully shy. To a man, Carter held the respect and the support of his teammates, but seldom their companionship. Carter could often be seen coming to the practice field alone, and departing the same way; head down, his long dreadlocks bobbing with each stride he took. He was always the first player to arrive for the team breakfast on Saturday morning game days, and many times lingered - always by himself - after a game, the last to leave the field, and later, the last to leave the locker room.

Well liked by all, but known by few, Carter did not appear to have even one close friend on the team. He simply did his thing in a quiet and unassuming but determined fashion, then disappeared into the south side streets where he resided with his father. The next day he would reappear and quietly repeat the same routine. He was the only senior star on the team whom Coach West had not labeled with a colorful and descriptive nick name. He was addressed by all as simply, Antonio.

Carter admitted he loved the locker room environment on Saturday morning game day - the anticipation of another opportunity to show the doubters of the world that despite a lack of size, he was the toughest football player in the city. "I can't describe how I would feel when I would wake up on Saturday mornings and start my pre game (preparation). I just felt zoned in, like this is where I am supposed to be, what I am supposed to do. It was like I was in my own world. It gave me a real calm and strong feeling. I am really going to miss that," said Carter.

Carter lived for fall Saturday afternoons, and one more chance to prove his worth to all those over the years who had questioned his lack of stature. He never failed to answer the bell. After he was tackled, no matter how hard he was hit by multiple players, some twice his size, Carter would bounce up from the ground and sprint back to his position in anticipation of the next play, a defiant show of toughness. In the locker room on Saturday game day morning, Carter felt safe, a calm washing over him - relishing in the preparation for the one activity in life that made him feel special – a Saturday afternoon football game at Roughrider Stadium.

By his own choice, Carter was a loner. The lack of constant companionship did not seem to bother him. He explained: "I have friends here, lots of them. It is just that I don't need people around me all the time. I like to go out, but also to stay focused on what is important. I have some big decisions to make, some big responsibilities to meet the next few years. The fun can wait. I got to stay focused on the important stuff: school and playing ball. That is my future. Not running around loud and acting (like) the fool."

Everyone at Roosevelt respected Carter's desire and admired his courage. Never once during the season did he back down from a challenge; on the field or off. "I like being the underdog," said Carter. When he ran the ball, he was a whirlwind of churning arms and legs. Bringing the compact Carter down, as many a battered PHL defender could attest to, was not an easy task. He was not a floater or a strider when he ran the football, he was a runaway miniature bull, always in full attack mode. Carter's balance was amazing. More than once a game he would produce a jaw dropping run; seemingly stopped and smothered by a multitude of defenders, only to somehow pop out of a scrum of players and continue his inexorable charge towards the opponent's goal line. He was a football warrior in the truest since. He was a joy for a spectator to watch and he deserved much more than the 2008 season gave him.

"It was just not in the cards for Antonio this year," said Coach Campbell, in a post season assessment of Carter's 2008 performance. "I really feel for him. He works so hard."

Several times during the season, Campbell had used his halftime speech to rip into his offensive lineman for what he felt was a less than stellar effort by his lineman to spring Carter. "Antonio is busting his ass out there, giving it everything he has, but you fat lazy asses will not give him (a fraction) of the effort he gives to this team," Campbell lectured his linemen during intermission of the Gateway Tech game. "Hold your blocks. You got the best running back in the PHL running behind you, but he can't do it alone."

Watching Carter at halftime was a study in determination and desire; but also pride and quiet confidence. He would find a spot away from his teammates, but within ear shot of the coaches, sitting quietly and motionless; conserving his energy and strength, preparing both mentally and physically for another 24 minutes of what was often an uphill fight. Carter never doubted his own skills. He held a fierce belief that it was just a matter of time, that his next highlight reel run was just one snap away. Only once - the halftime intermission of the Vashon game - did his frustration manifest itself into a verbal barrage of anger aimed at his teammates. At all other times, Carter remained calm, quiet and determined.

Carter's post Roosevelt future, by January 2009, was still very much undecided. He and Campbell had both known for over a year that his college travels would more than likely have to pass through some dusty and far off junior college outpost. "I have not been on any college visits yet." Carter admitted in January 2009, his eyes disclosing a developing concern for his future.

"I know Coach is still talking to some people for me. I got a good film from (Coach Campbell) and we are getting it out there. I still think I can get through the (NCAA) Clearinghouse," Carter said in reference to the NCAA office that certified a high school athlete as academically sufficient to be recruited by NCAA Division I and II member schools.

Those familiar with Carter's academic standing knew he was in denial. No way was he going to make it through the NCAA Clearinghouse and receive a football scholarship for the 2009 season from an NCAA Division I or II school.

In December 2008, Carter had mentioned one NCAA Division III school he thought was a possibility, Blackburn College in nearby Carlinville, IL. As a Division III school, the Beavers could offer Carter no athletic scholarship, but felt they could, their coaches had told him, based on his financial need, parlay together an attractive financial aid package. With no athletic money to give, Division III schools were exempt from the restrictions of the NCAA Clearinghouse, removal of an insurmountable hurdle in Carter's path to college. Carter seemed hopeful. Two weeks later, the President of Blackburn College announced that the small school was, for financial reasons, disbanding its football program.

"Junior College is the route right now for Antonio," said Campbell. "He knows that, he just has not yet totally accepted the fact. We think a Community College in Iowa is going to offer him. It is a Junior College, but like I told him the other day, 'listen, there are a lot of dudes out there right now making big money playing on Sundays that had to do the same thing, had to overcome the same problems that you now face.' A lot of great players had to go to JUCOs. It can be done and we are working hard to get Antonio that chance. We owe him that. There is not a better kid with a better heart you will ever find than Antonio. He just waited too long to get started with the books and now he is paying the price."

Before his spring graduation departure, Carter speaks of a desire to hammer home a lesson to the younger Roughriders. "Get busy right now, on the books. That is what I tell them," said Carter of his advice to younger teammates. "It is important for me to set a good example for the younger players. Coach Campbell tried hard with me to show me the right path and, I want to give back some of that to the younger guys. I will always support Roosevelt football. I am proud to have played here. I could have gone to one of the county schools. When I was a freshman here, one of the Kirkwood coaches was after me to transfer there. I am glad I didn't."

Carter expresses no remorse, no regrets, and no second thoughts about his years at Roosevelt. "It has been hard, all the shit we have to put up with here, that they don't have to at the private and county schools. But it has made me a better person to have gone to Roosevelt and fight for everything I want. Maybe we didn't win a state or even a district championship, but we were brothers and we gave it all we had. We are a family and nothing, no matter how much bad (luck) we had this year will ever make me not love the players and the coaches here. That last game, when Coach took me out in the 4th quarter, I looked up at the clock and I got real emotional. I knew it was over. I went over to (sophomore running back Stephen) Wallace and said, 'its' you now, Cuz. I am turning it over to you.'" Three months later, on a cold January morning, memories of the torch passing moment at Vianney caused an emotional rise in the normally stoic Carter's voice, a telltale sign of the quiet young man's sincerity, when reminiscing on his years as a Roughrider.

Spend much time with Antonio Carter, and a stranger will soon realize the burning desire of the quiet young man's passion for a productive future. "I just want out of here, you know. I just want to show Coach Campbell and Mr. Houston and all the others here who have believed in me that they didn't waste their time. I want them in the future to look back and see that trying to help me was time well spent."

In many ways Carter, as a finished project and RHS graduating senior, both exemplified the noble efforts of those at Roosevelt who toil relentlessly to better the lot in life of the students entrusted to their care, and epitomized the endless and frustrating struggle against overwhelming odds that so many at RHS daily endure.

Carter's unassuming nature, along with his genuine and honest demeanor, made for a very likeable and humble young man. Everyone at Roosevelt wanted to see the diminutive running back succeed; to fight his way through life's challenges with the same determination he displayed in tearing with reckless abandon through an opponent's defense. All concerned wanted Carter out of an inner city environment that had stymied the dreams of so many before him.

Carter knew college was his only hope for a route to a better life, his only alternative to being swallowed up by the mean streets of the big city. Unfortunately, by early 2009, the question had become a simple one: is there a road to any college open for a 5'4" running back with the heart of a champion, but a 14 on the ACT?

Chapter 7: The Post Season

"Right now, "Man-Child" is bull shit," was the candid assessment of Coach Campbell in regard to the January, 2009 status of his enigmatic mountain of an offensive lineman, junior Rene Faulk. "It is all up to him, but since football been over he has been sliding," said Campbell. In what way, Campbell was asked. "Ask him," Campbell uttered between clenched teeth.

Rene Faulk, aka "Man-Child" - a sobriquet assigned by Coach West in deference to the young lineman's tremendous physical prowess, tempered by his irritating immaturity - was, for his coaches, a constant source of both hope and torment.

The 6'3" 315 lb nephew of former St. Louis Rams future Hall of Fame running back Marshall Faulk had shown promise throughout the 2008 season. Campbell had noted in October, "Man-Child" is really starting to get it, starting to realize where this game can take him. He just has to get better, and if he continues as he is now, he will."

Assistant coach Darren West, who worked with Faulk each day during the season as his position coach, described the potential future for Faulk as "scary, man, just nothing but scary. That big old boy can destroy people on the football field. His potential is out of this world. When he wants to play nobody, and I mean nobody, will stop him. He is a beast on both sides of the ball. The only person who can stop "Man-Child" is "Man-Child," said West.

And, by the turn of the 2009 New Year, that is precisely what Faulk was doing.

Never an accomplished student, a problem exasperated by a diagnosis of behavioral disorders, Faulk had shown progress with his school decorum throughout the first semester of the 2008-09 school year. Faulk freely discussed his educational struggles in an off campus interview in October, 2008. He candidly described an early age diagnosis of a behavioral disorder and willingly shared his plight and his struggles with a diagnosed condition that had him labeled as a special educational student. "I don't mind talking about it," he admitted, "I got problems controlling my temper. I ain't ashamed of that. It is just something I need to work on." Faulk admitted to a recent remission into behavior the staff at Roosevelt had hoped the hulking young man had put behind him. "It was my fault. I got moved our of BD (behavioral disorder) class and into regular classes this fall," Faulk said, in regard to his start of the school year transfer from a self contained classroom to a regular classroom setting. In a behavioral disorder, or BD classroom, Faulk would spend his entire school day within the small setting of the same room. Under the arrangement that allowed him to return to regular classes, Faulk had more freedom and less adult supervision. "I didn't handle it well," he admitted.

Limited students, limited movement and consistency of the same teacher the entire day, experts felt was the most appropriate learning environment for students diagnosed with BD. Teachers and aides specially trained in helping students such as Faulk, would work one on one with Rene. The goal of any such special arrangement was to help the student master the skills necessary to control their inappropriate behavior, always with the goal of developing the social skills necessary to return to a regular classroom setting.

By the start of the 2008-2009 school year, the Behavioral Disorder teachers at Roosevelt, in conjunction with Faulk's counselor and parents, felt he was prepared for such a move. At first, the transition went smoothly, but by the time the football season ended in November, old inappropriate and unacceptable behaviors by Faulk were beginning to reappear.

By the start of the second semester in January, Faulk was back in a self contained classroom. What did he think of the change? "Gets me out of school at 12:30, so yeah, it ain't a bad deal. No complaints from me," Faulk said with a shrug of his powerful shoulders. "I know Coach Campbell is not happy with me," Faulk stated. "I can do better. I was doing better. But when football ended I kind of lost my way. But no problem man, I can get it back (together). I am not worried about it."

Faulk's potential as a big time college football player began to emerge in a more crisp and sharpened focus as the 2008 season unfolded. When motivated, he was the best player in the PHL. When not, he was a bitter example of wasted talent, a calamity so commonly found in the PHL.

Early in the season, to the constant irritation of the coaching staff, Faulk would dominate one play then take the next two off. "Man-Child," roared Coach West one day in the middle of an afternoon practice, "you have got to be the sorriest excuse for a football player I have ever seen. Get out of my sight, get off of my field and I hope to never see a lazier fat ass than you in my entire coaching career. Get on back to your buddies who are going nowhere, cause you ain't either," West concluded as he banished, for that day at least, Faulk from the team.

But as the year wore on, the transformation of Rene Faulk from out of shape, over weight underachiever to the "Man-Child" - capable of dominating the game from either side of the line of scrimmage - materialized in a startling short period of time. As Faulk's practice habits improved, so did his game day performance and, as Campbell liked to point out, also his off field behavior. Faulk began getting to practice on time and working hard, if not on every practice snap, at least most.

The coaching staff was almost giddy with anticipation of how good the monstrous Faulk could become. "That big old rascal has all the tools," gushed Campbell in October. "Wait until the college coaches see his tape. If he keeps getting things in order the way he is now, he will be one of the most heavily recruited linemen in the country next year."

True to Campbell's prediction, as the season wore on, interest in Faulk from Division I football coaches grew. At first, Faulk was a mere curiosity because of his last name and relationship to his famous uncle, compounded by his compelling story of surviving Hurricane Katrina, uprooted from his New Orleans home and arriving at Roosevelt High School as a football project in need of much work. But by the end of the 2008 season, Faulk was a legitimate Division I prospect.

On a winter day Faulk pulls from his overstuffed backpack several crumpled letters. "I got more of these somewhere, but a bunch of coaches have been by to talk to me," Faulk informs a visitor. The letters he produces are a short list of major college football powers: Nebraska, Missouri, Colorado and Oklahoma, among others, all properly engraved with the logos and letterhead of a who's who of Division I powers, introducing themselves to Faulk as potential suitors for his football talents. But, as Coach Campbell has incessantly preached to the "Man-Child," it could all disappear as quickly as it materialized. And it certainly appeared in January 2009, that Faulk was the one with his finger squarely on the eject button of his future college football career.

As the Fall 2008 transition from mild mannered Rene into the unbridled "Man-Child" played out, another benefit became obvious, Faulk was becoming a team leader. During the off season workouts of 2008, many senior Roughriders did little to hide their contempt for the lazy habits Faulk, a junior, more often than not brought with him to the practice field. Senior linebacker George Bell was often the most outspoken critic of Faulk.

"All that talent, wasted on a fat lazy ass like you," Bell told Faulk during a summer 2008 weight lifting session. Faulk would always give the outward appearance of being unfazed by such criticism from teammates, always maintaining a stoic front to such peer condemnation. Faulk would, however, admit in private that the stinging barbs and jabs of his older teammates hurt.

"They think it all comes easy for me because of my name and my size, but it ain't that way," Faulk said in August. "But it also helps motivate me. I know that is what George is doing when he gets on me. Same thing with Coach West. He is on me all the time, always pushing me. I know that is because they care. I have problems, but I am working hard to get better."

Faulk's sincerity, when addressing in a soft and almost child like voice his dreams and desires, betrays the public persona he often showed: an angry and undisciplined underachiever throwing away the many special athletic gifts bestowed upon him, always to the criticism and consternation of those less blessed. Faulk was becoming much too easy to peg by many who did not know him personally, as just another undisciplined underachiever from Roosevelt, throwing away a chance for a brighter future.

"Sure I want to play college football," Faulk said in January, 2009, "but I don't know if I want to go to college." His reference to a college football future without attending college were just the kind of irrational thoughts that Faulk would utter that drove crazy his coaches, and those who cared about his future.

By January 2009, it was clear to all at Roosevelt, that the future fortunes of the often brooding Faulk could fall either way. He was a fence sitter. Which way he would fall, and where he would land, would be determined over the next year. He could be on his way to college, becoming a well known and big time football star. Or Faulk could allow his bad attitude to destroy his hopes and dreams, casting him adrift; just another dead end loser from the neighborhood.

By the New Year, the red flags of concern were blowing fiercely in another gathering storm in the ongoing saga of the "Man-Child." But Faulk, when in the midst of a good day, would regularly pledge to disprove all the critics. "You know what got me going and thinking over the Christmas break, was when I saw Obama on TV." The oversized youth's sleepy eyes suddenly sparkle, alive with life; as Faulk continued, "Man ain't this something. A brother as President. If he can do something great like that, you know what, then I can go to college. I just got to believe. Man, when I think about Obama, it makes me feel real good, like I can do something with my life. 'Just watch me,' that's what I tell the dudes now who doubt me, 'just watch me.'"

Quadricous Sanford would finish the season as the most decorated of the Roughriders. He was named to the Class 5 Missouri Sportswriters first team as a defensive back. More notably, he was listed by the St. Louis Post Dispatch as the 28th best college football prospect among the area senior stars. This placed Sanford in elite company as most college scouts had rated the current senior class of the St. Louis metro area as one of the strongest in years. Sanford, by January 2009, was the only Roughrider senior committed to a college program, casting his lot with Arkansas-Pine Bluff, site unseen.

"I am going down there early next month," Sanford said in January 2009. "They want me to play defensive back and I think that is my best position. They like my speed and they told coach that after watching film of me, they think I can come in and play right away and not have to take a redshirt year. They said that my kick returning alone should get me on the field next year. That is important to me. I don't want to redshirt. I can't imagine what it would be like to not play for a whole year. Football keeps me straight. I live for it."

Sanford was well known throughout the area football community for his all around skills. Nicknamed "Mississippi" because of his roots in the northern Mississippi community of Batesville, the hard hitting, but soft spoken, young man seldom came off the field in the 2008 season. He led the team in punt returns and kickoff returns, was second on the team in rushing yards, and led the team in pass receptions and receiving yards. He was a ball hawking defensive back that led the Riders in interceptions and played all over the field on offense. He was the deep snapper on both punts and field goals and even was the backup quarterback, being pressed into service at the conclusion of the Webster Groves game when regular QB Arlando Bailey was knocked out of the contest with a concussion.

It was no understatement when Coach Campbell said after the season, "we are going to need a lot of players to replace Mississippi. He did it all for us. And he did it all well. He will be a good player at Pine Bluff. They will love his attitude."

Sanford had seen the bright lights of big time high school football. No other teammate at Roosevelt had experienced life on the uptown side of the high school football landscape. Sanford had left South Panola, Mississippi High School to enroll at Roosevelt at the conclusion of the summer vacation between his freshman and sophomore years. South Panola was in the midst of a four year undefeated string when Sanford pulled up roots to move to St. Louis and live with his maternal grandmother. The winning at South Panola would continue, reaching 89 straight victories before the Tigers tasted defeat in the December, 2008 Mississippi state title game. It was the nation's fifth longest winning streak in high school football, ever.

Several of Sanford's first cousins were stars on the South Panola 2008 team. Many of the senior Tigers were in the midst of the whirlwind and head turning courtship of the Division I college football powers. "Lots of my boys down there are going big time. Good for 'em, I say. I am not jealous, I got what I wanted by staying right here at Roosevelt," said Sanford.

To his credit and, after having been several opportunities during the 2008 season to speculate on what if, Sanford never once indicated a longing to return to the high powered program in Mississippi. "Everything there is real nice, I know," Sanford said in his distinctive southern drawl. "Equipment, field, weight room, you name it, at South Panola it was the best. But you know, that don't bother me, I mean leaving all that behind. I liked playing for Roosevelt and I am sorry it is over. If I had to choose between Roosevelt and South Panola again, I would pick Roosevelt again. No regrets. We were a family here. My teammates, and my coaches, here had my back. I didn't feel that at South Panola. As long as I could play, the coaches were behind me. As soon as I had problems, they just bring in another player. Here at Roosevelt, if I had a problem, people cared and they tried to help me, not just replace me. "

Sanford, ever the polite and polished young man, never waivered in his stated appreciation of his adopted high school and its school leaders. "We have a good school here," he said. "People not here everyday always dissing us. But they not here, they not see the good that goes on. My teachers here have been very dedicated to me. They want to see me succeed. Yeah, we had bigger and nicer things in the school at South Panola, but the caring was not there, not like it is here."

Sanford was always vague when asked why he left the only home he had ever known, just as he was set to emerge as a star football player in a community where high school football was king, star players, gods. When pressed, he would simply say, "I needed to get out. Coming up here was the best for my future."

Sanford readily admits that his landing in the best football program in the PHL was simply a matter of luck. "My Grandma lives on the south side, so I came to Roosevelt."

Coach Campbell was more than happy to accept his new player. "Mississippi and I both came at the same time. What a great welcoming gift! We are going to miss him around here. Mississippi never gets down. This is a hard job (coaching) under the best of conditions. But when you deal with all the stuff we have to, down here, it is good to have a kid with an attitude like Mississippi. He just loves to play football. State championship game or touch in the park, don't matter, he just wants to play football."

Sanford's love for the game never faltered nor dissipated in the face of adversity. "This was a tough year," Sanford said in January of 2009. "But we worked as hard as we could. We never quit on the coaches and they never quit on us. We battled all the way to the end. We should have won more. I know we were good enough, it just wasn't meant to be."

Despite the enjoyment of his days as a Roughrider, Sanford was looking confidently to the future. "I get to go home now, back down south," he observed of his commitment to the Historically Black College (HBC). Arkansas-Pine Bluff University played in Division I-AA of the NCAA. (While the majority of their athletic teams competed on the highest level - NCAA Division I - APB's football team was anchored in Division I-AA, a kind of purgatory of college football, not banging helmets each Saturday on the highest echelons of the sport, but still above those of the lower levels of Division II and Division III. One advantage the I-AA teams held over their larger brothers was a playoff to determine a true national champion. In the sub class of Division I there were no BCS yearly controversy, but a winner decided on the playing field after a sixteen team, end of the season, tournament. In December 2008; the Richmond Spiders, at the completion of the post season tournament, were the last man standing in Division I AA football.)

Before closing the Roosevelt chapter of his life, Sanford – who planned to major in Business - gave one quick glance back over his shoulder to revisit the last three years. "It is time to move on and I am ready to move on, but I will always remember my (high school) days here as good days. We have improved so much here. People need to know the work that people like Mr. Houston and Coach Campbell have done. How hard my teachers work. They get no credit. Everybody says 'oh Roosevelt, just a bunch of gang bangers. Why worry about that place. Just let them kill each other.' But that is so untrue here. This is a good school and the reason is that students here are told they matter. Maybe we don't have the fanciest of buildings and the greatest of equipment. Maybe we didn't win a state championship in football. Don't matter to me. What matters is that people here care and that is what I will remember about this school. Man, it has been three fast years, and now it is time to move on."

Of all of the Roughriders who entered the 2008 season harboring dreams of college football scholarships, the two who least needed to finance a college degree on the back of their football ability were quarterback Arlando Bailey and linebacker George Bell. Both were bright young men whose college test scores and, at least in Bailey's case, grade point averages were of significant strength to gain them admission, with or without football, into all but the most stringent and prestigious of America's colleges and universities.

Still, by January 2009, both were nervously assessing their potential college football suitors and options. While one, by early winter was frustrated to the pointed of expressing disappointed resignation at the lack of football choices on his table; the other was wrestling with making the right choice between several attractive educational institutions.

Both Bell and Bailey were well respected and recognized in the academic circles of Roosevelt as two of the school's brightest academic stars. When taking the state's mandated math skills test as juniors, both Bailey and Bell were members of an exclusive group at Roosevelt - whose membership could be counted on one hand - students who scored at what the state determined as the "proficient" level on the standardized test given by all Missouri public schools.

Bailey and Bell had seen their potential noted at a young age, and subsequent educational advantages were duly presented to both. The opportunities were readily snatched up and the college doors now swinging open to Bailey and Bell provided significant validation for time and funds invested at an early age in bright young African American males.

Bailey's association with his "adopted" white foster parents, the Hutchersons, had presented him with opportunities during his crucial adolescent developmental years that had awoken in him a desire for knowledge and education. He had attended exclusive private schools from the 7th through the 10th grade.

Upon Bailey's educational return to the SLPS for his junior year at Roosevelt, his foundation for learning, along with a newfound quest for intellectual mastery, had been solidified by the intense previous four years of high level instruction. He returned to the public school system for his junior year as a role model student.

Having mastered the tricky task of standing out academically in a way that did not cause resentment among his peers, the quarterback walked the hallways of Roosevelt High School with a quiet and steady confidence, secure in the respect bestowed upon him by students and faculty alike. Always cool, calm and in control, Bailey observed, "I like to learn and I think there are areas I achieve well in. I am not ashamed of that. Some here try to hide their intelligence to try and fit in socially. I don't."

Football however, as the calendar turned from 2008 to 2009, was a part of Bailey's world he no longer felt in control of, and that was eating at him with a growing sense of helplessness and frustration. He had in hand, in January 2009, not one solid offer to play college football.

Coach Campbell preached patience to Bailey. "People take longer to buy into the type of talent CBC has," said Campbell in a post season interview. "He doesn't look like a quarterback, and he doesn't just (overwhelm) you when you first watch him play. But the more you watch him on film, the more he grows on you. It is the whole package that gives him value. He doesn't rattle easy. He will take a hit. He is very accurate (as a passer), even if he doesn't have the cannon type arm to throw it a mile or through a brick wall. He is smart and he makes good decisions. And he is a leader. He has a presence on a team and in the huddle. Players just respect him. He came in here as a junior in a tough situation, but he never backed down and he earned the respect of everyone here."

During the summer before his senior year, Bailey was non committal and lackadaisical about his football future beyond the high school level, almost to the point of being flippant.

In August he had said, "I could have left football behind when I left CBC. I could have stayed at CBC and not played football. I like football, but it is not why I will go to college. If I get a good offer, great, if not, oh well. I will just concentrate on my studies."

That cavalier and carefree attitude of a summer that, by January, seemed so long ago, had dissipated as Bailey's senior season wore on, and his college football prospects were not materializing to his liking. Always in a state of calm control, Bailey would not openly admit concern. But for those who knew him, the cracks were beginning to show. His foster father, Ron Hutchinson, had said days after Christmas 2008, "I know it is bothering him that the colleges are not coming after him like he thought they would."

By January, Bailey's future career plans had also taken a sudden shift and football was now a very big part of the equation. Expressing a desire over the previous summer to explore the field of engineering as his first choice of study in college, by the time Bailey's last semester of high school had began, his career path focus had changed. "I would like to be a math teacher and a football coach," he confided in January. "I learned a lot here at Roosevelt because of football. The season did not go like any of us wanted it to, but we didn't let all the problems keep us from giving our best effort everyday. We fought and we kept fighting, even when we knew it was hopeless. I definitely want to continue to play football." Walking off the field at Vianney after the last game of his high school career, Bailey turned to an assistant coach and defiantly said, "my high school football career is over. Now my college football career starts. This was not my last game."

Several months later, Bailey's confident frame of mind had waned; replaced by a daily growing concern that his football career may well have in deed ended with the loss at Vianney. The lack of interest shown by college coaches for his future services was, by January, weighing heavily on the mind of the introspective young man.

For one who had taken the path less traveled to his spot on the 2008 Roosevelt Roughriders, blazing his own trail - always in command of his environment and circumstances - Bailey now faced a situation he could not control. His future as a football player, a role he had grown to realize was a defining part of the life he hoped to create for himself, was now in the fickle hands of uncompromising and brutally honest college coaches. To his growing agitation, their silence spoke volumes.

"Missouri State in Springfield has talked to me about walking on. But I don't know," Bailey related. Walk ons - athletes who did not receive a scholarship, but chose to try out for the team - are a mainstay in many college programs. They provide numbers to fill out a roster, and in some cases, practice cannon fodder for the scholarship players. These wannabes are given a uniform and a chance to prove their worth, with a promise from the coaches of the slight possibility that, in the future, some financial aid in the form of an athletic scholarship might be forthcoming.

Missouri State, like Arkansas-Pine Bluff, was an NCAA Division I-AA member. The Bears, never a football power, gave out the allotted number of 60+ football scholarships. Most I-AA schools would have at least two quarterbacks on full scholarship, and maybe even a third.

"I was told that the hardest position to walk on at is quarterback," said Bailey. He now understood that many college coaches show a reluctance to play a nonscholarship walk on athlete ahead of a scholarship player, for fear that such a move would beget the question of who made the decision to give scholarships to players who could not even beat out a non-scholarship player. This was especially true for the high profile position of quarterback. Maybe a walk on offensive lineman could play ahead of a scholarship teammate without raising the question of dubious evaluation of talent, but not at the glamorous and high profile quarterback position.

The life of a walk on QB did not seem appealing to Bailey. Most would be relegated to the non glamorous role of a "camp arm," providing a fresh arm for passing drills to receivers. Or worse, a tackling dummy running the scout team in practice each week, emulating the opposition for the preparation of the first team defense. A walk on QB would be expected to endure the many practice session poundings necessary to prepare the starting defensive unit for each Saturday.

Never at a loss for words, and displaying the stinging honesty of youth, teammate George Bell, without prompting, offered his insight into the predicament faced by his friend and senior classmate: "Maybe no college wants a fat quarterback."

George Bell was the Roughrider toughest to peg, to label, neatly fold and store in the appropriate drawer of the ridged caste system of the time honored high school social order. He was, at times, a loud and defiant voice to those in power. More than any other team member, Bell was quick to voice his opinion, requested or not, to the coaching staff. Sometimes his contribution was ignored by the coaches, sometimes it was met with agreement. To the point of insolence, George Bell was the unspoken spokesman of the 2008 Roosevelt Roughriders. The coaches knew it, his fellow seniors were cognizant of it, and with no doubt, so was George.

There was a presence about Bell - a moxie so common to the self assured high school athlete - that exuded self confidence and respect. When the coaches wanted to bridge a gap and address a problem, George Bell was often the liaison they sought out. His opinion mattered and he took his role of team leader seriously.

"I have had a lot of leadership training," Bell said during a break in an October 2008 weight lifting session. "Starting back in 7th grade, I have been in organized leadership developmental programs. I like to think of myself as a leader. I lead by example, not by words. I learned that a long time ago. Anybody can talk, but those who earn your respect as a leader, do so by actions."

Unlike his kindred spirit and senior friend Bailey, the football offers to Bell by early 2009 were promising. "I am looking at Missouri Southern right now for football and maybe Northern Iowa. Southern has offered me, but I have not visited yet," Bell said in reference to the Joplin, MO University that participated on the NCAA Division II level. Northern Iowa was nested one rung higher, on the NCAA Division I-AA level.

"I am also looking at Kansas State for their architectural program. But if I would go there, I probably would not play football. I am just not good enough for that level," said Bell.

How hard would it be for Bell to walk away from football? "I would miss it, but I would not have that hard of a time with not playing. I am just going to sit down in the spring, look at all of my options and then go with what is best for me. If my football days are over, then it was fun, but it's time to move on."

Surprisingly, Bell's GPA at Roosevelt was not that high, hovering around the 2.0 level, that of a C average student. Those educational statistics made Bell a rarity among the grade inflation so common at Roosevelt. Many of his classmates would boast of GPAs in the high B range, 3.5- 3.7; but standardized test scores – both in achievement tests and state mandated competency tests - that fell well below the state and national norms. Bell's academic record was just the opposite; some of the highest standardized test scores in the school, but a woefully average grade point average.

"I just get bored sometimes," was Bell's explanation, shrugging off his underachieving grade average. "The grades are not that important to me. It is the knowledge that I work for. Sometimes I get the knowledge but the teachers don't ask the right questions on the test, you know what I mean," explained Bell with a laugh.

If there was a Renaissance Man of Roosevelt High School, it would be George Bell. Always nattily dressed, never at a loss for words, the quintessential cool dude who was always in control; Bell would never show outward emotion or stress. He called the signals for the defense and he took his role as a coach on the field seriously. Never shy to point out a teammate's mistake or blown defensive coverage, criticism from George Bell was never once during the season answered with resentment from the scolded teammate. That, in itself, in an inner city environment, was amazing.

During the 2008 season, most on the field arguments, and occasional scuffles amongst the Roughriders, were almost always rooted in a perceived lack of respect being shown to the offended player. But with Bell, it was different. Players respected his authority and status in an unquestioning way. The level of confidence he displayed when openly questioning coaching strategy, placed him in awe by his team mates, especially the underclassmen. When one sophomore was asked by a fellow underclassman teammate during a practice in which he had raised the ire of Bell, "why do you let him talk to you like that," the answer was: "because he is George. If he can diss the coaches, I guess he can diss me too."

Bell was also the spiritual leader of the team. He would gather his teammates prior to each game in the end zone for a team prayer. His high pitched voice was a contrast to his macho style of faith. "Dear Lord," he began before one game, "we know who the better team is today. We need not your help there, because they don't have a chance. But please don't let us hurt anyone out there today as we play in your glory and your honor, Amen."

"George is going to be hard to replace next year," said Coach Campbell in October. "He has done a very good job for us as a football player. George is just one of those kids that grows on you. We know we are going to miss him, but I don't think we will realize how much until we start practice next August and George is not there to lead the cadence in calisthenics. Then it will hit home."

What are Bell's memories of the 2008 season, his fourth and final year as a starter for the Roosevelt High School Roughriders varsity football team? "It has been fun, you know. No regrets from me. We did all we could, we just had some tough breaks. But hey, I am proud of what we did for this school. I think we brought some pride to the students here. I think we brought some pride to the neighborhood. And it was not like that when I was a freshman. Nobody cared about football around here then. Nobody, back then, really cared much about anything at Roosevelt High School. Now people in school speak to you with respect if you are on the football team. Even teachers know you are special and you have high standards for your school work if you are a football player. And that is a nice change. We had a lot of pride with our team this year. We seniors are real close. We all stuck together, so I will not say this season was a disappointment. It was a growing experience. And that is never bad. If I never play football again, that is ok. I was a member of the Roosevelt Roughriders, a great bunch of dudes with cool coaches and the best damn football team in the PHL. Just think how good we could have been if the coaches had put me at running back, or at least had me run back kicks. Misused my whole career," as Bell stated for at least the 100th time his long held and ongoing complaint of the coaching staff's lack of recognition of his self proclaimed talents as a ball carrier.

With his patented high pitched laugh accentuating his final statement, the Renaissance Man of Roosevelt High School was out the door, down the hallway and, as always, the first in line for an early lunch.

CHAPTER 8
EPILOGUE

Nobody can give you freedom. Nobody can give you equality or justice or anything. If you're a man, you take it.
— Malcolm X

There is no human reason why a child should not admire and emulate his teacher's ability to do sums, rather than the village bum's ability to whittle sticks and smoke cigarettes. The reason why the child does not is plain enough - the bum has put himself on an equality with him and the teacher has not.
— Floyd Dell

Equality...is the result of human organization. We are not born equal.
— Hannah Arendt

"What it takes," Roosevelt High School Principal Terry Houston told me on an unseasonable warm February, 2009 morning, "is for a student to know someone cares." Leaning back in his office chair, with hands clasped tightly behind his head, Houston took a deep breath to momentarily release the ever present tension born from filling the role of Principal of an inner city high school. The head Roughrider was taking a short break from his normally hectic day to share with me his thoughts on the turn around of Roosevelt High School. Under Houston's whirlwind and energetic approach, in just over two years, Roosevelt had undergone a complete and total metamorphosis. From the worst high school in perhaps the worst public school system in the United States - Roosevelt was now viewed by many in the world of urban educational academia as a template for the rebirth of an inner city high school. Praise for Houston's efforts had come from far and wide. Over the past year, accolades, and awards had been bestowed on Houston at a head spinning pace of regularity. Faculty, students and area residents, by late winter 2009, were all singing the praises of Terry Houston and the work he had done at RHS.

Houston is quick to point out that the transformation of Roosevelt from a sluggish and dying school, to its seemingly overnight and mercurial rise in stature and public perception was still a work in progress. "If kids learn to trust you as an educator, then the battle will be won," said Houston. "And our kids trust us. They know we care, and that is important. And just as important, we trust our kids. Our students know we have a plan, but we also first have a goal. And our goal is to help these boys and girls - who come to us everyday eager to learn - prepare themselves for the rest of their lives. Think about it. What an immense responsibility we have: the very future of these kids is in our hands. I want everyone here at Roosevelt to realize this, to stop and think about the huge responsibility we have been (entrusted) with. If the immensity of this responsibility does not take your breath away, then I don't want you working with my students at Roosevelt High School. These kids deserve the best, and it is my job to see that they get nothing less."

Hope is life. Without hope, we have no life. No one should ever be deprived of hope. For many of the young athletes on the Roosevelt High School football team, hope was all they had. The "Forgotten Boys," as I came to refer to my football playing friends at RHS, were not dealt the strongest hand in the game of life. Privilege was not a term one would use to describe the family fortunes pinned to the chest of any of the Roosevelt players.

Despite the gloomy economical conditions of the everyday life of these young men, the hopes they espoused to me as they grew comfortable with my presence were, for the most part, well grounded in a strong optimism for the future. My fear is that, as time passes and these young men continue to suffer the societal kicks to the stomachs of their dreams, that an accumulative reality will set in, their present hopes supplanted by the cynicism born of repeated failure. The odds of escaping the stark limitations of the inner city life they know, I fear, are not stacked in their favor. Yet still they dream.

Labor Activist Marshall Ganz said that young people have an almost biological destiny to dream. I found that Ganz's wisdom rang true at Roosevelt High School. The optimism I found among its' students was uplifting to the very core of mankind's soul – the human spirit.

During my time at Roosevelt, the United States did what only twenty years ago would have been deemed improbable, the election of a black man as President of the United States. I watched the pride that Barack Obama's historical accomplishment brought to the African American citizens of Roosevelt - from the posters in Principal Terry Houston Office, to the campaign button I saw hanging from the bulletin board on the inside of a janitorial closet - the empowerment of Obama's victory resonated in a strong wind of hope that blew throughout the Roosevelt campus in the Fall of 2008.

In the August acceptance speech of his nomination at the Democratic National Convention Obama, in his own eloquent and succinct way, verbalized that spirit: "We have been told we cannot do this by a chorus of cynics. They will only grow louder and more dissonant in the weeks to come. We've been asked to pause for a reality check we've been warned against offering the people of this nation false hope. But in the unlikely story that is America, there has never been anything false about hope."

My experiences at Roosevelt High School brought about within me a wide spectrum of personal emotions. When asked how I felt at the completion of my year long endeavor, I would often comment on the extreme continuum that held the range of my feelings, best describe with the usage of two contradictory adjectives: invigorated and infuriated.

I found personal spiritual invigoration as I witnessed the everyday trials and tribulations of the Roosevelt High School football team. Their never wavering commitment to each other, displayed as they strived relentlessly for success, would warm the heart of the most stoic cynic.

I grew, through the year, to greatly respect the players, their coaches and the local school administration. Their story is uplifting by its simple but noble intentions - their stubborn unwillingness to surrender to the overwhelming societal forces they daily battled. The adult educators responsible for the daily operation of Roosevelt High School are top notch. I would have been proud, and felt fortunate, if they would have educated my own children. That is the highest compliment I can give to any educator.

However, the retroversion of my uplifting experience was the profound sense of infuriation at the total lack of any concern shown by the SLPS and its athletic operatives - the Public High League - for the well being and best interests of Arlando Bailey, Antonio Carter, George Bell, Rene Faulk and the rest of their Roughrider teammates. Any fair-minded person who saw what I did would share in my outrage. President Woodrow Wilson said almost 100 years ago: "You are not here merely to make a living. You are here to enable the world to live more amply, with greater vision, and with a finer spirit of hope and achievement. You are here to enrich the world. You impoverish yourself if you forget this errand." Such high gleaming of idealistic public service, above the building level of the SLPS hierarchy, I found to be non-existent.

If the SLPS employs a performance based system of job evaluation for its personnel, it would be interesting to see their criteria. From my observation, the primary route to long term employment and promotion within the SLPS system was to simply cover your own ass and don't rock the boat.

Thomas Szasz, the 20th century psychiatrist observed, "Men are afraid to rock the boat in which they hope to drift safely through life's currents when, actually, the boat is stuck on a sandbar. They would be better off to rock the boat and try to shake it loose." Within the current regime of educational "leaders" in St. Louis, MO, analogues to Szasz's descriptive sandbar, I see no intent or plan for breaking loose from the constraints that both doom and hinder SLPS's stated mission of providing a quality education for its students. Changing the status quo, regardless of the six Superintendents employed within a five year time frame, nor the multiple millions spent by the SLPS on "studies" and "consultants," is not - and has not been for years - a priority with the SLPS. With the SLPS its politics - not educating poor inner city children - that mans the helm, guiding what often seemed to me a rudderless ship.

I will be candid and cut to the bone; the upper level administration of the SLPS - and by default, the PHL - did not give a damn about the athletes on the Roosevelt High School football team. It became very transparent early in my year at Roosevelt that students were never priority within the overall system. In the SLPS, it is "stuff first, kids second."

Little was done to give the youngsters in the PHL the feeling that they were special, or that upper level administrators had their best interest at heart. In actuality, just the opposite was true. I hearken back, still shaking my head in disbelief, to the day before the Roosevelt football team's scheduled jamboree in August. For the first time during the season, the Roughriders would have the opportunity to scrimmage other schools. Although the event was just an exhibition and no score would be kept, it was very important for the players and coaches as they prepared for the upcoming season's schedule. The coaches and players both spoke throughout the week leading up to the jamboree of their excitement in anticipation of the Saturday evening event to be held under the lights of Gateway Tech Stadium.

Adding even more significance to the jamboree for Roosevelt was the absence of a game for the subsequent first weekend of the regular season. The PHL had not found Roosevelt a suitable opponent. The Riders would have to open the season one week late, and against a strong Eureka team that would have already played a regular season game, thus having worked out all first game bugs and jitters. As any coach will tell you, the most difficult game of any season is the first. Roosevelt would be at a huge disadvantage against a strong and experienced Eureka squad that had already played one game.

But at least Roosevelt would have the jamboree and they would need to use the opportunity to their best advantage. Wrong.

On the Friday afternoon before the jamboree, Coach Campbell received a short e-mail from the downtown offices of the SLPS. Due to the "chance" of rain he was informed, the jamboree was canceled.

No call to Coach Campbell asking for his input. No inquiry from the downtown administration as to how this cancellation would affect his team and their preparation for the upcoming season. No brain storming for an alternative plan. No collaboration with Roosevelt in any way, at any level. Could the deep sixing of the event not have at least waited until the day of the scrimmage – Saturday - to see if the "chance" of rain really did develop? (Saturday turned out to be a picture perfect late summer St. Louis day- not a cloud in the sky and not a drop of rain).

In the end, the SLPS did what it seemed to always do: take the option that required the least amount of effort. The jamboree was called off, and the kids be damned. The SLPS chose the grass at Gateway Tech Stadium over the well being of the student athletes of Roosevelt High School. This was a pattern I saw repeated by the district's downtown administration again and again throughout my time at Roosevelt. What is best for the student athletes was, most times, never even a blip on the SLPS radar screen of priorities. In short, in my opinion, based on my 12 months at Roosevelt, both the SLPS and the PHL are a disgrace to any basic standard of caring for kids.

In the spring of 2008, I spent an enlightening afternoon with a man of real vision, Tom Kuhn, of PHL, Inc. As stated earlier in this work, I have a great deal of respect and admiration for the philanthropically orientated good his private sector group has done on behalf of the athletes of the St. Louis Public High League. (The wisest move PHL, Inc. made, in my opinion, was to refuse to turn over money they had raised to the SLPS, as they were first told they must). During that first meeting, Kuhn made a statement that I would mull over in my mind many times during my year at Roosevelt. When I would become dispirited by the lack of concern and the often horrific conditions PHL athletes were forced to endure, I remembered Kuhn's words: "Every kid, and I don't care where they are from, deserves better than what the kids of the PHL are given."

I found no evidence, at any level, of any effort by the PHL to galvanize the positives of high school athletics - to uplift the experience of PHL athletes. I never once, at any PHL event I attended over a three year period (boy's soccer, girls soccer, boys basketball, girls basketball, baseball, softball and volleyball) found a game program or team roster made available to the attending public. How hard is it to type up a roster and photo copy a couple of hundred for the fans? Go to any suburban school, and you will always, at the least, find a program listing player's names and numbers. Often, you will find a slick multi page program highlighting the accomplishments of the host school and its athletic teams. The PHL and SLPS could certainly use some of this type of positive PR. But first, it would take a downtown administrator willing to get off of his or her ass and give a damn.

Seldom could I find PHL scores in the following day's paper. The only exception was football. In most of the other PHL sports, I am going to assume, the coaches just didn't take the time to call in the scores. If a public address announcer showed up for any PHL event, it was a rarity. The scorekeepers and timekeepers assigned by the PHL to games were, at best late, at worst, no shows. And when in attendance, were so lacking and deficient in their performance it was almost laughable. (Coach Campbell at one home football game, turned to the press box, after the latest in a number of miscues by the clock keeper, and yelled in a loud and exasperated voice, "do I have to run the clock, too?").

What is in overabundance at PHL contests are security guards.

In all fairness, there were a few notable exceptions of PHL programs, besides the Roosevelt Football team, that were led by coaches who cared. Metro High School's Girl's Basketball Coach, Gary Glasscock, being one. His team was one of the few bright stars still shining in the PHL. Entering the 2008-2009 season, Glasscock's squads had won two state titles while having made four consecutive state final four appearances. His interest and efforts, along with his setting of high expectations, allowed him to will his teams to rise above the levels of sub mediocrity that were so commonly accepted by the PHL. I must also note that Metro's scores appeared on a regular basis in the local press. In short, Glasscock gave a damn and it showed. The simple but passionate commitment that is common to all outstanding leaders, seemed to me to be all too lacking in most coaches and athletic administrators employed by the PHL.

Viewed by an outsider, the lack of game day preparation and concern for details in the PHL was alarming. After some acclimation brought on by long tenure, for many coaches who worked in the PHL, the lack of the basic necessities needed to administrate an athletic contest became nothing more than the reality of working for the SLPS. Like scratches on a pair of old and well worn eye glasses, PHL coaches had endured for so long the lack of simple amenities that suburban and out state coaches took for granted, they no longer noticed.

With the exception of *PHL, Inc* taking it upon themselves the responsibility of preparing game sites and providing useable equipment, field preparation and game equipment was either non existent in the Public High League, or at best, to the lowest forms of substandard levels imaginable. Instead of pylons in the end zones to mark the out of bounds lines at Roughrider Stadium, orange construction type cones were used in substitute. The cones in the Roosevelt end zones bore the labels "wet floor." How expensive is it to by pylons for the end zones? And this from a district that spent over $625,000 in the fall of 2008 for another in an endless line of "facility studies" to determine which neighborhood schools would proceed to the district's latest hit list for mothballing? (Due to public pressure, in the Spring of 2009, the Superintendent and the SAB ignored many of the school closings the $625,000 consultant recommended, and allowed certain politically connected schools on the hit list to stay open, prompting many observers to ask, "then why pay over 1/2 million for the study?")

Roosevelt Stadium being a prime example, sufficient locker room space was unheard of at most of the city schools playing venues. Soldan High School's field was the exception. The Soldan Stadium was built with home and visiting locker rooms located under the enclosed East stadium stands. However, when Roosevelt played Sumner High School at Soldan for the second game of the season, the locker rooms remained locked. Why? A simple answer: no one knew who had a key.

Sam Dunlap, Commissioner of the PHL and head of the athletic department of the SLPS, was in attendance that hot September Saturday afternoon. Roosevelt spent the pregame and halftime periods lying on the grass behind their sideline (there were no team benches) with no water, no shade and no bathroom facilities. This total lack of concern was on display with the Commissioner of the PHL in attendance and no effort by anyone to provide the most basic of necessities to the athletes. (Someone find the damn key!)

When Coach Campbell asked that afternoon for a bench to be provided on his sideline, three battered metal folding chairs (labeled "Soldan Band") materialized. Campbell was not even upset. He shrugged his shoulders and told me that is life in the PHL. But why is such a low standard permitted, or accepted? Where are the people whose job is to provide the basic necessities to the athletes of the PHL? Who is holding them accountable?

No recantation of my year with the Roughriders would be complete without some mention of the caliber of officiating provided by the PHL. My best descriptor of the work I witnessed in most all contests I attended: the worst officiating this side of hell.

At best, most officials the PHL hired were incompetent - didn't know the rules - and presumptuous -"we have to get this game under control (by calling a penalty on every other play) or we will have a riot with these type kids" (insert the word black).

My most serious concern is that, at worst, some officials were blatant racists - "you are the only one these animals will listen too." That statement made to Roosevelt senior lineman Tyler Clubb by a white official (hired by the PHL) during the game with Chaminade, still infuriates me, as it would anyone who spent time with the Roosevelt players.

How dare anyone call these kids animals? This was said by an adult who was hired to "serve' these children and help provide for them the benefits that justify organized athletics in our schools. To me, having gotten to know these young men through daily interaction over a one year period, they were great kids, and certainly not "animals." I don't believe it to be happenstance that this official's comment was made to Clubb, the only white player on the field for Roosevelt, nor do I have any doubt that it was, in fact, made.

What I found the most disparaging about the day to day operations of the PHL was that all the harm and lost opportunity to impact the lives of students that frustrated me so, was self inflicted by the very system itself. This was no outside conspiracy by a group with racist intent to deny the opportunities for personal growth that a strong athletic program would provide the black students of the PHL. In sharp contrast, all the harm, all the lost opportunities I witnessed, were inflicted by the PHL onto its own students. Even more disconcerting is that football, for the 2008-09 school year, was the flagship program of the PHL. Think of the sorry state of affairs of the "minor" sports in the Public High

League. It is almost impossible to describe the miserable state of the PHL. No words on the wretched conditions can do the subject justice. It is that bad.

Most of the "minor" sports within the oversight of the PHL: softball, baseball, volleyball, tennis and soccer; played only limited schedules- as few as five games- and at times did not even bother to compete in the state sponsored district tournaments at the end of the regular season. Most volleyball teams in the PHL played a round robin five or six game schedule against the other woeful city league teams. The level of volleyball play I witnessed was approximate to a weak suburban junior high team.

Despite the lack of skills or organization, when the volleyball game would begin, the PHL kids would play with a spirited degree of effort equal to that of their more skilled counterparts in the suburbs. So it is all relevant, right? Wrong. The PHL has reduced its athletic program, in most sports, to the level of glorified intramurals. A few games against other inept programs of fellow PHL members, played in the middle of the afternoon when few parents or other interested spectators can attend, and, presto, the PHL leadership has fulfilled its mandated mission of providing an "equitable and adequate" athletic program for its students. In reality, nothing could be farther from the truth.

Demetrious Johnson, well known St. Louis community activist and local sports personally, told me early in my project that the degrading condition of athletics in the PHL was part of a racial plot and conspiracy, orchestrated by a power structure that did not want strong city public school athletic programs, if they were controlled by strong black coaches who would symbolize proud role models for the impressionable African American athletes of the PHL. "They know what they are doing and it is being done to destroy the athletic programs of the city schools," Johnson said. "By doing this, they take away the only area left for these kids, where local pride and accomplishment can still be achieved by disadvantaged students," Johnson told me.

My initial reaction to Johnson's claims, before I had experienced everyday life in the PHL, was one of skepticism. It is just DJ fanning the flames of racial disharmony and discontent, an action that white suburbanites will tell you they have come to expect from Johnson. In hindsight I now can say, DJ, I not only agree with you, I think you have dramatically understated the severity of the problem.

It is sickening that the very adults entrusted and empowered to give the students of the SLPS the positive and impacting values athletics teach, have committed to the athletes of the PHL such little in the way of effort, leadership and vision. The PHL, as it currently exists, is nothing short of an apartheid system - equality in name only. Athletic programs for city black kids in today's PHL are separate but unequal by default, limiting opportunities based upon student residential, racial and socio-economic status.

Twenty Five years of busing the most talented - athletic and academic - black city students to the county schools, has left a shambles of the public education provided for the shrinking number of those - who for various reasons, but most notable adult apathy - are left behind to flounder in the educational cesspool that has become the SLPS. Teamed with the embarrassment of an athletic program provided by the PHL, I found no one outside the building level who seemed to care about those left behind, these "Forgotten Boys," the football players at Roosevelt High School.

I would have liked to have set aside several of these final pages to tell the SLPS and the PHL's side of the story. However, getting a member of the higher administration of either of these two organizations to return a phone call or answer an e-mail is akin to a solar eclipse – it might happen, if you are lucky, once in a lifetime. In other words, don't sit by the phone or the computer, holding your breath.

When I first started this project, I spoke to a man who told me a story that in time I could relate well too. The gentleman was a retired business executive who was at a point in his life that he felt an empowering need to give back to society. He had a strong sense of community activism, through volunteerism, fostering a desire to help the kids of the SLPS. He sought to become a volunteer at a local elementary school.

This gentleman wrote a long letter to the principal of the local elementary school, detailing his experience, background and talents. A reading tutor for a child needing that extra one on one help that the school system always bemoaned itself as too financially strapped to provide, he suggested, would be an effective use of his time and talents. He heard nothing back.

In time, he sent the same letter to multiple offices of the administration of the SLPS. Still he received no response. Later, he tried making phone calls. None were returned. Finally in desperation, he appeared, unannounced, at the downtown SLPS Administrative Offices. The person he needed to see, he was told, was out. He left his contact numbers with the receptionist. No one ever contacted him.

"I finally gave up," he told me in 2007. "What a terrible system we have in this city to educate the kids who cannot afford to go to the private schools. I was appalled at the way I was treated. What does this say about those in charge of this school district? What does this say about their concerns for betterment of these kid's lives? Education is a poor child's only hope to a better life, and the system that is in place to provide this education to the children of St. Louis, stinks."

I left numerous messages, e-mails, voice mails, as well as sending letters to a multitude of administrators of both the SLPS and the PHL. I explained in detail my project. I received only one response back - an e-mail from an Assistant Superintendent, informing me that I would need to get permission from the public relations office of the SLPS in order to talk to any students or SLPS employees. Sorry, too late for that - but I, at least, did get a response.

Make me King of the PHL for a day, and heads would roll. My initial action for improving the lot of the PHL athletes under my domain would begin with the extreme. When I first heard Demetrious Johnson's plan to clean house in the PHL, I thought, "what an overreaction from a well known radical." Not any more.

The only way to rebuild the PHL is to blow it up, completely wipe out the status quo and start anew. I would, as Johnson first suggested to me, fire everyone, coaches and athletic directors alike. I would open up every position in the PHL and those employed in the past would be welcome to reapply. I would hire back maybe 5% of the current staff. The others can find some other form of employment. That may sound harsh, but the lost student opportunities, under the current PHL regime, is almost criminal for the damage it is inflicting upon the students under its auspices, and thus pleadingly calls for such drastic, but justifiable, measures.

If you are to coach in my PHL, then you must put kids first. I want boat rockers. I want advocates for kids. I want professional educators who have a driving passion for their athletes; willing to invest their emotional blood, sweat, and tears for the betterment of their players. I want a whole staff full of Coach Campbells. I would demand that every coach set high expectations, willing to lead the athletes they coach to the commitment and the self discipline needed to be a champion.

My coaches and athletic directors will refuse to accept "no" for an answer. The athletes in my PHL deserve the best and it is their coaches and athletic directors' responsibility to see that the athletes receive nothing less, and raise hell until they get their just due. I want coaches who will demand better equipment, better uniforms, safe and adequate practice and game venues. (Where will I get this money, I am sure I will be asked? Lets go one year without hiring a "consultant" to do a "facilities study", would be my recommendation. The cool million or so we save will nicely revamp my PHL). I want coaches who will promote their athletes. That starts with the simple task of reporting scores to the media. (In my PHL, you can bet that scores will be called in to the media).

In my PHL, coaches would bring pride into their player's lives. I want coaches who will work tirelessly to help those children under their leadership visualize that athletics can be a means to an end. My coaches will be expected to network with college coaches to get their students the exposure they need to attract a college scholarship. I was told the story of one varsity basketball coach in the PHL, who had held his position for 13 years and had sent a grand total of three athletes to college basketball programs. If true, then this is totally unacceptable in my PHL.

And yes, winning does play into the evaluation equation. Wins and losses should never be the final and only evaluation tool for validating a high school athletic program, but it is important. In my PHL, coaches will be evaluated on the performance of their teams. It happens all the time in high school sports around this nation, coaches are dismissed because of losing performances by their teams. In the 2008-2009 season, from the best data I could find, since few scores were ever reported to the media, the Roosevelt girls basketball team played only 13 games – county schools played up to 32 – losing all 13, several where they scored, as a team, under 10 points. One game they lost 66-5. Why have a program? Who is benefiting from such a travesty? My message: we can do better – and we must do better.

What I saw unfold over the course of a year with the Roosevelt High School Football team was that Head Coach DeAndre Campbell set himself up for failure, and I admire him for it. He set expectations high and would not accept that it was impossible for a PHL team to dream of state titles. Improbable: yes. Impossible: never. In reality, his team is not yet in the class of the district foes he encounters from the county and private schools. In 2008, that was proven on the football field. I confided in a friend as early as the middle of September that this Roosevelt team would not win a district game. The schedule was too loaded with long time powerhouse programs, and Roosevelt is just not yet at that level.

But the gap is narrowing. Every Rider district game was competitive; and the post game respect of the opposing coaches for the improvement Campbell's teams had made, was genuine and sincere. "In due time," one county coach told me. If Campbell stays at Roosevelt, he predicted, in due time the Riders would no longer be a breather on anyone's district dance card. Regardless of his team's shortcomings, because Coach Campbell set the bar high, his players never stopped dreaming, never stopped working.

Coach Campbell told me many times that the day of the re-emergence of Roosevelt and the other PHL football programs was not far off – in essence, a return to a time that 40 year veteran of the PHL wars Coach Simmons remembers fondly as, "when they feared us."

As this project progressed, another personal experience from deeper into my recessed past popped to the forefront of my memories, aiding me as I developed an understanding and empathy for what inner city kids endure everyday: low expectations, often originating with the very adults entrusted with facilitating a child's education.

In 1971, when I was a freshman in high school, I chose to write for, an English class assignment, a review of that fall's Attica Prison Riots in upstate

New York. I discussed the overcrowding, the despair and brutality brought on by the forced dehumanized conditions that the inmates lived in. I tended then, as I do now, to root for the underdog. My insights were deep felt, punctuated with the idealism of an impressionable 14 year old coming of age in an impressionable time.

I hoped for a good grade on my writing assignment. Instead, I received an F and a scolding with a warning from my teacher: "if you ever plagiarize a paper in this class again, you will be removed from class, placed in Study Hall for the remainder of the year and forced to retake freshman English over again as a sophomore."

As a child, I liked to read; therefore I also like to write, two hobbies rather strange for someone of my age and background. With the hindsight of an adult who spent nearly 30 years laboring in public schools, I now have a professional understanding of the rigid caste system - both socially and academically - that develops in American high schools. I see now that I was viewed by many of my teachers as "a nobody;" one of the legions of invisible kids who for four years float through high schools across this nation, bothering no one and learning little. My English teacher had me academically pigeon holed, with the appropriate label assigned: "No Future."

I did not plagiarize that paper, or any other assignment I ever wrote for my freshman English class. I remember the after-class dressing down from my teacher that I received as clear today as I did at the time of its occurrence, almost 40 years ago. Distinctly, I remember one phrase hurled at me: "This reads like something you would find in Time Magazine." In a different context, this could have been the ultimate inspiring compliment to a young and aspiring writer, but the intent of this teacher's stinging comment (made with obvious sarcasm) was very clear to me, and it was not meant to elicit aspirations of future writing successes. The conclusion drawn from the admonishment was simple and clear: there was no way someone like me could write something that good and "don't think for a minute you have me fooled."

Today, with anti-plagiarism software programs that uncover academic deceit so widely available, it is much easier to police student writing. In 1971, it took a lot of legwork and tedious research to substantiate a charge of plagiarism. The punishment for my "crime" was not more severe for the simple reason that my teacher was too lazy to prove that I had, indeed, been dishonest. I should have been outraged (today I am), but in 1971 I was just another skinny white kid with a bad haircut who just wanted to be left alone. Come third hour every Monday, Wednesday, and Friday morning, I had to strip buck naked after PE class and take a shower with 75 other boys, some of them seniors. I had bigger worries than the total disrespect and arrogant put down I had received from my ass of an English teacher. Instead of anger, I chose survival.

To not have to repeat freshman English my sophomore year, I intentionally "dumbed down" every paper I turned in to this teacher for the remainder of that school year. I made sure that the composition of my work was of the low level expected from someone of my lowly status. As I look back nearly 40 years later, I think only; "how sad."

I witnessed this same social "beat down" pattern repeated often with the Roosevelt students of 2008-2009. Their survival instincts are finely honed with a type of street "smarts" and moxie that makes it easy to brush aside societies put downs. On an afternoon in October 2008, outside of Mr. Houston's Office at RHS, I heard one adult female admonish a male Roosevelt student: "Your Auntie says you are just like your Daddy, just a no good, never amount to nothing, just waiting to go to prison thug." So why should a student who is constantly told they have no future be upset about a bad grade? "Ain't like I am ever going to be a brain surgeon, anyway," was the response one Roughrider football player gave me when I asked if he was upset about failing a Biology class.

It takes a special teacher and a special person to nurture and mentor a student and propel him or her to break the cycle of self fulfilling prophecies of failure that many inner city kids, especially males, face on a frequent and daily basis. Fortunately, I can look back on my own student experiences and be thankful that as my education progressed, I found teachers who were there to encourage and enrich; prod and challenge; and in the end, congratulate and celebrate student achievement. I am proud to say as a retired educator, teaching is indeed, the noblest of professions.

As a teacher, I attempted to remain always cognizant that one can never know when the simplest, and what may seem at the moment the most mundane, of actions can have a life changing impact upon a student. By my senior year of high school, I had become fascinated with the process of recording and composing my thoughts on paper. When alone and out of sight of a disbelieving world, I would write thoughts in a notebook I kept hidden. Amazement would sweep over me as I would construct my abstract thoughts into a tangible product recorded in my journal. Adjusting, tweaking, paraphrasing and editing, I would shake my head in wonderment when reading my finished work. Like a painter, I would step back to admire my creations. I had, by the time I reached the age of 17, gathered the self confidence, brought on by several years of maturity, to display my writing efforts at the finest level I could produce, no longer feeling a need to "dumb down" my work to fit some societal mode of expectations.

Early in my senior year of high school, once again during English class, we were assigned to take a selected paragraph and rewrite it twice: once from a formal stand point with the appropriate rigid use of the language, and from an informal angle incorporating the use of current cultural slang. During the following day's class period, when asked for volunteers to share their work, I raised my hand, a first in many a year. As I completed my reading, and to the audible (to me at least) comments from fellow students of "did he really write that," I have a crystal clear recall of my teacher's comment: "David, that is really good." Five little words I doubt this teacher has any recollection of uttering today; but five little words that changed my life. "You know what", I thought, "maybe I can achieve. Maybe I do have a future." All it took was a small amount of encouragement and praise from a teacher.

Now a tough question for a recovering liberal: Was the court ordered 1981 Desegregation of the St. Louis Public Schools a success? Indeed, a very hard question to answer. In his 1993 work, <u>Is Reality Optional</u>, Thomas Sowell wrote: "Much of the social history of the Western world over the past three decades has involved replacing what worked, with what sounded good. In area after area - crime, education, housing, and race relations - the situation has gotten worse after the bright new theories were put into operation. The amazing thing is that this history of failure and disaster has neither discouraged the social engineers nor discredited them."

Based on the factual based reality of school desegregation in St. Louis, MO, Sowell is right. It is hard for a liberal to admit, but in every modern American attempt to right the wrongs of urban school segregation, when attempted through the course of forced busing; the exact opposite of the desired effect has resulted: a more racially segregated system than was found in the pre busing days. To argue any other point is a total disregard for the facts of reality.

From an academic approach, who could argue with the gains made in racial relations - fueled by a more equitable system of public education - in the USA over the past generation? No question that desegregation and affirmative action programs instituted in mass a generation ago, have through the educational opportunities provided; played a major role in the growth of the middle class of African American citizens now found so common in today's American society. A viable and growing middle class of black Americans within the Metro St. Louis area exists today that did not in the 1970s. Visual proof can be made by surveying the student body makeup of many former all white suburban schools, that in 2009 contained not only black students who are bussed from the city, but also a growing segment of students whose parents – ironically, some former desegregation students themselves – have bought homes in these former lily white districts; now living the American Dream of middle class life in the suburbs.

But what about those youngsters left behind in the decaying inner cities? What has happened to the once thriving inner city neighborhoods built upon the history and heritage of a stable urban education system? Today, drive through the streets of north St. Louis and pay witness to the boarded up buildings along the trash lined streets of a dying city, and you will have your answer.

Until the same resources, opportunities and concern are given to the students left behind in the underfunded inner city schools - the "Forgotten Boys" of Roosevelt High School's football team, for example - the success of public school desegregation in the United States will remain a question open to serious societal debate.

Are charter schools the answer? My opinion on this matter has transgressed, due to my year at Roosevelt, from clear to murky. I started this project looking to validate the importance of the neighborhood school in the inner city communities, and demonize what I perceived as the most serious threat to urban public schools- charters. In some ways, I feel I succeeded. The work done at Roosevelt High School by a dedicated group of educators could serve as a template for the rest of the SLPS. But it will not. The racially polarized politics of the City of St. Louis will not allow for such. Nor will the total lack of leadership within the current structure and organization of the SLPS.

Charter schools have themselves, both on the local St. Louis scene, and on the national level, proven to be ripe with corruption. The problems of charter schools are well documented, but so are its successes. The inherent problem with charters is that they remove local oversight from the process. Local citizens lose control. There is no elected local school board to infuse the values of the community into the local education system. The benefit of the charter system, we are told by its proponents, is the removal of the red tape - the academic and political autocracy that has ham strung so many educators with high standards and ideals. But the test scores for charter schools in the city of St. Louis are no better than those of the SLPS. Stories of corruption and financial irresponsibility involving charter schools are just as prevalent as those involving the SLPS. Pick your poison, is the option now left to city parents without the resources to enroll their children in the private or county schools.

Despite my optimism for the continued improvement of Roosevelt High School, in my opinion, the SLPS continues to be a flawed system. Even if the state take over and the SAB succeeds in creating some semblance of turnaround that can be quantitatively validated with test data; along with the establishment of a solid economic structure and base for public education in St. Louis, what happens then? Turn the system back over to local control for the recreation of the same educational travesty that had existed, before the take over, for years?

Maybe that question is moot. From what I experienced with the SAB, I see little difference from dealing with them or the SLPS under the former elected board of education. Neither will return phone calls.

Despite the election of an African American as President of the United States, and regardless of the creation of a black middle class with economic clout that was only a dream a generation ago, to say that we are now a color blind society would be a very misleading and inaccurate statement. In the time I spent at Roosevelt, race was the most important dynamic involved in every relationship I developed. The fact that I felt I could speak openly about race with the many African Americans I came to know as friends at Roosevelt, was a great deal of benefit to raising, for me, the clarity of the picture of the school and its inhabitants.

Never once did I feel uneasy or in danger at Roosevelt. But to say that my white skin was not a factor in the interactions I engaged in on a daily basis would be patently false. I was always conscious of my minority status, that I was different.

I tried very hard, when at Roosevelt, to avoid any personal behavior that could be perceived by the students and staff as an attempt on my part to "be black." I have learned over the years from African American friends that this type of behavior from whites trying to "fit in" is often seen by blacks as patronizing and insulting. With that being said, I will admit that it did not take long for me to enjoy my immersion into the black culture at Roosevelt.

I promised Coach Campbell, in the beginning of my year with his team, that in time he, his players and coaching staff, would became comfortable with my presence. I would become invisible, I pledged, my low key presence creating no distractions for him or his team. I failed on that promise, miserably. During the crucial Gateway Tech game, my mouth got Roosevelt flagged by an official for a 15 yard unsportsmanlike conduct penalty. Coach Campbell is a big guy who I knew could become very emotional during a game. Once he learned the identity of the culprit responsible for the untimely penalty flag, he came looking for me. Despite my best attempt to practice my claim of invisibility by hiding on the sidelines behind the "Man-Child," it didn't take Campbell long to locate my white face. Before I could express my innocence and the referee's total over-reaction to my suggestions for improving his craft; Campbell grabbed me by the shoulders and said, "Dave, you are one of us. You can tell the refs anything you want. Give 'em hell! I don't care, just wait until we get the game a little more under control before you do it again, Ok?" No problem, Coach.

The election of Barack Obama has in many ways raised the hopes of both races for a more colorblind future. A 2008 Gallup poll reported that blacks' views have improved a bit when it comes to equality in employment and housing, though a wide gap with whites' views remains. In 2008, 52% of African Americans say blacks have as good a chance as whites to get any housing they can afford, a jump of 8 percentage points from 2007. Furthermore, 43% of African Americans say blacks have as good a chance to get any kind of job they're qualified for, up 5 points from 2007, and 10 points from 2005. The gap between blacks and whites in assessing race relations seems to be narrowing. In 2007, 75% of whites and 55% of blacks said black/white relations were good, a 20-point gap. This year (2008), that difference of opinion drops to 9 points.

Encouraging news? Yes. An indication that we are now a color blind society and race is no longer a social dynamic of concern? Not even close. According to the above mentioned Gallup Poll, black and white Americans continue to see a different society in terms of treatment along racial lines. Two-thirds of non-Hispanic whites say they are satisfied with the way blacks are treated in the USA; two-thirds of blacks say they are dissatisfied.

Will we ever reach as a society in my lifetime a true color blind existence? I doubt it. In my children's lifetime? Maybe. There does appear to be hope. The Gallop Poll referenced above found that most Americans say race relations are getting better. Eight in 10 whites and seven in 10 blacks say civil rights for blacks have improved in the past decade. Nearly as many say civil rights will improve over the next decade. Time will tell. We may not yet have the right answers, but we as a society seem to be learning the right questions to ask. We do have hope.

Surprisingly, the most difficult task I have encountered in completing this project is deciding where to stop. The lives of Antonio, Arlando, Quadricous, George, Rene, Tyler and the rest of the 2008 Roosevelt Roughrider football team is an ongoing story. The jury is still very much out in deliberating the future of this self proclaimed band of brothers. In four years, I hope to attend multiple college graduation ceremonies where the ultimate combatant to a life sentence of inner city poverty - an education - is bestowed upon these young men in the form of a college diploma.

Terry Houston told me once, with a chuckle, that his goal was to make Roosevelt High School so successful that "the white kids will come back." I hope to see in the not too distant future, a fully refurbished and rebuilt Roosevelt High School, returning the old building to its former grandeur as a proud anchor of a thriving Tower Grove Neighborhood. I want to stand under those arched entryways of an architectural treasure that has served well so many past generations of students and witness "the white kids come back."

I worry not about Roosevelt High School's ability, under its current leadership, to survive. Left to the site based management and leadership of Principal Houston, RHS, I have no doubt, will not only survive, but thrive. However, what I fear is the total systemic failure of the SLPS and thus the shuttering of Roosevelt due to the accompanying collapse from above.

Every student I encountered in my year at Roosevelt High School, athlete and non-athlete alike, had a story to tell. The problem - and the tragedy - was that outside of the brick walls of the old south side high school, I found few in the St. Louis Public School System who cared enough to listen.

Without a change in direction, fueled by the elimination of the racially polarizing politics that has doomed the SLPS for at least the last generation, public education in the city of St. Louis, MO will continue its slow slide into oblivion, drowning under the weight of its own incompetency.

The 2008 football season of the Roosevelt High School Roughriders was, in many ways, a disappointment. I sensed early on that this was never destined to be a story with a fairy tale ending. Never once did I enter Roosevelt High School without a numbing feeling of reality, always cognizant of the harsh environment and the accompanying constant challenges of survival under such stark circumstances that dominate – and wear down - the lives of those in the Roosevelt family.

There was to be no "Hoosiers" like ending for this team; Hollywood would have never written the script for the fate bestowed upon this edition of Roughriders. Regardless, the story of this football team is one worth telling. Within these pages I have attempted to record a true documentation of more than just a football season. To say that this story is about only football would be akin to saying that Moby Dick is a story about only fishing. It is much more. I have tried to expose - through an admitted empathetic and biased eye - the day to day struggles in the battle to educate inner city kids, burdened by a system hamstrung by the political agendas that stunt any real attempt at progress. It is often not a pretty picture I have drawn, but as Coach West would say, "it is, Dude, what it is."

Was 2008 a successful year for Coach Campbell's team, one he toiled so long and hard to mold into a proud and disciplined unit? I have not yet the answer. I do gain some sense of optimism for this group's future, due to the resilience I observed depicted by them on a daily basis. When knocked down - as they were often in the 2008 season - without fail, this team pulled its collective self up and jumped back into the fray, a character trait that will serve these young men well in the adult world they are about to enter.

In the end, any evaluation of the success or failure of a public education entity must always be based on one simple component: the success or failure of the students in its care. The young men I came to know at Roosevelt are a good and hearty bunch - coached, taught, prodded and guided by some excellent and caring educators. I hope life will treat them all with kindness.

As I look back over my year of *Riding the Storm Out*, I walk away with a simple hope: that the validation of the efforts of those who guided these boys through a challenging final year of high school will emerge in due time, based on the future life successes of these "Forgotten Boys." As the toughest 5 foot 4 inch running back I have ever witnessed play the great game of high school football told me, "I just want to show Coach Campbell and Mr. Houston, and all the others here who have believed in me, that they didn't waste their time. I want them, in the future, to look back and see that helping me was time well spent."

I pray it was.

David Almany – June, 2009

APPENDIX
SEASON BOX SCORES

September 6 vs. Eureka @ Roosevelt

Eureka	7	3	7	7	24
Roosevelt	0	0	7	0	7

First quarter
E_Cole Toti 6 run (Corey Smith kick), 8:36
Second quarter
E_Corey Smith 36 FG 1:29
Third quarter
R_Dashaun Moss 37 interception (Muhammad Dukley Kick), 7:18
E_Brandon Richards 30 run (Corey Smith kick), 5:29
Fourth quarter
E_Cole Toti 2 run (Corey Smith kick), 5:03

Roosevelt Passing	Comp	Att	Yds	TD	Int
Arlando Bailey	12	27	308	0	2
Totals	12	27	308	0	2

Roosevelt Receiving	Rec	Yds	Avg
Antonio Carter	2	14	7.0
Quadricous Sanford	5	192	38.4
Robert Scott	1	4	4.0
Harold Brown	2	44	22.0
Jerome Finner	1	39	39.0
Zebedee Williams	1	16	16.0
Totals	12	309	25.8

Roosevelt Kickoff Returns	Ret	Yds
Quadricous Sanford	3	88
Totals	3	88

Roosevelt Punt Returns	Ret	Yds
Quadricous Sanford	2	35
Totals	2	35

September 13 vs Sumner @ Soldan

Teams	Score by Quarters				F
Roosevelt	14	0	7	0	21
Sumner	0	0	0	0	0

First quarter
R_Arlando Bailey 5 run (Mohammad Dukly kick), 8:32
R_Antonio Carter 15 pass from Arlando Bailey (Mohammad Dukly kick), 4:46
Third quarter
R_Antonio Carter 25 run (Mohammad Dukly kick), 3:38

Roosevelt Rushing	Rush	Yds	Avg
Antonio Carter	18	125	6.9
Quadricous Sanford	1	35	35.0
Arlando Bailey	4	25	6.3
Zebedee Williams	2	8	4.0
Robert Scott	1	8	8.0
Totals	26	201	7.7

Roosevelt Passing	Comp	Att	Yds	TD	Int
Arlando Bailey	18	24	308	1	1
Totals	18	24	308	1	1

Roosevelt Receiving	Rec	Yds	Avg
Antonio Carter	2	35	17.5
Quadricous Sanford	6	121	20.2
Zebedee Williams	5	70	14.0
Robert Scott	2	15	7.5
Harold Brown	2	47	23.5
Jerome Finner	1	20	20.0
Totals	18	308	17.1

Roosevelt Kickoff Returns	Ret	Yds
Quadricous Sanford	1	35
Totals	1	35

Roosevelt Punt Returns	Ret	Yds
Totals	0	0

September 20 @ Gateway Tech

Teams	Score by Quarters				F
Roosevelt	6	9	0	14	29
Gateway Tech	6	0	6	0	12
First quarter					
R_Harold Brown 20 pass from Arlando Bailey (kick failed), 8:34					
G_Anthony Pierson 79 run (kick failed), 8:16					
Second quarter					
R_Mohammad Dukly 27 FG, 10:08					
R_Robert Scott 65 pass from Arlando Bailey (kick failed), 3:18					
Third quarter					
G_Anthony Pierson 36 run (kick failed), 4:45					
Fourth quarter					
R_Quadricous Sanford 15 pass from Arlando Bailey (Mohammad Dukly kick), 5:15					
R_Antonio Carter 5 run (Mohammad Dukly kick), :56					

Roosevelt Rushing	Rush	Yds	Avg
Antonio Carter	13	38	2.9
Quadricous Sanford	2	9	4.5
Robert Scott	1	9	9.0
Arlando Bailey	1	1	1.0
Totals	17	57	3.4

Roosevelt Passing	Comp	Att	Yds	TD	Int
Arlando Bailey	19	33	333	3	3
Totals	19	33	333	3	3

Roosevelt Receiving	Rec	Yds	Avg
Antonio Carter	2	2	1.0
Quadricous Sanford	9	112	12.4
Robert Scott	3	158	52.7
Harold Brown	4	41	10.3
Zebedee Williams	1	20	20.0
Totals	19	333	17.5

Roosevelt Kickoff Returns	Ret	Yds
Quadricous Sanford	2	90
Charles Weatherspoon	1	12
Totals	3	102

Roosevelt Punt Returns		Ret	Yds
Quadricous Sanford		5	90
George Bell		1	35
Totals		6	125

September 27 vs. Beaumont @ Southwest

Teams	Score by Quarters				F
Roosevelt	27	13	0	6	46
Beaumont	0	0	0	0	0

First quarter
R_Antonio Carter 12 run (Mohammad Dukly kick), 10:47
R_Zebedee Williams 40 run (Mohammad Dukly kick), 8:06
R_Antonio Carter 20 run (Mohammad Dukly kick), 6:10
R_Arlando Bailey 1 run (kick failed), 2:22
Second quarter
R_Antonio Carter 6 run (kick failed), 9:10
R_Quadricous Sanford 50 pass from Arlando Bailey (Mohammad Dukly kick), 1:51
Fourth quarter
R_Quadricous Sanford 5 run (kick failed), 2:49

Roosevelt Rushing	Rush	Yds	Avg
Antonio Carter	12	121	10.1
Quadricous Sanford	6	70	11.7
Zebedee Williams	1	40	40.0
Charles Banks	2	35	17.5
Arlando Bailey	3	20	6.7
Harold Brown	1	8	8.0
Totals	25	294	11.8
Season Totals	225	1748	7.8

Roosevelt Passing	Comp	Att	Yds	TD	Int
Arlando Bailey	7	10	195	1	0
Totals	7	10	195	1	0
Season Totals	121	210	0.0	11	0.0

Roosevelt Receiving	Rec	Yds	Avg
Quadricous Sanford	3	85	28.3
Zebedee Williams	1	55	55.0
Harold Brown	2	43	21.5
Robert Scott	1	12	12.0
Totals	7	195	27.9
Season Totals	121	2002	16.5

Roosevelt Kickoff Returns	Ret	Yds
Quadricous Sanford	1	30
Totals	1	30
Season Totals	25	0.0

Roosevelt Punt Returns	Ret	Yds
Quadricous Sanford	1	3
Charles Weatherspoon	1	5
Totals	2	8

October 4 vs. Vashon @ Roosevelt

Score by Quarters					F
Vashon	0	12	0	0	12
Roosevelt	7	0	0	12	19

First quarter
R_Robert Scott 10 pass from Arlando Bailey (Mohammad Dukly kick), 1:48
Second quarter
V_Michael Tyler 2 run (kick failed), 8:02
V_Terrell Craig 26 pass from Raynell Ferguson (run failed), 4:57
Fourth quarter
R_Harold Brown 6 pass from Arlando Bailey (run failed), 6:54
R_Quadricous Sanford 31 run (kick failed), 1:45

Roosevelt Passing	Comp	Att	Yds	TD	Int
Arlando Bailey	16	24	181	2	2
Totals	16	24	181	2	2

Roosevelt Receiving	Rec	Yds	Avg
Quadricous Sanford	6	62	10.3
Zebedee Williams	1	15	15.0
Robert Scott	5	70	14.0
Harold Brown	4	34	8.5
Totals	16	181	11.3

Roosevelt Kickoff Returns	Ret	Yds
Charles Weatherspoon	3	87
Totals	3	87

Roosevelt Punt Returns	Ret	Yds
Totals	0	0

October 11 vs. Career Academy @ Roosevelt

Teams	Score by Quarters				F
Miller	0	8	0	6	14
Roosevelt	14	0	6	7	27

First quarter
R_Antonio Carter 1 run (kick failed), 8:46
R_Quadricous Sanford 65 pass from Arlando Bailey (Antonio Carter run), 5:17
Second quarter
M_Avion Kincade 1 run (Demarco Billups run), 5:00
Third quarter
R_Antonio Carter 6 run (kick failed), 7:34
Fourth quarter
M_Avion Kincade 2 run (run failed), 7:00
R_Antonio Carter 25 run (Mohammad Dukly kick), 2:31

Roosevelt Rushing	Rush	Yds	Avg
Antonio Carter	17	85	5.0
Arlando Bailey	5	54	10.8
Quadricous Sanford	5	20	4.0
Robert Scott	1	18	18.0
Totals	28	177	6.3

Roosevelt Passing	Comp	Att	Yds	TD	Int
Arlando Bailey	11	23	206	1	1
Totals	11	23	206	1	1

Roosevelt Receiving	Rec	Yds	Avg
Antonio Carter	2	30	15.0
Quadricous Sanford	3	97	32.3
Robert Scott	2	20	10.0
Harold Brown	4	59	14.8
Totals	11	206	18.7

Roosevelt Kickoff Returns	Ret	Yds
Quadricous Sanford	2	60
Christopher Woods	1	3
Totals	3	63

Roosevelt Punt Returns	Ret	Yds
Quadricous Sanford	2	61
Totals	2	61

October 18 vs. Webster Groves @ Roosevelt

Teams	Score by Quarters				F
Webster	0	14	20	0	34
Roosevelt	6	0	0	0	6

First quarter
R_Robert Scott 6 pass from Arlando Bailey (kick failed), 8:32
Second quarter
W_Marquis Clemons 3 run (Conor Barker kick), 11:23
W_Joseph Thomas 13 pass from Derrick Dilworth (Conor Barker kick), 7:24
Third quarter
W_Joseph Thomas 3 pass from Marquis Clemons (Conor Barker kick), 11:10
W_Jaremy Harris 26 pass from Derrick Dilworth (kick failed), 8:23
W_Jaremy Harris 45 pass from Derrick Dilworth (Conor Barker kick), 2:11

Roosevelt Rushing	Rush	Yds	Avg
Antonio Carter	13	92	7.1
Arlando Bailey	4	61	15.3
Quadricous Sanford	1	18	18.0
Totals	18	171	9.5

Roosevelt Passing	Comp	Att	Yds	TD	Int
Arlando Bailey	10	18	123	1	0
Totals	10	18	123	1	0

Roosevelt Receiving	Rec	Yds	Avg
Antonio Carter	1	3	3.0
Quadricous Sanford	2	40	20.0
Harold Brown	2	16	8.0
Jerome Finner	1	20	20.0
Robert Scott	4	44	11.0
Totals	10	123	12.3

Roosevelt Kickoff Returns	Ret	Yds
Quadricous Sanford	2	65
Totals	2	65

Roosevelt Punt Returns	Ret	Yds
Quadricous Sanford	1	18
Totals	1	18

October 25 vs Chaminade @ Roosevelt

Teams	Score by Quarters				F
Chaminade	14	3	14	7	38
Roosevelt	7	0	0	6	13

First quarter
R_Antonio Carter 5 run (Mohammad Dukly kick), 4:02
C_Rob Standard 3 run (Mason Hutson kick), 3:05
C_Rob Standard 2 run (Mason Hutson kick), :45
Second quarter
C_Mason Hutson 37 FG, 4:15
Third quarter
C_Trevor LaBarge 4 run (Mason Hutson kick), 5:05
C_Rob Standard 19 run (Mason Hutson kick), 4:50
Fourth quarter
R_Arlando Bailey 4 run (run failed), 9:12
C_Rob Standard 45 run (Mason Hutson kick), 7:30

Roosevelt Rushing	Rush	Yds	Avg
Arlando Bailey	8	111	13.9
Antonio Carter	13	84	6.5
Quadricous Sanford	3	18	6.0
George Bell	2	7	3.5
Totals	26	220	8.5

Roosevelt Passing	Comp	Att	Yds	TD	Int
Arlando Bailey	9	20	117	0	0
Totals	9	20	117	0	0

Roosevelt Receiving	Rec	Yds	Avg
Quadricous Sanford	5	62	12.4
Harold Brown	3	38	12.7
Robert Scott	1	17	17.0
Totals	9	117	13.0

Roosevelt Kickoff Returns	Ret	Yds
Antonio Carter	3	96
Totals	3	96

Roosevelt Punt Returns	Ret	Yds
Quadricous Sanford	1	7
Totals	1	7

October 31 @ Vianney

Teams	Score by Quarters				F
Roosevelt	15	0	7	20	42
Vianney	15	26	14	7	62

First quarter
R_Robert Scott 22 pass from Arlando Bailey (Mohammad Dukly kick), 6:13
V_Chris Starkey 6 run (Chris Starkey run), 5:07
V_James Gladstone 23 pass from Dalton Hewitt (Brett Hassenmueller kick), 4:55
R_Harold Brown 16 pass from Arlando Bailey (Antonio Carter pass from Arlando Bailey), :45

Second quarter
V_James Gladstone 12 pass from Dalton Hewitt (Brett Hassenmueller kick), 11:23
V_DeMarco Moorehead 6 run (run failed), 6:28
V_James Gladstone 35 pass from Dalton Hewitt (Brett Hassenmueller kick), 1:11
V_DeMarco Moorehead 42 interception (kick failed), :50
Third quarter
V_James Gladstone 19 pass from Dalton Hewitt (Brett Hassenmueller kick), 10:01
R_Quadricous Sanford 12 run (Mohammad Dukly kick), 7:51
V_DeMarco Moorehead 20 pass from Dalton Hewitt (Brett Hassenmueller kick), 1:45
Fourth quarter
V_Matt Grimes 50 interception (Brett Hassenmueller kick), 8:48
R_Stephen Wallace 18 run (kick failed), 3:59
R_Arlando Bailey 2 run (kick failed), 1:45
R_George Bell 35 interception (Quadricous Sanford pass from Arlando Bailey), 1:01

Roosevelt Rushing	Rush	Yds	Avg
Antonio Carter	17	143	8.4
Quadricous Sanford	6	72	12.0
Arlando Bailey	8	37	4.6
Zebedee Williams	2	30	15.0
Stephen Wallace	2	27	13.5
Totals	35	309	8.8

Roosevelt Passing	Comp	Att	Yds	TD	Int
Arlando Bailey	19	31	230	2	0
Totals	19	31	230	2	0

Roosevelt Receiving	Rec	Yds	Avg
Antonio Carter	2	16	8.0
Quadricous Sanford	5	56	11.2
Zebedee Williams	4	28	7.0
Harold Brown	5	71	14.2
Robert Scott	3	59	19.7
Totals	19	230	12.1

Roosevelt Kickoff Returns	Ret	Yds
Quadricous Sanford	2	65
Antonio Carter	3	55

APPENDIX II
CUMULATIVE SEASON STATISTICS

Scoring

	TD	FG	2 pt	XP	Safety	
Antonio Carter	10	0	2	0	0	64
Quadricous Sanford	5	0	1	0	0	32
Robert Scott	4	0	0	1	0	25
Arlando Bailey	4	0	0	0	0	24
Harold Brown	4	0	0	0	0	24
Mohammad Dukly	0	1	0	14	0	17
George Bell	1	0	0	0	0	6
Dashaun Moss	1	0	0	0	0	6
Stephen Wallace	1	0	0	0	0	6
Zebedee Williams	1	0	0	0	0	6

PASSING

	Comp	Att	PCT	Yds	TDs	Ints	Rating
Arlando Bailey	121	210	57.62	2001	11	9	102.876

RUSHING

	Att	Yds	TDs	Avg
Antonio Carter	132	829	9	6.3
Arlando Bailey	44	387	4	8.8
Quadricous Sanford	29	306	3	10.6
Zebedee Williams	6	94	1	15.7
Robert Scott	6	54	0	9.0
Charles Banks	2	35	0	17.5
Stephen Wallace	2	27	1	13.5
Harold Brown	2	9	0	4.5
George Bell	2	7	0	3.5

RECEIVING

	Att	Yds	TDs	Avg
Quadricous Sanford	44	827	2	18.8
Robert Scott	22	399	4	18.1
Harold Brown	28	393	4	14.0
Zebedee Williams	13	204	0	15.7
Antonio Carter	11	100	1	9.1
Jerome Finner	3	79	0	26.3

TOTAL YARDS

	Rush	Rec	Tot
Quadricous Sanford	306	827	1133
Antonio Carter	829	100	929
Robert Scott	54	399	453
Harold Brown	9	393	402
Arlando Bailey	387	0	387
Zebedee Williams	94	204	298
Charles Banks	35	0	35
Stephen Wallace	27	0	27
George Bell	7	0	7

KICKOFFS

	Att	Yds	Avg
Mohammad Dukly	16	805	50.31

PUNTING

	Att	Yds	Avg
Robert Scott	19	627	33.00

KICKOFF RETURNS

	Att	Yds	Avg
Quadricous Sanford	13	433	33.31
Antonio Carter	6	151	25.17
Charles Weatherspoon	5	114	22.80
Christopher Woods	1	3	3.00

PUNT RETURNS

	Att	Yds	Avg
Quadricous Sanford	12	214	17.83
George Bell	1	35	35.00
Charles Weatherspoon	1	5	5.00